AUTOCAD 2005 AND
AUTOCAD LT 2005

NO EXPERIENCE REQUIRED

AUTOCAD® 2005 AND AUTOCAD LT® 2005

NO EXPERIENCE REQUIRED®

David Frey

SYBEX®

San Francisco • London

Associate Publisher: Dan Brodnitz
Acquisitions Editor: Willem Knibbe
Developmental Editor: Mariann Barsolo
Production Editor: Mae Lum
Technical Editor: Sam Sol Matzkin
Copyeditor: Pat Coleman
Compositor: Franz Baumhackl
Proofreaders: Laurie O'Connell, Nancy Riddiough
Indexer: Ted Laux
Book Designer: Franz Baumhackl
Cover Designer: Design Site
Cover Illustrator: Jack D. Myers

An earlier version of this book was published under the
title *AutoCAD 2004 and AutoCAD LT 2004: No Experience
Required* © 2003 SYBEX Inc.

Library of Congress Card Number: 2004104123
ISBN: 0-7821-4341-5

Manufactured in the United States of America

10 9 8 7 6 5 4 3 2

To Irv and Ruth, Shirley and Sol,
Phyllis and Jonas, and to Dick and Sylvia,
for their enthusiasm and support
for my writing this book.

Acknowledgments

Many people deserve acknowledgment and gratitude for their contribution to the development and publication of this book. Many thanks to the folks at Sybex who were involved in this project. Monica Baum of the contracts and licensing team helped me finalize the contract. Thanks also to Willem Knibbe, acquisitions editor, for his efforts to gain support for the publication of this book and for his help in getting me started. Mariann Barsolo served well as developmental editor through most of the project and gave excellent answers to my numerous questions. I appreciate the efforts of Pat Coleman, who, returning in her role as copyeditor, continued to be diligent at improving the readability of the book. Mae Lum served (for the third time!) as production editor and has again done wonders to coordinate everything, keep me well informed, and make sure the book got done on time. Also, thanks to Sam Sol Matzkin, who served as the technical editor; his generosity in lending his experience as a civil engineer and as an AutoCAD trainer to this project is greatly appreciated.

I also want to mention the production team at Sybex: compositor Franz Baumhackl; proofreaders Laurie O'Connell and Nancy Riddiough; and indexer Ted Laux. They've been successful in maintaining the standards of high quality that Sybex is known for, and I appreciate their work on this book.

CONTENTS AT A GLANCE

CONTENTS

CHAPTER 6   Using Layers to Organize Your Drawing   169

CHAPTER 7   Grouping Objects into Blocks   215

INTRODUCTION

This book was born of the need for a simple yet engaging tutorial that would help beginners step into the world of AutoCAD or AutoCAD LT without feeling intimidated. That tutorial has evolved over the years into a full introduction to the way in which architects and civil and structural engineers use AutoCAD to increase their efficiency and ability to produce state-of-the-art computerized production drawings and designs.

Because AutoCAD and AutoCAD LT are so similar, it makes sense to cover the basics of both programs. For most of the book, the word *AutoCAD* stands for both AutoCAD and AutoCAD LT.

When you come to a section of a chapter that applies to AutoCAD only, an icon (shown here) is displayed in the margin to alert you. Then, at the end of that section, extra information for AutoCAD LT users is provided to give you a workaround or otherwise keep you in step with the tutorial.

The appendix, which is an introduction to drawing in 3D, applies only to AutoCAD, because AutoCAD LT does not have the 3D commands and features. LT users, be assured: other than the 3D features, LT is much the same program as AutoCAD, with minor differences. You'll be prompted when those differences come along.

This book is directed toward AutoCAD and AutoCAD LT novices—users who know how to use a computer and do basic file-managing tasks, such as creating new folders and saving and moving files, but who know nothing or little about AutoCAD or LT, as we'll be calling AutoCAD LT throughout the book. If you are new to the construction and design professions, this book will be an excellent companion as you're learning AutoCAD. If you're already practicing in those fields, you'll immediately be able to apply the skills you'll pick up from this book to real-world projects. The exercises have been successfully used to train architects, engineers, and contractors, as well as college and high-school students, in the basics of AutoCAD.

For those of you in other trades and professions, the project that runs through the book—drawing a small cabin—has been kept simple so that it does not require any special training in architecture or construction. Also, most chapters have additional information and exercises specifically designed for non-AEC users. So anyone wanting to learn AutoCAD will find this book helpful.

> **A note like this will provide you with information on AutoCAD LT, as well as other helpful information.**

What Will You Learn from This Book?

Learning AutoCAD, like learning any complex computer program, requires a significant commitment of time and attention and, to some extent, a tolerance for repetition. You must understand new concepts to operate the program and to appreciate its potential as a drafting and design tool. But to become proficient at AutoCAD, you must also use the commands enough times to gain an intuitive sense of how they work and how parts of a drawing are constructed.

At the end of most chapters, you will find one or more additional exercises and a checklist of the tools you have learned (or should have learned!). The steps in the tutorial have a degree of repetition built into them that allows you to work through new commands several times and build up confidence before you move on to the next chapter.

Progressing through the book, the chapters fall into four general areas of study:

► Chapters 1 through 3 familiarize you with the organization of the screen, go over a few of the most basic commands, and equip you with the tools necessary to set up a new drawing.

► Chapters 4 and 5 develop drawing strategies that will help you use commands efficiently.

► Chapters 6 through 11 work with AutoCAD's major features.

► Chapters 12 through 14 and the Appendix examine intermediate and advanced AutoCAD features.

In the process of exploring these elements, you will follow the steps involved in laying out the floor plan of a small, three-room cabin. You will then learn how to generate elevations from the floor plan and, eventually, how to set up a title block and print your drawing. Along the way, you will also learn how to do the following:

► Use the basic drawing and modify commands in a strategic manner

► Set up layers

► Put color into your drawing

► Define and insert blocks

► Generate elevation views

► Place hatch patterns and fills on building components

► Use text in your drawing

► Dimension the floor plan

Chapters in the last part of the book touch on more advanced features of AutoCAD, including:

▶ Drawing a site plan

▶ Using external references

▶ Setting up a drawing for printing with layouts

▶ Making a print of your drawing

▶ Working in three dimensions, for AutoCAD users

All these features are taught using the cabin as a continuing project. As a result, you will build up a set of drawings that document your progress through the project and that you can use later as reference material if you find that you need to refresh your-self with material in a specific skill.

At the end of the book is a glossary of terms that are used in the book and are related to AutoCAD and building design, followed by an index.

Files on the Website

If you are already somewhat familiar with AutoCAD and reading only some of the chapters, you can pull accompanying files for this book from Sybex's website at www.sybex .com. Use the Catalog or Search tool to find this book's web page, and then click the Downloads button.

Also on Sybex's website, in addition to the .dwg files that accompany the book, you can download a bonus chapter, "Making the Internet Work with AutoCAD" and a bonus appendix, "An Introduction to Attributes." These introduce you to tools for working online with AutoCAD and demonstrate a method for defining attributes and construct-ing a title block using attributes, respectively.

Hints for Success

Because this book is essentially a step-by-step tutorial, it has a side effect in common with any tutorial of this type. After you finish a chapter and see that you have progressed further through the cabin project, you may have no idea how you got there and are sure you couldn't do it again without the help of the step-by-step instructions.

This feeling is a natural result of this kind of learning tool, and you can do a couple of things to get past it. You can do the chapter over again. This may seem tedious, but it has a great advantage. You gain speed in drawing. You'll accomplish the same task in half the time it took you the first time. If you repeat a chapter a third time, you'll halve your time again. Each time you repeat a chapter, you can skip more and more of the explicit instructions, and eventually you'll be able to execute the commands and finish the chapter by just looking at the figures and glancing at the text. In many ways this is just like learning a musical instrument. You must go slow at first, but over time and through practice, your pace picks up.

Another suggestion for honing your skills is to follow the course of the book, but apply the steps to a different project. You might draw your own living space or design a new one. If you have a real-life design project that isn't too complex, that's even better. Your chances for success in learning AutoCAD or any computer program are greatly increased when you are highly motivated, and a real project of an appropriate size can be the perfect motivator.

Ready, Set...

When I started learning AutoCAD about 17 years ago, I was at first surprised how long I could sit at a workstation and be unaware of time passing. Then, shortly afterward, I experienced a level of frustration that I never thought I was capable of feeling. When I finally "got over the hump" and began feeling that I could successfully draw with this program after all, I told myself that I would someday figure out a way to help others get over the hump. That was the primary motivating force for writing this book. I hope it works for you and that you too get some enjoyment while learning AutoCAD. As the title says, there is "No experience required," only an interest in the subject and a willingness to learn!

CHAPTER 1

Getting to Know AutoCAD

- ▶ Opening a new drawing

- ▶ Getting familiar with the AutoCAD and AutoCAD LT Graphics windows

- ▶ Modifying the display

- ▶ Displaying and arranging toolbars

Your introduction to AutoCAD and AutoCAD LT begins with a tour of the features of the screens used by the two programs. In this chapter, you will also learn how to use some tools that help you control the screen's appearance and how to find and start commands. For the material covered in this chapter, the two applications are almost identical in appearance. Therefore, as we tour AutoCAD, I'll point out any differences between AutoCAD and AutoCAD LT. In general, LT is a 2D program, so it doesn't have the 3D features that come with AutoCAD, such as solids modeling and rendering. The other differences are minor. As mentioned in this book's Introduction, when I say "AutoCAD," I mean both AutoCAD and AutoCAD LT. I'll also refer to AutoCAD LT as "LT" throughout this chapter and the rest of the book. Starting up AutoCAD is the first task at hand.

Starting Up AutoCAD

If you installed AutoCAD or LT using the default settings for the location of the program files, start AutoCAD by choosing Start ➢ All Programs ➢ Autodesk ➢ Auto-CAD 2005 ➢ AutoCAD 2005. For LT, choose Start ➢ All Programs ➢ Autodesk ➢ AutoCAD LT 2005 ➢ AutoCAD LT 2005. If you customized your installation, find and click the AutoCAD 2005 or the AutoCAD LT 2005 icon to start the program.

The Startup Dialog Box

If AutoCAD or LT opens with the Startup dialog box sitting in front of the Auto-CAD Graphics window, your screen will look like Figure 1.1. If the Startup dialog box doesn't open, read on a little—you'll see how to display it and then how to suppress it.

The Startup dialog box has four buttons in the upper-left corner. The first two buttons let you set up a new drawing and choose an existing drawing to revise or update. The second two buttons use templates and wizards to initiate advanced setup routines. The contents of the middle portion of the dialog box depend on which of the four buttons you choose. By beginning a new drawing, you can get past this dialog box to the AutoCAD Graphics window.

> **Dialog boxes with various combinations of buttons and text boxes are used extensively in AutoCAD and LT. You will learn their many functions as you progress through the book.**

> **Radio buttons are round and come in a list or a group. You can activate only one radio button at a time.**

1. Click the Start From Scratch button, the second button from the left.

2. In the Default Settings section, click the Imperial (Feet And Inches) radio button.

3. Click OK to close the Startup dialog box. Your monitor displays the AutoCAD or LT Graphics window, sometimes called the Graphical User Interface, or GUI (see Figure 1.2).

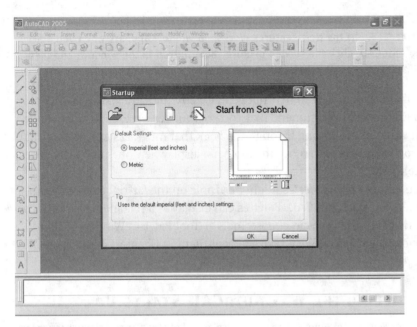

FIGURE 1.1: The Startup dialog box

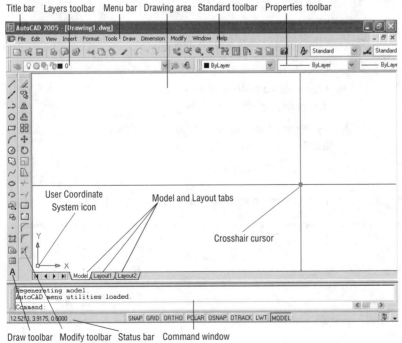

FIGURE 1.2: The AutoCAD Graphics window

N O T E   If the New Features Workshop window appears when you start up AutoCAD, click the second or third radio button in the window, and then click OK to remove it. You can always access it on the Help menu.

The toolbars on your screen may not be in exactly the same places as they are shown in Figure 1.2. I recommend that you set your screen to look like the one here, as it will make following through the book that much easier. Later in this chapter, you will see how to move the toolbars, display new ones and place them, and delete them.

Another feature called *palettes* might be visible on the far-right side of your screen when you start AutoCAD. Palettes can display as a rectangular area or as a vertical title bar. If they appear, choose Tools ➤ Tool Palettes Window to temporarily close the palettes. We'll take a look at them in Chapters 7 and 9.

CONTROLLING THE WAY AUTOCAD STARTS UP

You can set AutoCAD and LT to display or hide the Startup dialog box when you start AutoCAD.

1. From the menu bar, choose Tools ➤ Options to open the Options dialog box.

2. Click the System tab to bring it forward.

3. In the General Options section, open the Startup drop-down list.

   ▶ If you want AutoCAD to display the Startup dialog box, click Show Startup Dialog Box.

   ▶ If you want AutoCAD to start up with a blank drawing, click Do Not Show A Startup Dialog.

4. Click Apply, and then click OK.

The next time you start up AutoCAD, your preference will be used.

Introduction to the AutoCAD Graphics Window

At the top of the Graphics window sit the title bar, the menu bar, and three toolbars.

Title bar   Layers toolbar   Menu bar   Standard toolbar   Properties toolbar

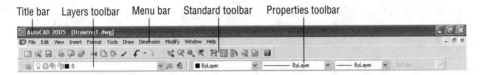

The title bar is analogous to the title bar in any Windows program. It contains the program name (AutoCAD or AutoCAD LT) and the title of the current drawing with its *path*. Below the title bar is the menu bar, where you will see the drop-down menus. Among the drop-down menus, the first two on the left and the last one on the right are Windows menus (meaning that they appear on most Windows applications). These Windows menus also contain a few commands specific to AutoCAD. The rest of the menus are AutoCAD menus.

Below these menus is the *Standard toolbar*, which contains 22 command buttons (LT has only 21). Several of these buttons will be familiar to Windows users; the rest are AutoCAD commands. Just below the Standard toolbar are the *Layers toolbar* and the *Properties toolbar*, which together contain three command buttons and five drop-down lists.

The blank middle section of the screen is called the *drawing area*. Notice the movable *crosshair cursor*. The crosshairs on your cursor may not extend completely across the screen. I recommend that you set them to look like they do in the figures in this book, and I will show you how to do this when we make a few changes later in this chapter.

Notice the little box at the intersection of the two crosshair lines. This is one of several forms of the AutoCAD and LT cursor. When you move the cursor off the drawing area, it changes to the standard Windows pointing arrow. As you begin using commands, it will take on other forms, depending on which step of a command you are in.

The icon with a double arrow in the lower-left corner of the drawing area is the *User Coordinate System icon*. It indicates the positive direction for the X and Y coordinates. You won't need it for most of the chapters in this book, so you'll learn how to make it invisible in Chapter 3.

◄

The title bar and menu bar at the top of the LT screen are identical to those of AutoCAD except that *AutoCAD LT* appears in the title bar rather than *AutoCAD*.

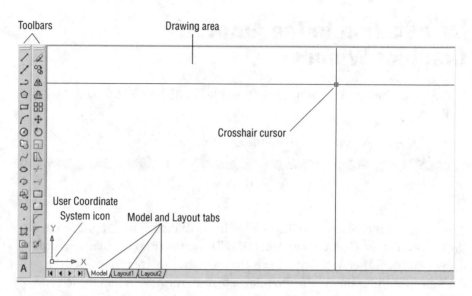

At the bottom of the drawing area are three tabs: a Model tab and two Layout tabs. You use these tabs to switch between viewing modes. (I'll discuss viewing modes in Chapter 13.) Our example shows no toolbars floating in the drawing area, but there are two docked toolbars at the left of the drawing area. Your screen may or may not have the toolbars, or they may be in a different position. If the toolbars are within the drawing area, they will have a colored title bar. For specifics, see the section "The Toolbars" later in this chapter.

Below the drawing area is the *Command window*.

```
Regenerating model.
AutoCAD menu utilities loaded.
Command:
```

The Command window in LT is identical to the one in AutoCAD.

The Command window is where you tell the program what to do and where the program tells you what's going on. It's an important area, and you will need to learn how it works in detail. Three lines of text should be visible. If your screen displays fewer than three lines, you will need to make another line or two visible. You'll learn how to do this later in this chapter in the section "The Command Window."

Below the Command window is the *status bar*.

| 6.3464, 3.0266, 0.0000 | | SNAP | GRID | ORTHO | POLAR | OSNAP | OTRACK | LWT | MODEL |

On the left end of the status bar, you'll see a coordinate readout window. In the middle are eight readout buttons (LT has only seven) that indicate various drawing modes. It is important to learn about the coordinate system and most of these drawing aids (Snap, Grid, Ortho, and Osnap) early as you learn to draw in AutoCAD or LT. They will help you create neat and accurate drawings. Polar and Otrack are advanced drawing tools and will be introduced in Chapter 5. Lwt stands for Lineweight and will be discussed in Chapter 14 in the discussion on plotting. The Model button is an advanced aid that will be covered in Chapter 13. At the far right of the status bar are small icons that indicate the presence of various features for a drawing session. These features are beyond the scope of this book.

LT does not display the Otrack button on the status bar.

This has been a quick introduction to the various parts of the Graphics window. I didn't mention a couple of items that might be visible on your screen. You might have scroll bars below and to the right of the drawing area, and you might have a menu on the right side of the drawing area. Both features can be useful, but they can also be a hindrance and can take up precious space in the drawing area. They won't be of any use while working your way through this book, so I suggest that you remove them for now.

To temporarily remove these features, follow these steps:

1. Choose Tools ➤ Options to open the Options dialog box (shown in Figure 1.3). It has nine tabs (LT has only eight) across the top that act like tabs on file folders.

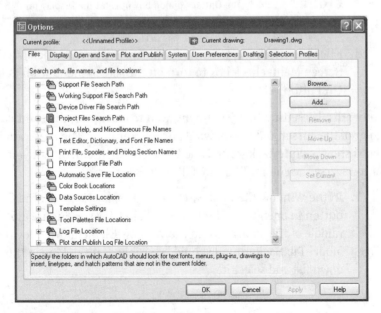

FIGURE 1.3: The Options dialog box

2. Click the Display tab, which is shown in Figure 1.4. Focus on the rectangular area titled Window Elements. If scroll bars are visible on the lower and right edges of the drawing area, the Display Scroll Bars In Drawing Window check box will be checked.

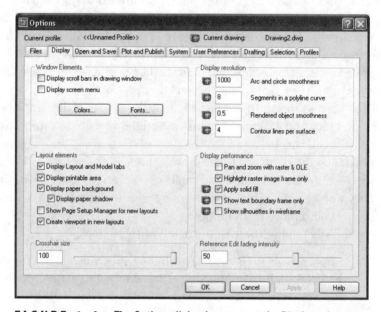

FIGURE 1.4: The Options dialog box open at the Display tab

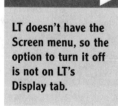

LT doesn't have the Screen menu, so the option to turn it off is not on LT's Display tab.

3. Click the check box to turn off the scroll bars. Also click the Display Screen Menu check box to turn off the screen menu. Don't click the OK button yet.

Another display setting that you might want to change at this point controls the color of the cursor and the drawing area background. The illustrations in this book show a white background and black crosshair cursor, but you might prefer to reverse the colors. To do so, follow these steps:

1. In the Window Elements area of the Display tab, click the Colors button to open the Color Options dialog box (see Figure 1.5). In the middle of the dialog box, in the Window Element drop-down list box, Model Tab Background should be visible. If it's not, open the drop-down list and select it.

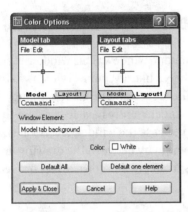

FIGURE 1.5: The Color Options dialog box

2. Move to the Color drop-down list, which is below the Window Element drop-down list. If your drawing area background is currently white, a square followed by the word *White* is displayed. Open the Color drop-down list. Scroll to Black (or the background color you want) and select it. The drawing area will now be that color, and the cursor color will change to white, as shown in the Model Tab preview window in the upper-left corner of the dialog box.

3. Click the Apply & Close button to close the Color Options dialog box.

4. Don't close the Options dialog box yet.

5. If you want the lines of your crosshair cursor to extend completely across the screen, go to the lower-left corner of the Display tab (lower-right for LT) and move the slider to change the Crosshair Size setting to 100.

6. Click OK to close the Options dialog box.

Your screen and crosshair cursor will take on their newly assigned colors, and the crosshair lines should extend across the drawing area.

T I P If you choose a color other than black as the drawing area background color, the color of the crosshair cursor remains the same as it was (black). To change the crosshair color, in the Color Options dialog box, open the Window Element drop-down list, and select Model Tab Pointer. Then select a color from the Color drop-down list.

The Command Window

Just below the drawing area is the Command window. This window is actually separate from the drawing area and behaves like a Windows window—that is, you can drag it to a different place on the screen and resize it, although I don't recommend that you do this at first. If you currently have fewer than three lines of text in the window, you will need to increase the window's vertical size. To do so, move the cursor to the horizontal boundary between the drawing area and the Command window until it changes to an up-and-down arrow broken by two parallel horizontal lines.

Hold down the left mouse button and drag the cursor up by approximately the amount that one or two lines of text would take up, and then release the mouse. You should see more lines of text, but you might have to try this a couple of times to display exactly three lines. When you close the program, the new settings will be saved, and the next time you start up AutoCAD, the Command window will display three lines.

The Command window is where you give information to AutoCAD and where AutoCAD prompts you for the next step in executing a command. It is a good practice to get into the habit of keeping an eye on the Command window as you work on your drawing. Most errors occur when you are not taking a look at it frequently.

Before you begin to draw, take a close look at the menus, toolbars, and keyboard controls.

N O T E In many cases, you can start AutoCAD commands in a number of ways: from drop-down menus, from the toolbars, and from the keyboard. When you get used to drawing with AutoCAD, you will learn some shortcuts that start commands quickly, and you will find the way that is most comfortable for you.

Drop-Down Menus

The menu bar, just below the title bar (see Figure 1.2 earlier in this chapter), consists of 11 words and an icon. Click any of these to display a drop-down menu. The icon on the left end and the File and Edit menus are included with all Windows-compatible applications, although they are somewhat customized to work with AutoCAD. The menu associated with the icon contains commands to control the appearance and position of the drawing area.

Commands in the File menu are for opening and saving new and existing drawing files, printing, linking on the Internet, exporting files to another application, choosing basic utility options, and exiting the application. The Edit menu contains the Undo and Redo commands, the Cut and Paste tools, and options for creating links between AutoCAD files and other files. The Help menu (the last menu on the right) works like all Windows Help menus and contains a couple of AutoCAD-specific entries as well, including some online resources and a context-sensitive help feature called the Info Palette.

The other eight menus contain the most-often-used AutoCAD commands. You will find that if you can master the logic of how the commands are organized by menu, you can quickly find the command you want. Here is a short description of each of the other AutoCAD drop-down menus:

View   Contains tools for controlling the display of your drawing file.

Insert   Contains commands for placing drawings and images or parts of them inside other drawings.

Format   Contains commands for setting up the general parameters for a new drawing.

Tools   Contains special tools for use while you are working on the current drawing, such as those for finding the length of a line or for running a special macro.

Draw   Contains commands for creating new objects (such as lines or circles) on the screen.

Dimension   Contains commands for dimensioning a drawing.

Modify   Contains commands for changing existing objects in the drawing.

Window   Contains commands for displaying currently open windows and lists currently open drawing files.

The Toolbars

Just below the drop-down menus is the most extensive of the toolbars—the Standard toolbar.

The 22 icons on the AutoCAD Standard toolbar don't appear as buttons until you point to them, and they are arranged into seven logical groups. The icons on the left half of the Standard toolbar are mostly for commands used in all Windows-compatible applications, so you might be familiar with them. The icons on the right half of the Standard toolbar are AutoCAD commands that you use during your regular drawing activities for a variety of tasks. You use these commands to take care of a number of tasks, including the following:

▶ Changing the view of the drawing on the screen

▶ Changing the properties of an object, such as color or linetype

▶ Borrowing parts of an unopened drawing to use in your current drawing

▶ Displaying a set of palettes that contain objects you can use in your drawing

> **LT has only 21 Standard toolbar buttons. It's missing the Sheet Set Manager button because it doesn't have this feature.**

Toolbar Flyouts

Notice that one icon on the Standard toolbar has a little triangular arrow in the lower-right corner. This arrow indicates that clicking this icon displays more than one command. Follow these steps to see how this special icon works.

1. Move the cursor up to the Standard toolbar, and point to the icon that has a magnifying glass with a rectangle in it.

2. Rest the arrow on the button for a moment without clicking. A small window opens just below it, displaying the command the button represents. In this case, the window should say "Zoom Window." This is a tool tip—all buttons have them. Notice the small arrow in the lower-right corner of the icon. This is the multiple-command arrow mentioned earlier.

3. Place the arrow cursor on the button and hold down the left mouse button. A column of eight buttons drops down vertically below the

original button. The top button in the column is a duplicate of the button you clicked. This column of buttons is called a *toolbar flyout*.

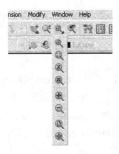

4. While still holding down the mouse button, drag the arrow down over each button until you get to the one that has a magnifying glass with a piece of white paper on it. Hold the arrow there until you see the tool tip. It should say "Zoom All." Now release the mouse button. The flyout disappears, and AutoCAD executes the Zoom All command. Look in the Command window at the bottom of the screen.

At the end of the top line of text is "_all." This tells you that you have used the All option of the Zoom command. This flyout is called the *Zoom flyout* because it contains tools for changing views of the drawing, or "zooming around in the drawing."

5. Look at the Standard toolbar where the Zoom Window button was previously. Notice that it's been replaced by the Zoom All button.

The Zoom All command changes the view of your drawing to include special pre-set parameters. We'll look at this command in Chapter 3.

T I P On a toolbar flyout, the button you select replaces the button that was on the toolbar. This arrangement is handy if you are going to be using the same command several times, because the button for the command is readily available and you don't have to open the flyout to select it again. The order of the flyout buttons remains the same, so when you open the Zoom flyout again, the Zoom Window button will be at the top of the list. You will need to become familiar with any flyout buttons you use, because the last one used becomes the representative button on the home toolbar.

The behavior of the Zoom flyout on the Standard toolbar is the same as the behavior of flyouts in general.

 N O T E Whenever you start up AutoCAD or LT for a new drawing session, the toolbars are reset and contain the original flyout buttons.

The toolbar flyouts are actually regular toolbars that have been attached to another toolbar. There are 29 toolbars in all, and only 2 are flyouts—the Zoom flyout I just discussed, and the Insert flyout on the Draw toolbar. You can display the Zoom and Insert flyouts as regular toolbars, independent of the Standard and Draw toolbars.

LT has 22 toolbars compared with AutoCAD's 29. The additional toolbars in AutoCAD are almost all for 3D and rendering tools.

Displaying and Arranging Toolbars

In this section, I'll use the Zoom toolbar to show you some ways you can control and manipulate toolbars. Follow these steps:

1. Right-click any toolbar button on the screen to open the Toolbars menu (see Figure 1.6).

FIGURE 1.6: The Toolbars menu

2. Click Zoom to display the Zoom toolbar in the form of a floating box in the drawing area.

Notice that the Zoom toolbar now has a title bar. Toolbars that are positioned on the drawing area have title bars. By placing the cursor on the title bar and holding down the left mouse button, you can drag the toolbar around the screen. Try this with the Zoom toolbar.

3. Click and drag the Zoom toolbar to the right side of the screen. You will notice that as you drag it, the toolbar stays put, and you are dragging a rectangle of the same size as the toolbar (see Figure 1.7). As you drag the rectangle to the right of the drawing area and begin to move it off the drawing area onto the right side of the screen, the rectangle becomes taller and thinner.

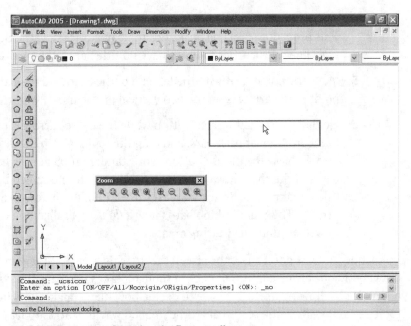

FIGURE 1.7: Dragging the Zoom toolbar

4. Release the left mouse button once the toolbar is out of the drawing area. The rectangle changes to the Zoom toolbar, which is now positioned off the drawing area without its title bar.

This procedure is called *docking* a toolbar. Notice how the Standard and Object Properties toolbars have no title bars—they are docked.

5. Move the cursor arrow to the left end of the Standard toolbar so the point of the arrow is on the two vertical grab bars.

6. Hold down the left mouse button while the cursor arrow is on the Standard toolbar grab bars, and drag the toolbar onto the drawing area. Release the mouse button. The Standard toolbar now has a title bar, and the space it was occupying at the top of the screen has been filled, making the drawing area a little larger, as you can see in Figure 1.8. The Standard toolbar is now a *floating* toolbar and can be moved around the drawing area.

Floating toolbars don't affect the size of the drawing area, but they cover your drawing. Each row or column of docked toolbars takes up space that would otherwise be drawing area. You have to decide how many docked and floating toolbars you need on the screen at a time. A good way to start is to leave the Standard, Layers, and Properties toolbars docked at the top of the screen and the Draw and Modify toolbars docked on the left side of the screen, as shown earlier in Figure 1.2.

Grab bars are the two lines at the left end of a horizontal toolbar or at the top of a vertical one. They represent the one place to grab a docked toolbar to move it. You can also change a docked toolbar into a floating toolbar by double-clicking its grab bars.

FIGURE 1.8: The Standard toolbar on the drawing area

To put the Standard toolbar back where it was and delete the Zoom toolbar, follow these steps:

1. Drag the Standard toolbar up to its former position above the Layers and Properties toolbars.

2. Drag the Zoom toolbar back onto the drawing area, using the grab bars. You can easily change the shape of any floating toolbar by dragging its edge. Let's change the shape of this toolbar.

3. Move the cursor to the far-right edge of the Zoom toolbar until the crosshair cursor changes to a two-way arrow.

Hold down the left mouse button with the cursor on the right edge of the toolbar, and drag the arrow to the left until the rectangle changes shape. Release the mouse button.

You can reshape and reposition each floating toolbar to fit on the drawing area just as you like it. You won't need the Zoom toolbar just now, so remove it.

4. Move the cursor up to the title bar and click the box with an × in it to close the Zoom toolbar.

If your Draw and Modify toolbars are positioned on the left side of the drawing area as shown earlier in Figure 1.2, continue with the next section. If these toolbars are in another location on the drawing area, try the steps you used in this section to dock them on the left side. If the toolbars are not visible, right-click any visible toolbar button, and then choose Draw. Drag the Draw toolbar to the left side of the drawing area and dock it. Do the same with the Modify toolbar, positioning it next to the Draw toolbar.

This arrangement of the toolbars will be convenient because you often use commands on these five toolbars. When you need other toolbars temporarily, you can use the Toolbars menu to display them in the drawing area and let them float.

Custom Toolbars

You can customize each toolbar, and you can build your own custom toolbars with only the command buttons you use. You can even design your own buttons for commands that aren't already represented by buttons on the toolbars. These activities are for more advanced users, however, and are not covered in this book. To find out more about how to customize toolbars, see *Mastering AutoCAD 2005 and AutoCAD LT 2005* by George Omura (Sybex, 2004).

Profiles

 As you become accustomed to working with AutoCAD, you will develop your own preferences for the layout of the AutoCAD Graphics window, including:

▶ Which toolbars are docked and where

▶ The shape of the crosshair cursor

▶ The background color of the drawing area

You control these features from the Options dialog box. If you share your workstation with others, you will find it convenient to set up a profile and save it. That way, if someone changes the organization of your Graphics window, you can quickly restore your preferences. Here's how to do this:

1. Set the toolbars on your screen as you prefer them.

2. Choose Tools ➤ Options to open the Options dialog box, click the Display tab, and make any changes you want to the color of the background and cursor or to the visibility of slide bars.

3. Click the Profiles tab, which is shown in Figure 1.9.

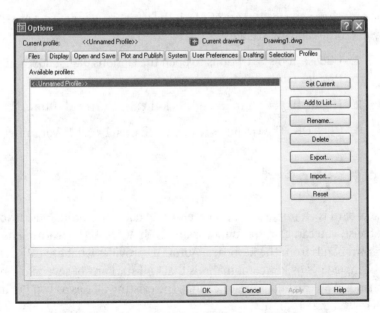

FIGURE 1.9: The Profiles tab in the Options dialog box

> **LT does not have the Profiles feature. LT users can skip ahead to "The Keyboard" section.**

4. Click the Add To List button to open the Add Profile dialog box, which is shown in Figure 1.10.

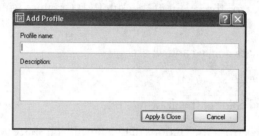

FIGURE 1.10: The Add Profile dialog box

5. In the Profile Name box, type the name of your profile. You also have the option of entering a description below the name.

6. Click Apply & Close. Your new profile appears in the Available Profiles list. This new profile is the arrangement of the screen that was current when you added your profile to the list.

7. Click OK to close the Options dialog box.

The next time you start up AutoCAD, if the Graphics window is not set up the way you want, follow these steps:

1. Choose Tools ➤ Options to open the Options dialog box, and click the Profiles tab.

2. Highlight your profile, and click the Set Current button.

3. Click OK. The Graphics window will then be set to your preferences.

The Keyboard

The keyboard is an important tool for entering data and commands. If you are a good typist, you can gain speed in working with AutoCAD by learning how to enter commands from the keyboard. AutoCAD provides what are called *alias keys*—single keys or key combinations that will start any of several often-used commands. You can add more or change the existing aliases as you get more familiar with the program.

In addition to the alias keys, you can use several of the F keys (function keys) on the top row of the keyboard as two-way or three-way toggles (switches) to turn AutoCAD functions on and off. Although buttons on the screen duplicate these functions (Snap, Grid, and so on), it is sometimes faster to use the F keys.

Finally, you can activate commands on the drop-down menus from the keyboard, rather than using the mouse. If you press the Alt key, an underlined letter, called a *hotkey*, appears on each menu. Pressing the key for the underlined letter activates the menu. Each command on the menu also has a hotkey. Once you activate the menu with the hotkey combination, you can type the underlined letter of these commands. For a few commands, this method can be the fastest way to start them up and to select options.

While working in AutoCAD, you will need to key in a lot of data, such as dimensions and construction notes, answer questions with "yes" or "no," and use the arrow keys. You will use the keyboard constantly. It may help to get into the habit of keeping the left hand on the keyboard and the right hand on the mouse—if you are right-handed—or the other way around, if you are left-handed.

The Mouse

Your mouse will most likely have two or three buttons. (If it's an IntelliMouse, it will have two or more buttons with a wheel between them.) So far in this chapter, you have used the left mouse button for choosing menus, commands, or command options or for holding down the button and dragging a menu, toolbar, or window. The left mouse button is the one you will be using most often, but you will also use the right mouse button.

While drawing, you will use the right mouse button for the following three operations:

> ▶ To display a menu containing options relevant to the particular step you are in at the moment

> ▶ To use in combination with the Shift or Control key to display a menu containing special drawing aids called Object Snaps (see Chapter 10)

> ▶ To display a menu of toolbars when the pointer is on any icon of a toolbar that is currently open

If you have a three-button mouse, the middle button is usually programmed to display the Object Snap menu, instead of using the right button with the Shift key. If you have an IntelliMouse, you can use the wheel in several ways to control the view of your drawing. I'll cover those methods in subsequent chapters.

AutoCAD makes extensive use of toolbars and the right-click menu feature. This makes your mouse an important input tool. The keyboard is necessary for inputting numeric data and text, and it has hotkeys and aliases that can speed up your work. But the mouse is the primary tool for starting commands, selecting options, and controlling toolbars.

The next chapter will familiarize you with a few basic commands that will enable you to draw a small diagram. If you are going to take a break and want to close AutoCAD, choose File ➢ Exit, and choose not to save the drawing.

Are You Experienced?

Now you can...

- ☑ **open a new drawing using the Start Up dialog box**

- ☑ **recognize the elements of the AutoCAD Graphics window**

- ☑ **understand how the Command window works and why it's important**

- ☑ **use drop-down menus**

- ☑ **call up and control the positioning of toolbars**

- ☑ **save a profile of your screen setup in AutoCAD**

CHAPTER 2

Basic Commands to Get Started

- ▶ Understanding coordinate systems
- ▶ Drawing your first figure
- ▶ Erasing, offsetting, filleting, extending, and trimming lines in a drawing

N ow that you have taken a quick tour of the AutoCAD and LT screens, you are ready to begin drawing. In this chapter, you will be introduced to a few basic commands used in drawing with AutoCAD and AutoCAD LT. To get you started, I will guide you through the process of drawing a box (see Figure 2.1).

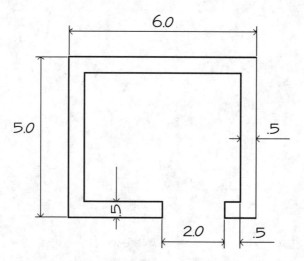

FIGURE 2.1:   The box to be drawn

You need to use only five or six commands to draw the box. First, you'll become familiar with the Line command and how to make lines a specific length. Then I'll go over the strategy for completing the box.

The Line Command

In traditional architectural drafting, lines were often drawn to extend slightly past their endpoints (see Figure 2.2). This is no longer done in CAD except for special effects.

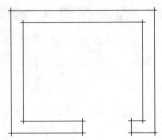

FIGURE 2.2: The box drawn with overlapping lines

The *Line command* draws a line between locations on existing lines, between geometric figures, or between two points that you can choose anywhere within the drawing area. You can designate these points by clicking them on the screen, by entering the X and Y coordinates for each point in the Command window, or by entering distances and angles at the command line. After you draw the first segment of a line, you can end the command or draw another line segment from the end of the first one. You can continue to draw adjoining line segments for as long as you like. Let's see how this works.

To be sure that you start with your drawing area set up the way it is set up for this book, choose File ➢ Close to close any open drawings. If multiple drawings are open, repeat the Close command for each drawing until you have no drawings open. Your drawing area will be gray and blank with no crosshair cursor, your toolbars will disappear except for five buttons on the Standard toolbar, and you will have only four drop-down menus.

1. Click the New button at the left end of the Standard toolbar. In the Create New Drawing dialog box, click the Start From Scratch icon, if it's not already selected, and click OK. The menus, crosshair cursor, and toolbars return, and you now have a blank drawing in the drawing area.

2. Glance down at the status bar at the bottom of your screen. All buttons except Model should be off—that is, in an unpushed state. If any of the others appear to be pushed, click them to turn them off.

3. Be sure that the Draw and Modify toolbars are docked on the left side of the drawing area, as shown in Figure 2.3. Refer to Chapter 1 if you need a reminder on how to display or move toolbars.

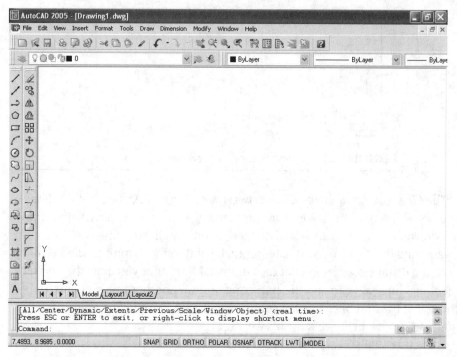

FIGURE 2.3: The Draw and Modify toolbars docked on the left side of the drawing area, and all status bar buttons except Model turned off

You can also start the Line command by choosing Draw ➢ Line or by typing L and pressing the Enter key.

4. Click the Line button at the top of the Draw toolbar.

Look at the bottom of the Command window and see how the Command: prompt has changed.

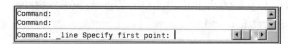

The prompt now tells you that the Line command is started (Command: _line) and that AutoCAD is waiting for you to designate the first point of the line (Specify first point:).

5. Move the cursor onto the drawing area, and using the left mouse button, click a random point to start a line.

6. Move the cursor away from the point you clicked, and notice how a line segment appears that stretches like a rubber band from the point

you just picked to the cursor. The line changes length and direction as you move the cursor.

7. Look at the Command window again, and notice that the prompt has changed.

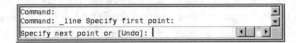

It is now telling you that AutoCAD is waiting for you to designate the next point (Specify next point or [Undo]:).

8. Continue picking points and adding lines as you move the cursor around the screen (see Figure 2.4). After you draw the third segment, the Command window repeats the Specify next point or [Close/Undo]: prompt each time you pick another point.

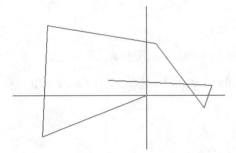

FIGURE 2.4:   Drawing several line segments

9. When you've drawn six or seven line segments, press Enter to end the Line command. The cursor separates from the last drawn line segment. Look at the Command window once again.

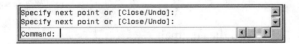

The Command: prompt has returned to the bottom line. This tells you that no command is running.

In this exercise, you used the left mouse button to select the Line button from the Draw toolbar and also to pick several points in the drawing area to make the line segments. You then pressed Enter (⏎) on the keyboard to end the Line command.

N O T E   In the exercises that follow, the Enter symbol (⏎) will be used. When I say to "type" or "enter" something, it means to type the data that follows the word *type* or *enter* and then to press the Enter key (⏎). For example, rather than writing "type L and press the Enter key," I'll write "type L⏎."

Using Coordinates

Try using the Line command again, but instead of picking points in the drawing area with the mouse as you did before, this time enter X and Y coordinates for each point from the keyboard. To see how, follow these steps:

1. Click the Erase button on the Modify toolbar.

2. Type all⏎.

3. Press ⏎ to clear the screen.

> You can also start the Erase command by typing e⏎ or by choosing Modify ➢ Erase.

Now start drawing lines again by following these steps:

1. Start the Line command again by clicking the Line button on the Draw toolbar.

2. Type 2,2⏎.

3. Type 6,3⏎.

4. Type 4,6⏎.

5. Type 1,3⏎.

6. Type 10,6⏎.

7. Type 10,1⏎.

8. Type 2,7⏎.

9. Press ⏎ again to end the command.

The lines will be similar to those you drew previously, but this time you know where each point is located relative to the 0,0 point. In the drawing area, every point has an absolute X and Y coordinate. In steps 2 through 8, you entered the X and Y coordinates for each point. For a new drawing, such as this one, the origin (0,0 point) is in the lower-left corner of the drawing area, and all points in the drawing area have positive X and Y coordinates (see Figure 2.5).

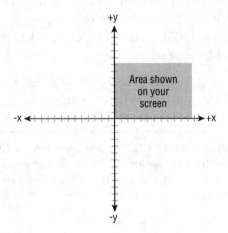

FIGURE 2.5: The X and Y coordinates on the drawing area

Let's explore how the cursor is related to the coordinates in the drawing.

1. Move the cursor around, and notice the left end of the status bar at the bottom of the screen. This is the coordinate readout, and it displays the coordinates of the cursor's position.

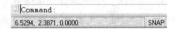

2. Move the cursor as close to the lower-left corner of the drawing area as you can without it changing into an arrow. The coordinate readout should be close to 0.0000,0.0000,0.0000.

NOTE   In AutoCAD, you will see a readout for the Z coordinate as well, but you can ignore it for now because you will be working in only two dimensions for the majority of this book. The Z coordinate will always read 0 until you work in three dimensions (see the Appendix). AutoCAD LT does not have the readout for the Z coordinate.

3. Move the cursor to the top-left corner of the drawing area. The readout will change to something close to 0.0000,9.0000,0.0000, indicating that the top of the screen is 9 units from the bottom.

4. Move the cursor one more time to the upper-right corner of the drawing area. The readout will still have a Y coordinate of approximately 9.0000, and the X coordinate will now have a value between 12.0000 and 16.0000, depending on the size of your monitor and how the various parts of the AutoCAD Graphics window are laid out on your screen. (See Chapter 1 for a recap.)

The drawing area of a new drawing is preset to be 9 units high and 12–16 units wide, with the lower-left corner of the drawing at the coordinates 0,0.

 N O T E   For the moment, it doesn't matter what measure of distance these units represent. I'll address that topic in Chapter 3. And don't worry about the four decimal places in the coordinate readout. The number of places is controlled by a setting you will learn about soon.

Relative Coordinates

Once you understand the coordinate system used by AutoCAD, you can draw lines to any length and in any direction. Look at the box shown earlier in Figure 2.1. Because you know the dimensions, you can calculate, by adding and subtracting, the absolute coordinates for each *vertex*—the connecting point between two line segments—and then use the Line command to draw the shape by entering these coordinates from the keyboard. But AutoCAD offers you several tools for drawing this box much more easily. Two of these tools are the relative Cartesian and the relative polar coordinate systems.

When drawing lines, these systems use a set of new points based on the last point designated, rather than the 0,0 point of the drawing area. They are called "relative" coordinate systems because the coordinates used are *relative* to the last point specified. If the first point of a line is located at the coordinate 4,6, and you want the line to extend 8 units to the right, the coordinate that is relative to the first point is 8,0 (8 units in the positive X direction and 0 units in the positive Y direction), while the actual—or *absolute*—coordinate of the second point is 12,6.

The *relative Cartesian coordinate system* uses relative X and Y coordinates in just the manner shown, and the *relative polar coordinate system* relies on a distance and an angle relative to the last point specified. You will probably favor one system over the other, but you need to know both systems because at times, because of the information you have at hand, you will be able to use only one of the two. A limitation of this nature will be illustrated in Chapter 4.

When entering relative coordinates, you need to type an "at" symbol (@) before the coordinates. In the previous example, you would enter the relative Cartesian coordinates as @8,0. The @ lets AutoCAD know that the numbers following it represent coordinates that are relative to the last point designated.

Relative Cartesian Coordinates

The Cartesian system of coordinates, named after the philosopher René Descartes, who invented the X,Y coordinate system in the 1600s, uses a horizontal (X) and vertical (Y) component to locate a point relative to the 0,0 point. The relative Cartesian system uses the same components to locate the point relative to the last point picked, so it's a way of telling AutoCAD how far left or right and up or down to extend a line or to move an object from the last point picked (see Figure 2.6). If the direction is to the left, the X coordinate will be negative. Similarly, if the direction is down, the Y coordinate will be negative. Use this system when you know the horizontal and vertical distances from point 1 to point 2. To enter data using this system, use this form: @x,y.

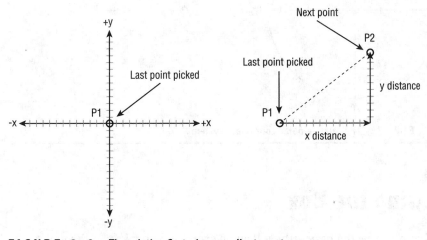

FIGURE 2.6: The relative Cartesian coordinate system

Relative Polar Coordinates

This system requires a known distance and direction from point 1 to point 2. Calculating the distance is straightforward: it's always positive and is simply the distance away from point 1 that point 2 will be placed. The direction requires a convention for determining an angle. AutoCAD defines right (toward three o'clock) as the direction of the 0° angle. All other directions are determined from a counterclockwise rotation (see Figure 2.7). On your screen, up is 90°, left is 180°, down is 270°, and a full circle is 360°. To let AutoCAD know that you are entering an angle and not a relative Y coordinate, use the "less than" symbol (<) before the angle and after the distance. So in the previous example, to designate a point 8 units to the right of the first point, you would enter @8<0.

 N O T E   Remember, use the relative polar coordinates method to draw a line from the first point when you know the distance and direction to its next point. Enter data using this form: **@distance<angle**.

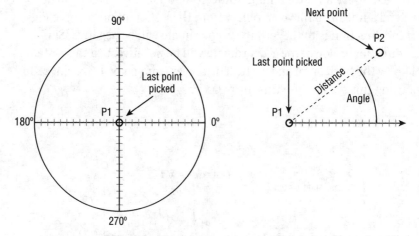

FIGURE 2.7: The relative polar coordinate system

Drawing the Box

Now that you have the basics, the following exercises will take you through the steps to draw the four lines that form the outline of the box using both relative coordinate systems.

Using Relative Cartesian Coordinates

To begin drawing the box, we'll use the same drawing.

1. If your drawing is already blank, jump to step 2. If you still have lines on your drawing, start the Erase command, type all↵, and then press ↵ again.

2. Click the Line button at the top of the Draw toolbar.

3. At the Specify First point: prompt in the Command window, type 3,3↵. This is an absolute Cartesian coordinate and will be the first point.

4. Type @6,0↵.

5. Type @0,5↵.

6. Type @-6,0↵.

7. Type c↵. The letter *c* stands for *close*. Entering this letter after drawing several lines closes the shape by extending the next line segment from the last point specified to the first point (see Figure 2.8). It also ends the Line command. Notice that in the Command window the prompt is Command:. This signifies that AutoCAD is ready for a new command.

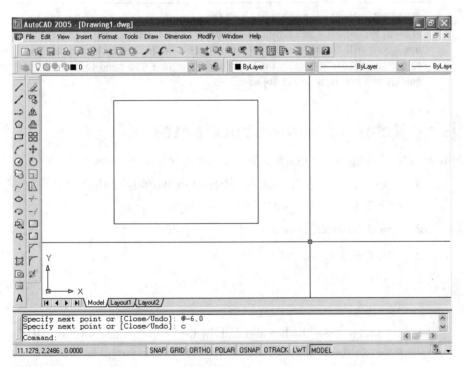

FIGURE 2.8: The first four lines of the box

Erasing Lines

To prepare to draw the box again, use the Erase command to erase the four lines you have just drawn.

1. Start the Erase command. Notice how the cursor changes from the crosshair to a little square. This is called the *pickbox*. When you see it on the screen, it's a sign that AutoCAD is ready for you to select objects on the screen. Also, notice the Command window. It is prompting you to select objects.

2. Place the pickbox on one of the lines and click. The line changes to a dashed line. This is called *ghosting* or *highlighting*.

3. Do the same thing with the rest of the lines.

4. Press ↵. The objects are erased, and the Erase command ends.

N O T E   You have been introduced to two methods of selecting lines to be erased: typing all↵ and using the pickbox to select them. Throughout the book, you will be introduced to several other ways to select objects. The selection process is important in AutoCAD because you need to be able to quickly and precisely select objects.

Using Relative Polar Coordinates

Now draw the box again using the polar method by following these steps:

1. Start the Line command. (Click the Line button on the Draw toolbar.)

2. Type 3,3↵ to start the box at the same point.

3. Type @6<0↵.

4. Type @5<90↵.

5. Type @6<180↵.

6. Type c↵ to close the box and end the Line command. Your box will once again resemble the box shown earlier in Figure 2.8.

You can see from this exercise that you can use either method to draw a simple shape. When the shapes you are drawing get more complex and the amount of available information about the shapes varies from segment to segment, one of the two relative coordinate systems will turn out to be more appropriate. As you start drawing the floor plan of the cabin in Chapters 3 and 4, you will get more practice using these systems.

Some additional tools make the process of drawing simple, *orthogonal* lines like these much easier. I'll introduce these tools in the following three chapters.

The Offset Command

The next task is to create the lines that represent the inside walls of the box. Because they are all equidistant from the lines you have already drawn, the *Offset command* is the appropriate command to use. You will offset the existing lines 0.5 units to the inside.

The Offset command involves three steps:

▶ Setting the offset distance

▶ Picking the object to offset

▶ Indicating the offset direction

Here's how it works:

1. Be sure the prompt line in the Command window reads `Command:`. If it doesn't, press the Esc key until it does. Then click the Offset button on the Modify toolbar. The prompt changes to `Specify offset distance or [Through] <1.0000>:`. This is a confusing prompt, but it will become clear soon. For now, let's specify an offset distance through the keyboard.

You can also start the Offset command by choosing Modify ➢ Offset or by typing o↵.

W A R N I N G   As important as it is to keep an eye on the Command window, some of the prompts may not make sense to you until you get used to them.

2. Type .5↵ for a distance. Now you move to the second stage of the command.

Note that the cursor has changed to a pickbox, and the prompt changes to say `Select object to offset or <exit>:`.

3. Place the pickbox on one of the lines and click. The selected line ghosts (see Figure 2.9), the cursor changes back to the crosshair, and the prompt changes to `Specify point on side to offset:`. Auto-CAD is telling you that to determine the direction of the offset, you must specify a point on one side of the line or the other. You make the choice by picking anywhere in the drawing area, on the side of the line where you want the offset to occur.

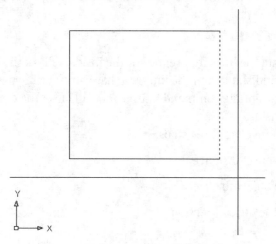

FIGURE 2.9: The first line to be offset is selected.

4. Pick a point somewhere inside the box. The offset takes place, and the new line is exactly 0.5 units to the inside of the chosen line (see Figure 2.10). Notice that the pickbox comes back on. The Offset command is still running, and you can offset more lines the same distance.

FIGURE 2.10: The first line is offset.

You have three more lines to offset.

5. Click another line; then click inside the box again. The second line is offset.

6. Click a third line, click inside the box, click the fourth line, and then click again inside the box (see Figure 2.11).

F I G U R E 2 . 1 1 : Four lines have been offset.

  N O T E   The offset distance stays set at the last distance you specify— 0.5, in this case—until you change it.

7. Press ↵ to end the Offset command.

This command is similar to the Line command in that it keeps running until it is stopped. With Offset, after the first offset, the prompts switch between Select object to offset or <exit>: and Specify point on side to offset: until you press ↵ to end the command.

The inside lines are now drawn, but to complete the box, you need to clean up the intersecting corners. To handle this task efficiently, we will use a new tool called the Fillet command.

SPECIFYING DISTANCES FOR THE OFFSET COMMAND

The prompt you see in the Command window after starting the Offset command is:

```
Specify offset distance or [Through] <1.0000>:
```

This prompt is actually describing several options for setting the offset distance.

▶ Enter a distance from the keyboard.

▶ Pick two points on the screen to establish the offset distance as the distance between those two points.

▶ Press ↵ to accept the offset distance that is displayed in the prompt in the angle brackets.

▶ Type **t**↵ to use the Through option. When you select this option, you are prompted to select the line to offset. You are then prompted to pick a point. The line will be offset to that point. When you pick the next line to offset, you then pick a new point to locate the position of the new line. The Through option allows each line to be offset a different distance.

As you get used to using Offset, you will find uses for each of these options.

The Fillet Command

The *Fillet command* lets you round off a corner formed by two lines. You control the radius of the curve, so if you set the curve's radius to zero, the lines will form a sharp corner. In this way, you can clean up corners such as the ones formed by the lines inside the box.

You can also start the Fillet command by choosing Modify ➤ Fillet or by typing f↵.

1. At the Command: prompt, click the Fillet button on the Modify toolbar. Notice the Command window:

```
Command: _fillet
Current settings: Mode = TRIM, Radius = 0.0000
Select first object or [Polyline/Radius/Trim/mUltiple]:
```

The default fillet radius should be 0.0000 units. Like the Offset distance, the Fillet radius remains set at whatever length you specify until you change it.

2. If your command window displays a radius of 0.0000, go on to step 3. Otherwise, type **r⏎**, and then type)⏎ to change the radius to zero.

3. Move the cursor—now a pickbox—to the box, and click two intersecting lines, as shown in Figure 2.12. The intersecting lines will both be trimmed to make a sharp corner (see Figure 2.13). The Fillet command automatically ends.

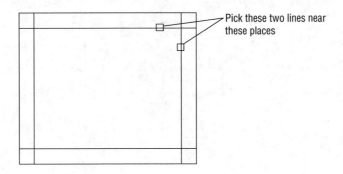

Pick these two lines near these places

FIGURE 2.12: Pick two lines to execute the Fillet command.

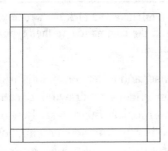

FIGURE 2.13: The first cleaned-up corner

4. Press ⏎ to restart the command, and then fillet two more lines in a similar fashion.

Once a command has ended, you can restart it by pressing either ⏎ or the spacebar or by right-clicking and choosing Repeat from the shortcut menu.

5. Continue restarting the command and filleting the lines for each corner until all corners are cleaned up (see Figure 2.14).

T I P   In most cases, you will get the same effect by pressing the spacebar as you get by pressing ⏎. The exception is when you are entering data in the Command window; in that case, pressing the spacebar just makes a space.

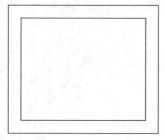

F I G U R E 2 . 1 4 : The box with all corners cleaned up

N O T E   If you make a mistake and pick the wrong part of a line or the wrong line, press Esc to end the command and then type u⏎. This will undo the effect of the last command.

Used together like this, the Offset and Fillet commands are a powerful combination of tools to lay out walls on a floor plan drawing. Because these commands are so important, let's take a closer look at them to see how they work. Both commands are on the Modify toolbar or drop-down menu, both have the option to enter a numeric value or accept the current value—for offset distance and fillet radius—and both hold that value as the default until it is changed. However, the Offset command keeps running until you stop it, and the Fillet command stops after each use and must be restarted for multiple fillets. These two commands are probably the most frequently used tools in AutoCAD. You will learn about more of their uses in later chapters.

The Fillet command has a sister command, the Chamfer command, that is used to bevel corners with straight lines. When the distances for the Chamfer command are set to 0, you can use it to clean up corners in the same way that you use the Fillet command. Some users prefer to use Chamfer rather than Fillet because they don't bevel corners but may at times use Fillet to round off corners. By using Chamfer to clean up corners, Fillet can have any radius and won't have to constantly be reset to 0. You will develop your own preference.

Completing the Box

The final step in completing the box (see Figure 2.1 earlier in this chapter) is to make an opening in the bottom wall. From the diagram, you can see that the opening is 2 units wide and set off from the right inside corner by 0.5 units. To make this opening, you will use the Offset command twice, changing the offset distance for each offset, to create marks for the opening.

Offsetting Lines to Mark an Opening

Follow these steps to establish the precise position of the opening:

1. At the Command: prompt, start the Offset command, either from the Modify toolbar or the Modify menu. Notice the Command window. The default distance is now set at 0.5, the offset distance you previously set to offset the outside lines of the box to make the inside lines. You want to use this distance again. Press ⏎ to accept this preset distance.

2. Pick the inside vertical line on the right, and then pick a point to the left of this line. The line is offset to make a new line 0.5 units to its left (see Figure 2.15).

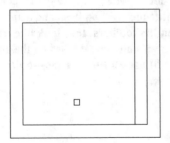

FIGURE 2.15: Offsetting the first line of the opening

3. Press ↵ to end the Offset command, and then press it again to restart the command. This will allow you to reset the offset distance.

4. Enter 2 as the new offset distance and press ↵.

5. Click the new line, and then pick a point to the left. Press ↵ to end the Offset command (see Figure 2.16).

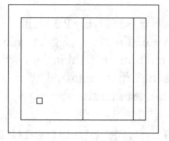

FIGURE 2.16: Offsetting the second line of the opening

You now have two new lines indicating where the opening will be. You can use these lines to form the opening using the Extend and Trim commands.

> **TIP** The "buttons" you have been clicking in this chapter are also referred to as "icons" and "tools." When they are in dialog boxes or on the status bar, they have icons (little pictures) on them and actually look like buttons to push. When they are on the toolbars, they look like icons. But when you move the pointer arrow cursor onto one, it takes on the appearance of a button with an icon on it. I will use all three terms—*button*, *icon*, and *tool*—interchangeably in this book.

Extending Lines

You use the *Extend command* to lengthen (extend) lines to meet other lines or geometric figures (called *boundary edges*). Executing the Extend command may be a little tricky at first until you see how it works. Once you understand it, however, it will become automatic. The command has two steps: first, you pick the boundary edge or edges, and second, you pick the lines you want to extend to meet those boundary edges. After selecting the boundary edges, you must press ↵ before you begin selecting lines to extend.

1. To begin the Extend command, click the Extend button on the Modify toolbar. Notice the Command window.

```
Current settings: Projection=UCS Edge=None
Select boundary edges ...
Select objects:
```

The bottom line says Select objects:, but in this case you need to observe the bottom two lines of text in order to know that AutoCAD is prompting you to select boundary edges.

2. Pick the very bottom horizontal line (see Figure 2.17) and press ↵.

You can also start the Extend command by choosing **Modify ➣ Extend** from the Modify drop-down menu or by typing ex↵.

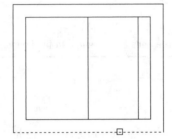

FIGURE 2.17: Selecting a line to be a boundary edge

T I P   The Select Objects: prompt would be more useful if it said, "Select objects and press Enter when finished selecting objects." But it doesn't. You have to train yourself to press ↵ when you finish selecting objects in order to get out of selection mode and move on to the next step in the command.

3. Pick the two new vertical lines created by the Offset command. Be sure to place the pickbox somewhere on the lower halves of these lines, or AutoCAD will ignore your picks. The lines are extended to the boundary edge line. Press ↵ to end the Extend command (see Figure 2.18).

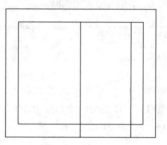

FIGURE 2.18: The lines are extended to the boundary edge.

Trimming Lines

The final step is to trim away the horizontal lines to complete the opening. To do this, you use the *Trim command*. As with the Extend command, there are two steps. The first is to select reference lines—in this case, they're called *cutting edges* because they determine the edge or edges to which a line is trimmed. The second step is to pick the lines that are to be trimmed.

1. Click the Trim button on the Modify toolbar to start the Trim command. Notice the Command window. Similar to the Extend command, the bottom line prompts you to select objects, but the second line up tells you to select cutting edges.

2. Pick the two vertical offset lines that were just extended as your cutting edges, and then press ↵ (see Figure 2.19).

You can also start the Trim command by choosing Modify ➢ Trim from the Modify drop-down menu or by typing **tr**↵.

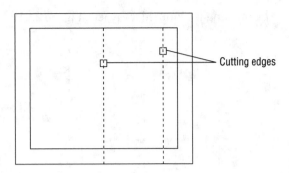

Cutting edges

FIGURE 2.19: Lines selected to be cutting edges

3. Pick the two horizontal lines across the opening somewhere between the cutting edge lines (see Figure 2.20).

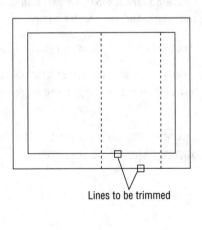

Lines to be trimmed

FIGURE 2.20: Lines selected to be trimmed

The opening is trimmed away (see Figure 2.21).

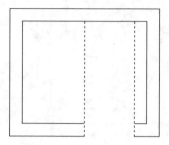

FIGURE 2.21: Lines are trimmed to make the opening.

 N O T E   If you trim the wrong line or wrong part of a line, you can click the Undo button on the Standard toolbar. This will undo the last trim without canceling the Trim command, and you can try again.

Now let's remove the extra part of our trimming guide lines.

1. Press ↵ twice—once to end the Trim command and again to restart it. This will allow you to pick new cutting edges for another trim operation.

2. Pick the two upper horizontal lines next to the opening as your cutting edges, shown in Figure 2.22, and press ↵.

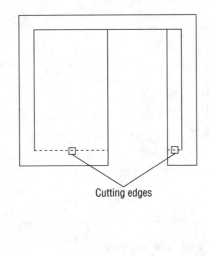

FIGURE 2.22: Lines picked to be cutting edges

3. Pick the two vertical lines that extend above the new opening. Be sure to pick them above the opening (see Figure 2.23). The lines are trimmed away, and the opening is complete. Press ↵ to end the Trim command (see Figure 2.24).

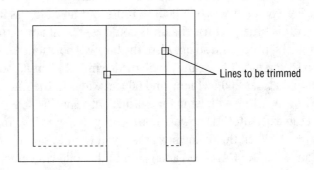

FIGURE 2.23: Lines picked to be trimmed

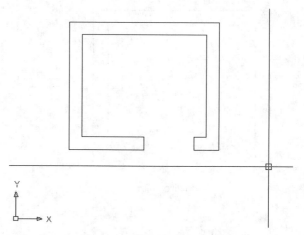

FIGURE 2.24: The completed trim

Congratulations! You have just completed the first drawing project in this book and have covered all the tools in this chapter. These skills will be useful as you learn how to work on drawings for actual projects.

A valuable exercise at this time would be to draw this box two or three more times, until you can do it without the instructions. This will be a confidence-builder and will get you ready to take on new information in the next chapter, in which you will set up a drawing for a building.

The box you drew was 6 units by 5 units, but how big was it? You really don't know at this time, because the units could represent any actual distance: inches, feet, meters, miles, and so on. Also, the box was positioned conveniently on the screen so you didn't have any problem viewing it. What if you were drawing a building that was 200 feet long and 60 feet wide? In the next chapter, you will learn how to set up a drawing for a project of a specific size.

You can exit AutoCAD now without saving this drawing. To do so, choose File ➢ Exit. When the dialog box asks if you want to save changes, click No. Or you can leave AutoCAD open and go on to the following practice section or the next chapter.

If You Would Like More Practice...

Draw the following object shown in Figure 2.25.

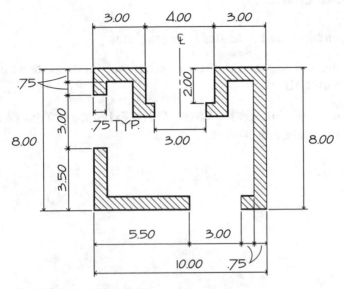

FIGURE 2.25: Practice drawing

You can use the same tools and strategy used to draw the box. Choose File ➤ New to start a new drawing, and click the Start From Scratch button in the Create New Drawing dialog box. Here's a summary of the steps to follow:

▶ Ignore the three openings at first.

▶ Draw the outside edge of the shape using one of the relative coordinate systems. To make sure the box fits on your screen, start the outline of the box in the lower-left corner at the absolute coordinate of 1,0.5.

▶ Offset the outside lines to create the inside wall.

▶ Fillet the corners to clean them up.

▶ Use the Offset, Extend, and Trim commands to create the three openings.

▶ Don't worry about trying to put in the dimensions, center line, or hatch lines. You'll learn how to create those objects later in the book.

Are You Experienced?

Now you can...

☑ **understand the basics of coordinates**

☑ **discern between the two relative coordinate systems used by AutoCAD**

☑ **use the Line, Erase, Offset, Fillet, Extend, and Trim commands to create a drawing**

Setting Up a Drawing

I n Chapter 2, we explored the default drawing area that is set up when you open a new drawing. It is probably 9 units high by 12 to 16 units wide, depending on the size of your monitor. You drew the box within this area. If you drew the additional diagram offered as a supplemental exercise, the drawing area was set up the same way.

For most of the rest of this book, you will be developing drawings for a cabin with outside wall dimensions of 25' × 16', but the tools you use and the skills you learn will enable you to draw objects of any size. In this chapter, you will learn how to set up the drawing area to lay out the floor plan for a building of a specific size. The decimal units with which you have been drawing until now will be changed to feet and inches, and the drawing area will be transformed so that it can represent an area large enough to display the floor plan of the cabin you will be drawing.

You will be introduced to some new tools that will help you visualize the area your screen represents and allow you to draw lines to a specified incremental distance, such as to the nearest foot. Finally, you will save this drawing to a floppy disk or to a special folder on your hard disk. At the end of the chapter is a general summary of the various kinds of units that AutoCAD supports.

Drawing Units

When you draw lines of a precise length in AutoCAD, you use one of five kinds of linear units. Angular units can also be any of five types. You can select the type of units to use, or you can accept the default Decimal units that you used in the last chapter.

When you start a new drawing, AutoCAD displays a blank drawing called Drawing*n*.dwg with the linear and angular units set to decimal numbers. The units and other basic setup parameters applied to this new drawing are based on a prototype drawing with default settings—including those for the units. This chapter will cover some of the tools for changing the basic parameters of a new drawing so you can tailor it to the cabin project or for your own project. You will start by setting up new units.

1. With AutoCAD running, close all drawings, and then click the New button (on the Standard toolbar) to start a new drawing. Depending on the way AutoCAD is set up, you will see either the Create New Drawing dialog box or the Select Template dialog box. If you see the Create New Drawing dialog box, be sure the Start From Scratch option is selected and click OK. If you see the Select Template dialog

box, click the arrow to the right of the Open button and select Open With No Template - Imperial.

To get started with the steps in this chapter, check to be sure that, for now, all the status bar buttons except Model are clicked to the Off position—that is, they will appear unpushed.

When we get to Chapter 10, you will see how to use templates to set up drawings.

2. Choose Format ➤ Units to open the Drawing Units dialog box (see Figure 3.1). In the Length area, Decimal is currently selected. Similarly, in the Angle area, Decimal Degrees is the default.

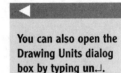

You can also open the Drawing Units dialog box by typing un.↵.

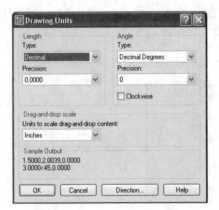

FIGURE 3.1: The Drawing Units dialog box

3. In the Length area, click the arrow in the Type drop-down list and select Architectural. These units are feet and inches, which you will be using for the cabin project.

Notice the two Precision drop-down lists at the bottom of the Length and Angle areas. When you changed the linear units specification from Decimal to Architectural, the number in the Precision drop-down list on the left changed from 0.0000 to 0'-0¹/₁₆". At this level of precision, linear distances are displayed to the nearest ¹/₁₆".

4. Select some of the other Length unit types from the list and notice the way the units appear in the Sample Output area at the bottom of the dialog box. Then select Architectural again.

N O T E   Drop-down lists are lists of choices with only the selected choice displayed. When you click the arrow, the list opens. When you make another selection, the list closes, and your choice is displayed. You can choose only one item at a time from the list.

5. Click the arrow in the Precision drop-down list in the Length area to display the choices of precision for Architectural units (see Figure 3.2). This setting controls the degree of precision to which AutoCAD will display a linear distance. If set to $\frac{1}{16}$", any line that is drawn more precisely—such as a line 6'-3$\frac{1}{32}$" long—is displayed to the nearest $\frac{1}{16}$" or, in the example, as 6'-3$\frac{1}{16}$". But the line will still be 6'-3$\frac{1}{32}$" long.

If you change the precision setting to $\frac{1}{32}$" and then use the Distance command (explained in Chapter 7) to measure the line, you will see that its length is 6'-3$\frac{1}{32}$".

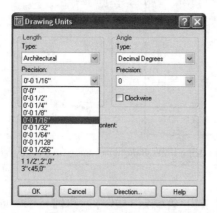

F I G U R E 3 . 2 :   The Precision drop-down list for Architectural units

6. Click 0'-0$\frac{1}{16}$" to maintain the precision for display of linear units at $\frac{1}{16}$".

If you open the Type drop-down list in the Angle area, you see a choice between Decimal Degrees and Deg/Min/Sec, among others. Most drafters find the decimal angular units the most practical, but the default precision setting is to the nearest degree. This might not be accurate enough, so you should change that to the nearest hundredth of a degree.

1. Click the arrow in the Precision drop-down list in the Angle area.

2. Click 0.00.

   The Drawing Units dialog box will now indicate that, in your drawing, you plan to use Architectural units with a precision of ¹⁄₁₆" and Decimal angular units with a precision of 0.00 (see Figure 3.3).

FIGURE 3.3: The Drawing Units dialog box after changes

Clicking the Direction button at the bottom of the Drawing Units dialog box opens the Direction Control dialog box that has settings to control the direction of 0 degrees. By default, 0 degrees is to the right—or east—and positive angular displacement goes in the counterclockwise direction. (See Figure 2.7 in Chapter 2 for an explanation of this.) These are the standard settings for most uses of CAD. There is no need to change these from the defaults. If you want to take a look, open the Direction Control dialog box, note the choices, and then click OK to close it. You won't have occasion in the course of this book to change any of those settings.

N O T E   **You will have a chance to work with the Surveyor angular units later in the book, in Chapter 12, when you develop a site plan for the cabin.**

3. Click OK in the Drawing Units dialog box to close it. Notice the coordinate readout in the lower-left corner of the screen. It now reads out in feet and inches.

This tour of the Drawing Units dialog box has introduced you to the choices you have for the types of units and the degree of precision for linear and angular measurement. The next step in setting up a drawing is to determine its size.

N O T E   If you accidentally click the mouse when the cursor is on a blank part of the drawing area, AutoCAD starts a rectangular window. I'll talk about these windows soon, but for now, just press the Esc key to close the window.

Drawing Size

As you discovered earlier, the default drawing area on the screen for a new drawing is 12 to 16 units wide and 9 units high. After changing the units to Architectural, the same drawing area is now 12 to 16 *inches* wide and 9 *inches* high.

You can check this by moving the crosshair cursor around on the drawing area and looking at the coordinate readout, as you did in the previous chapter.

T I P   When you change Decimal units to Architectural units, one Decimal unit translates to one inch. Some industries, such as civil engineering, often use Decimal units to represent feet instead of inches. If the units in their drawings are switched to Architectural, a distance that was a foot now measures as an inch. To correct this, the entire drawing must be scaled up by a factor of 12.

The drawing area is defined as the part of the screen in which you draw. You can make the distance across the drawing area larger or smaller through a process known as zooming in or out. To see how this works, you'll learn about a tool called the grid that helps you to draw and to visualize the size of your drawing.

The Grid

The *grid* is a pattern of regularly spaced dots used as an aid to drawing. You can set the grid to be visible or invisible. The area covered by the grid depends on a setting called Drawing Limits. To learn how to manipulate the grid size, you'll make the grid visible, use the Zoom In and Zoom Out commands to vary the view of the grid, and then change the area over which the grid extends by resetting the drawing limits. Before doing this, however, let's turn off the User Coordinate

System icon that currently sits in the lower-left corner of the drawing area. You'll display it again and learn how to use it in Chapter 8.

1. At the Command: prompt, type **ucsicon**↵, and then type **off**↵. The icon will disappear.

2. At the Command: prompt, move the crosshair cursor to the status bar at the bottom of the screen and click the Grid button. The button will appear to have been pushed down, and dots will appear on most of the drawing area (see Figure 3.4). These dots are the grid. They are preset by default to be ½" apart, and they extend from the 0,0 point (the Origin), out to the right, and up to the coordinate point 1'-0",0'-9". Notice that rows of grid dots run right along the left edge, top, and bottom of the drawing area, but the dots don't extend all the way to the right side. The grid dot at the 0,0 point is positioned exactly at the lower-left corner of the screen, and the grid at 1'-0",0'-9" is on the top edge, not too far from the upper-right corner.

You can also control the visibility of the UCS icon by choosing View ➤ Display ➤ UCS Icon ➤ On. If On has a check mark, clicking it turns off the UCS icon. If it doesn't, clicking turns the icon back on.

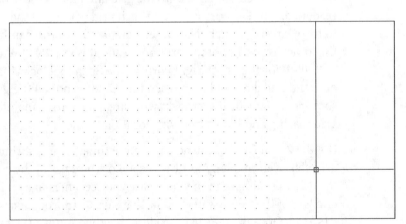

FIGURE 3.4: The AutoCAD default grid

3. For a better view of the entire grid, use the Zoom Out command. From the drop-down menu, choose View ➤ Zoom ➤ Out. The view changes, and the grid appears smaller (see Figure 3.5). Move the crosshair cursor to the lower-left corner of the grid, and then move it to the upper-right corner. Notice the coordinate readout in the lower left of your screen. These two points should read as approximately 0'-0",0'-0" and 1'-0",0'-9", respectively.

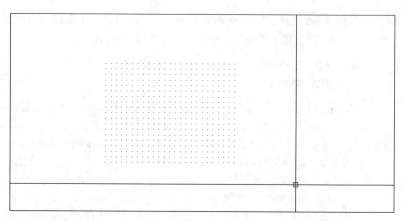

FIGURE 3.5: The grid after zooming out

4. On the status bar, next to the Grid button, click the Snap button, and then move the cursor back onto the grid and look at the coordinate readout again. The cursor stops at each grid point, and the readout is to the nearest half inch. Now when you place the crosshair cursor on the lower-left corner of the grid, the readout is exactly 0'-0",0'-0", and 1'-0",0'-9" for the upper-right corner. The Snap tool locks the cursor onto the grid dots, and even when the cursor is not on the grid but somewhere outside it on the drawing area, the cursor maintains the grid spacing and jumps from one location to another.

5. Use the Zoom Out command a few more times. The first time, the grid gets even smaller. After the second or third use of the command, the grid may disappear, in which case you see a message on the second line of the Command window that says Grid too dense to display. Once the dots get too close together, AutoCAD lets you know that the monitor can't display them.

6. On the same menu, use the Zoom In tool enough times to bring the view of the grid back to the way it was in Figure 3.5. You are not changing the size of the grid, just the view of it. It's like switching from a normal to a telephoto lens on a camera.

The grid is more a guide than an actual boundary of your drawing. You can change a setting to force lines to be drawn only in the area covered by the grid, but this is not ordinarily done. For most purposes, you can draw anywhere on the screen. The grid merely serves as a tool for visualizing how your drawing is going to be laid out.

Because it will serve as a layout tool for this project, you need to increase the area covered by the grid from its present size of 1' × 9" to 60' × 40'. Because the Drawing Limits setting controls the size of the grid, you need to change it.

Drawing Limits

The Drawing Limits setting records the coordinates of the lower-left and upper-right corners of the grid. The coordinates for the lower-left corner are 0,0 by default and are usually left at that setting. You need to change only the coordinates for the upper-right corner.

1. At the Command: prompt, choose Format ➤ Drawing Limits from the drop-down menu. Notice the Command window:

   ```
   Command: '_limits
   Reset Model space limits:
   Specify lower left corner or [ON/OFF] <0'-0",0'-0">:
   ```

   The bottom command line tells you that the first step is to decide whether to change the default X and Y coordinates for the lower-left limits, both of which are currently set at 0',0". There is no need to change these.

2. Press ↵ to accept the 0',0" coordinates for this corner. The bottom command line changes and now displays the coordinates for the upper-right corner of the limits. This is the setting you want to change.

3. Type 60',40'↵. Be sure to include the foot sign (').

N O T E   AutoCAD requires that, when using Architectural units, you always indicate when a distance is feet by using the foot sign ('). You do not have to use the inch sign (") to indicate inches.

The grid now appears to extend to the top-right edge of the drawing area (see Figure 3.6), but it actually extends way past the edges. It was one foot wide and now it's 60 times that, but the drawing area is showing us only the first foot or so. To bring the whole grid onto the screen, use the Zoom command again, but this time you will use the All option.

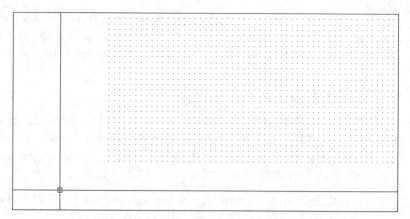

FIGURE 3.6: The same view with the grid extended to 60' × 40'

4. Choose View ➤ Zoom ➤ All. The grid disappears, and you get the `Grid too dense to display` message in the Command window.

Remember that you found the grid spacing to be ½", by default. If the drawing area is giving us a view of a 60' × 40' grid with dots at ½", the grid is 1440 dots wide and 960 dots high. If the whole grid were to be shown on the screen, the dots would be so close together that they would only be about one pixel in size and would solidly fill the drawing area. So AutoCAD won't display them at this density. For this reason, you need to change the spacing for the dots.

You need to change the spacing for another reason: for the drawing task ahead, it will be more useful to have the spacing set differently. Remember how we turned Snap on, and the cursor stopped at each dot? If you set the dot spacing to 12", you can use Grid and Snap modes to help you draw the outline of the cabin because the dimensions of the outside wall line are in whole feet: 25' × 16'. Here's how:

1. Right-click the Grid button on the status bar, and choose Settings from the small menu that opens. The Drafting Settings dialog box opens, and the Snap And Grid tab is active (see Figure 3.7). The settings in both the Grid and Snap areas include X and Y Spacing settings. Notice that they are all set for a spacing of ½". The other settings in the dialog box don't concern us right now.

FIGURE 3.7: The Snap And Grid tab of the Drafting Settings dialog box

2. In the Grid area, click in the GridX Spacing text box and change the ½" to 0. If you set the grid spacing to 0, it will then take on whatever spacing you set for the SnapX Spacing text box. This is how you lock the two together. When the GridX Spacing text box reads 0, click the ½" in the GridY Spacing text box. It changes to match the GridX Spacing text box.

3. In the Snap section, change the SnapX Spacing setting to 12. The inch sign is not required. Then click the SnapY Spacing setting. It automatically changes to match the SnapX Spacing and changes both text boxes to display as 1' instead of 12".

4. In the Snap Type & Style area, be sure Grid Snap and Rectangular Snap are selected. The Snap On and Grid On check boxes at the top of the dialog box should be checked. If they aren't, click them.

5. Click OK. The grid is now visible (see Figure 3.8). Move the cursor around on the grid—be sure Snap is on. (Check the Snap button on the status bar. It will be pressed when Snap is on.) Notice the coordinate readout. It is displaying coordinates to the nearest foot to conform to the new grid and snap spacing.

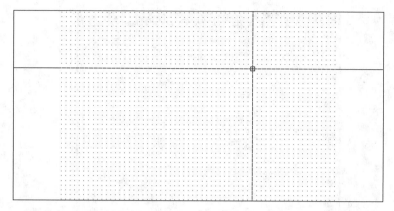

FIGURE 3.8: The new 60' × 40' grid with 12" dot spacing

6. Move the crosshair cursor to the upper-right corner of the grid and check the coordinate readout. It should display 60'-0", 40'-0", 0'-0". (In LT, you won't have the third coordinate.)

Drawing with Grid and Snap

Your drawing area now has the proper settings and is zoomed to a convenient magnification. You should be ready to draw the first lines of the cabin.

1. At the Command: prompt, start the Line command. (Click the Line button on the Draw toolbar.) Pick a point on the grid in the lower-left quadrant of the drawing area (see Figure 3.9).

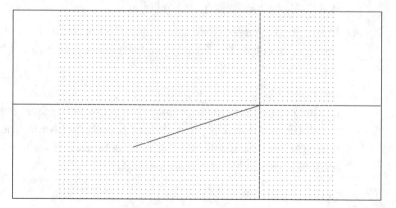

FIGURE 3.9: One point picked on the grid

2. Hold the crosshair cursor to the right of the point just picked, and look at the coordinate readout. It may be displaying relative polar coordinates from the first point picked, but probably not. If it isn't, try clicking once on the coordinate readout. If that doesn't work, clicking one more time will do the job, because a three-way toggle controls the coordinate readout.

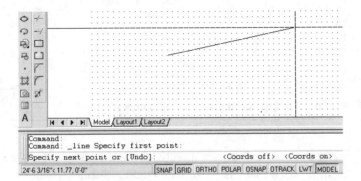

3. Now hold the crosshair cursor directly out to the right of the first point picked, and look at the coordinate readout. It will be displaying a distance in whole feet and should have an angle of 0.00. (For Auto-CAD users, ignore the extra Z coordinate.)

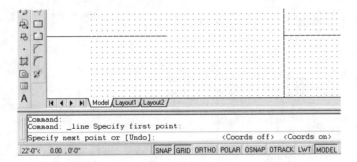

4. Continue moving the crosshair cursor left or right until the readout displays 25'-0"<0.00. At this point, click the left mouse button to draw the first line of the cabin wall (see Figure 3.10).

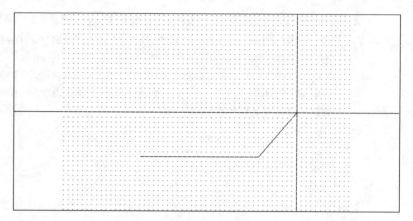

FIGURE 3.10: The first line of the cabin wall is drawn.

5. Move the crosshair cursor directly above the last point picked to a position such that the coordinate readout displays 16'-0"<90.00, and pick that point.

6. Move the crosshair cursor directly left of the last point picked until the coordinate readout displays 25'-0"<180.00, and pick that point (see Figure 3.11).

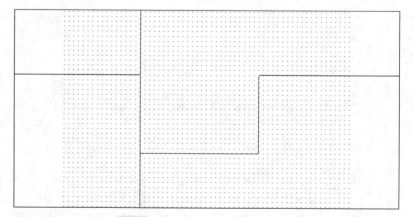

FIGURE 3.11: Drawing the second and third wall lines

7. Finally, type c↵ to close the box. This tells AutoCAD to draw a line from the last point picked to the first point picked and, in effect, closes the box. AutoCAD then automatically ends the Line command (see Figure 3.12).

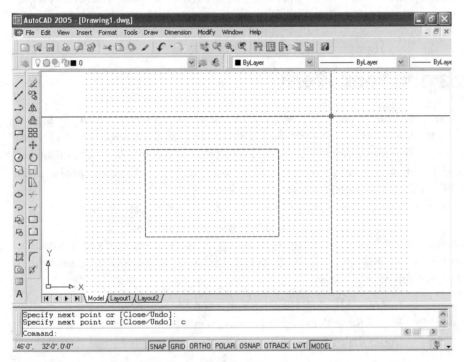

FIGURE 3.12: The completed outside wall lines

This method for laying out building lines by using Snap and Grid and the coordinate readout is quite useful if the dimensions all conform to a convenient rounded-off number, such as the nearest 6 inches or, as in this case, the nearest foot. It is not necessary to keep Snap and Grid set to the same spacing, as they were in this example, as long as the grid spacing is a whole multiple of the snap spacing. In this project, you could have kept the snap spacing at 1' and set the grid spacing to 4'. You then wouldn't have so many dots on the screen, and Snap would still have forced the crosshair cursor to stop at quarter intervals (every 12") between the 4-foot–spaced grid dots. This would have been a slightly more elegant way to accomplish the same thing.

The key advantage to this method over just typing the relative coordinates—as was done with the box in Chapter 2—is that you avoid having to type the numbers.

You should, however, assess whether the layout you need to draw has characteristics that lend themselves to using Grid, Snap, and the coordinate readout area or whether just typing the relative coordinates would be more efficient. As you get more comfortable with AutoCAD, you will see that this is the sort of question that comes up often: which way is the most efficient? This happy dilemma is inevitable in an application with enough tools to give you many strategic choices. In Chapters 4 and 5, you will learn other techniques for drawing rectangles.

Saving Your Work

As with all Windows-compatible applications, when you save a file for the first time by choosing File ➤ Save, you can designate a name for the file and a folder in which to store it. Normally, you use Windows Explorer to designate file and folder information before you start a new drawing; but for the cabin project, you will do that now, after the drawing has been started.

I recommend that you create a special folder, called something like Training Data, for storing the files you will generate as you work your way through this book. This will keep them separate from project work already on your computer, and you will always know where to save or find a training drawing. To save your drawing, follow these steps.

1. In AutoCAD, click the Save button on the Standard toolbar or choose File ➤ Save. Because you haven't named this file yet, the Save Drawing As dialog box opens.

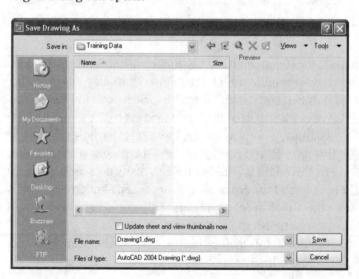

N O T E   The actual folders and files may be different on your computer.

2. In the Save In drop-down list, designate the drive and folder where you want to save the drawing. If you are saving it on the hard drive or server, navigate to the folder in which you want to place the new Training Data folder.

 3. Click the Create New Folder button near the top-right corner of the dialog box. The folder appears in the list of folders. It is called New Folder. Right-click the new folder and choose Rename from the shortcut menu that opens.

4. Enter **Training Data** (or whatever name you want to give the new folder) ↵.

5. Double-click the new folder to open it.

6. In the File Name box, change the name to `Cabin03`. You're not required to enter the `.dwg` extension in this case.

 N O T E   From now on, when you are directed to save the drawing, save it as `Cabin`x, with x indicating the number of the chapter. This way, you will know where in the book to look for review, if necessary. Name multiple saves within a chapter `Cabin`xa, `Cabin`xb, and so on.

7. Click Save. Notice that the title bar now displays the new name of the file along with its path. It is now safe to exit AutoCAD.

8. If you want to shut down AutoCAD at this time, choose File ➢ Exit. Otherwise, keep your drawing up and read on.

The tools covered in this chapter will be your key to starting a new drawing from scratch and getting it ready for a specific project.

USING THE WIZARD TO SET UP A NEW DRAWING

AutoCAD comes with two Setup wizards, Quick and Advanced. Neither helps you set up Grid and Snap, but they do help you with setting the Units and the Drawing Limits. Here is a summary of how the wizards work.

When you select Use A Wizard in the Startup dialog box, you are prompted to choose Quick or Advanced.

The Quick Wizard

▶ Units: Select Units, and then click the Next button.

▶ Area: Here you set the Drawing Limits by specifying the X and Y coordinates of the upper-right corner. You do this by entering the *x* value for the Width, and the *y* value for the Length. For example, if the coordinates of the upper-right corner are 60', 40' as they are for the cabin drawing, enter 60' for the width and 40' for the length. Then click Finish.

▶ Now you will need to Zoom to All, and specify your Grid and Snap settings. They stay at the default setting of ½", and both remain off. Use the procedure shown in this chapter.

The Advanced Wizard

▶ Units: Select the Linear Units and the Precision. Then click Next.

▶ Angle: Select the Angular Units and the Precision. Then click Next.

▶ Angle Measure: Ignore this and click the Next button.

▶ Angle Direction: Ignore this and click the Next button.

▶ Area: Here you set the Drawing Limits by specifying the X and Y coordinates of the upper-right corner. You do this by entering the *x* value for the Width and the *y* value for the Length. For example, if the coordinates of the upper-right corner are 60', 40' as they are for the cabin drawing, enter 60' for the Width and 40' for the Length. Then click Finish.

▶ Now you will need to Zoom to All, and specify your Grid and Snap settings, as they stay at the default setting of ½", and both remain off. Use the procedure shown in this chapter.

A Summary of AutoCAD's Units

The following is a brief description of each of the linear and angular unit types that AutoCAD offers the user and how they are used. The example distance is 2'-6½". The example angle is 126°35'10".

Linear Units

The linear unit types that AutoCAD uses are as follows:

Architectural   This unit type uses feet and inches with fractions. You must use the foot sign ('), for example, 2'-6½". For this distance, enter 2'6-½ or 2'6.5. For the most part, these are the units that will be used in this book.

Decimal   Uses decimal units that can represent any linear unit of measurement. You do not use the foot sign, the inch sign, or fractions. For example, if each decimal unit equals 1 inch, to specify a line to be 2'-6½" long, you must convert feet to inches and enter a length of 30.5. But if each decimal unit equals 1 foot, you must convert the inches to the decimal equivalent of a foot and enter 2.5417.

Engineering   This unit is equivalent to Architectural units except that inches are displayed as decimals rather than fractions. For a distance of 2'-6½", enter 2'6.5 or 2.5417'. In either method, the resulting distance will be displayed as 2-6.5".

Fractional   These units are just like Architectural units except there is no use of feet. Everything is expressed in inches and fractions. If you enter 30-½ or 30.5, the resulting distance displays as 30½.

Scientific   This unit system is similar to the Decimal unit system except for the way in which distances are displayed. If you enter 3.05E+01, that is what is displayed. The notation always uses an expression that indicates a number from 1 to 10 that is to be multiplied by a power of 10. In this case, the power is 1, so the notation means 3.05×10 or 30.5 in Decimal units.

Angular Units

The angular unit types that AutoCAD uses are as follows:

Decimal   This type uses 360 degrees in a circle in decimal form, with no minutes and no seconds. All angles are expressed as decimal degrees. For example, an angle of 126°35'10" is entered as **126.586** or **126d35'1"** and displays as 126.5861. AutoCAD uses a *d* instead of the traditional degree symbol (°).

Deg/Min/Sec   This is the traditional system for measuring angles. In Auto-CAD's notation, degrees are indicated by the lowercase d, the minutes use the traditional ', and the seconds use the traditional ". The system is clumsy. Most users now use decimal angles instead of this system and choose their preference for precision.

Grads   This unit is based on a circle being divided into 400 grads, so 90° equals 100 grads. One degree equals 1.11 grads, and 1 grad equals 0.90 degrees. Auto-CAD uses g as the symbol for grads.

Radians   The radian is the angle from the center of a circle made by the radius of the circle being laid along the circumference of the circle. One radian equals 57.3 degrees, and 360 degrees equals 6.28 radians or 2π radians. AutoCAD uses r as the symbol for radians.

Surveyor   These units use bearings from the north and south directions, toward the east or west directions, and are expressed in degrees, minutes, and seconds. They will be discussed in Chapter 12. In the example we are using, 126° 35' 10" translates to N 36d35'10" W in bearings, or Surveyor units.

The next chapter will focus on adding to the drawing, modifying commands you learned as part of Chapter 2, and creating strategies for solving problems that occur in the development of a floor plan.

If You Would Like More Practice...

Set up a few more new drawings. Use parameters that you might use in your own profession if it isn't architecture. Following are three practice setup challenges and a summary of steps described in this chapter. Use this procedure, or feel free to try the Use A Wizard options in the Startup dialog box.

Architecture Project:	**Building size:**	125' × 85'
	Units:	Architectural
	Drawing Limits:	200', 150'
	Grid/Snap Spacing:	5'
Civil Project:	**Building Size:**	87' × 60'
	Units:	Decimal
	Drawing Limits:	120', 90'
	Grid/Snap Spacing:	10'

Mechanical Project:	Block Size:	6" × 10"
	Units:	Decimal
	Drawing Limits:	1' × 2'
	Grid/Snap Spacing:	1"

Summary of the procedure:

▶ Set the units.

▶ Set the drawing limits.

▶ Set Grid Spacing to 0, and set Snap Spacing to the given distance.

▶ Turn on Grid and Snap.

▶ Zoom to All.

▶ Draw the rectangle using relative Cartesian or polar coordinates.

Are You Experienced?

Now you can...

☑ **set up linear and angular units for a new drawing**

☑ **make the grid visible and modify its coverage**

☑ **use the Zoom In and Zoom Out features**

☑ **activate the Snap mode and change the Snap and Grid spacings**

☑ **use the Zoom All function to fit the grid on the drawing area**

☑ **draw lines using Grid, Snap, and the coordinate readout**

☑ **create a new folder on your hard drive from within AutoCAD**

☑ **name and save your file**

CHAPTER 4

Gaining Drawing Strategies: Part 1

▶ Making interior walls

▶ Zooming in on an area using various zoom tools

▶ Making doors and swings

▶ Using Object Snaps

▶ Using the Copy and Mirror commands

Assuming that you have worked your way through the first three chapters, you have now successfully drawn a box (Chapter 2) as well as the outer wall lines of the cabin (Chapter 3). From here on, you will develop a floor plan for the cabin and in Chapter 8, elevations (views of the front, back, and sides of the building that show how the building will look if you're facing it). The focus in this chapter is on gaining a feel for the strategy of drawing in Auto-CAD and on how to solve drawing problems that come up in the course of laying out the floor plan. As you work your way through this chapter, your activities will include making the walls, cutting doorway openings, and drawing the doors (see Figure 4.1). In Chapter 5, you will add steps and a balcony and place fixtures and appliances in the bathroom and kitchen.

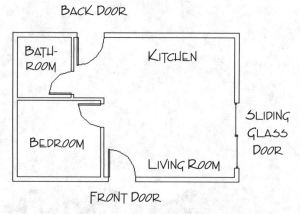

FIGURE 4.1: The basic floor plan of the cabin

Each exercise in this chapter presents opportunities to practice using commands you already know from previous chapters and to learn a few new ones. The most important goal is to begin to use strategic thinking as you develop methods for creating new elements of the floor plan.

Laying Out the Walls

For most floor plans, the walls come first. The first lesson in this chapter is to understand that you will not be putting many new lines in the drawing, at least not as many as you might expect. You will create most new objects in this chapter from items already in your drawing. In fact, you will draw no new lines to make walls. You'll generate all new walls from the four exterior wall lines you drew in the last chapter.

You will need to create an inside wall line for the exterior walls (because the wall has thickness) and then make the three new interior walls (see Figure 4.2). The thickness will be 4" for interior walls and 6" for exterior walls, because exterior walls have an additional layer or two of weather protection, such as shingles or stucco. Finally, you will need to cut five openings in these walls (interior and exterior) for the doorways.

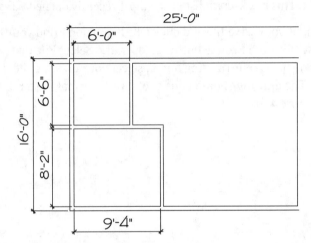

FIGURE 4.2: The wall dimensions

All the commands used for this exercise were presented in Chapters 2 and 3. If you need a refresher, glance back at these chapters.

The Exterior Wall Lines

The first step is to offset the existing four wall lines to the inside to make the inside wall lines for the exterior walls. You will then need to fillet them to clean up their corners, just like you did for the box in Chapter 2.

This procedure is identical to the one you performed in Chapter 2 on the box.

 T I P Buildings are usually—but not always—dimensioned to the outside edge of exterior walls and to the center line of interior walls. Wood-frame buildings are dimensioned to the outside edges of their frames and to the center lines of the interior walls.

If you are starting AutoCAD and if you have chosen Do Not Show A Startup Dialog on the System tab of the Options dialog box, follow the instructions at the beginning of step 1.

1. If AutoCAD is already running, choose File ➢ Open. In the Select File dialog box, navigate to the folder you designated as your training folder and select your cabin drawing. (You named it Cabin03.dwg at the end of Chapter 3.)

   Then click Open. If you are starting AutoCAD, and if you have chosen Show Startup Dialog Box on the System tab of the Options dialog box, the Startup dialog box opens. Be sure the Open A Drawing button is selected, and then look for the Cabin03 drawing in the Select A File list box. This box keeps a list of the most recently opened .dwg files.

   Highlight your .dwg file and click OK. If you don't find your file in the list, click the Browse button to open the Select File dialog box. Find and open your training folder, select your drawing file, and click Open. The drawing should consist of four lines making a rectangle (see Figure 4.3).

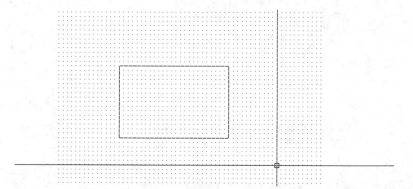

FIGURE 4.3: The cabin as you left it in Chapter 3

2. On the status bar, click the Grid and Snap buttons to turn them off. Then start the Offset command by clicking the Offset button on the Modify toolbar.

3. At the Offset distance: prompt, type 6↵.

N O T E You do not have to enter the inch sign ("), but you are required to enter the foot sign (').

4. At the Select object to offset: prompt, click one of the four lines.

5. Click in a blank area inside the rectangle. The first line is offset 6"
to the inside (see Figure 4.4). The Offset command is still running,
and the Select object to offset: prompt is still in effect.

F I G U R E 4 . 4 : **The first line is offset.**

6. Select another outside wall line and click in a blank area on the
inside again. Continue doing this until you have offset all four outside wall lines to the inside at the set distance of 6". Then press ⏎ to
end the Offset command (see Figure 4.5). Now you will clean up the
corners with the Fillet command.

F I G U R E 4 . 5 : **All four lines are now offset 6" to the inside.**

7. Start the Fillet command by clicking the Fillet button on the Modify
toolbar.

8. Look at the Command window to see whether the radius is set to
zero. If it is, go on to step 9. Otherwise, type r⏎, and then type 0⏎ to
set the Fillet radius to zero.

9. Click any two lines that form an inside corner. Be sure to click the
part of the lines you want to remain after the fillet is completed.
(Refer to Chapter 2 to review how the Fillet command is used in a
similar situation.) Both lines will be trimmed to make an inside corner (see Figure 4.6). The Fillet command automatically ends after
each fillet.

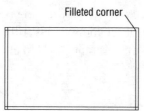

Filleted corner

FIGURE 4.6: The first corner is filleted.

10. Press ↵ or the spacebar to restart the Fillet command.

11. Pick two more lines to fillet, and then restart the Fillet command. Continue doing this until all four corners are cleaned up (see Figure 4.7). After the last fillet, the Fillet command will end automatically.

FIGURE 4.7: The four inside corners have been cleaned up.

> You can restart the most recently used command by pressing the spacebar or ↵ at the Command: prompt or by right-clicking and choosing the first item on the shortcut menu that opens.

CHARACTERISTICS THAT OFFSET AND FILLET HAVE IN COMMON

▶ Both are on the Modify toolbar and on the Modify drop-down menu.

▶ Both have a default distance setting—offset distance and fillet radius—that you can accept or reset.

▶ Both require you to select object(s).

You will find several uses for Offset and Fillet in the subsequent sections of this chapter and throughout the book.

The Interior Walls

Create the interior wall lines by offsetting the exterior wall lines.

1. At the Command: prompt, start the Offset command.

2. At the Offset distance: prompt, type 9'4↵. Leave no space between the foot sign (') and the 4.

N O T E   AutoCAD requires that you enter a distance containing feet and inches in a particular format: no space between the foot sign (') and the inches, and a hyphen (-) between the inches and the fraction. For example, if you are entering a distance of 6'-4¾", you type 6'4-¾. The measurement is displayed in the normal way, 6'-4¾", but you must enter it in the format that has no spaces.

3. Click the inside line of the left exterior wall (see Figure 4.8).

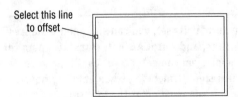

Select this line to offset

FIGURE 4.8:   Selecting the wall line to offset

4. Click in a blank area to the right of the selected line. The line is offset 9'-4" to the right.

5. Press ↵ twice, or press the spacebar twice. The Offset command is now restarted, and you can reset the offset distance.

T I P   In the Offset command, your opportunity to change the offset distance comes right after you start the command. So if the Offset command is already running, and you need to change the offset distance, you need to stop and then restart the command. To do so, press ↵ or the spacebar twice.

6. Type 4↵ to reset the offset distance.

7. Click the new line that was just offset, and then click in a blank area to the right of that line. You have created a vertical interior wall (see Figure 4.9). Press ↵ twice to stop and restart the Offset command.

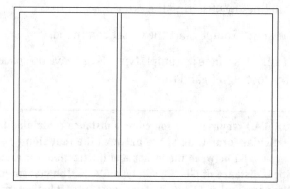

FIGURE 4.9:   The first interior wall

8. Type 6.5'↵ to set the distance for offsetting the next wall.

N O T E   With Architectural units set, you can still enter distances in decimal form for feet and inches, and AutoCAD will translate them into their appropriate form. For example, you can enter 6'-6" as 6.5', and you can enter 4½" as 4.5 without the inch sign. Remember, when entering figures, you can leave off the inch sign ("), but you must enter the foot sign (').

9. Pick a point on the inside, upper exterior wall line (see Figure 4.10).

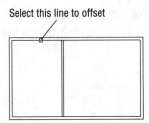

Select this line to offset

FIGURE 4.10: Selecting another wall line to offset

10. Click in a blank area below the line selected. The inside exterior wall line is offset to make a new interior wall line. Press the spacebar twice to stop and restart the Offset command.

11. Type 4↵. Click the new line and click again below it. A second wall line is made, and you now have two interior walls. Press the spacebar to end the Offset command.

These interior wall lines form the bedroom and one side of the bathroom. You need to clean up their intersections with each other and with the exterior walls. If you take the time to do this now, it will be easier to make the last interior wall and thereby complete the bathroom. Refer to Figures 4.1 and 4.2 earlier in this chapter to see where we're headed.

Cleaning Up Wall Lines

Earlier, you used the Fillet command to clean up the inside corners of the exterior walls. You can use that command again to clean up some of the interior walls, but you will have to use the Trim command to do the rest of them. You'll see why as you progress through the next set of steps.

1. It will be easier to pick the wall lines if you make the drawing larger on the screen. Type z↵, and then type e↵. Press ↵, and then type .6x↵. The drawing is bigger. You've just used two options of the Zoom command: First, you zoomed to *Extents* to fill the screen with your drawing. You then zoomed to a scale (.6x) to make the drawing 0.6 the size it had been after zooming to Extents. This is a change in magnification on the view only; the building is still 25 feet long and 16 feet wide.

2. Click the Fillet button on the Modify toolbar to start the Fillet command, and after checking the Command window to be sure that the

radius is still set to zero, click two of the wall lines as shown in Figure 4.11a. The lines will be filleted, and the results will look like Figure 4.11b.

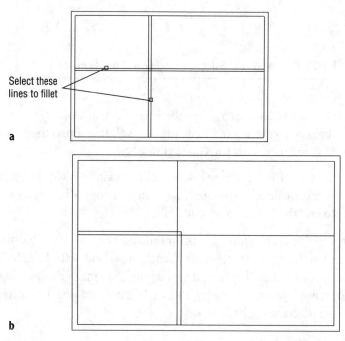

a

b

FIGURE 4.11: Selecting the first two lines to fillet (a), and the result of the fillet (b)

3. Press the spacebar to restart the Fillet command. Select the two lines as shown in Figure 4.12a. The results are shown in Figure 4.12b.

The two new interior walls are now the right length, but you will have to clean up the areas where they form T intersections with the exterior walls. The Fillet command won't work in T intersections because too much of one of the wall lines gets trimmed away. You'll have to use the Trim command in T-intersection cases. The Fillet command does a specific kind of trim and is easy and quick to execute, but its uses are limited (for the most part) to single intersections between two lines.

The best rule for choosing between Fillet and Trim is the following: If you need to clean up a single intersection between two lines, use the Fillet command. For other cases, use the Trim command.

Label in figure: Select these lines to fillet

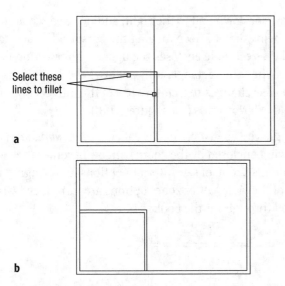

Select these
lines to fillet

a

b

FIGURE 4.12: Selecting the second two lines to fillet (a), and the result of the second fillet (b)

Using the Zoom Command

To do this trim, you need a closer view of the T intersections. Use the Zoom command to get a better look.

1. Type z↵. Then move the crosshair cursor to a point slightly above and to the left of the upper T intersection (see Figure 4.13), and click in a blank area outside the floor plan.

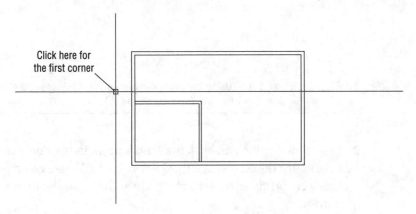

Click here for
the first corner

FIGURE 4.13: Positioning the cursor for the first click of the Zoom command

When you start the Zoom command by typing z↵ and then picking a point on the screen, a zoom window begins.

2. Move the cursor down and to the right, and notice a rectangle with solid lines being drawn. Keep moving the cursor down and to the right until the rectangle encloses the upper T intersection (see Figure 4.14a). When the rectangle fully encloses the T intersection, click again. The view changes to a closer view of the intersection of the interior and exterior walls (see Figure 4.14b).

The rectangle you've just created is called a *zoom window*. The part of the drawing enclosed by the zoom window becomes the view on the screen. This is one of several zoom options for changing the magnification of the view. Other zoom options are introduced later in this chapter and throughout the book.

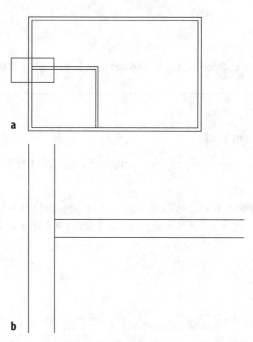

FIGURE 4.14: Using the zoom window option: positioning the rectangle (a), and the new view after the Zoom command (b)

3. On the Modify toolbar, click the Trim button. In the Command window, notice the second and third lines of text. You are being prompted to select cutting edges (objects to use as limits for the lines you want to trim).

4. Select the two interior wall lines and press the spacebar. The prompt changes, now asking you to select the lines to be trimmed.

5. Select the inside exterior wall line at the T intersection, between the two intersections with the interior wall lines that you have just picked as cutting edges (see Figure 4.15a). The exterior wall line is trimmed at the T intersection (see Figure 4.15b). Press the spacebar to end the Trim command.

In the Trim command, click the part of the line that needs to be trimmed away when picking lines to be trimmed. In the Fillet command, select the part of the line that you want to keep.

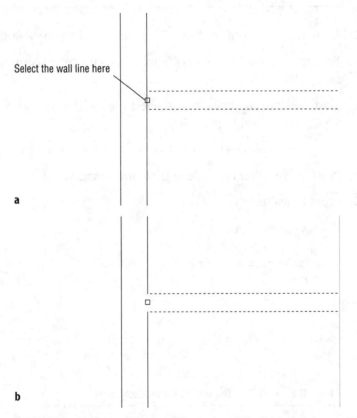

Select the wall line here

a

b

F I G U R E   4 . 1 5 : Selecting a line to be trimmed (a), and the result of the Trim command (b)

6. Return to a view of the whole drawing by typing z↵ and then p↵. This is the Zoom command's Previous option, which restores the view that was active before the last use of the Zoom command (see Figure 4.16).

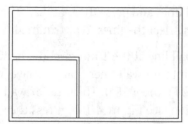

F I G U R E 4 . 1 6 : The result of the Zoom Previous command

Repeat this procedure to trim the lower T intersection. Follow these steps:

1. Type z↵ and click two points to make a rectangular zoom window around the intersection.

2. Start the Trim command again, select the interior walls as cutting edges, and press the spacebar.

3. Select the inside exterior wall line between the cutting edges.

4. Press the spacebar or ↵ to end the Trim command.

5. Zoom Previous by typing z↵p↵.

Figure 4.17 shows the results.

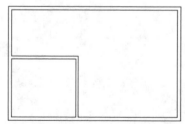

F I G U R E 4 . 1 7 : The second trim is completed.

You need to create one more interior wall to complete the bathroom.

Finishing the Interior Walls

You will use the same method to create the last bathroom wall that you used to make the first two interior walls. Briefly, this is how it's done:

1. Offset the upper-inside line of the left exterior wall 6' to the right; then offset this new line 4" to the right.

2. Use Zoom Window to zoom into the bathroom area.

T I P   Make a zoom window just large enough to enclose the bathroom. The resulting view should be large enough to allow you to trim both ends of the interior wall without re-zooming.

3. Use the Trim command to trim away the short portion of the inter- sected wall lines between the two new wall lines. This can be accom- plished in one use of the Trim command: once you select the new wall lines as cutting edges, you can trim both lines that run across the ends of the selected lines to those same cutting edges.

4. Use Zoom Previous to restore the full view.

The results should look like Figure 4.18.

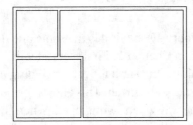

FIGURE 4.18: The completed interior walls

You used Offset, Fillet, Trim, and a couple of zooms to create the interior walls. The next task is to create five doorway openings in these walls. If you need to end the drawing session before completing the chapter, choose File ➢ Save As, and then change the name of this drawing to Cabin04a.dwg and click Save. You can then exit AutoCAD. To continue, do the same save and move on to the next section.

Cutting Openings in the Walls

Of the five doorway openings needed, two are on interior and three are on exterior walls (see Figure 4.19). Four of them will be for swinging doors, and one will be for a sliding glass door. We won't be doing the hatchings and dimensions shown in the figure—those features will be covered in future chapters.

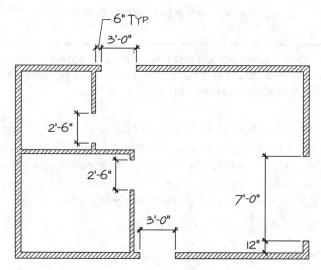

FIGURE 4.19: The drawing with doorway openings

The procedure used to make each doorway opening is the same one that you used to create the opening for the box in Chapter 2. First, you establish the location of the *jambs*, or sides, of an opening. One jamb for each swinging door opening will be located 6" from an inside wall corner. This allows the door to be positioned next to a wall and out of the way when swung open. When the jambs are established, you will trim away the wall lines between the edges. The commands used in this exercise are Offset, Extend, and Trim. You'll make openings for the 3'-0" exterior doorways first.

The Exterior Openings

These openings are on the front and back walls of the cabin and have one side set in 6" from an inside corner.

1. Click the Offset button on the Modify toolbar to start the Offset command, and then type 6↵ to set the distance.

2. Click one of the two lines indicated in Figure 4.20, and then click in a blank area to the right of the line that you selected. Now do the same thing to the second wall line. You have to offset one line at a time because of the way the Offset command works.

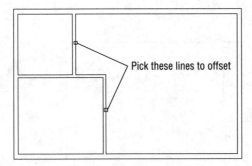

FIGURE 4.20: The lines to offset for 3'-0" openings

3. End and restart the Offset command by pressing the spacebar or ↵ twice; then type 3'↵ to set a new offset distance, and offset the new lines to the right (see Figure 4.21). Next, you will need to extend these four new lines through the external walls to make the jamb lines.

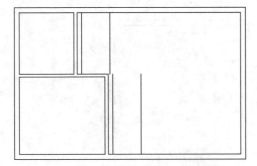

FIGURE 4.21: The offset lines for 3'-0" openings

4. Be sure to end the Offset command by pressing the spacebar or ↵; then start the Extend command. You use Extend here exactly as you used it in Chapter 2. Select the upper and lower horizontal outside, external wall lines as boundary edges for the Extend command, and press the spacebar or ↵.

T I P If you start a new command by entering letters on the keyboard, you must first be sure that the previous command has ended. On the other hand, if you start a new command by clicking its icon on a toolbar or by choosing it from the menu bar, it doesn't matter if the previous command is still running. AutoCAD will just cancel it.

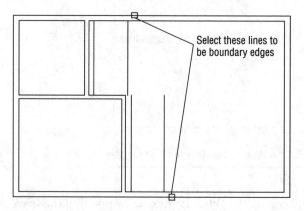

Select these lines to be boundary edges

5. Click the four lines to extend them. The lines are extended through the external walls to make the jambs (see Figure 4.22). End the Extend command by pressing the spacebar or ↵.

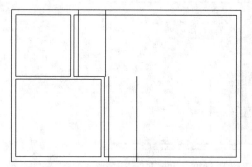

FIGURE 4.22: The lines after being extended through the external walls

T I P   You must pick the lines to be extended on the half of them nearest the boundary's edge; if you do not, they will extend to the opposite boundary edge.

To complete the openings, we will continue with steps 6 and 7. First, we'll trim away the excess part of the jamb lines, and then we'll trim away the wall lines between the jamb lines. You'll use the Trim command the same way you used it in Chapter 2, but this time you'll do a *compound* trim to clean up the wall and jamb lines in one cycle of the command.

6. Type tr↵ to start the Trim command, and select the three lines at each opening (six lines total) as shown in Figure 4.23. Then press the spacebar or ↵ to tell AutoCAD you are finished selecting objects to serve as cutting edges.

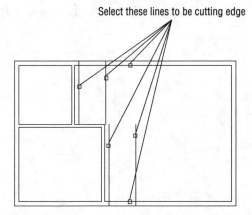

Select these lines to be cutting edge

FIGURE 4.23: Selecting the cutting edges

7. Pick the four wall lines between the jamb lines, and then pick the jamb lines—the lines you just extended to the outside exterior walls, as shown in Figure 4.24.

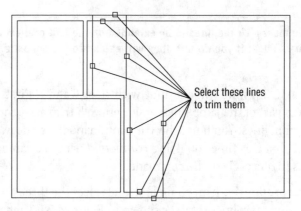

FIGURE 4.24: The lines to be trimmed

8. Each time you pick a line, it is trimmed. Press the spacebar or ↵ to end the command. Your drawing should look like Figure 4.25.

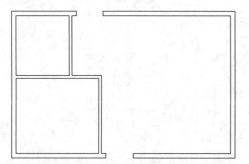

FIGURE 4.25: The finished 3'-0" openings

  T I P   When picking lines to be trimmed, remember to pick the lines on the portion to be trimmed away.

You can construct the two interior openings using the same procedure.

The Interior Openings

These doorways are 2'-6" wide and also have one jamb set in 6" from the nearest inside corner. Figure 4.26 shows the three stages of fabricating these openings. Refer to the previous section on making openings for step-by-step instructions.

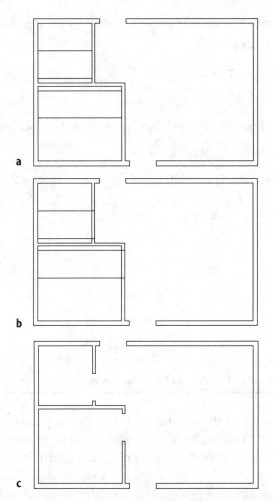

FIGURE 4.26: Creating the interior openings: the offset lines that locate the jamb lines (a), the extended lines that form the jamb lines (b), and the completed openings after trimming (c)

Construct the 7'-0" exterior opening using the same commands and technique.

The 7'-0" Opening

Notice that in Figure 4.19, earlier in this chapter, the opening on the right side of the building has one jamb set in 12" from the inside corner. This opening will be for the sliding glass door.

You've done this procedure before, so here's a summary of the steps:

1. Offset a wall line 12".

2. Offset the new line 7'-0".

3. Extend both new lines through the wall.

4. Trim the new lines and the wall lines to complete the opening.

5. Save this drawing as Cabin04b.dwg.

This completes the openings. The results should look like Figure 4.27.

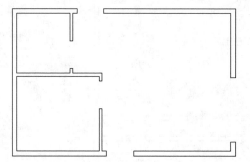

FIGURE 4.27: The completed doorway openings

As you gain more control over the commands you used here, you will be able to anticipate how much of a task can be done for each use of a command. Each opening required offsetting, extending, and trimming. You constructed these openings by drawing two at a time except for the last one, thereby using each of the three commands three times. It is possible to do all the openings using each command only once. In this way, you do all the offsetting, then all the extending, and finally all the trimming. In cutting these openings, however, the arrangement of the offset lines determined how many cycles of the Trim command were most efficient to use. If lines being trimmed and used as cutting edges cross each other, the trimming gets complicated. For these five openings, the most efficient procedure is to use each command twice. In Chapter 8, you'll get a chance to work with more complex multiple trims when you draw the elevations.

Now that the openings are complete, you can place doors and door swings in their appropriate doorways. In doing this, you'll be introduced to two new objects and a few new commands, and you'll have an opportunity to use the Offset and Trim commands in new, strategic ways.

WHAT TO DO WHEN YOU MAKE A MISTAKE

When you are offsetting, trimming, and extending lines, it's easy to pick the wrong line. Here are some tips on how to correct these errors and get back on track:

▶ You can always cancel any command by pressing the Esc key until you see the Command: prompt in the Command window. Then click the Undo button on the Standard toolbar to undo the results of the last command. If you undo too much, click the Redo button. You can click it more than once to redo several undos.

▶ Errors made with the Offset command include setting the wrong distance, picking the wrong line to offset, or picking the wrong side to offset toward. If the distance is correct, you can continue offsetting, end the command when you have the results you want, and then erase the lines that were offset wrong. Otherwise, press Esc and undo your previous offset.

▶ Errors made with the Trim and Extend commands can sometimes be corrected on the fly, so you don't have to end the command, because each of these has an Undo option. If you pick a line and it doesn't trim or extend the right way, you can undo that last action without stopping the command and then continue trimming or extending. You can activate the Undo option used while the command is running in three ways: click the Undo button on the Standard toolbar; type **u↵**; or right-click and choose Undo from the shortcut menu that opens. Each of these will undo the last trim or extend, and you can try again without having to restart the command. Each time you activate the Undo option *from within the command*, another trim or extend is undone.

▶ The Line command also has the same Undo option as the Trim and Extend commands. You can undo the last segment drawn (or the last several segments) and redraw them without stopping the command.

Creating Doors

In a floor plan, a rectangle or a line for the door and an arc showing the path of the door swing usually indicates a swinging door. The door's position varies, but it's most often shown at 90° from the closed position (see Figure 4.28). The best rule I have come across is to display them in such a way that others working with your floor plan will be able to see how far, and in what direction, the door will swing open.

FIGURE 4.28: Possible ways to illustrate doors

The cabin has five openings. Four of them need swinging doors, which open 90°. The fifth is a sliding glass door. Drawing it will require a different approach.

Drawing Swinging Doors

The swinging doors are of two widths: 3' for exterior and 2'-6" for interior (refer to Figure 4.1 earlier in this chapter). In general, doorway openings leading to the outside are wider than interior doors, with bathroom and closet doors usually being the narrowest. For the cabin, we'll use two sizes of swinging doors. You will draw one door of each size and then copy these to the other openings as required. Start with the front door at the bottom of the floor plan. To get a closer view of the front door opening, use the Zoom Window command.

1. Before you start drawing, check the status bar at the bottom of the screen and make sure only the Model button at the far right is pressed. All other buttons should be in the Off position—that is, up. If any are pressed, click them once to turn them off.

2. Choose Tools ➤ Drafting Settings to open the Drafting Settings dialog box. Then click the Object Snap tab to activate it, if it's not already on top.

◀

LT does not have the Extension and the Parallel Osnap modes, and it also does not have Object Snap Tracking.

3. Be sure all check boxes are unchecked. If any boxes have check marks in them, click the Clear All button to uncheck them. Then click OK to close the dialog box.

4. At the Command: prompt, move the cursor to the Standard toolbar and click the Zoom Window button.

5. Pick two points to form a window around the front doorway opening, as shown in Figure 4.29a. The view changes, and you now have a close-up view of the opening (see Figure 4.29b). You'll draw the door in a closed position and then rotate it open.

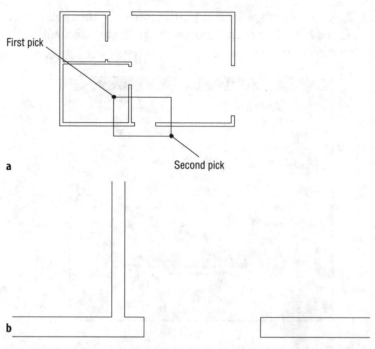

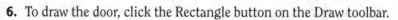

FIGURE 4.29: Forming a zoom window at the front door opening (a), and the result (b)

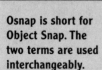

6. To draw the door, click the Rectangle button on the Draw toolbar.

   Notice the Command window prompt. Several options are in brackets, but the option Specify first corner point (before the brackets) is the default and is the one you want. You form the rectangle in the same way that you form the zoom window—by picking two points to represent opposite corners of the rectangle. In its closed position, the door will fit exactly between the jambs, with its upper corners coinciding with the upper endpoints of the jambs. To make the first corner of the rectangle coincide with the upper endpoint of the left jamb exactly, you will use an Object Snap to assist you. *Object Snaps* (or *Osnaps*) allow you to pick specific points on objects such as endpoints, midpoints, the center of a circle, and so on.

> You can also start the Rectangle command by choosing Draw ➤ Rectangle or by typing rec↵ in the Command window.

7. Type end↵. This activates the Endpoint Osnap for one pick.

> Osnap is short for Object Snap. The two terms are used interchangeably.

8. Move the cursor near the upper end of the left jamb line. When the cursor gets very close to a line, a colored square appears at the nearest endpoint. This shows you which endpoint in the drawing is closest to the position of the crosshair cursor at that moment.

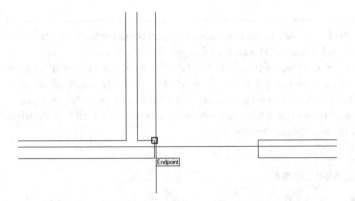

9. Move the cursor until the square is positioned on the upper end of the left jamb line, as shown, and then click that point. The first corner of the rectangle now is located at that point. Move the cursor to the right and slightly down to see the rectangle being formed (see Figure 4.30a). To locate the opposite corner, let's use the relative Cartesian coordinates discussed in Chapter 2.

10. When the Command window shows the Specify other corner point or [Dimensions]: prompt, type @3',-1.5↵ in the command line. The rectangle is drawn across the opening, creating a door in a closed position (see Figure 4.30b). The door now needs to be rotated around its hinge point to an opened position.

◄

Because of the way AutoCAD displays the crosshair cursor, both the lines and the crosshair disappear when its lines coincide with lines in the drawing. This makes it difficult to see the rectangle being formed.

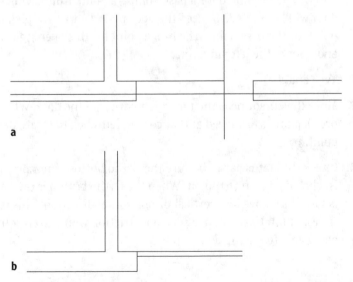

FIGURE 4.30: The rectangle after picking the first corner (a), and the completed door in a closed position (b)

N O T E   You could have used the Rectangle command to lay out the first four wall lines of the cabin in Chapter 3. Then you could have offset all four lines in one step to complete the exterior walls, and the corners would have been automatically filleted. It would have been faster than the method we used, but a rectangle's lines are all one object. In order to offset them to make the interior walls, they would have to be separated into individual lines using the Explode command.

Rotating the Door

This rotation will be through an arc of 90° in the counterclockwise direction, making it a rotation of +90. By default, counterclockwise rotations are positive, and clockwise rotations are negative. You'll use the Rotate command to rotate the door.

 1. Click the Rotate button on the Modify toolbar. You'll see a prompt to select objects. Click the door and press ↵.

You can also start the Rotate command by choosing Modify ≻ Rotate on the drop-down menu or by typing ro↵.

 N O T E   When you select the door, one pick selects all four lines. Rectangles are made of a special line called a *polyline* that connects all segments into one object. You will learn more about them in Chapter 10.

You will be prompted for a base point—a point around which the door will be rotated. To keep the door placed correctly, pick the hinge point for the base point. The hinge point for this opening is the upper endpoint of the left jamb line.

2. Type end↵.

3. Move the cursor near the upper-left corner of the door. When the colored square is displayed at that corner, left-click to locate the base point.

4. Check the status bar to be sure the Ortho button is not pressed. If it is, click it to turn Ortho off. When the Ortho button is on, the cursor is forced to move in a vertical or horizontal direction. This is useful at times, but in this instance such a restriction would keep you from being able to see the door rotate.

5. Move the cursor away from the hinge point, and see how the door rotates as the cursor moves (see Figure 4.31a). If the door swings properly, you are reassured that you correctly selected the base point. The prompt reads Specify rotation angle or [reference], asking you to enter an angle.

6. Type 90↲. The door is rotated 90∞ to an open position (see Figure 4.31b).

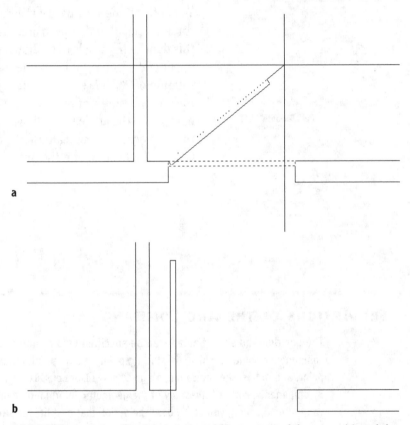

FIGURE 4.31: The door rotating with movement of the cursor (a), and the door after the 90° rotation (b)

To finish this door, you need to add the door's swing. You'll use the Arc command for this.

Drawing the Door Swing

The *swing* shows the path that the outer edge of a door takes when it swings from closed to fully open. Including a swing with the door in a floor plan helps to resolve clearance issues. You draw the swings using the *Arc command*, in this case using the Endpoint Osnap. This command has many options, most of which are based on knowing three aspects of the arc, as you will see.

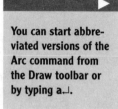

You can start abbreviated versions of the Arc command from the Draw toolbar or by typing a↵.

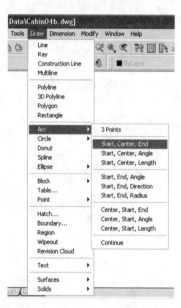

1. Choose Draw ➤ Arc to open the Arc menu. Ten of the 11 options have combinations of three aspects that define an arc. The arc for this door swing needs to be drawn from the upper end of the right jamb line through a rotation of 90°. We know the start point of the arc, the center of rotation (the hinge point), and the angle through which the rotation occurs, so we can use the Start, Center, Angle option on the Arc menu.

THE OPTIONS OF THE ARC COMMAND

The position and size of an arc can be specified by a combination of its components, some of which are starting point, ending point, angle, center point, and radius. The Arc command gives you 11 options, 10 of which use 3 components. With a little study of the geometric information available to you on the drawing, you can choose the option that best fits the situation.

Choosing Draw ➤ Arc on the drop-down menu displays 10 options with their 3 components, and an 11th option is used to continue the last arc drawn. For that reason, this is the best way to start the Arc command when you are first learning it.

When you start the Arc command by clicking the Arc button on the Draw toolbar or by typing **a**↵, you get an abbreviated form of the command in the Command window. You can access all 11 options of the command through this prompt, but you have to select the various components along the way.

2. From the Arc menu, choose Start, Center, Angle. The command prompt now reads _arc Specify start point of arc or [Center]:. The default option is Specify start point of arc. You can also start with the center point, but you have to typ e c↵ before picking a point to be the center point.

3. Activate the Endpoint Osnap (type end↵) and pick the upper endpoint of the right jamb line.

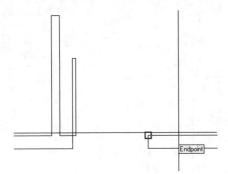

The prompt changes to read: Specify second point of arc or [Center/End]: _c Specify center point of arc.

This may be confusing at first. The prompt gives you three options: Second Point, Center, and End. (Center and End are in brackets.) Because you previously chose the Start, Center, Angle option, Auto-CAD automatically chooses Center for you. That is the last part of the prompt.

4. Activate the Endpoint Osnap again and select the hinge point. The arc is now visible, and its endpoint follows the cursor's movement (see Figure 4.32a). The prompt displays a different set of options and then ends with the Included angle option.

5. Type 90↵. The arc is completed, and the Arc command ends (see Figure 4.32b).

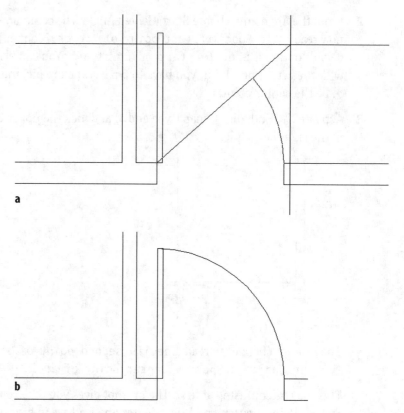

FIGURE 4.32: Drawing the arc: the ending point of the arc follows the cursor's movements (a), and the completed arc (b)

The front door is completed. Because the back door is the same size, you can save time by copying this door to the other opening. You'll see how to do that next.

Copying Objects

The *Copy command* makes a copy of the objects you select. You can locate this copy either by picking a point or by entering relative coordinates from the keyboard. For AutoCAD to position these copied objects, you must designate two points: a base point, which serves as a point of reference for where the copy move starts; and then a second point, which serves as the ending point for the Copy command. The copy is moved the same distance and direction from its original that the second point is moved from the first point. When you know the actual distance and direction to move the copy, the base point isn't critical because you will specify the second point with relative polar or Cartesian coordinates. But in this situation, you don't know the exact distance or angle to move a copy of the front door to the back door opening, so you need to choose a base point for the copy carefully.

In copying this new door and its swing to the back door opening of the cabin, you need to find a point somewhere on the existing door or swing that can be located precisely on a point at the back door opening. There are two points like this to choose from: the hinge point and the start point of the door swing. Let's use the hinge point. You usually know where the hinge point of the new door belongs, so this is easier to locate than the start point of the arc.

1. Click the Copy button on the Modify toolbar. The prompt asks you to select objects to copy. Pick the door and swing, and then press ↵. The prompt reads `Specify base point or displacement, or [Multiple]:`.

   Activate the Endpoint Osnap and pick the hinge point. A copy of the door and swing is attached to the crosshair cursor at the hinge point (see Figure 4.33). The prompt changes to `Specify second point of displacement or <use first point of displacement>:`. You need to pick where the hinge point of the copied door will be located at the back door opening. To do this, you need to change the view back to what it was before you zoomed into the doorway opening.

You can also start the Copy command by choosing Modify ➤ Copy on the dropdown menu or by typing cp↵.

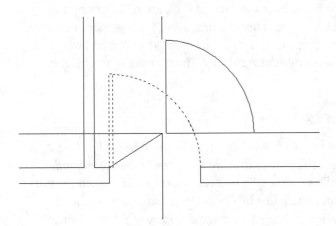

FIGURE 4.33: The copy of the door and swing attached to the crosshair cursor

2. From the Standard toolbar, click the Zoom Previous button to restore the full view of the cabin. Move the crosshair cursor with the door in tow up to the vicinity of the back door opening. The back door should swing to the inside and be against the wall when open, so the hinge point for this opening will be at the lower end of the left jamb line.

3. Activate the Endpoint Osnap and pick the lower end of the left jamb line on the back door opening. The copy of the door and swing is placed in the opening (see Figure 4.34), and by looking at the Command window, you can see that the Copy command has ended.

> The Copy command ends when you pick or specify the second point of the move, unless you're copying the same object to multiple places. You'll do that in Chapter 5 when you draw the stove top.

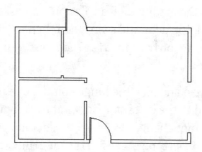

FIGURE 4.34:   The door is copied to the back door opening.

The door is oriented the wrong way, but you'll fix that next.

When you copy doors from one opening to another, often the orientation doesn't match. The best strategy is to use the hinge point as a point of reference and place it where it needs to go, as you have just done. Then flip and/or rotate the door so that it sits and swings the right way. The flipping of an object is known as *mirroring*.

Mirroring Objects

> You were able to use the Zoom command while you were in the middle of using the Copy command. You can use most of the display commands (Zoom, Pan, and so on) in this way. This is called using a command *transparently*.

You have located the door in the opening, but it needs to be flipped so that it swings to the inside of the cabin. To do this, we'll use the *Mirror command*.

The Mirror command allows you to flip objects around an axis called the *mirror line*. You define this imaginary line by designating two points on the line. Strategic selection of the mirror line ensures the accuracy of the mirroring action, so it's critical to visualize where the proper line lies. Sometimes you will have to draw a guideline in order to designate one or both of the endpoints.

1. Choose the Zoom Window icon from the Standard toolbar, and create a window around the back door and its opening.

2. Click the Mirror button on the Modify toolbar. Select the back door and swing, and press ↵. The prompt line changes to read `Specify first point of mirror line:`.

3. Activate the Endpoint Osnap, and then pick the hinge point of the door. The prompt changes to read `Specify second point of mirror line:`, and you will see the mirrored image of the door and the swing moving as you move the cursor around the drawing area. You are rotating the mirror line about the hinge point as you move the cursor. As the mirror line rotates, the location of the mirrored image moves (see Figure 4.35).

You can also start the Mirror command by choosing **Modify ➤ Mirror** on the drop-down menu or by typing **mi↵**.

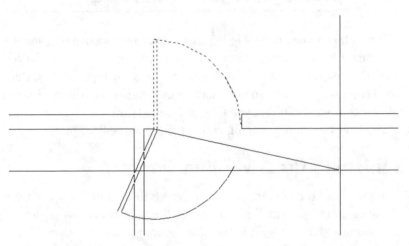

FIGURE 4.35: The mirror image moves as the mirror line rotates.

4. Hold the crosshair cursor directly to the right of the first point picked, along the inside wall line. The mirror image appears where you want the door.

5. Activate the Endpoint Osnap again and pick the lower end of the right jamb line. The mirror image disappears, and the prompt changes to read `Delete source objects? [Yes/No] <N>:`. You have two choices. You can keep both doors by pressing ↵ and accepting the default (No). Or you can discard the original one by typing y (for yes) in the command line and pressing ↵.

6. Type y↵. The flipped door is displayed, and the original one is deleted (see Figure 4.36). The Mirror command ends. Like the Copy command, the Mirror command ends automatically after one mirroring operation.

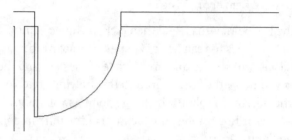

FIGURE 4.36: The mirrored door and swing

It may take some practice to become proficient at visualizing and designating the mirror line, but once you are used to it, you will have learned a very powerful tool. Because many objects—including building layouts, widgets, steel beams, road cross sections, and so on—have some symmetry to them, wise use of the Mirror command can save you a lot of drawing time.

You have two more swinging doors to place in the floor plan.

Finishing the Swinging Doors

You can't copy the existing doors and swings to the interior openings because the sizes don't conform, but you can use the same procedure to draw one door and swing and then copy it to the other opening.

 N O T E   We could have used the Stretch command to lengthen the door, but that's an advanced Modify command and won't be introduced until Chapter 9. Besides, the arc would have to be modified to a larger radius. It's easier to just draw another door and swing to a different size.

1. Click the Zoom Previous button on the Standard toolbar. Then click the Zoom Window button right next to the Zoom Previous button, and make a zoom window to magnify the view of the interior door openings. Be sure to make the zoom window large enough to leave some room for the new doors to be drawn (see Figure 4.37).

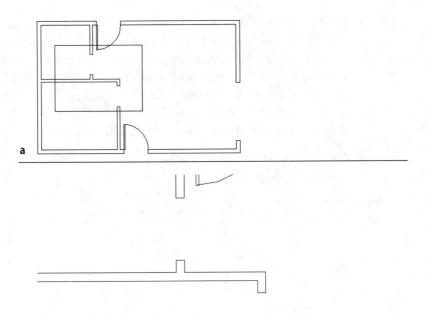

FIGURE 4.37: A zoom window in the interior door opening area (a), and the results of the zoom (b)

2. Follow the same procedure to draw the door and swing in the lower opening. Here is a summary of the steps:

   A. Use the Rectangle command and Endpoint Osnap to draw the door from the hinge point to a point @1.5,-2'6.

   B. Rotate the door around the hinge point to an open position. You will have to use a rotation angle of –90°.

   C. Use the Start, Center, Angle option of the Arc command to draw the door swing, starting at the upper-left corner of the door and using Endpoint Osnap for the two picks.

3. Use the Copy command to copy this door and swing to the other interior opening. The base point will be the hinge point, and the second point will be the left end of the lower jamb line in the upper opening. Use the Endpoint Osnap for both picks.

The Start, Center, Angle options, as well as a few others, of the Arc command require that you choose the start point for the arc in such a way that the arc is drawn in a counter-clockwise direction. If you progress in a clockwise direction, use a negative number for the angle.

4. Use the Mirror command to flip up this copy of the door and swing. The mirror line will be different from the one used for the back door. The geometrical arrangement at the back opening required that the door and its swing be flipped across the opening. For this one, the door and its swing must flip in a direction parallel to the opening. For this opening, the mirror line is the lower jamb line itself, so pick each end of this line (using Endpoint Osnap) to establish the mirror line.

5. Use the Zoom Previous button to see the four swinging doors in place (see Figure 4.38).

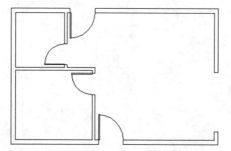

FIGURE 4.38: The four swinging doors in place

The last door to draw is the sliding glass door. This kind of door requires an entirely different strategy, but you'll use commands familiar to you by now.

 N O T E   The buttons you have been clicking in this chapter are also referred to as icons and tools. When they are in dialog boxes or on the status bar, they actually look like buttons to push that have icons on them. When they are on the toolbars, they look like icons, that is, little pictures. But when you move the Pointer Arrow cursor onto one, it takes on the appearance of a button with an icon on it. All three terms—*button*, *icon*, and *tool*—will be used interchangeably in this book.

Drawing a Sliding Glass Door

Sliding glass doors are usually drawn to show their glass panels within the door frames.

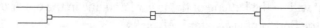

To draw the sliding door, you will apply the Line, Offset, and Trim commands to the 7' opening you made earlier. It's a complicated exercise but it will teach you a lot about the power of using these three commands in combination.

1. Click the Zoom Window button on the Standard toolbar, and make a zoom window closely around the 7' opening. In making the zoom window, pick one point just above and to the left of the upper door-jamb and below and to the right of the lower jamb. This will make the opening as large as possible while including everything you will need in the view (see Figure 4.39).

FIGURE 4.39: The view when zoomed in as closely as possible to the 7' opening

2. You will be using several Osnaps for this procedure, so it will be convenient to have the Osnap Flyout toolbar more immediately available. Here's how:

   A. Right-click any button on any of the toolbars on your screen to open the Toolbar menu.

   B. Click Object Snap. The Toolbar menu closes, and the Object Snap toolbar is displayed in the drawing area. It is in floating mode.

   C. Put the cursor on the colored title bar of the Object Snap toolbar, and holding down the left mouse button, drag the toolbar to the right side of the drawing area. Dock it there by releasing the mouse button (see Figure 4.40). Now you can easily select all Object Snaps as needed.

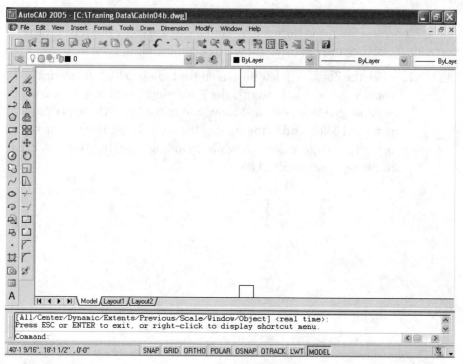

FIGURE 4.40: The Object Snap toolbar docked to the right of the drawing area

3. Offset each jamb line 2" into the doorway opening (see Figure 4.41).

FIGURE 4.41: Jamb lines offset 2" into the doorway opening

4. Type L↵ to start the Line command. Click the Midpoint Osnap button on the Object Snap toolbar, and then place the cursor near the midpoint of the upper doorjamb line. Notice that a colored triangle appears when your cursor is in the vicinity of the midpoint. A symbol with a distinctive shape is associated with each Osnap. When the triangle appears at the midpoint of the jamb line, left-click. Click the Midpoint Osnap button again, move the cursor to the bottom jamb line, and, when the triangle appears at that midpoint, click again. Press ↵ to end the Line command.

5. Start the Offset command and type 1.5↵ to set the offset distance. Pick the newly drawn line, and then pick a point anywhere to the right side. Then, while the Offset command is still running, pick the original line again, and pick another point in a blank area somewhere to the left side of the doorway opening (see Figure 4.42). Press ↵ to end the Offset command.

A line *offset* from itself, that is, a copy of the selected line, is automatically made at a specified perpendicular distance from the selected line.

FIGURE 4.42: The offset vertical line between the jambs

6. Check the status bar to see if Ortho is on. If it's not, click it to activate it. Type L↵ to start the Line command. Click the Midpoint Osnap button, and then move the cursor near the midpoint of the left vertical line. When the colored triangle appears at the midpoint of this leftmost line, click. Hold the cursor out directly to the right of the point you just selected to draw a horizontal line through the three vertical lines. When the cursor is about two feet to the right of the three vertical lines, pick a point to set the endpoint of this guideline. Press ↵ to end the Line command (see Figure 4.43).

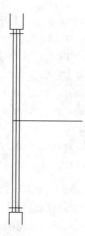

FIGURE 4.43: The horizontal guideline drawn through vertical lines

7. Type o↵ to start the Offset command. Type 1↵ to set the offset distance. Select this new line, and then pick a point in a blank area anywhere above the line. Pick the new horizontal line again, and then pick anywhere below it. The new line has been offset 1" above and below itself (see Figure 4.44). Now you have placed all the lines necessary to create the sliding glass door frames in the opening. You still need to trim back some of these lines and erase others. Press ↵ to end the Offset command.

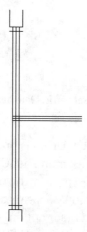

FIGURE 4.44: The offset horizontal guideline

8. Start the Trim command by typing **tr**↵. When you are prompted to select cutting edges, pick the two horizontal lines that were just created with the Offset command. Then press ↵.

9. Now trim the two outside vertical lines by selecting them as shown in Figure 4.45a. The result is shown in Figure 4.45b.

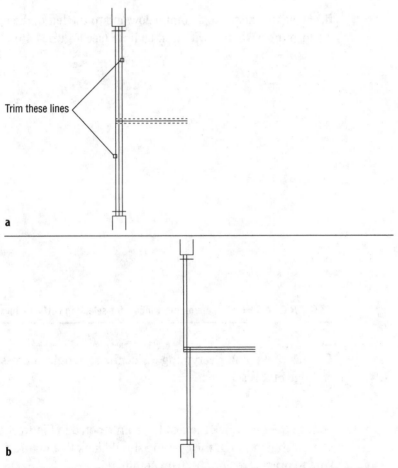

FIGURE 4.45: Picking the vertical lines to trim (a), and the result (b)

10. Press ↵ twice to stop and restart the Trim command. When you are prompted to select cutting edges, use a special window called a *crossing window* to select all the lines visible in the drawing. A crossing window will select everything within the window or crossing it. Here's how to do it:

A. Pick a point above and to the right of the opening.

B. Move the cursor to a point below and to the left of the opening, forming a window with dashed lines (see Figure 4.46).

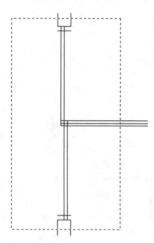

F I G U R E   4 . 4 6 :   The crossing window for selecting cutting edges

C. Pick that point. Everything inside the rectangle or crossing an edge of it is selected.

D. Press ↵.

11. To trim the lines, pick them at the points noted in Figure 4.47a. When you finish trimming, the opening should look like Figure 4.47b. Be sure to press ↵ to end the Trim command.

N O T E   If all lines don't trim the way you expect them to, you may have to change the setting for the Edgemode system variable. Cancel the trim operation and undo any trims you've made to the sliding glass door. Type edgemode↵, and then type 0↵. Now start the Trim command and continue trimming.

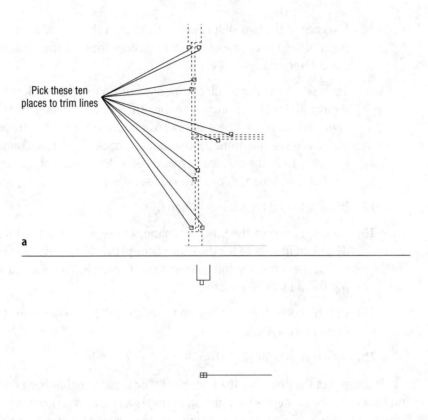

Pick these ten
places to trim lines

a

b

FIGURE 4.47: Lines to trim (a), and the result (b)

12. Start the Erase command and erase the remaining horizontal guideline.

To finish the sliding glass doors, you need to draw in two lines to represent the glass panes for each door panel. Each pane of glass is centered inside its frame, so the line representing the pane will run between the midpoints of the inside edge of each frame section.

13. Type L↵ to start the Line command, and pick the Midpoint button on the Object Snap toolbar.

14. For each of the two sliding door frames, put the cursor near the mid-point of the inside line of the frame section nearest the jamb. When the colored triangle appears there, click.

Then select the Perpendicular Osnap button from the Object Snap toolbar and move the cursor to the other frame section of that door panel. When you get near the horizontal line that represents both the inside edge of one frame section and the back edge of the frame section next to it, the colored Perpendicular Osnap symbol will appear on that line. When it does, select that point.

15. Press ↵ to end the Line command.

16. Press ↵ to restart the Line command, and repeat the procedure described in step 14 for the other door panel, being sure to start the line at the frame section nearest the other jamb. The finished opening should look like Figure 4.48a.

17. Use the Zoom Previous button to see the full floor plan with all doors (see Figure 4.48b).

18. Save this drawing as Cabin04c.

This completes the doors for the floor plan. The focus here has been on walls and doors and the strategies for drawing them. As a result, you now have a basic floor plan for the cabin, and you will continue to develop this plan in the next chapter.

The overall drawing strategy that has been emphasized in this chapter is using objects already in the drawing to create new ones. You started with four lines that constituted the outside wall lines. By offsetting, filleting, extending, and trimming, you drew all the walls and openings without drawing any new lines. For the swinging doors, you made two rectangles and two arcs. Then by copying, rotating, and mirroring, you formed the other two swinging doors. For the sliding glass door, you drew two new lines; then you used Offset, Trim, and Erase to finish the door. So you used four lines and created six new objects to complete the walls and doors. This is a good start in learning to use AutoCAD wisely.

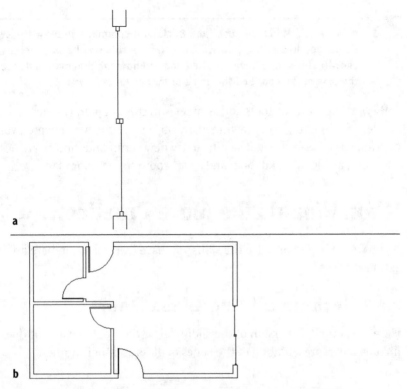

FIGURE 4.48: The finished sliding glass doors (a), and the floor plan with all doors finished (b)

Throughout this chapter, I have indicated several instances when you can press the spacebar instead of the ↵ key. This can be handy if you keep one hand resting on the keyboard while the other hand controls the mouse. For brevity, I will continue to instruct you to use ↵ and not mention the spacebar, but as you get better at drawing in AutoCAD, you may find the spacebar a useful substitute for ↵ in many cases. You will find your preference. You can substitute the spacebar for ↵ when handling the following tasks:

- ▶ Restarting the previous command

- ▶ Ending a command

- ▶ Moving from one step in a command to the next step

- ▶ Entering a new offset distance or accepting the current offset distance

- ▶ Entering relative or absolute coordinates

- ▶ Entering an angle of rotation

N O T E   When you used the Rectangle command to draw the swinging doors, you had to use relative Cartesian coordinates because relative polar coordinates would have required you to know the diagonal distance across the plan of the door and the angle of that distance as well.

By working with the tools and strategies in this chapter, you now should have an idea of an approach to drawing many objects. In the next chapter, you will continue in the same vein, learning a few new commands and strategies as you add steps, a balcony, a kitchen, and a bathroom to the floor plan.

If You Would Like More Practice...

If you would like to practice the skills you have learned so far, here are some extra exercises.

An Alternate Sliding Glass Door

Here is a simplified version of the sliding glass door of the cabin. It doesn't include any representation of the panes of glass and their frames.

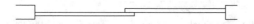

To draw it, use a technique similar to the one described in the previous section. Copy the jambs for the 7' opening to the right, and draw this door between them.

An Addition to the Cabin

This addition is connected to the cabin by a sidewalk and consists of a remodeled two-car garage in which one car slot has been converted into a storage area and an office (see Figure 4.49). Use the same commands and strategies you have been using up to now to draw this layout adjacent to the cabin. Save this exercise as Cabin04c-addon.dwg.

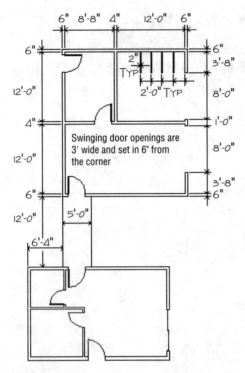

FIGURE 4.49: The garage addition

Refer to this chapter and the previous one for specific commands. Here is the general procedure:

1. Draw the two lines that represent the walkway between the two buildings.

2. Draw the outside exterior wall line.

3. Use Offset, Fillet, and Trim to create the rest of the walls and wall lines.

4. Use Offset, Extend, and Trim to create the openings.

5. Use Rectangle and Arc to create a swinging door.

6. Use Copy, Rotate, and Mirror to put in the rest of the doors.

7. Use Offset, Line, and Copy to draw the storage partitions.

Draw Three Views of a Block

Use the tools you have learned in the last few chapters to draw the top, right side, and front views of the block shown in Figure 4.50.

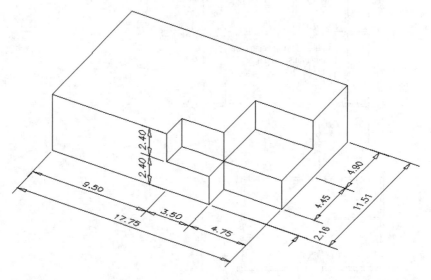

FIGURE 4.50: The block

Below is a graphic representation of the twelve steps necessary to complete the exercise.

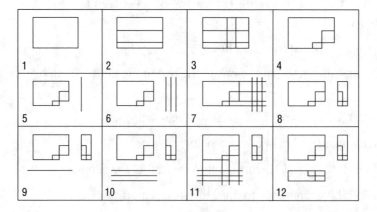

Here are the 12 steps in summary that correspond to the 12 drawings. Start with the top view:

1. Start a new drawing. Leave all settings at the defaults. Use relative polar or relative Cartesian coordinates and the Line command to draw a rectangle 17.75 wide and 11.51 high.

2. Offset the bottom horizontal line up 2.16 and the new line up 4.45.

3. Offset the right vertical line 4.75 to the left and the new line 3.50 to the left.

4. Use the Trim command to trim back lines and complete the view.

Next, do the right side view:

5. Draw a vertical line to the right of the top view. Make it longer than the top view is deep.

6. Offset the vertical line 2.4 to the right, and then offset the new line 2.4 to the right also.

7. Use Endpoint Osnap to draw lines from the corner points of the top view across the three vertical lines.

8. Trim the lines back to complete the side view.

Finally, draw the front view:

9. Draw a horizontal line below the top view. Make it longer than the top view is wide.

10. Offset this line 2.4 down, and then offset the new line 2.4 down.

11. Use Endpoint Osnap to draw lines from the corner points of the top view, down across the three horizontal lines.

12. Trim the lines back to complete the view.

This ends the exercise. There are ways to rotate and move each view relative to the other views. We will look at those commands later in the book, and draw more views in Chapter 8.

Are You Experienced?

Now you can...

- ☑ offset exterior walls to make interior walls

- ☑ zoom in on an area with the Zoom Window command and zoom back out with the Zoom Previous command

- ☑ use the Rectangle and Arc commands to make a door

- ☑ use the Endpoint, Midpoint, and Perpendicular Object Snap modes

- ☑ use the Crossing Window selection tool

- ☑ use the Copy and Mirror commands to place an existing door and swing in another opening

- ☑ use the Offset and Trim commands to make a sliding glass door

CHAPTER 5

Gaining Drawing Strategies: Part 2

- ▶ Using Object Snaps
- ▶ Using Polar Tracking
- ▶ Zooming and panning with Realtime
- ▶ Copying and moving objects
- ▶ Using Direct Entry of distances
- ▶ Creating circles and ellipses

T he previous chapter emphasized using existing geometry (or objects) in a drawing to create new geometry. In this chapter, we'll look at new tools for forming an efficient drawing strategy. Before we get back to the cabin, I want to give you a brief overview of the tools available for starting and running commands.

Developing a drawing strategy begins with determining the best way to start or when to start a command. AutoCAD provides several ways to start most of the commands you will be using. You have seen how the Offset, Fillet, Trim, and Extend commands can be found on either the Modify toolbar or the Modify drop-down menu. You can also start them by typing the first letter or two of the command and then pressing Enter.

T I P   Here's a quick recap. To start the Offset command, type **o**. To enter the Fillet command, type **f**. To execute the Trim command, type **tr**, and to execute the Extend command, type **ex**. You can also start almost all AutoCAD commands by typing the full name of the command, for example, **extend**↵. And don't forget that you can access the drop-down menus by pressing the Alt key and then the hotkey—the letter that becomes underlined in the menu name when the Alt key is pressed. For example, to open the Modify drop-down menu, press Alt and then **m**.

The choice of which method to use is determined, to an extent, by what you are doing at the time as well as by your command of the keyboard. When using the abbreviations, keyboard entry is generally the fastest method; but if your hand is already on the mouse and the Modify toolbar is docked on the screen, selecting commands from the toolbar might be faster. The drop-down menus are slower to use because they require more selections to get to a command, but they also contain more commands and command options than the toolbars.

Remember that if you have just ended a command, you can restart that command by pressing ↵ or the spacebar or by right-clicking the mouse. When you right-click, a *shortcut* menu appears near the cursor.

The top item on this menu is Repeat *command*, where *command* is the last command used. For example, if you just finished using the Erase command and you right-click your mouse, the top item of the shortcut menu is Repeat Erase. I'll introduce the other items on this shortcut menu throughout the rest of the book. The shortcut menu is also called a *context* menu because the items on it depend on the following:

▶ Whether a command is running

▶ Which command you are using

▶ Where you are in a command

In this chapter, you will be introduced to several new commands and, through the step-by-step instructions, be shown some alternate methods for accomplishing tasks similar to those you have previously completed. You will add front and back steps, thresholds, a balcony, and kitchen and bath fixtures to the cabin floor plan (see Figure 5.1). For each of these tasks, the focus will be on noticing which objects and geometry are already in the drawing that can make your job easier and on tools to help you accomplish the tasks more quickly and efficiently.

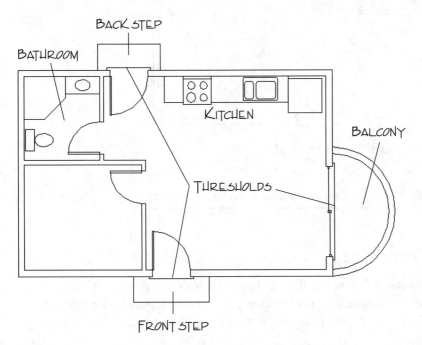

FIGURE 5.1: The cabin with front and back steps, thresholds, balcony, kitchen, and bathroom

Drawing the Steps and Thresholds

The steps and thresholds are each drawn with three simple lines. The trick is to see which part of the drawing you can effectively use to generate and position those lines. Use a width of 2' for the front and back steps, and use a length of 6' for the front step and 5' for the back step. The three thresholds extend 2" beyond the outside wall line and run 3" past either jamb line (see Figure 5.2). These are simple shapes to draw, but you will learn a few new techniques as you create them.

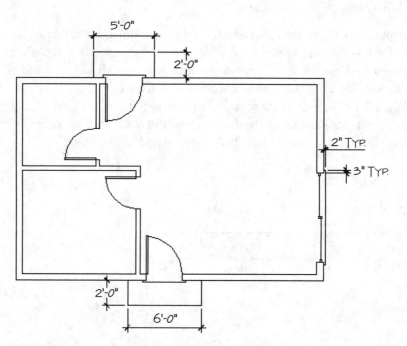

FIGURE 5.2: The steps and thresholds with their dimensions

The Front Step

As you can see in Figure 5.2, the front step is 2' wide and 6' long. Because you know the width of the doorway opening, you can determine how far past the opening the step extends, assuming it to be symmetrical. You can draw a line from the endpoint of one of the jamb lines, down 2', and then offset the proper distance left and right to create the sides of the step. Here's how it's done:

1. With AutoCAD running, open your cabin drawing (last saved as Cabin04c), and use the Zoom command options to achieve a view similar to Figure 5.3.

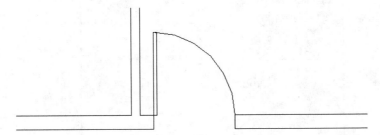

FIGURE 5.3: Zoomed in to the front opening

2. Check to be sure all buttons on the status bar except Model are in the off position. Start the Line command, activate the Endpoint Osnap, and pick a point at the lower end of the left jamb line.

WAYS TO USE THE OBJECT SNAP TOOLS

You can access the Object Snap tools in several ways:

▶ The Object Snap toolbar might be docked on the right side of the drawing area. If not, you can display it and dock it.

▶ The Object Snap menu also contains Object Snaps. To open this menu, hold down the Shift key and click the right mouse button.

▶ If you're using an Intellimouse or have a mouse with three buttons, you might be able to open the Object Snap menu by clicking the Intellimouse wheel or clicking the third mouse button.

▶ You can type the first three letters of any Object Snap to activate it, as in **end**↵ for Endpoint.

3. Right-click the Polar button on the status bar at the bottom of the screen, and then choose Settings from the shortcut menu to open the Drafting Settings dialog box. By default, the Polar Tracking tab is active.

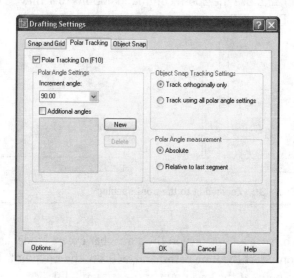

4. In the Polar Angle Settings area, check whether Increment Angle is set to 90.00. If it's not, open the drop-down list and select 90.00. On the right side, be sure that Absolute is selected in the Polar Angle Measurement area. Finally, in the upper-left corner, click the Polar Tracking On check box. Click OK.

5. Hold the crosshair cursor so that it is below the first point picked. Do not pick a point yet (see Figure 5.4). A dashed line called a *temporary alignment path* is displayed along with a tool tip that identifies the alignment path as a Polar path; a relative polar coordinate confirms the angle to be 270°. As you move the cursor from left to right, notice that the alignment path and tool tip disappear when you get too far from a point directly below the first point of the line, and they reappear as you get back close to vertical.

For LT users, your Polar Tracking tab in the Drafting Settings dialog box won't have the Object Snap Tracking Settings area because LT doesn't have this feature.

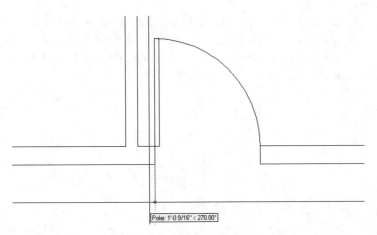

Polar: 1'-0 9/16" < 270.00°

FIGURE 5.4: The Line command running with Polar Tracking on

6. While the alignment path and tool tip are visible, type 2'↵. A vertical line is drawn that is 2 feet long. When the Line command is running and the crosshair cursor is held away from the last point picked in a particular direction, you can enter a distance, and the line is drawn to the desired length in the direction of the crosshair cursor. This is called the *Direct Entry* method of entering distances. Because you want the line to be vertical, Polar Tracking assisted you by producing an alignment path in the vertical direction.

When Polar Tracking mode is on, temporary alignment paths assist you in drawing lines at angles that are multiples of the increment angle, in this case, 90°.

7. Press ↵ to end the Line command. Type o↵ to start the Offset command. Type 1'6↵ for an offset distance, and offset this line to the left.

8. Press ↵ twice to stop and restart Offset. Type 6'↵ and offset this new line to the right (see Figure 5.5). Press ↵ to end the Offset command.

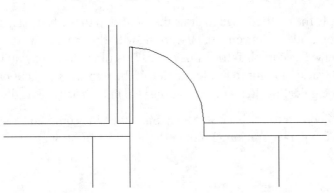

FIGURE 5.5: The sides of the front step after offsetting

9. Erase the original line, and then draw a line from the lower endpoints of these two new lines to represent the front edge of the step. Use the Endpoint Osnap for each point picked. Press ↵ to end the Line command. Your drawing should look like Figure 5.6.

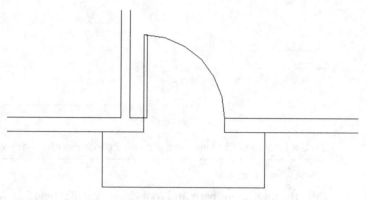

F I G U R E   5 . 6 :   The completed front step

10. Zoom Previous to view the entire floor plan.

The strategy here was to recognize that a line drawn from the jamb line can be used to determine the location of the sides of the step. Using Polar Tracking to draw is a quick way to enter distances when the lines are at angles that are multiples of the Polar Tracking increment angle that you set. For the back step, you'll build on this by adding the Temporary Tracking Point aid to your bag of tools.

The Back Step

You can apply the method used to draw the front step to the back step as well. The situation is identical: you will be working with the same geometry in the drawing and will accomplish the same thing. This time, however, you'll use a Temporary Tracking Point to locate the side of the step. This will cut out the need to use a guideline. Remember that the step in the back is 5' wide.

1. Zoom in to the back step area. Start the Line command and click the Temporary Tracking Point button on the Object Snap toolbar.

LT does not have the Temporary Tracking Point tool, so LT users should skip to the sidebar in the middle of the following steps to get alternate instructions for steps 1 through 3.

The prompt line in the Command window will read _line Specify first point: _tt Specify temporary OTRACK point:. This is actually three prompts grouped together:

▶ _line signifies the start of the Line command.

▶ Specify first point is the first prompt for the Line command.

▶ _tt Specify temporary OTRACK point signifies that the Temporary Tracking Point option has been selected.

In this case, because the step is 5' long, we want to begin the side of the step 1' to the left of the doorway opening. So the temporary tracking point that you need is the starting point from which you will measure the 1' distance—in this case, it is the upper end of the left jamb line.

2. Select the Endpoint Osnap and pick the upper end of the left jamb line. A small cross appears at the point you just picked, and the prompt line now has _endp of Specify first point: added to it. This is actually two more prompts grouped together:

▶ _endp signifies that the Endpoint Osnap was selected.

▶ Specify first point is the second prompt for the Temporary Tracking Point option. AutoCAD has recorded the temporary tracking point and waits for you to specify the first point of the line that is to be the left side of the back step. You will do this by using Polar Tracking and Direct Entry, telling AutoCAD how far and in what direction from the temporary tracking point you want to begin the line—in this case, it's 1' to the left.

3. Hold the cursor to the left of the temporary tracking point. When the temporary alignment path appears with the tool tip, as shown in Figure 5.7, type 12↵. A line begins 1' to the left of the opening on the outside wall line. Hold the crosshair cursor directly above the beginning of the line, and when you see the vertical alignment path with the tool tip, type 2'↵. The side of the step is drawn using the Direct Entry technique with Polar Tracking. The Line command is still running.

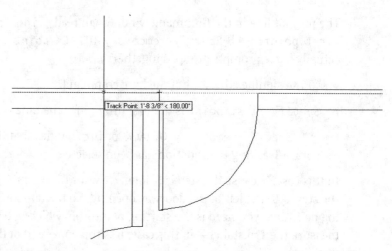

Track Point: 1'-8 3/8" < 180.00°

F I G U R E   5 . 7 : Using a temporary tracking point with Polar Tracking and Direct Entry

STEPS 1 THROUGH 3 FOR LT USERS

Here are instructions for LT users:

1. Zoom in to the back step area. Start the Line command and click the Tracking button on the Object Snap toolbar. (The Tracking button is the one at the top.)

2. Select the Endpoint Osnap and pick the upper end of the left jamb line.

3. Hold the cursor out to the left of the point you picked, past the edge of the building, and type **12⏎**. Then hold the cursor directly above the point that was selected until the Polar Tracking lines and tool tips appear. Type **24⏎**.

Now continue with step 4.

4. Hold the crosshair cursor directly to the right from the last point; then, when you see the alignment path and tool tip, type 5'⏎. The front edge of the step is drawn. You used Direct Entry with Polar Tracking again, and you didn't have to enter either the relative polar or the Cartesian coordinates.

5. Select Perpendicular Osnap from the Object Snap toolbar, and move the cursor to the outside wall line (see Figure 5.8). When the perpendicular icon appears on the wall line, click the mouse button. The right edge of the step is drawn, and the back step is complete. Press ↵ to end the Line command.

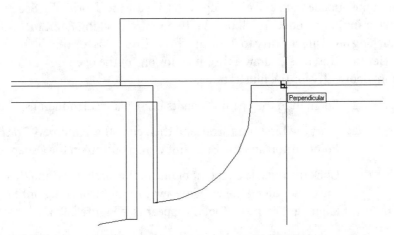

F I G U R E 5 . 8 : Completing the back step with the Perpendicular Osnap

6. Zoom Previous to view the completed back step with the whole floor plan.

Temporary Tracking is a handy tool for AutoCAD users. We'll use it a few more times in this book. When you combine it with the technique of using Polar Tracking to help enter distances, as you have for the back step, you will be surprised at how quickly you can lay out orthogonal walls in a floor plan. The Polar Tracking technique, used by itself, powerfully facilitates drawing the footprint of a building. When you work through the next section, you'll get to practice using the Temporary Tracking tool once more.

I'm sure this seems complicated, but you'll get a chance to try the technique three more times, because you now have to do the thresholds for the three external openings.

The Thresholds

Thresholds generally are used on doorway openings when the level changes from one side of the opening to the other. This usually occurs at entrances that open from or to the outside. Though quite different in shape, each threshold for the cabin has the same geometry as the steps. The lip of each threshold is offset 2" from the outside wall, and each edge runs 3" past the doorjamb. (See Figure 5.2 earlier in this chapter.) You'll use the Temporary Tracking Point tool with Polar Tracking and Direct Entry to draw the three thresholds for the cabin.

Here are the steps to draw a threshold for one of the openings. I'll use the front door entry for the illustrations.

> For LT users, reuse the steps in the "Steps 1 through 3 for LT Users" sidebar in the previous section to complete the exercise in this section. You draw the thresholds using the same procedure you used for the back step.

1. Zoom in to the opening and its immediate surroundings.

2. Start the Line command, and then click the Temporary Tracking Point button and the Endpoint Osnap button on the Osnap toolbar.

3. Click the outside endpoint of one of the jamb lines, and then move the cursor along the wall line away from the opening until the Polar alignment path and tool tip appear (see Figure 5.9a).

4. Enter the distance that the threshold extends past the jamb. (It's 3".) This begins the first line.

5. Move the crosshair away from the wall line in a horizontal or vertical direction (depending on which opening you are drawing) until the Polar alignment path and tool tip appear (see Figure 5.9b).

6. Enter the overhang distance of the threshold. (It's 2".)

7. Move the crosshair in a direction perpendicular to the last point of the last segment drawn, until the Polar alignment and tool tip appear.

8. Enter the length of the threshold. (It's the length of the opening + 6".)

9. Invoke the Perpendicular Osnap and hold the crosshair back on the wall line; then click. Press ↵ to end the Line command (see Figure 5.9c).

10. When finished, Zoom Previous to view the finished thresholds with the rest of the drawing.

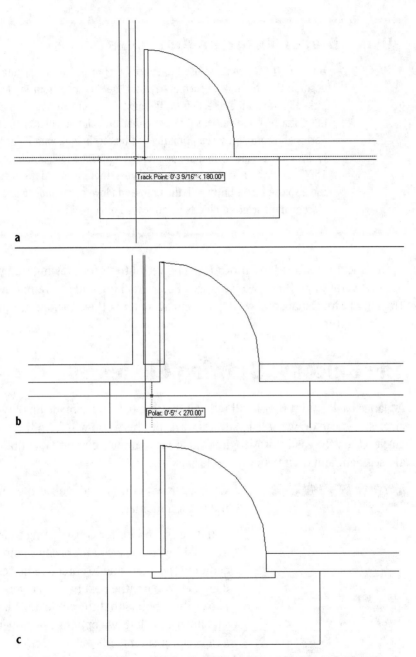

Track Point: 0'-3 9/16" < 180.00°

a

Polar: 0'-5" < 270.00°

b

c

F I G U R E 5 . 9 : The tracking path and Track Point tool tip (a), the first threshold line is started (b), and the completed threshold (c)

USING DIRECT ENTRY OF DISTANCES

Direct Entry is a method used to specify distances for line segments. You position the crosshair in such a way that the direction from the last point picked indicates the direction for the next line segment. You then just type the distance. There's no need to use either the relative polar or the relative Cartesian coordinates. You primarily use this technique with Polar Tracking to draw line segments that are oriented at a preset angle, in this case, 90°, 180°, 270°, and 0°. It saves time because there is less data to type. You can also use Direct Entry with the Copy and Move commands to specify displacement of selected objects being moved or copied.

The tracking features in AutoCAD are powerful tools for drawing that you can use in several ways. So far we have used Polar Tracking and the Temporary Tracking Point Osnap, and we'll use them again and other tracking features later in this chapter.

The Balcony: Drawing Circles

A glance back at Figure 5.1 will tell you that the balcony is made up of two semi-circles. You can draw these in several ways, but here you will form them from a circle. Often the easiest way to draw an arc is to draw a circle that contains the arc segment and then trim the circle back.

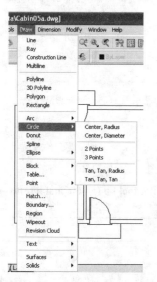

1. Choose Draw ➤ Circle and look at the Circle menu for a moment.

   You have six options for constructing a circle. The first two require you to specify a point as the center of the circle and to enter a radius or a diameter. You use the next two when you know two or three points that the circle must intersect. And finally, the last two options use tangents and a radius or just tangents to form a circle.

2. The balcony has a radius of 5', so choose the Center, Radius option. The Command window prompts you to specify a point as the center of the circle. The actual center for the balcony will be 5' above the lower-right corner of the outside

wall line, but for this exercise, we will draw the circle in the living room and then move it into position later.

3. Pick a point in the middle of the largest room of the cabin. The center is now established, and as you move the cursor, the circle changes size and becomes attached to the crosshair cursor (see Figure 5.10). You could pick a point to establish the radius, but in this case, you know exactly what you want the radius to be.

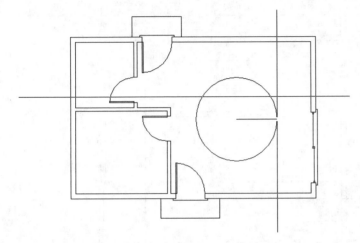

FIGURE 5.10: The circle attached to the crosshair cursor

4. Type 5'↵. The circle is drawn, and the command ends.

5. Click the Move button on the Modify toolbar. The cursor changes to a pickbox. Select the circle and press ↵.

6. On the Object Snap toolbar or flyout, click the Quadrant button. Select the circle somewhere near its bottom extremity (see Figure 5.11a). An image of the circle is attached to the crosshair cursor. Turn Polar Tracking off by clicking the Polar button on the status bar.

7. Move the crosshair cursor around to see that the lowest point on the circle is attached at the crosshair (see Figure 5.11b). You need to place this point on the circle at the lower-right corner of the outside wall line.

8. Select the Endpoint Osnap, and then pick the lower-right corner of the cabin. The circle is positioned correctly for the balcony (see Figure 5.11c). Now you can use the existing wall lines to trim the circle into a semicircle.

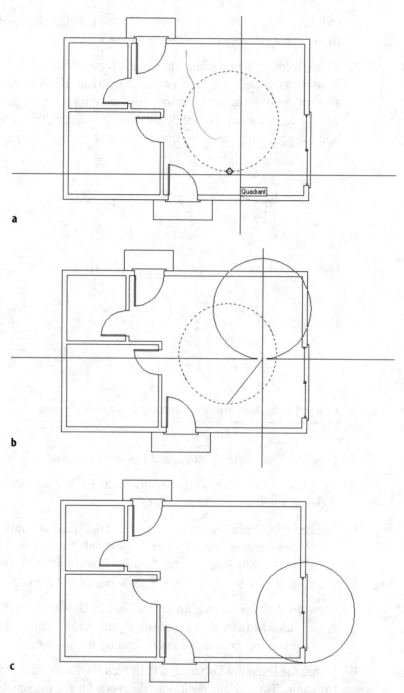

a

b

c

FIGURE 5.11: Selecting the base point with Quadrant Osnap (a), the circle attached to the crosshair cursor at its lowest point (b), and the circle positioned for the balcony (c)

9. Zoom in to the area of the balcony and start the Trim command.

10. Select the two outside wall lines on the far right, as shown in Figure 5.12, and then right-click.

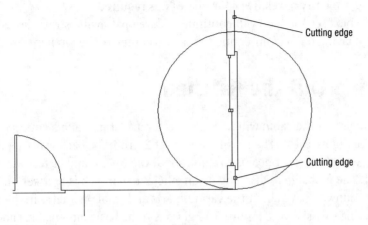

FIGURE 5.12: Selecting wall lines to be cutting edges

11. Select the portion of the circle that is inside the cabin. The circle is trimmed into a semicircle. Press ↵ to end the Trim command.

12. Start the Offset command, set the distance for 6", and offset the semicircle to the inside. Press ↵ to end the Offset command. The balcony is complete. Zoom Previous to view the floor plan with the completed balcony. Save the drawing as Cabin05a.dwg (see Figure 5.13).

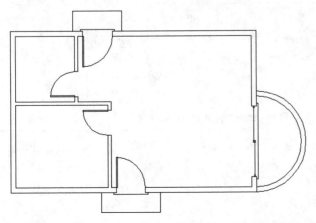

FIGURE 5.13: The floor plan with the balcony completed

As mentioned at the beginning of this section, you can use several techniques to draw the balcony. The one you used gave you the opportunity to use the Move command and the Quadrant Osnap, and it let you see how using the lowest quadrant snap point on the circle is an easy way to locate the balcony on the building. No entry of relative coordinates was required.

In the next section, you will continue to develop drawing strategies as you focus on laying out a counter and fixtures to complete the kitchen.

Laying Out the Kitchen

The kitchen for the cabin will have a stove, a refrigerator, and a counter with a sink (see Figure 5.14). The refrigerator is set 2" from the back wall. Approaching this drawing task, your goal is to think about the easiest and fastest way to complete it. The first step in deciding on an efficient approach is to ascertain what information you have about the various parts and what geometry in the drawing will be able to assist you. Figure 5.14 gives you the basic dimensions, and you will get more detailed information about the sink and stove as we progress through the exercise.

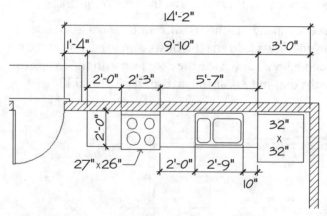

FIGURE 5.14: The general layout of the kitchen

The Counter

Although the counter is in two pieces, you will draw it as one piece and then cut out a section for the stove. Try two ways to draw the counter to see which method is more efficient.

Using Polar Tracking and Direct Entry with a Temporary Tracking Point

1. Use a zoom window to zoom your view so it is about the same magnification as Figure 5.15. On the status bar, click the Polar button to turn Polar Tracking back on if it is not already on. The Model and Polar buttons should be in the on position. The rest of the buttons should be off.

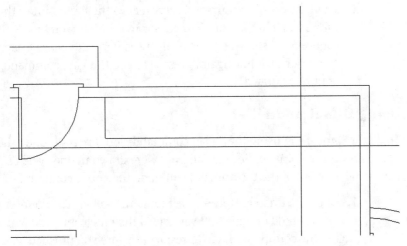

FIGURE 5.15: Drawing the counter using the Direct Entry technique

2. Start the Line command. Activate the Temporary Tracking Point Osnap and click Endpoint Osnap. Then pick the lower end of the right back doorjamb line. A small cross is placed on the point you choose.

3. Hold the crosshair cursor directly to the right of that point. When the Track Point tool tip and the dotted-line tracking path appear, type 1'4↵. The line for the left side of the counter is begun.

LT users should use steps 2 and 3 in the following "Steps 2 and 3 for LT Users" sidebar instead of these.

Steps 2 and 3 for LT Users

Here are instructions for LT users:

2. Start the Line command. Click the Tracking button at the top of the Object Snap toolbar, and click Endpoint Osnap. Then pick the lower end of the right back doorjamb line.

3. Hold the cursor directly to the right of the point you picked and type **1'4**↵. Then press ↵ again. This begins the counter line on the inside wall line 1'-4" to the right of the point you originally picked.

Now continue with step 4 to complete the counter.

4. Hold the crosshair cursor directly below the first point of the line and type 2'↵. Hold the crosshair cursor to the right and type 9'10↵ (see Figure 5.15, shown earlier). Select the Perpendicular Osnap and pick the inside wall line again. Press ↵ to end the Line command. The counter is drawn.

Using Offset and Fillet

To do the same thing using the Offset command, you'll need to undo the effects of the previous command. Because all lines were drawn in one cycle of the Line command, one use of the U command will undo the entire counter.

 1. Click the Undo button on the Standard toolbar. The counter you just drew should disappear. If you ended the Line command while drawing the counter and had to restart it before you finished, you might have to click the Undo button more than once. If you undo too much, click the Redo button, which is just to the right of the Undo button.

Now draw the counter again, this time using the Offset and Fillet commands.

2. Offset the right inside wall line 3' to the left. Then offset this new line 9'-10" to the left. Finally, offset the upper inside wall line 2' down (see Figure 5.16).

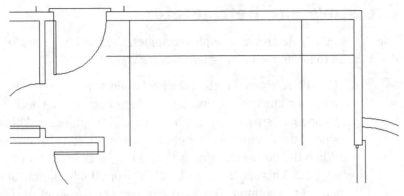

FIGURE 5.16: Offsetting wall lines to create the counter

3. Use the Fillet command with a radius of zero to clean up the two corners.

You can decide which of the two methods is more practical for you. Both are powerful techniques for laying out orthogonal patterns of lines for walls, counters, and other objects.

UNDOING AND REDOING IN AUTOCAD

AutoCAD has two Undo commands, and they operate quite differently.

▶ When you click the Undo button on the Standard toolbar, you are using AutoCAD's U command. You can also start it by typing **u**↵. The U command works like the Undo command for Windows-compatible applications by undoing the results of commands one step at a time.

▶ The Undo command in AutoCAD has many options, and you start it by typing **undo**↵. You use this approach when you want to undo everything you've done since you last saved your drawing or to undo back to a point in your drawing session that you marked earlier. Be careful when you use the Undo command; you can easily lose a lot of your work.

The Redo command will undo the effect of several undos. So if you undo a few steps too many, you can still get them back.

The Stove and Refrigerator

The stove and refrigerator are simple rectangles. Use the Temporary Tracking Point Osnap to locate the first corner of each shape.

LT users should use steps 1 through 3 in the following "Steps 1 through 3 for LT Users" sidebar instead of these.

1. For the refrigerator, click the Rectangle button on the Draw toolbar, and then click the Temporary Tracking Point Osnap option. Use Endpoint Osnap to select a base point at the upper end of the right side of the counter. Then hold the cursor directly below that point. When the dotted tracking path and the Track Point tool tip appear, type 2↵. This starts the rectangle 2" from the back wall, along the side of the counter. To specify the opposite corner of the rectangle, type @32,-32↵.

2. For the stove, right-click the mouse, and choose Repeat Rectangle from the shortcut menu that opens. Use the technique that was used in step 1, but pick the upper end of the left side of the counter as the tracking point. Hold the cursor directly to the right of that point and type 2'↵. Then type @27,-26 to complete the rectangle.

3. Use the Trim command to trim away the front edge of the counter at the stove (see Figure 5.17).

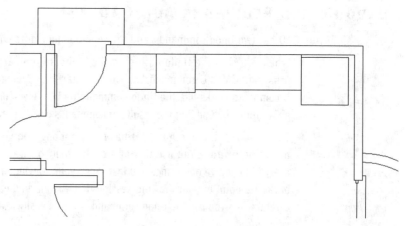

FIGURE 5.17: The stove and refrigerator made with rectangles

STEPS 1 THROUGH 3 FOR LT USERS

Here are instructions for LT users:

1. For the refrigerator, click the Rectangle button on the Draw toolbar, and then click the Tracking button at the top of the Object Snap toolbar. Use Endpoint Osnap to select a base point at the upper end of the right side of the counter. Then hold the cursor directly below that point and type **2**↵. This starts the rectangle 2" from the back wall, along the side of the counter. To specify the opposite corner of the rectangle, type **@32,-32**↵.

2. For the stove, right-click the mouse and choose Repeat Rectangle from the shortcut menu that opens. Use the technique that was used in step 1, but pick the upper end of the left side of the counter as the tracking point. Hold the cursor directly to the right of that point and type **2'**↵. Then type **@27,-26** to complete the rectangle.

3. Use the Trim command to trim away the front edge of the counter at the stove (see Figure 5.17, shown earlier).

N O T E   Because the stove rectangle is drawn as a *polyline*—a special line in which all segments compose one unique entity—you need to select only one segment of it for all sides of the rectangle to be selected and, in this case, to become cutting edges.

Completing the Stove

The stove needs a little more detail. You will need to add circles to represent the burners and to add a line off the back to indicate the control panel (see Figure 5.18). The burners are located by their centers.

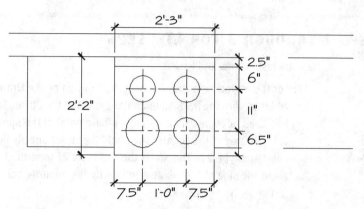

FIGURE 5.18: The details of the stove

1. Zoom in to a closer view of the stove using the zoom window. You need to draw a line along the back of the stove that is 2.5" in from the wall line. Offsetting seems like the right command to use.

2. Offset the wall line down 2.5". When you pick the line, pick it somewhere to the right or left of the stove. Then after it's offset, trim it back to the sides of the stove (see Figure 5.19).

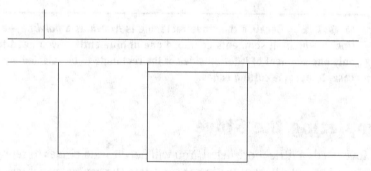

FIGURE 5.19: The stove with the control panel drawn

W A R N I N G   The back segment of the stove coincides with the wall. If you try to pick the wall line where the two lines coincide, you might pick the rectangle of the stove instead. You don't want to offset a line of the stove because it is a polyline. When any segment of a polyline is offset, all segments are offset, and all corners are filleted automatically. This would be an inconvenience in this situation because only one line segment needs to be offset. When you draw the sink, you'll learn a technique for selecting the line you want when two or more lines overlap or coincide.

3. The next step is to lay out guidelines to locate the centers of the burners. Offset the line you created for the control panel in step 2 down 6". Then offset this new line down 11". Next you need vertical guidelines. Use tracking to draw the first guideline.

4. Start the Line command and select Temporary Tracking Point Osnap and then Endpoint Osnap. Then pick the upper-left corner of the stove.

5. Hold the cursor directly to the right of this point. When the dotted tracking path and the Track Point tool tip appear, type 7.5↵. The first guideline is started.

6. Hold the crosshair cursor below the first point of the guideline and pick a point just below the stove. Press ↵ to end the Line command.

7. Offset this line 12" to the right (see Figure 5.20). The guidelines are set in place.

LT users need to use the Tracking tool for Steps 4 and 5. Use the same method you used for the refrigerator and the counter.

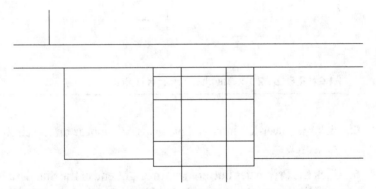

FIGURE 5.20: The guidelines for the centers of the burner circles

The next step is to draw a circle for one burner, copy it to the other three burner locations, and then change the radius of the left front burner.

1. Using the Intersection Osnap and the Circle command, draw a circle with its center at the lower-left intersection of the guidelines and with a radius of 3.5".

2. Start the Copy command. Select the circle and then press ↵.

3. Type m↵ to start the Multiple option. Choose Intersection Osnap. Select the intersection of the guidelines at the center of the circle as a base point.

4. Select the Intersection Osnap again, and pick the intersection of guidelines above the first circle (see Figure 5.21). Select the Intersection Osnap again, and pick one of the intersections on the right side. Then select the Intersection Osnap one more time, and pick the fourth intersection of guidelines. Press ↵ to end the Multiple Copy command. The burners are in place. Now you need to change the size of the lower-left burner.

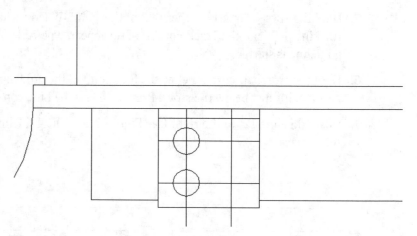

FIGURE 5.21:   The first burner is copied.

5. Pick the lower-left burner. Five grips will appear on the circle and at its center.

6. Click the Properties button near the right end of the Standard toolbar to open the Properties palette. It will fill most of the left part of the screen (see Figure 5.22). Notice the drop-down list at the top of the Properties palette. This tells you that the currently selected object is a circle.

7. Move down the categorized list of properties and click Radius.

8. Highlight the 3.5" Radius setting. Change it to 4.5" and press ↵. The burner in the drawing is enlarged.

9. Click the X in the upper-left corner of the Properties palette to close it. Then press the Esc key to turn off the five grips that were on the circle.

10. Erase the guidelines, and the stove is completed (see Figure 5.23). Zoom Previous to see the whole kitchen with the completed stove.

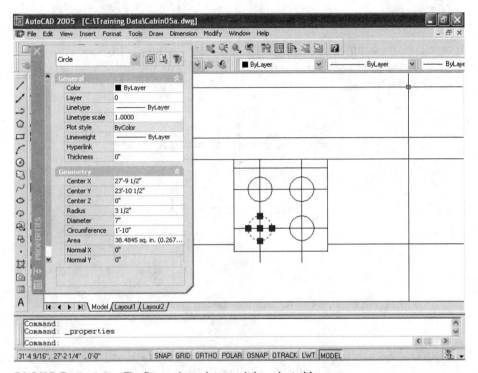

FIGURE 5.22: The Properties palette and the selected burner

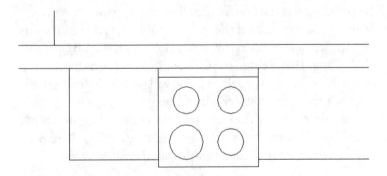

FIGURE 5.23: The completed stove

With the stove finished, the final task in the kitchen is to draw the sink.

 N O T E The Properties palette is an important tool for working with objects in a drawing. You will learn more about it in Chapter 6, and you will use it throughout the rest of this book.

The Kitchen Sink

You will draw a double sink, with one basin larger than the other (see Figure 5.24). You will use Offset, Fillet, and Trim to create the sink from the counter and wall lines.

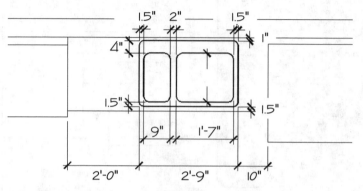

FIGURE 5.24: The sink with dimensions

1. Zoom in to the sink area, keeping the edges of the refrigerator and stove in view. Offset the wall line 1" down and the front edge of the counter 1.5" up.

2. Start the Offset command, and set the offset distance to 10". We're going to offset the right side of the counter 10" to the left, but it coincides with the left side of the refrigerator. Hold down the Ctrl key as you pick that line. Then release the Ctrl key. If the refrigerator ghosts, pick the same line again. The selected line will switch to the line representing the edge of the counter. When the counter edge is selected, press ↵, and then complete the offset by picking a point to the left of the selected line. This selection technique is called *cycling*. It allows you to select a line that may coincide with another line.

3. Offset this new line 2'-9" to the left. This forms the outside edge of the sink (see Figure 5.25a).

4. Fillet the corners of this rectangle to clean them up, using a radius of zero.

5. Offset the left side, bottom, and right side of the sink 1.5" to the inside. Offset the top side 4" to the inside. Then offset the new line on the left 9" to the right and then again 2" farther to the right. This forms the basis of the inside sink lines (see Figure 5.25b).

> When we drew the detail onto the stove, we could have used cycling to select the wall line where it coincided with the stove outline. We didn't need to because we could easily select the wall line at a point where the stove outline wasn't interfering.

6. Trim away the horizontal top and bottom inside sink lines between the two middle vertical sink lines. Then fillet the four corners of each sink with a 2" radius to clean them up.

7. Fillet all outside sink corners with a 1.5" radius. This will finish the sink (see Figure 5.25c). Zoom Previous to view the whole kitchen with the completed sink.

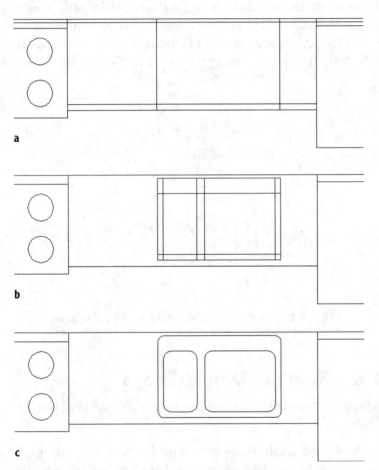

a

b

c

FIGURE 5.25: The offset lines to form the outside edge of the sink (a), the offset lines to form the inside edges of the sink (b), and the finished sink (c)

This completes the kitchen area. You drew few new lines to complete this task because most of them were created by offsetting existing lines and then trimming or filleting them. Keep this in mind as you move on to the bathroom.

Constructing the Bathroom

The bathroom has three fixtures: a sink, a shower, and a toilet (see Figure 5.26). In drawing these fixtures, you will be using a few Object Snaps over and over again. You can set one or more of the Osnap choices to be continually running until you turn them off. That way, you won't have to select them each time.

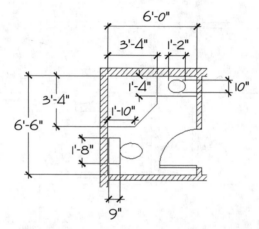

FIGURE 5.26: The bathroom fixtures with dimensions

Setting Running Object Snaps

You will set only two Osnaps to run continually for now, until you get used to how they work.

    1. Right-click the Osnap button on the status bar, and choose Settings from the shortcut menu to open the Drafting Settings dialog box. By default, the Object Snap tab is on top.

Each of the 13 Osnap options (11 options for LT) has a check box and a symbol next to it. The symbol appears in the drawing when a particular Osnap is selected and the cursor is near a point where that Osnap can be used. You can check any number of Osnaps to be running at a time.

 N O T E The symbols or icons that appear on an object when an Osnap is active and when you move the cursor near the object are called *AutoSnaps*. They're quite helpful, and you can choose a different color for them if you want. If you're using a dark background in the drawing area, use a bright color, such as yellow. For a white background, try blue.

2. In the lower-left corner of the Drafting Settings dialog box, click Options to open the Options dialog box; the Drafting tab should be on top. Then on the left side in the AutoSnap Settings area, open the AutoSnap Marker Color drop-down list and select a color. While you're in this area, make sure the Marker, Magnet, and Display

LT users' Object Snap tab will not have all the Object Snap modes, the Object Snap Tracking On check box, and the Osnap tracking explanation at the bottom, because LT doesn't have these features. We're not using any of these features right now, anyway.

AutoSnap Tool Tip check boxes are selected. Also make sure that the Display AutoSnap Aperture Box is unchecked. Then click OK.

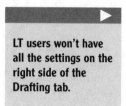

LT users won't have all the settings on the right side of the Drafting tab.

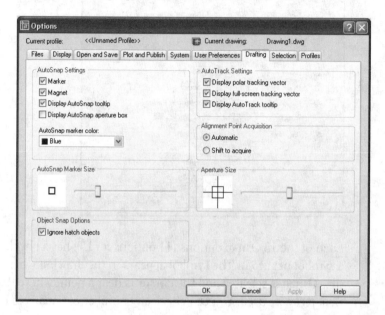

3. Back in the Object Snap tab of the Drafting Settings dialog box, click the check boxes next to Endpoint and Midpoint. Then above the list and to the left, be sure there's a check mark in the box next to Object Snap On. Click OK to close the dialog box. These Osnaps will now be active any time you are prompted to select a point on the drawing.

Now you are ready to begin drawing the three fixtures for the bathroom. The shower determines the placement of the other two, so let's start there.

Drawing a Shower Unit

You will start the shower unit with a square and then trim away one corner. As you start this exercise, check the status bar. The Polar, Osnap, and Model buttons should be in the on position. The rest of the buttons should be off.

1. Type z↵p↵ to Zoom to Extents. Then use the zoom window to view the bathroom close-up. Start the Rectangle command. For the first point, move the cursor to the upper-left inside corner of the room. Notice the square that appears at the corner. This is the AutoSnap symbol for the Endpoint Osnap. As soon as it appears on the endpoint

you want to snap to, click the left mouse button. The first corner of the square is placed. For the second point, type @40,-40↵.

T I P   If you don't get the square you want after entering the relative coordinates for the second corner, check this setting. Choose Tools ≻ Options to open the Options dialog box. Click the User Preferences tab. In the upper-right corner of the Priority For Coordinate Data Entry area, be sure that the button next to Keyboard Entry Except Scripts is active. Then click OK. Try the square again.

2. Start the Line command, and move the cursor near the midpoint of the bottom line of the square. Notice that a triangle, the Midpoint AutoSnap symbol, appears when you get near the midpoint of the line. When you see the triangle on the midpoint you want, click.

3. Move the cursor near the midpoint of the right side of the rectangle until you see the triangle appear at the midpoint location (see Figure 5.27). Click again. Press ↵ to end the Line command.

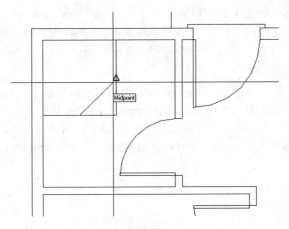

F I G U R E 5 . 2 7 : Using Midpoint Osnap to complete a line across the corner of the shower

4. Use this line as a cutting edge, and trim away the lower-right corner of the shower rectangle. The trimming will require only one pick because you are trimming a polyline. Press ↵ to stop the Trim command. This completes the shower.

Next, draw the sink to the right of the shower.

The Bathroom Sink

You will offset a line and draw an ellipse for this fixture, while practicing the Temporary Tracking Point Osnap option in the process. The Endpoint and Midpoint Osnaps are still running.

1. Zoom in to the sink area with a zoom window. Offset the top inside wall line down 16". Then use the shower wall as a cutting edge and trim back the line.

2. Click the Ellipse button on the Draw toolbar. Type c⏎ to select the Center option.

> ▶
>
> **LT users will need to follow steps 3 and 4 in the following "Steps 3 and 4 for LT Users" sidebar instead of these.**

3. Click the Temporary Tracking Point Osnap button, and then move the cursor near the midpoint of the newly offset line. When the AutoSnap symbol appears at the midpoint of this line, click. This establishes a tracking point (a small cross).

4. Move the crosshair cursor directly above the tracking point. When the dotted tracking path and the Track Point tool tip appear, type 8⏎ to locate the center of the counter. The Command window will prompt you for the location of the ends of two perpendicular axes. You will start with the left/right axis and enter the distance using Direct Entry and Polar Tracking, as you did for the steps earlier in this chapter.

5. Hold the crosshair cursor directly to the right of the center point. Type 7⏎. Hold the crosshair cursor directly above the center and type 5⏎. The ellipse is constructed, and the sink fixture is complete (see Figure 5.28). Leave the view on your screen as it is for a moment.

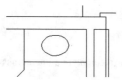

FIGURE 5.28: The completed sink fixture

Steps 3 and 4 for LT Users

Here are instructions for LT users:

3. Click the Tracking button at the top of the Object Snap toolbar, and then move the cursor near the midpoint of the newly offset line. When the AutoSnap symbol appears at the midpoint of this line, click. This establishes a tracking point.

4. Move the crosshair cursor directly above the tracking point and type **8**↵ to locate the center of the counter. Press ↵ again to end Tracking and continue with the Ellipse command. The Command window will prompt you for the location of the ends of two perpendicular axes. You will start with the left/right axis and enter the distance using Direct Entry and Polar Tracking, as you did for the steps earlier in this chapter.

Drawing the toilet is the final task in this chapter. You will use the Ellipse command again, along with the Rectangle command. You will also be introduced to a couple of new display options.

Positioning a Toilet

The toilet consists of a rectangle and an ellipse centered between the shower and the wall. The tank is offset 1" from the back wall and is 9" × 20". The ellipse representing the seat measures 18" in one direction and 12" in the other.

1. On the Standard toolbar, click the Pan Realtime button. The cursor changes to a small hand when you return it to the drawing area. Position it in the lower-left corner of the drawing area with the view still zoomed in on the sink.

2. Hold down the left mouse button and drag the hand up and to the right. When the toilet area comes into view, release the mouse button. The drawing slides along with the movement of the cursor. If necessary, do this again until you have the toilet area centered in the drawing area.

3. Right-click the mouse, and choose Zoom from the shortcut menu that opens. Back on the drawing, the cursor changes to a magnifying glass with a plus and minus sign.

With Zoom Realtime, moving the cursor to the left or right has no effect on the view. The magnification is controlled solely by the up-and-down motion.

4. Position the Zoom Realtime cursor near the top of the drawing and hold down the left mouse button. Drag the cursor down, and watch the view being zoomed out in real time. Move the cursor up, still holding the mouse button down. Position the cursor in such a way that you have a good view of the toilet area, and then release the mouse button. Right-click again, and choose Exit from the shortcut menu to end the Zoom Realtime command.

These zooming options are convenient tools for adjusting the view of your drawing. Let's move on to the toilet. You need to find a way to position the toilet accurately, centering it between the wall and shower. The midpoint of the left wall line won't be useful because the wall line runs behind the shower. You will have to construct a guideline.

1. With the Rectangle command, draw the toilet tank a few inches to the right of the wall, not touching any lines. (See Figure 5.26, shown earlier, for the dimensions.) Then offset the left wall line 1" to the right to make a guideline. Use the shower as a cutting edge, and trim this guideline down to the shower (see Figure 5.29a).

2. Start the Move command, select the tank, and then press ↵.

3. For the base point, move the cursor to the middle of the left side of the tank. When you see the triangle at the midpoint, click the left mouse button.

4. For the second point, move the cursor onto the guideline. When it gets closer to the midpoint than the endpoint, the triangle will appear at the midpoint. At this point, click the left mouse button. The rectangle is accurately positioned 1" from the left wall and centered between the shower and lower wall (see Figure 5.29b).

5. Erase the guideline.

6. Start the Ellipse command. The Command window displays a default prompt of Specify axis endpoint of ellipse or [Arc/Center]:. Using the Specify Axis endpoint option, you can define the first axis from one end of the ellipse to the other. This will help you here.

7. Move the cursor near the midpoint of the right side of the tank and, when the triangle shows up there, click. This starts the ellipse.

8. Hold the crosshair cursor out to the right of the rectangle and type 1'6.↵. The first axis is positioned. Now as you move the crosshair cursor, you will see that a line starts at the center of the ellipse, and the cursor's

movement controls the size of the other axis (see Figure 5.29c). To designate the second axis, you need to enter the distance from the center of the axis to the end of it, or half the overall length of the axis.

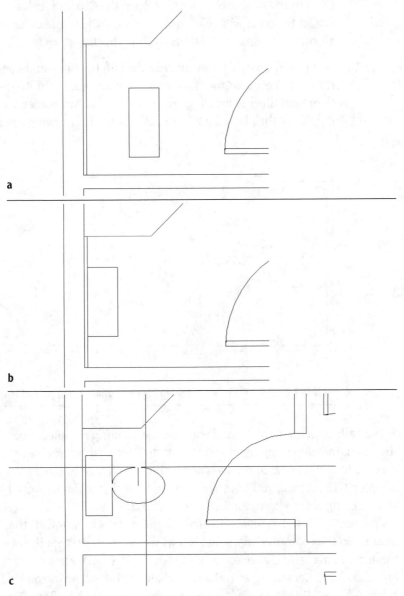

FIGURE 5.29: The toilet tank with an offset guideline (a), the tank correctly positioned (b), and the cursor controlling the size of the second axis for the toilet seat (c)

9. Hold the crosshair cursor directly above the center point and type 6↵. The ellipse is complete, and the toilet is finished.

10. In the status bar, right-click the Osnap button, and then choose Settings from the shortcut menu to open the Settings dialog box. The Object Snap tab will be in front. Click the Clear All button to turn off all running Osnaps. Click OK to close the dialog box.

11. Before you save this drawing, use the Pan Realtime and Zoom Realtime commands to zoom out and pan your drawing until the whole floor plan fills the drawing area, except for a thin border around the outside of the plan (see Figure 5.30). Save this drawing as Cabin05b.

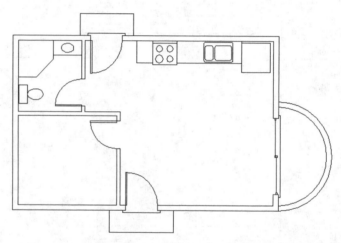

FIGURE 5.30: The completed floor plan zoomed and panned to fill the screen

The bathroom is complete, and you now have a fairly complete floor plan for the cabin. In completing the drawing tasks for this chapter, you have been exposed to several new commands and techniques to add to those introduced in Chapter 4. Combined, you now have a set of tools that will take you a long way toward being able to lay out a drawing of any size.

Chapters 1 through 5 fill out the basic level of skills in AutoCAD that allow you to draw on the computer approximately as you would with pencil and vellum, though you may already see some of the advantages CAD offers over traditional board drafting. Beginning with the next chapter, you will be introduced to concepts of AutoCAD that do not have a counterpart in board drafting. These features will take you to a new level of knowledge and skill, and you will start to get an idea of what sets computer drafting apart.

USING REALTIME PAN AND REALTIME ZOOM

The Realtime Pan and Zoom buttons are next to each other on the Standard toolbar. You can start Realtime Pan by typing **p**↵. You can start Realtime Zoom by typing **z**↵↵. You can also start Realtime Pan or Zoom by right-clicking at the Command: prompt and then choosing Pan or Zoom from the shortcut menu. If you try this, you will find that it is easier than clicking the Realtime Pan or Zoom buttons.

Once one of these Realtime commands is running, you can switch to the other one by clicking the other Realtime button or by right-clicking and choosing the other one from the shortcut menu. The shortcut menu also has other options that help make Realtime Pan and Zoom quite useful commands.

Exit   Ends the Realtime Zoom or Pan commands.

Pan   Switches to Realtime Pan from Realtime Zoom.

Zoom   Switches to Realtime Zoom from Realtime Pan.

3D Orbit   A special viewing tool for 3D that is covered in the Appendix.

Zoom Window   Allows you to make a zoom window without first ending Realtime Pan or Zoom. You pick a point, hold down the left mouse button, and then drag open a window in your drawing. When you release the button, you are zoomed into the window you made, and Realtime Pan or Zoom resumes.

Zoom Original   Restores the view of your drawing that you had when you began Realtime Pan or Zoom.

Zoom Extents   Zooms to the drawing Extents.

To end Realtime Pan or Zoom, press the Esc key, press ↵, or right-click and choose Exit from the shortcut menu.

When Realtime Pan or Zoom is running, AutoCAD is in a special mode that makes the status bar and the Grid (if it is on) invisible and therefore unusable.

If You Would Like More Practice...

Following are several additional exercises that will give you the opportunity to practice the skills and techniques you have learned up until now.

Draw the Cabin Again

As is true for almost any skill, the key to mastery is practice. Redrawing the entire cabin may seem daunting at this point when you think of how long it took you to get here. But if you try it all again, starting with Chapter 3, you will find that it will take about half the time that it did the first time, and if you do it a third time, half that time again. Once you understand the techniques and how the commands work, feel free to experiment with alternative techniques to accomplish tasks and with other options on the commands.

Draw Something Else

If you have a specific project in mind that you would like to draw in AutoCAD, so much the better—try it.

Draw Some Furniture for the Cabin

Once you put some furniture in the cabin, you will quickly see how small it is! But it can still accept some basic furniture without seeming too cramped. You should be able to add the following:

▶ Kitchen—a table and chairs

▶ Living room—a short couch, coffee table, and easy chair

▶ Bedroom—a double bed, dresser, and side table

Use a tape measure, and go around your office or home to determine the approximate dimensions of each piece. The goal here is not so much accuracy of scale but to practice drawing in AutoCAD. Figure 5.31 shows the floor plan with these items of furniture. If you draw the bed that I show here, try using the Spline tool for the curved, turned-down sheets. It's in the middle of the Draw toolbar. You'll see how it works after a little experimentation.

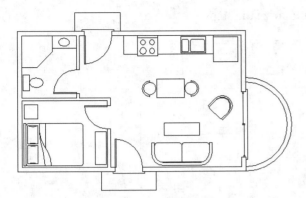

FIGURE 5.31: The floor plan with furniture

Draw a Gasket

Figure 5.32 shows a gasket that is symmetrical about its vertical and horizontal axes. This symmetry will allow you to use the Mirror command to create much of the drawing.

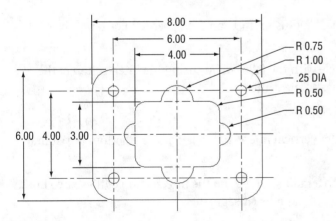

FIGURE 5.32: A gasket

The following diagrams summarize the steps.

To draw the gasket, set the Linear Units to Engineering with a precision of 0'-0.00". Set the Angular units to Decimal with a precision of 0.00. Now follow these steps:

1. Use the Line command to draw a rectangle 4" wide and 3" high.

2. Offset the upper horizontal line and the left vertical line 1" to the inside of the rectangle.

3. Use Fillet with a radius set to 1" on the upper-left corner of the original rectangle.

4. Draw the circle with the 0.25" radius using the intersection of the two offset lines as the center.

5. Erase the offset lines.

6. Offset the right vertical line 2" to the left and the bottom horizontal line 1.5" up.

7. Use Fillet with a radius of 0.50" on the intersection of these two lines, retaining the right and lower segments.

8. Trim back the lower-right corner of the original rectangle.

9. Draw circles with 0.50" and 0.75" radii on the bottom and right sides of the shape.

10. Use Trim and Erase to remove unneeded lines.

11. Use Mirror to flip the shape down.

12. Use Mirror again to flip the shape to the right.

13. Erase unneeded lines. (Each line to be erased is really two lines.)

Draw a Parking Lot

Here is a parking lot partially bordered by sidewalks and streets (see Figure 5.33).

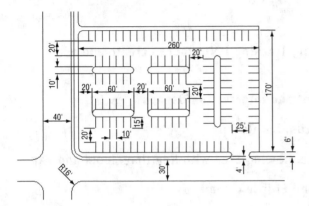

FIGURE 5.33: A parking lot

You will get a lot of practice using the Offset and Fillet commands. Guidelines will help you, so don't be afraid to use them. Here's a summary of the steps:

1. Set Linear and Angular units to Decimal, each with a precision of 0. Assume that 1 linear decimal unit equals 1'. Set Polar Tracking to 90° and turn it on. Set Endpoint and Midpoint Osnaps to be running. Set the Snap to 10, Grid to 0, and Drawing Limits to 400, 250. Zoom All.

2. Use Grid and Snap to draw the large 260' × 170' rectangle using the Line command and relative Cartesian coordinates as you did in Chapter 3. Offset three of the lines 6' to the outside to make the sidewalk.

3. On two sides, offset the outer sidewalk line 4' to the outside to make the curb. Then offset the curb lines 30' and 40' to make the street.

4. Draw extra lines to make the street intersection.

5. Fillet and Trim lines to create the curved corners of the intersection and sidewalks.

6. Offset the lines of the inner rectangle to the inside to make guidelines for the parking strips and islands.

7. Use Fillet and Trim to finish the drawing.

T I P   Using Fillet on two parallel lines creates a semicircle to connect them. Try it on the islands in the parking area.

Are You Experienced?

Now you can...

- ☑ use the Temporary Tracking Point tool to create and use tracking points

- ☑ use the Quadrant and Intersection Osnaps

- ☑ set up and use running Osnaps

- ☑ move around the drawing area with Realtime Zoom and Pan

- ☑ use the Circle and Ellipse commands

- ☑ move and duplicate objects with the Move and Copy Multiple commands

- ☑ use a circle and the Trim command to make a semicircle arc

- ☑ use guidelines to locate the center of circles for a stove top

CHAPTER 6

Using Layers to Organize Your Drawing

▶ Creating new layers

▶ Assigning a color and a linetype to layers

▶ Moving existing objects onto a new layer

▶ Controlling the visibility of layers

▶ Working with linetypes

In precomputer days, drafters used sets of transparent overlays on their drafting tables. These were sheets that stacked on top of one another, and the drafters could see through several at a time. Specific kinds of information were drawn on each overlay, all related spatially so that several overlays might all be drawn to the same floor plan. Each overlay had small holes punched near the corners so the drafter could position it onto buttons, called registration points, that were taped to the drawing board. Because all overlays had holes punched at the same locations with respect to the drawing, information on the set of overlays was kept in alignment.

To help you organize your drawing, AutoCAD provides you with an amazing tool, called *layers,* which is a computerized metaphor for the transparent overlays, only much more powerful and flexible. In manual drafting, you could use only four or five overlays at a time before the information on the bottom overlay became unreadable. In AutoCAD, you are not limited in the number of layers you can use. You can have hundreds of layers, and complex CAD drawings often do.

Layers as an Organization Tool

To understand what layers are and why they are so useful, think again about the transparent overlay sheets used in hand drafting. Each overlay is designed to be printed. The bottom sheet may be a basic floor plan. To create an overlay sheet for a structural drawing, the drafter traces over the lines of the floor plan that they need in the overlay and then adds new information pertinent to that sheet. For the next overlay, the same thing is done again. Each sheet, then, contains some information in common, in addition to data unique to that sheet.

In AutoCAD, using layers allows you to generate all the sheets for a set of overlays from a single file (see Figure 6.1). Nothing needs to be drawn twice or traced. The wall layout will be on one layer and the roof lines on another. Doors will be on a third. You can control the visibility of layers so that all objects residing on a layer can be made temporarily invisible. This feature lets you put all information keyed to a particular floor plan in one .dwg file and from that drawing, to produce a series of derived drawings, such as the foundation plan, the second floor plan, the reflected ceiling plan, and the roof plan, by making different combinations of layers visible for each drawing. When you make a print, you decide which layers will be visible. Consequently, in a set of drawings, each sheet based on the floor plan will display a unique combination of layers, all of which are in one file.

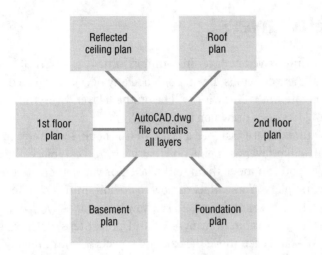

FIGURE 6.1: A diagram of several drawings coming from one file

Layers, as an organization tool, allow you to classify the various objects in a computerized drawing—lines, arcs, circles, and so on—according to the component of the building they represent, such as doors, walls, and windows. Each layer is assigned a color, and all objects placed on the layer take on that assigned color. This lets you easily distinguish between objects that represent separate components of the building (see Figure 6.2). And you can quickly tell what layer a given object or group of objects is on.

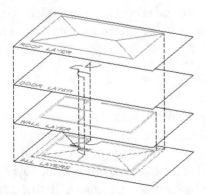

FIGURE 6.2: Separate layers combined to make a drawing

First, we'll look at the procedure for achieving this level of organization, which is to set up the new layers and then move existing objects onto them. Following that, you will learn how to create new objects on a specific layer.

Setting Up Layers

All AutoCAD drawings have one layer in common—the 0 layer. The 0 layer is the default layer in all new drawings. If you don't add any new layers on a drawing, everything you create in that drawing will be on the 0 layer. Everything so far in the cabin drawing has been drawn on the 0 layer.

All objects in AutoCAD are assigned a layer. In this book, I will refer to objects assigned to a particular layer as "being on" that layer. You can place objects on a layer in two ways: you can move them to the layer, or you can create them on the layer in the first place. You will learn how to do both in this chapter. But first you need to learn how to set up layers. To see how this is done, you will create seven new layers for your cabin drawing—Walls, Doors, Steps, Balcony, Fixtures, Headers, and Roof—and then move the existing objects in your drawing onto the first five of these layers. After that, you will create new objects on the Header and Roof layers. Let's begin by creating a few new layers.

1. Open AutoCAD, and then open Cabin05b.dwg. The Layers toolbar should be just above the drawing area on your screen on the left, and contains three buttons and a drop-down list for controlling layers. (The LT Layers toolbar has only two buttons.)

    To the right is the Properties toolbar with four drop-down lists for controlling linetypes, colors, and other layer properties. These are the default positions for these toolbars, but your screen may have a different arrangement.

2. Click the Layer Properties Manager button on the left end of the Layers toolbar to open the Layer Properties Manager dialog box (see Figure 6.3). Notice the large open area in the middle right of the dialog box with the 0 layer listed at the top. This is called the Layer List box. All the layers in a drawing are listed here, along with their states and properties. For Cabin5b, there is only one layer so far.

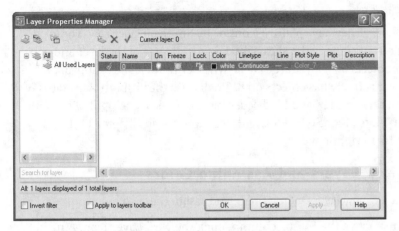

F I G U R E   6 . 3 : The Layer Properties Manager dialog box

The Layer Properties Manager Dialog Box

To the left of the Layer List box is the Layer Filters tree view box. Each box has three icons and buttons above it, and there are two check boxes and four buttons at the bottom of the dialog box. Before setting up new layers, look for a moment at the Layer List box.

We'll look more closely at the Layer Filters tree view box in Chapter 12.

The Layer List Box

Each layer has four properties: Color, Linetype, Lineweight, and Plot Style. Look at the 0 layer row in the list, and notice the square and the word *White* in the Color column. The square is black (or white if you have a black background for your drawing area), but the name of the color is White whether the square is black or white. Continuous is in the Linetype column. This tells us that the 0 layer has been assigned the color White (black or white) and the Continuous linetype by default.

N O T E   If you set up your drawing area so that the background is white, AutoCAD automatically changes the color assigned to White in the Layer List box to black, so lines that would normally appear as white on a black background now appear as black on the white background. When you then switch to a black background, the black line changes to a white line. This allows the line to be visible regardless of the background color, and AutoCAD doesn't have to assign a new color to a layer that has been assigned the White color when the user switches background colors.

The five columns to the left of the Color column are titled Status, Name, On, Freeze, and Lock. They have picture icons or text in the 0 layer row. These columns represent some of the status modes—or states—of the layer and control whether objects on a layer are visible, whether they can be changed, or whether a layer actually has objects on it. I'll discuss the visibility and status of layers later in this chapter, and I'll discuss the columns to the right of the Linetype column—Line, Plot Style, Plot, and Description—in Chapter 14. Don't worry about them right now.

Creating New Layers and Assigning Colors

Let's create a few new layers, name them, and assign them colors.

1. Just above the Status column, click the New Layer icon. A new layer called Layer1 appears in the list. The layer's name is highlighted, which means that you can rename it by entering another name now.

2. Type Walls↵. Layer1 changes to Walls. The row for the Walls layer should still be highlighted (see Figure 6.4).

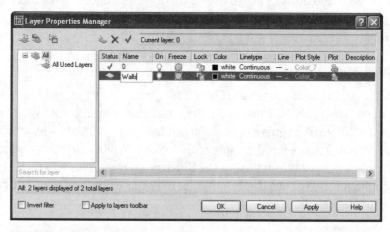

FIGURE 6.4: The Layer Properties Manager dialog box with a new layer named Walls

3. Click the word *White* in the Color column for the Walls row to open the Select Color dialog box (see Figure 6.5). Notice the three tabs at the top—Index Color, True Color, and Color Books. Be sure the Index Color tab is selected and on top. There are three sets of color swatches and two buttons for making color choices. In the row of 9 color swatches, below the large group of 240 choices, click the cyan (turquoise) square. In the Color text box, white changes to cyan, and one of the rectangles in the lower-right corner takes on the color cyan.

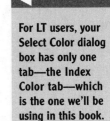

For LT users, your Select Color dialog box has only one tab—the Index Color tab—which is the one we'll be using in this book.

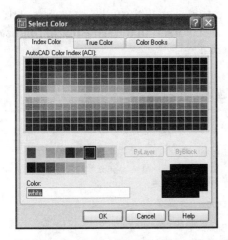

FIGURE 6.5: The Index Color tab in the Select Color dialog box

4. Click OK to close the Select Color dialog box. In the Layer List box of the Layer Properties Manager dialog box, you can see that the color square for the Walls layer has changed to cyan.

As you create your new list of layers and assign them colors, notice how each color looks in your drawing. Some are easier to see on a screen with a light background, and others do better against a dark background. In this book, I will be assigning colors that work well with a black background. If your system has a white background, you might want to use darker colors, which can be found in the array of 240 color swatches in the upper half of the Index Color tab.

Let's continue creating new layers and assigning them colors. You'll master this procedure as you add a new layer or two in each chapter throughout the rest of the book.

1. In the Layer Properties Manager dialog box, click the New Layer icon.

2. Type Doors↵ to change the name of the layer.

3. Pick the color square in the Doors row. When the Select Color dialog box opens, click the red square in the same row of color swatches where you previously found cyan. Click OK.

4. Repeat these steps, creating each of the following layers with their assigned colors. Pick the colors from the same row of color swatches that you have been using.

Layer Name	Color
Steps	9 (Light Gray)
Balcony	Green
Fixtures	Magenta
Headers	Yellow
Roof	Blue

   T I P   The color blue may or may not read well on a black background. If you don't like the way it looks, try picking a lighter shade of blue from the array of 240 colors on the Index Color tab.

When finished, the layer list should have eight layers with their assigned colors in the color squares of each row (see Figure 6.6). All layers are assigned the Continuous linetype by default. This is convenient because most building components are represented in the floor plan by continuous lines, but the roof—because of its position above the walls—needs to be represented by a dashed line. Later you will assign a Dashed linetype to the Roof layer.

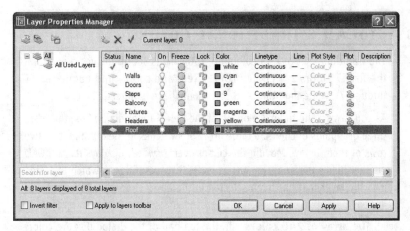

FIGURE 6.6: The Layer List box, in the Layer Properties Manager dialog box, with the seven new layers and the 0 layer

NAMING LAYERS

You can name layers in a variety of ways. With their different color assignments, layers make it possible for you to easily distinguish which objects in your drawing represent walls or other parts of your building. Most offices follow a standard for organizing layers by name, color, and linetype. The American Institute of Architects publishes Layering Standards, which are often adapted by architecture firms and customized to fit their specific needs. Before AutoCAD version 2000, lineweights in AutoCAD drawings were controlled by color, so the layer standards were developed around this determining factor. Since version 2000, this is no longer the case. As a result, you can expect that layering standards used for years will be changing. With the cabin drawing, you will start out developing a basic set of layers. Once you learn how to manage the set we are using here, tackling more complex layering systems will come naturally.

N O T E   When you name layers, you can use upper- and lowercase letters, and AutoCAD will preserve them. But AutoCAD does not distinguish between them and treats Walls, WALLS, and walls as the same layer.

In more complex drawings, you might need several layers for variations of the same building component, landscape element, or machine part. The Walls layer, for example, might be replaced by several layers, such as Existing Walls to Remain, Walls to Be Demolished, and New Walls. Once you acquire the skills presented here, you will have no difficulty progressing to a more complex layering system.

USING AUTOCAD'S TRADITIONAL COLORS

The traditional set of 255 colors for AutoCAD is set up in such a way that the first 7 colors are named (Blue, Red, and so on) and numbered (1 through 7), while the other 248 colors only have numbers.

As you saw on the Index Color tab of the Select Color dialog box, there are three groupings of colors: a large array of swatches in the top half, and two rows of them below. Moving the cursor over a swatch displays its AutoCAD number below the array, as well as its RGB values. Click a swatch to assign it to the layer that has been selected in the Layer Properties Manager dialog box.

The array of 240 colors   In the top half of the dialog box are colors numbered 10 through 249, arranged in an array of 24 columns, each having 10 swatches.

The row of 9 standard color swatches   This group includes colors 1 through 9. The first 7 colors in this group also have names: Red (1), Yellow (2), Green (3), Blue (4), Cyan (5), Magenta (6), and White/Black (7). Colors 8 and 9 have numbers only. Color 7 is named White, but will actually be black if you are using a white background color.

The row of 6 gray shades   These are colors that are often assigned screening values (such as 50%, 75%, and so on), numbering 250 through 255. As pure color assignments, they range from almost black to almost white.

These 255 colors, plus the background color, make up the traditional Auto-CAD 256-color palette. Two additional colors are in a group by themselves, Logical Colors, and are represented by buttons on the Index Color tab.

The two buttons in this grouping—ByLayer and ByBlock—represent two ways that a color can be assigned to objects—such as lines, circles, text, and so on—via the layer they are on or via the *block* they are part of, rather than to the objects themselves. (Blocks are covered in the next chapter.) When you assign the color cyan to the Walls layer and place all objects representing walls on that layer, all wall objects are automatically assigned the color ByLayer and take on the color of their layer, in this case, cyan.

Looking at the Other Tabs in the Select Color Dialog Box

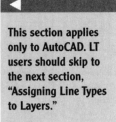 AutoCAD also supports a True Color palette and various PANTONE color groups. Although I won't cover these features in any depth in this book, let's take a quick look at them before we move on.

The True Color Tab   With the Layer Properties Manager dialog box open, click one of the color swatches in the Layer List box to open the Select Color dialog box again. Then click the True Color tab. In the upper-right corner, the Color Model drop-down list will display either RGB or HSL. The RGB (for Red, Green, Blue) color model looks like Figure 6.7a, and the HSL (Hue, Saturation, Luminance) model looks like Figure 6.7b.

> **This section applies only to AutoCAD. LT users should skip to the next section, "Assigning Line Types to Layers."**

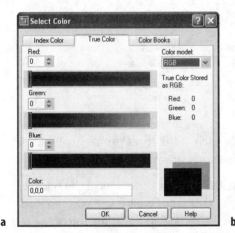 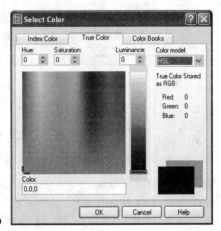

FIGURE 6.7:   The True Color tab with the RGB color model (a) and the HSL color model (b)

The RGB screen shows three horizontal color bands, one for each of the three primary colors. Move the sliders on each band to set a number from 0 to 255, or type a number in the counter box for each color. The three numbers that make up a color are displayed at the bottom and on the right side, and the rectangles in the lower-right corner show the currently selected and previously selected color.

The HSL screen displays a rectangle of colors and a vertical band with a slider. Click and drag the crosshair around on the rectangle. The color in the front rectangle in the lower-right corner changes as you move the crosshair. Moving it left or right takes the *hue* through a range of 360 values. Moving it up or down changes the percentage of *saturation*, or intensity, with the top of the rectangle representing 100%.

The slider to the right of the rectangle controls the *luminance*, which, like saturation, varies from 0%—representing the color black—to 100%, or white. A luminance of 50% maximizes a color's brightness.

The Color text box displays the currently selected color's three RGB numbers. You can also specify a color by entering numbers in the individual boxes for hue, saturation, and luminance—or the boxes for red, green, and blue in the RGB screen. And you can use the Up and Down arrows in these boxes to scroll through the possible settings.

If you select a color using the RGB or HSL screens, it is displayed in the Layer List box of the Layer Properties Manager dialog box by its three RGB numbers.

> The Color column might be compressed in such a way that the names of colors in the list may be abbreviated. You can widen the column by clicking and dragging the divider at the right of the title farther to the right.

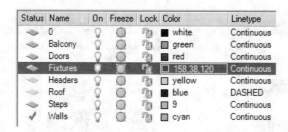

Status	Name	On	Freeze	Lock	Color	Linetype
	0				white	Continuous
	Balcony				green	Continuous
	Doors				red	Continuous
	Fixtures				158,38,120	Continuous
	Headers				yellow	Continuous
	Roof				blue	DASHED
	Steps				9	Continuous
	Walls				cyan	Continuous

With the combination of 255 values for each of the three primary colors, you now have more than 16 million colors to choose from in AutoCAD.

The Color Books Tab   The Color Books tab displays the colors of the selected *color book* (see Figure 6.8a). AutoCAD has nine color books, and you can load more. Each book is listed in the Color Book drop-down list at the top of the tab with the current book being displayed in the box. Below that, a set of colors that corresponds to the position of the slider is displayed in bars. Moving the slider to a new position displays another set of colors. Click a displayed color bar to select it, and then click OK. The color is displayed in the Layer Properties Manager Layer List box by its identifying name and number (see Figure 6.8b).

Later in the book, you will be asked to create new layers and assign them colors of your choice. Use this opportunity to explore the True Color and Color Books tabs of the Select Color dialog box, and try using some of these colors in your drawing. Keep the Layer Properties Manager dialog box open. You will use it to assign linetypes in the next section.

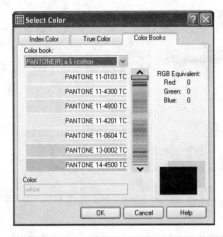

Status	Name	On	Freeze	Lock	Color	Linetype
	0				white	Continuous
	Balcony				green	Continuous
	Doors				red	Continuous
	Fixtures				PANTONE DS 160-1 C	Continuous
	Headers				yellow	Continuous
	Steps				9	Continuous
	Walls				cyan	Continuous
	Roof				blue	DASHED

F I G U R E 6 . 8 : The Color Books tab in the Select Color dialog box (a), and the Layer List with an assigned PANTONE number (b)

Assigning Linetypes to Layers

When you assign a color to a layer, you can choose any color supported by your system. Not so with linetypes. Each new drawing has only one linetype loaded into it by default (the Continuous linetype). You must load in any other linetypes you need from an outside file.

1. In the Layer Properties Manager dialog box, click Continuous in the row for the Roof layer to open the Select Linetype dialog box (see Figure 6.9). In the Loaded Linetypes list, only Continuous is displayed. No other linetypes have been loaded into this drawing.

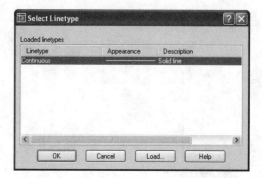

FIGURE 6.9: The Select Linetype dialog box

2. Click Load to open the Load Or Reload Linetypes dialog box. Scroll down the list to the Dashed, Dashed2, and DashedX2 linetypes (see Figure 6.10). Notice how, in this family, the dashed lines are different sizes.

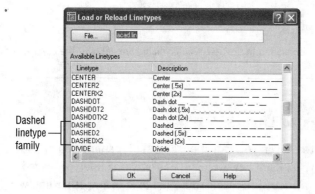

FIGURE 6.10: The list scrolled to the three Dashed linetypes

3. Click the word *Dashed* in the left column, and then click OK. You are returned to the Select Linetype dialog box. The Dashed linetype has been added to the Linetype list under Continuous (see Figure 6.11). Click Dashed to highlight it and click OK. In the Layer Properties Manager dialog box, the Roof layer has been assigned the Dashed linetype (see Figure 6.12).

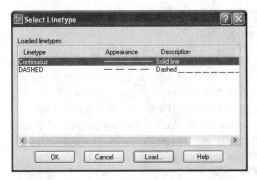

FIGURE 6.11: The Select Linetype dialog box with the Dashed linetype loaded

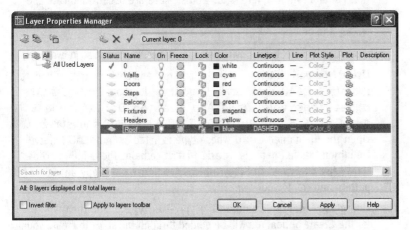

FIGURE 6.12: The Layer Properties Manager dialog box with the Roof layer assigned the Dashed linetype

AUTOCAD'S LINETYPES

In the Available Linetypes list in the Load Or Reload Linetypes dialog box, 45 linetypes are listed. They fall into three groups.

Acad_ISO   The first 14 linetypes are in the Acad_ISO family (International Organization for Standardization). They are set up to be used in metric drawings and have *lineweight,* or pen-width, settings.

Continued on next page

AutoCAD's Linetypes *(Continued)*

Standard AutoCAD   Below the ISO linetypes are eight families of three linetypes each, mixed with seven special linetypes that contain graphic symbols. Each family has one basic linetype and two that are multiples of it: one has dashes twice the size (called, for example, Dashed×2), and one has dashes half the size (called Dashed2). (See Figure 6.10, shown earlier.) Having an assortment of different sizes of one style of linetype is helpful for distinguishing between building components, such as foundation walls and beams, which, in addition to roof lines, may also need dashed lines.

Complex   Mixed in with the Standard linetypes are seven linetypes that contain symbols, letters, or words. These are used to indicate specific elements in the drawing, such as fences, hot-water lines, railroad tracks, and others.

It is not difficult to create your own custom linetypes. You can do so in two ways.

Using Notepad   Start the Notepad program and navigate to the Support folder for AutoCAD 2004, usually found at this location: C:\Documents & Settings*your name*\Application Data\Autodesk\ AutoCAD 2005 [or AutoCAD LT 2005]\R16.0\enu\support. Open the file named acad whose type is listed as "AutoCAD Linetype Definition." Its full name is acad.lin. It contains the definition codes for all the linetypes, and they are easy to figure out. Copy an existing pattern and create your own.

Using the Linetype Command   Type **-linetype**↵, and then type **c**↵ for the Create option. You will be guided through the steps to create your own .lin file or add to an existing file. To use the Linetype command, you need to know the definition codes. Use Notepad until you get a feel for the codes.

A Word about Lineweight

In the Layer Properties Manager dialog box is a column for the Lineweight property. When you first create a layer, it is assigned the default lineweight. Just as you assigned a color and a linetype for each new layer in the cabin drawing, you can also assign a lineweight. Once assigned, lineweights can be displayed so you can see how your drawing will look when printed. In Chapter 14 you will learn more about lineweights, about how to assign them to layers, and about how to view your drawing as it will look when printed or in WYSIWYG mode.

The Current Layer as a Drawing Tool

Now is a good time to look at what it means for a layer to be current. Notice the green check mark icon above the Layer List box in the Layer Properties Manager dialog box. The name of the current layer, in this case, 0, is displayed just above the Layer List box next to the green check mark.

At any time, one, and only one, layer is set as the current layer. When a layer is current, all objects you draw will be on that layer and will take on the properties assigned to it. Because the 0 layer is current—and has been current so far in this book—all objects that you have drawn so far are on the 0 layer and have the line-type and color that are specified by default for the 0 layer: Continuous and White (or Black), respectively. If you make the Walls layer current, any new lines you draw will be Cyan and Continuous. If the Roof layer is current, any new lines will be Blue and Dashed.

1. Click the Walls layer in the Layer List box to highlight it. Then click Current. The Walls layer replaces the 0 layer as the current layer.

2. Click OK to close the Layer Properties Manager dialog box and return to your drawing.

3. Look at the Layer Control drop-down list on the Object Properties toolbar. Most of the symbols you saw in the Layer List box, in the Layer Properties Manager dialog box, are on this drop-down list. The Walls layer is the visible entry on the list and has a cyan square (the color you assigned to the Walls layer earlier). The layer visible in this list when it is closed and no objects are selected is the current layer.

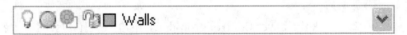

4. Now look at your drawing. Nothing has changed because the objects in the drawing are still on the 0 layer.

You need to move the objects in the drawing onto their proper layers. To do this, you'll use the Layer Control drop-down list on the Object Properties toolbar to assign each object to one of the new layers.

Assigning Objects to Layers

When assigning existing objects in the drawing to new layers, our strategy will be to begin by selecting all the objects that belong on the same layer and that are easiest to select. We'll reassign them to their new layer, using the Layer Control drop-down list. We'll then move to a set of objects that belong on a different layer and are slightly more difficult to select, and so on.

1. In the drawing, pick the two arcs of the balcony. Grips appear on the arcs, and the lines ghost. This signals that the lines have been selected (see Figure 6.13).

   Notice also that in the Layer Control drop-down list, the layer being displayed now is the 0 layer rather than Walls, the current layer. When objects are selected with no command running, the Layer Control drop-down list displays the layer to which the selected objects are currently assigned. If selected objects are on more than one layer, the Layer Control drop-down list goes blank.

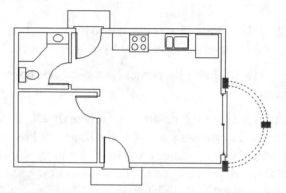

FIGURE 6.13: The balcony arcs, selected and displaying their grips

2. Click the Layer Control drop-down list to open it (see Figure 6.14).

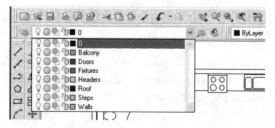

FIGURE 6.14: The opened Layer Control drop-down list

3. Click the Balcony layer. The list closes. The Balcony layer is displayed in the Layer Control drop-down list. The balcony arcs have been moved to the Balcony layer and are now green.

4. Press Esc to remove the grips. The current layer, Walls, returns to the Layer Control drop-down list.

This is the process you need to go through for each layer so that the new layers can receive objects that are currently on the 0 layer. In the next section, we'll move the threshold and steps to the Steps layer. You will select the threshold and steps by using a selection window.

Selecting Objects with Windows

AutoCAD provides many tools for selecting objects in your drawing. Two of the most powerful are the crossing and regular selection windows. You determine the size and location of these selection windows by picking points on your drawing to be opposite corners of a rectangle that will serve as the window. The *regular window* selects any objects completely enclosed by the window. The *crossing window* selects objects that are completely enclosed by or cross through an edge of the window. The crossing window is represented by dashed lines, and the regular window is represented by solid lines.

By default, AutoCAD is set up so that whenever no command is running and the prompt in the Command window is Command:, you can pick objects one at a time or start a regular or a crossing window. If you pick an object, it is selected, and its grips are displayed. If you select a blank area of the drawing, a selection window is started. If you then move the cursor to the right of the point just picked, a regular window is started. If you move the cursor to the left, a crossing window is started. You'll use a crossing window to select the sliding glass door threshold, and you'll use two regular windows to select the front and back steps and those thresholds.

1. Zoom into the sliding glass door area. Click the Osnap button on the status bar to put it in the off position, if it isn't already off.

2. Hold the crosshair cursor above and to the right of the upper-right corner of the balcony threshold—still inside the balcony wall—as shown in Figure 6.15a. Click that point, and then move the cursor down and to the left until you have made a tall, thin crossing window that completely encloses the right edge of the threshold and is crossed on its left edge by the short horizontal connecting lines, as shown in Figure 6.15b. Then click again. Click the Layer Control drop-down list to open it, and then click the Steps layer. The balcony threshold is now on the Steps layer.

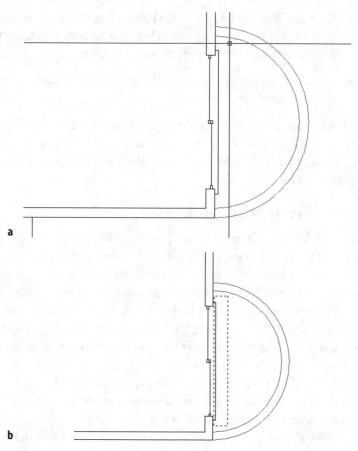

FIGURE 6.15: Starting the crossing selection window (a), and completing it (b)

3. Zoom Previous to return to a view of the entire drawing. Make two regular windows to select the front and back steps and their thresholds. Be sure your first pick starts a window at the left and finishes to the right of each step, so the window completely encloses the horizontal and vertical lines that make up each step and threshold. Figure 6.16 illustrates the two regular selection windows and the points to pick to create them. Once selected, the objects display their grips. For lines, grips appear at each endpoint and at the midpoint of each segment. When endpoints of lines coincide or when lines are very short, some of the grips overlap.

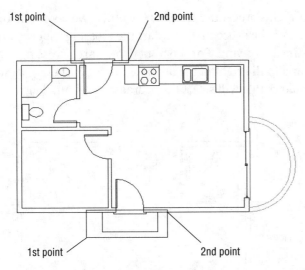

1st point   2nd point

1st point   2nd point

FIGURE 6.16: The two regular selection windows used to select the front and back steps and thresholds

4. Click the Layer Control drop-down list, and then click the Steps layer. The front and back steps and their thresholds are now on the Steps layer.

5. Press the Esc key to remove the grips.

Selecting the Doors and Swings

To select the doors and swings, you can use crossing windows. Let's examine this task closely to learn more valuable skills about how to select objects.

1. Place the crosshair cursor in a clear space below and to the right of the back door, and then pick that point to start the selection window. Move the cursor up and to the left until the crossing window crosses the back door and swing, but does not cross the wall line, as shown in Figure 6.17a.

2. When you have the crossing window positioned correctly, click again to select the back door and its swing.

3. Move to the bathroom, and position the crosshair cursor in the clear space directly above the swing. When the crosshair is positioned, click. Then move the cursor down and to the left until the window you are creating crosses the bathroom door and swing, without crossing any wall lines (see Figure 6.17b). Then click in a clear space again. The bathroom door and swing are selected.

Grips have uses other than signaling that an object has been selected. You'll learn about some of these as we progress through the chapters.

4. Continue this procedure to select the other two doors and their swings. For the bedroom door, start the crossing window directly below the door swing. For the front door, start a crossing window above and to the right of the door. Figure 6.17c shows the two crossing windows that will select the bedroom and front doors.

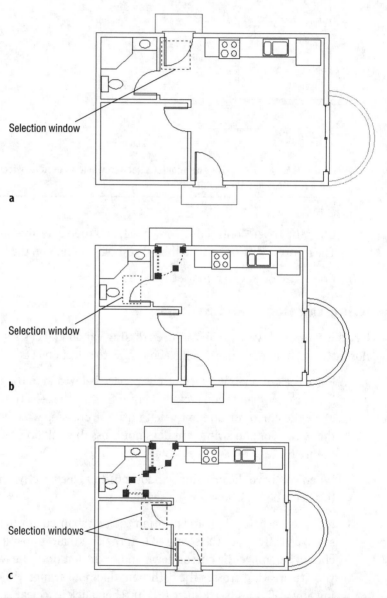

FIGURE 6.17: Using a crossing window to select the doors and swings: the back door (a), the bathroom door (b), and the bedroom and front doors (c)

5. Open the Layer Control drop-down list and select the Doors layer. Then press Esc to remove the grips. The swinging doors are now red and on the Doors layer.

For the sliding glass door, it is awkward to create a crossing window from left to right because it may be difficult to position the pickbox between the threshold lines and the sliding door. In this situation, use a regular window to select the objects.

1. Zoom in to the sliding glass door area. Pick a point to the left of the balcony opening, just above the upper jamb line. Move the crosshair down and to the right until the right edge of the window sits inside the wall but to the right of the sliding glass window frames. When your window is positioned as shown in Figure 6.18, click. The entire sliding glass door assembly will be selected, but not the jambs, walls, threshold, or balcony. Many grips appear: 13 lines make up the sliding glass door, and each has three grips. Many of the grips overlap.

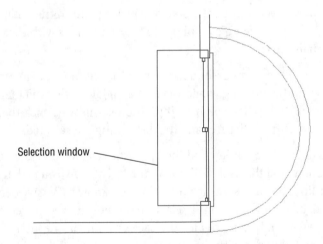

FIGURE 6.18: Using a regular selection window to select the sliding glass door

2. Open the Layer Control drop-down list and select the Doors layer. Back in your drawing, all doors are the color red and are on the Doors layer.

3. Press Esc to remove the grips, and then Zoom Previous. You will have a full view of the floor plan.

The next task is to move the kitchen and bathroom counters and fixtures onto the Fixtures layer. In doing this, you'll learn how to deselect some objects from a group of selected objects.

Selecting the Kitchen and Bathroom Fixtures

Sometimes it is more efficient to select more objects than you want and then deselect those you don't want. You'll see how this is done when you select the kitchen and bathroom fixtures.

1. Pick a point in the kitchen area just below the refrigerator to start a crossing window.

2. Move the cursor to the left and up until the upper-left corner of the crossing window is to the left of the left edge of the counter and inside the back wall, as shown in Figure 6.19a. When you have it correct, click that point. The entire kitchen counter area and the back wall line are selected.

3. Now move over to the bathroom and pick a point in the middle of the bathroom sink, being careful not to touch any lines with the crosshair cursor.

4. Move the crosshair cursor down and to the left until the lower-left corner of the crossing window is in the middle of the toilet tank (see Figure 6.19b). When you have it positioned this way, click that point. All the bathroom fixtures and the door swing are selected.

5. Hold down the Shift key and then pick the selected door swing in the bathroom and the back wall line in the kitchen. As you pick them, their lines become solid again, letting you know they have been deselected, or removed from the selection set, but their grips remain (see Figure 6.19c). Be sure to pick the back wall line in the kitchen where it doesn't coincide with the stove.

6. Release the Shift key. Open the Layer Control drop-down list and select the Fixtures layer. The fixtures are now on the Fixtures layer and are magenta in color.

7. Press the Esc key to remove the grips.

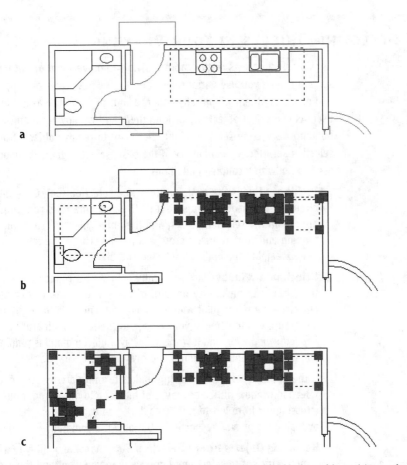

FIGURE 6.19: A crossing window to select the kitchen objects (a), another crossing window to select the bathroom objects (b), and the completed selection set after removing the door swing and back wall line (c)

The last objects to move onto a new layer are the wall lines. As the drawing is now, it will not be easy to select the wall lines because so many other objects in the drawing are in the way. However, these other objects are now on their own layers, while the wall lines are still on the 0 layer. If you make all your layers temporarily invisible except for the 0 and Walls layers, selecting the wall lines will be easy.

SELECTING OBJECTS IN YOUR DRAWING

As you select objects in the cabin drawing to move them onto their prescribed layers, you use various selection tools. These tools are important, and mastering them will greatly enhance your performance as an AutoCAD user. As you select objects by picking them and windowing them, you are building a *selection set*. You might later want to remove objects from that selection set. Here is a summary of the basic selection tools that you have used so far, with a couple of additions.

Picking   This is the basic, bottom-line selection tool. Click the line, circle, or other object to select it. If no command is running, grips appear on the selected object, and the object ghosts. If a command is running and you are being prompted to Select objects:, grips do not appear, but the object is selected and ghosts.

Selecting a Window Automatically   To start a window, click a location that is in an empty portion of the screen, where there are no objects. To form a regular window, move your cursor to the right. To form a crossing window, move your cursor to the left. This feature is called *implied windowing*, and it works this way if no command is running or if one is running and the prompt line says Select objects:.

If the geometry of your drawing makes forming a crossing or regular selection window difficult because of the need to move from right to left (crossing) or from left to right (regular), you can force one or the other by typing **c**↵ or **w**↵, respectively, but only if a command is running.

Removing Objects from a Selection Set   At some point, you will find it more efficient to select more objects than you want and then remove the unwanted ones. You can do this in two ways:

▶ To remove a couple of objects, hold down the Shift key and pick the objects.

▶ To remove many objects, type **r**↵, and then use the selection tools (picking, windows, and so on) to remove them from the selection set.

If you need to add objects back to the selection set after removing some, type **a**↵. This will put you back into selection mode, and you can continue adding objects to the set.

Turning Off and Freezing Layers

You can make layers invisible either by turning them off or by *freezing* them. When a layer is turned off or frozen, the objects on that layer are invisible. These two procedures operate the same way and do about the same thing. The difference between freezing and turning a layer off is technical and beyond the scope of this book. However, here is a good rule to follow: if you want a layer to be invisible for only a short time, turn it off; if you prefer that it be invisible semipermanently, freeze it. For the task at hand, we will turn off all the layers except the 0 layer and the Walls layer. We will then move the wall lines onto the Walls layer.

1. Click the Layer Properties Manager button on the Object Properties toolbar to open the Layer Properties Manager dialog box. Notice that the 0 layer is still first in the list and that the other layers have been reorganized alphabetically (see Figure 6.20a). Also notice the icons in the Status column: a green check mark signifies that the Walls layer is current; the dark blue layer icons signify that those layers (Balcony, Doors, Fixtures, and Steps) now have objects on them; and the light gray layer icons tell us that those layers (0, Headers, and Roof) do not have any objects on them.

NOTE Because the Walls is current and has a green check mark in the Status column, you can't tell if it has any objects on it. You have to make another layer current, and then check whether the Walls icon is blue or gray.

2. Click the Balcony layer to highlight it. Then hold down the Shift key and click the Steps layer. All layers have been selected except the 0 layer and the Walls layer.

3. Move the arrow cursor over to the On column, which has a lit light bulb as a symbol for each layer row.

4. Click one of the light bulbs of the selected layers. The lit light-bulb symbols have all changed to unlit bulbs except the ones for the 0 layer and the Walls layer (see Figure 6.20b).

> Layers beginning with numbers are listed first, in numeric order. Following those are the rest of the layers listed alphabetically.

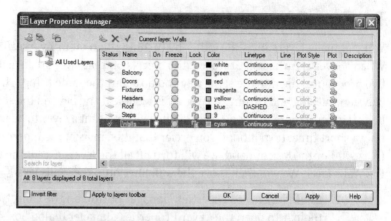

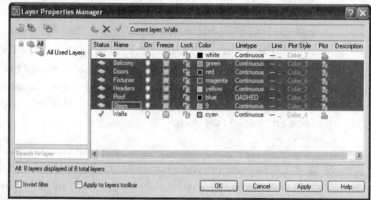

FIGURE 6.20: The layers, now listed alphabetically (a), and newly turned-off layers (b)

5. Click OK. All objects in your drawing are invisible except the wall lines (see Figure 6.21). The wall lines are still on the 0 layer.

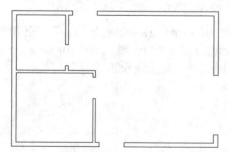

FIGURE 6.21: The floor plan with all layers frozen except the Walls layer and the 0 layer

6. Start a regular selection window around the cabin by clicking the upper-left corner of the drawing area, above and to the left of any lines. Then click the lower-right corner in the same way. All the wall lines are selected, and grips appear on all of them.

7. Open the Layer Control drop-down list, and then click the Walls layer. The walls move to the Walls layer and are now cyan. Press Esc to remove the grips.

8. Click the Layer Properties Manager button on the Object Properties toolbar. In the Layer Properties Manager dialog box, right-click any layer and choose Select All from the shortcut menu. All layers are highlighted.

9. Click one of the unlit bulbs in the On column. All unlit bulbs become lit. Click OK. Back in your drawing, all objects are now visible and on their correct layers (see Figure 6.22).

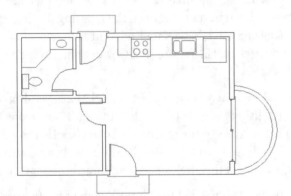

FIGURE 6.22: The floor plan with all layers visible and all objects on their correct layers

10. Save this drawing in your training folder as Cabin06a.

Two of your layers, Roof and Headers, still have no objects on them because these components haven't been drawn yet. We'll draw the headers now.

Drawing the Headers

Most door and window openings do not extend to the ceiling. The portion of the wall above the opening and below the ceiling is the *header*. The term comes from the name of the beam inside the wall that spans the opening. In a floor plan, wall lines usually stop at the door and window openings, but you need lines across the gap between jamb lines to show that an opening does not extend to the ceiling; hence, the header.

To draw headers, you need to make the Headers layer current. As you've seen, you can use the Layer Properties Manager dialog box. But there is a shortcut, the Layer Control drop-down list, which you have just been using to move objects from one layer to another.

1. Click anywhere on the drop-down list or the down-arrow button on the right end. The drop-down list opens, displaying a list of the layers in your drawing. If you have more than 10 layers, a scroll bar becomes operational, giving you access to all the layers.

2. Click the Headers layer. The drop-down list closes. Headers is now in the box; this tells you that the Headers layer has replaced Walls as the current layer.

3. Right-click the Osnap button on the status bar, and then choose Settings from the shortcut menu to open the Drafting Settings dialog box at the Object Snap tab. Be sure Endpoint is the only Object Snap mode with a check mark, be sure that Object Snap On is checked, and then click OK.

4. The doors and steps may be in your way. Click the Layer drop-down list. When the list of layers appears, click the light-bulb icons for the Doors and Steps layers to turn them off. Then click Headers at the top of the list. The drop-down list closes; the Headers layer is still current. The doors, steps, and thresholds have temporarily disappeared.

   You need to draw two parallel lines across each of the five openings, from the endpoint of one jamb line to the corresponding endpoint of the jamb on the opposite side of the opening.

5. To start the Line command, type L↵. Move the cursor near the upper end of the left jamb for the back door until the colored square appears at the upper endpoint of the jamb line, then click.

6. Move the cursor to the upper end of the right jamb, and do the same thing you did in the previous step.

7. Right-click once to open a shortcut menu near your cursor.

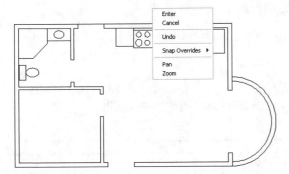

8. Choose Enter on the menu, and then right-click again to open another shortcut menu at the cursor.

9. Choose Repeat Line.

10. Move to the lower endpoint of the right jamb line for the back door and—with the same technique used in steps 5 through 9—draw the lower header line across the opening. The results are shown in Figure 6.23a.

11. Keep using the same procedure to draw the rest of the header lines for the remaining four doorway openings. Use a click, click, right-click, click, right-click, click pattern on your mouse that repeats for each header line. Here are the steps:

A. Click one of the jamb corners.

B. Click the opposite jamb corner.

C. Right-click to open a shortcut menu.

D. Press ↵ to end the Line command.

E. Right-click again to open another shortcut menu.

F. Choose Repeat Line.

G. Click one of the jamb corners.

H. And so on.

When you're finished, use the Layer drop-down list to turn on the Doors and Steps layers. The floor plan will look like Figure 6.23b.

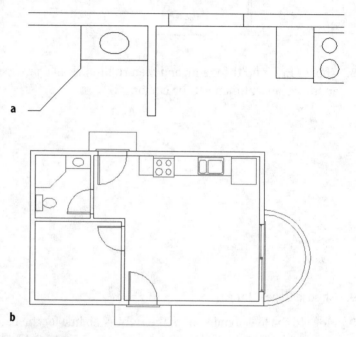

FIGURE 6.23: The header lines drawn for the back door opening (a), and for the rest of the doorway openings (b)

 N O T E   Shortcut menus—also called context menus and right-click menus—contain frequently used tools. The specific tools on a menu depend on what you're doing when you right-click. It was not terribly efficient to use them to draw the header lines, but it was a good way to introduce them to you. It's also a way to draw without using the keyboard.

The Layer drop-down list box is a shortcut that allows you to quickly pick a different layer as the current layer and to turn off or turn on individual layers. To create new layers or to turn off many layers at a time, use the Layer Properties

Manager dialog box. (Click the Layer Properties Manager button on the Object Properties toolbar.) You'll learn about another tool for changing the current layer as you draw the roof lines.

Drawing the Roof

Before starting to draw the roof lines, refer to Figure 6.24 and note the lines representing different parts of the roof:

▶ Four *eaves lines* around the perimeter of the building, representing the lowest edge of the roof

▶ One *ridgeline*, representing the peak of the roof

▶ Four *hip lines*, connecting the endpoints of the eaves lines to an endpoint of the ridgeline

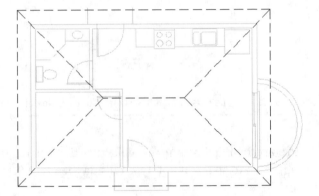

FIGURE 6.24: The floor plan with the roof lines

The roof for the cabin is called a *hip roof* because the end panels slope down to the eaves just as the middle panels do. The intersections of the sloping roof planes form the hip lines. We'll start with the eaves.

Creating the Eaves

Because the roof is cantilevered out beyond the exterior walls the same distance on all sides of the building, we can generate the eaves lines by offsetting the outside wall lines.

1. Start the Offset command. Then type **1'6**↲ to set the offset distance. Pick the left outside wall line, and then pick a point to the left of that line to offset it to the outside.

2. Move to another side of the building, pick one of the outside wall lines, and offset it to the outside.

3. Repeat this for the other two sides of the building until you have offset one outside wall line to the outside of the building on each side of the cabin (see Figure 6.25). Press ↵ to end the Offset command. Be sure you have only one line offset on each side of the building. If you offset two lines on one side, erase one.

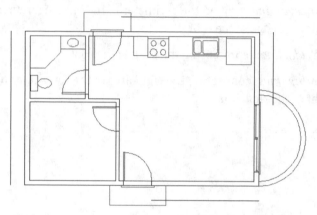

FIGURE 6.25: One outside wall line is offset to each side of the building.

4. Type f↵ to start the Fillet command. Make sure that the radius is set to zero. If it is, go to step 5. If not, type r↵, and then type 0↵ to reset the radius.

5. Click any two of these newly offset lines that are on adjacent sides of the building. Click the half of the line nearest the corner where the two selected lines will meet (see Figure 6.26a). The lines extend to meet each other and form a corner (see Figure 6.26b). The Fillet command ends.

6. Press ↵ to restart the Fillet command. Pick two more adjacent lines that will meet at another corner.

7. Start the Fillet command again, and keep picking pairs of lines until all the corners are filleted and the result is a rectangle that represents the eaves of the roof surrounding the building, offset 1'-6" from the outside exterior walls (see Figure 6.27).

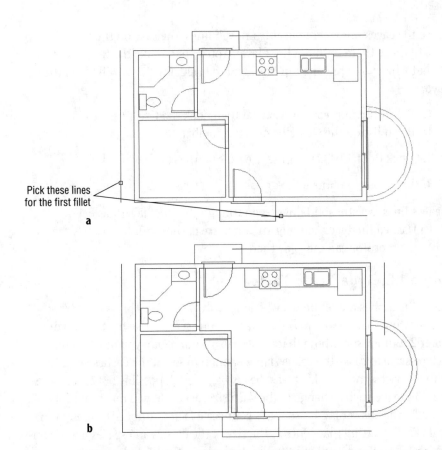

Pick these lines
for the first fillet

a

b

FIGURE 6.26: Picking lines to fillet one of the eaves' corners (a), and the result (b)

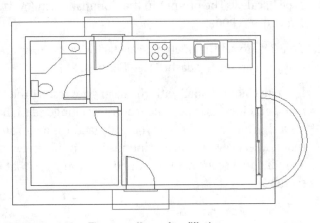

FIGURE 6.27: The eaves lines after filleting

Because the eaves lines were offset from wall lines, they are on the Walls layer. You need to move them onto the Roof layer. You'll then make the Roof layer current so that when you draw the hip lines and the ridgeline, they will be on the Roof layer.

1. Select the four eaves lines, and then click the Layer Control dropdown list on the Object Properties toolbar.

2. Click Roof. The eaves lines are now on the Roof layer.

3. Press Esc to remove the grips.

The eaves lines are still solid lines, even though the Roof layer has been assigned a Dashed linetype. Actually, the lines are dashed, but the dashes are so small that the monitor can't display them.

Setting a Linetype Scale Factor

By default, the dashes are set up to be ½" long with ¼" spaces. This is the correct size for a drawing that is close to actual size on your screen, like the box you drew in Chapter 2. But for something that is the size of your cabin, you must increase the linetype scale to make the dashes large enough to see. If the dashes were 12" long with 6" spaces, they would at least be visible, though possibly not exactly the right size. To make such a change in the dash size, ask what you must multiply ½" by to get 12". The answer is 24—so that's your scale factor. AutoCAD stores a Linetype Scale Factor setting that controls the size of the dashes and spaces of noncontinuous linetypes. The default is 1.00, which gives you the ½" dash, so you need to change it to 24.00.

1. Type ltscale↵. The prompt in the Command window reads New scale factor <1.0000>:.

2. Type 24↵ to set the linetype scale factor to 24. Your drawing changes, and you can see the dashes (see Figure 6.28).

   If you are not satisfied with the dash size, restart the Ltscale command and increase the scale factor for a longer dash or decrease it for a shorter one. This linetype scale factor is a global one, meaning that it affects every noncontinuous line in the drawing. There is also an individual scale factor for linetypes. You'll see that in the next section.

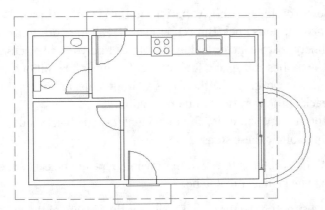

FIGURE 6.28: The eaves lines on the Roof layer with visible dashes

Assigning an Individual Linetype Scale Factor

Although the Ltscale command sets a linetype scale factor for all noncontinuous lines in the drawing, you can adjust the dash and space sizes for individual lines. If you want to change the dash and space size for one of the eaves lines of the roof to make them larger, follow these steps:

1. Select an eaves line to display grips.

2. Click the Properties button on the Standard toolbar to open the Properties palette.

3. Click Linetype Scale. Highlight the current scale of 1.0000 and type 3↵.

4. Close the Properties palette and press Esc to remove the grips. The dashes and spaces of the previously selected eaves line are three times larger than those for the rest of the roof lines.

5. Click the Properties button and use the same procedure to change the current linetype scale factor for the eaves line back to 1.

 N O T E   If no objects are selected, and you set Linetype Scale in the Properties palette to a number other than 1.000, any noncontinuous lines that are subsequently drawn will be controlled by this new Linetype Scale.

This tool allows you to get subtle variations in the size of dashes and spaces for individual, noncontinuous lines. But remember that all lines are controlled by an individual linetype scale factor and by the global linetype scale factor. The actual size of the dashes and spaces for a particular line is a result of the two linetype scale factors working together. This additional flexibility requires you to keep careful track of the variations you are making.

To find out the current values for the individual (called object) and global linetype scale factors, follow these steps:

1. With `Cabin06a` as the current drawing, type **linetype**⏎ to open the Linetype Manager dialog box.

2. Make sure the Details area is visible at the bottom of the dialog box. If it isn't, click Show Details in the upper-right corner.

3. Note the bottom-right corner. The current global and object linetype scales are displayed here. They can also be modified here.

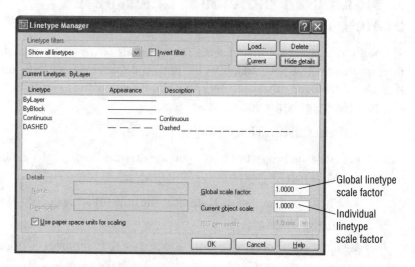

4. For now, click Cancel.

Drawing the Hip and Ridge Lines

Next, you'll draw two of the diagonal hip roof lines and then use the Mirror command to create the other two. To do this, you need to assign the Roof layer as the current layer. Because you have moved the lines you just offset to the Roof layer, you can use the Make Object's Layer Current button to make the Roof layer current.

1. Click the Make Object's Layer Current button on the Layers toolbar, just to the right of the Layer Control drop-down list. You will get the `Select object whose layer will become current:` prompt.

2. Pick one of the dashed eaves lines. The Roof layer replaces Header in the Layer drop-down list, telling you the Roof layer is now the current layer.

   Look at the Linetype Control drop-down list on the Properties toolbar. A dashed line with the name ByLayer appears there. ByLayer tells you that the current linetype is going to be whatever linetype has been assigned to the current layer. In the case of the Roof layer, the assigned linetype is dashed. You will read more about ByLayer at the end of this chapter.

3. The Endpoint Osnap should still be running. How can you tell? Type os.⏎ to open the Drafting Settings dialog box at the Osnap tab. You can easily see which Osnaps are checked. First, be sure Object Snap On is checked. Then, if Endpoint is checked, click the Polar Tracking tab. Otherwise, click the Endpoint check box and then click the Polar Tracking tab (see Figure 6.29).

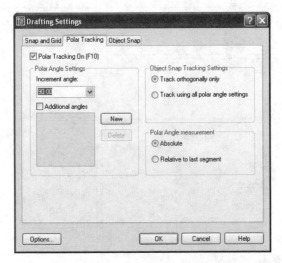

FIGURE 6.29: The Polar Tracking tab in the Drafting Settings dialog box

4. At the top, click the Polar Tracking On (F10) check box to turn on Polar Tracking.

5. In the Polar Angle Settings area, open the Increment Angle drop-down list and select 45.

6. Click OK to close the Drafting Settings dialog box.

7. Start the Line command. Move the crosshair cursor to the lower-left corner of the rectangle representing the roof until the square appears on the corner, and then click. A line is started.

8. Move the crosshair cursor up and to the right at a 45° angle from the lower-left corner of the roof. When the angle of the line being drawn approaches 45°, a tracking path and a Polar tool tip will appear, along with a small *x* near the crosshair cursor (see Figure 6.30a).

9. While the tracking path is visible, type 15'↵↵. The first hip line is drawn, and the Line command ends (see Figure 6.30b).

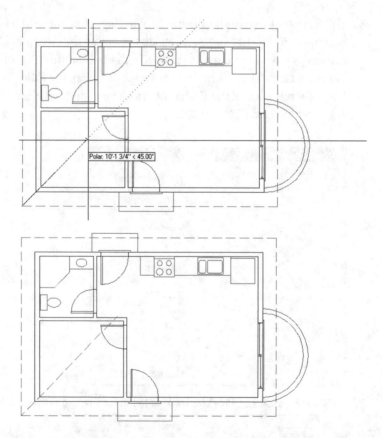

FIGURE 6.30: The 45° tracking path for the first hip line of the roof (a), and the completed first hip line (b)

Use the same procedure to draw another hip line from the upper-left corner of the roof. Here's a summary of the steps:

1. Restart the Line command, and start a line at the upper-left corner of the roof.

2. Hold the crosshair cursor down and to the right at an angle of approximately 45° until the Polar Tracking path with its tool tip appears. (The tool tip will confirm that the actual angle is 315°.)

3. Type 15'↵↵. The second hip line is completed.

The two hip lines need to be filleted together at their intersection, but the bedroom door is in the way.

1. Open the Layer Control drop-down list and turn off the Door layer. Then click the Roof layer in the list to close the list.

2. Start the Fillet command. The radius should still be set to zero. Click the two diagonal lines at a place that is close to their intersection. The lines are filleted together (see Figure 6.31a). Now you need to mirror these two diagonal lines to the right side of the roof.

3. Start the Mirror command. At the prompt to select objects, select the two diagonal lines, and then press ↵. Click the Midpoint Osnap button and place the cursor on the horizontal eaves line above the cabin. When the triangle appears at the midpoint of the eaves line, click.

4. Move the crosshair cursor down into the living room, keeping it directly below the point just picked, and when the tracking line and Polar tool tip appear, click in a clear space. Press ↵ when asked whether to delete old objects. The diagonal lines from the left are mirrored to the right (see Figure 6.31b). The Mirror command automatically ends. To finish the roof, we'll draw in the ridgeline.

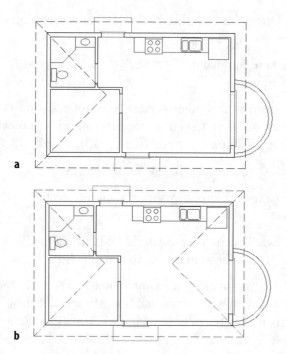

a

b

FIGURE 6.31: The first two hip lines are filleted together (a) and then mirrored to the right (b).

5. Start the Line command. Endpoint Osnap is still running. Pick the two intersections of the diagonal lines, and then press ↵. Open the Layer Control drop-down list and turn on the Doors layer. Then click the roof layer to close the drop-down list. This completes the ridgeline and finishes the roof (see Figure 6.32). Save this drawing as Cabin06b.

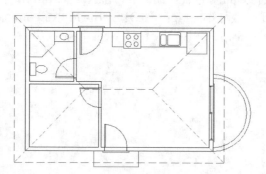

FIGURE 6.32: The completed roof

By drawing the roof lines, you have completed the exercises for this chapter. The cabin floor plan is almost complete. In the next chapter, you will complete the floor plan by placing windows in the external walls using a new grouping tool called the *block*. The rest of this chapter contains a short discussion on color, linetypes, and lineweights and how they work with layers and objects.

Properties of Layers and Objects

Here are a few concepts to consider when assigning properties to layers and objects.

Selecting Colors for Layers and Objects

First, you must decide whether you prefer a light or dark background color for the drawing area. This is generally a personal preference, but the lighting in your work area can be a contributing factor. Bright work areas usually make it difficult to read monitors easily, and with a dark background color on your screen in a brightly lit room, you will often get distracting reflections on the screen. Eyestrain can result. Darkening your work area will usually minimize these effects. If that's not possible, you might have to live with a lighter background.

Next, look at the colors in your drawing. If the background of your drawing area is white, notice which colors are the easiest to read. For most monitors, yellow, light gray, and cyan are somewhat faded, while blue, green, red, and magenta are read easily. If your drawing area background is black, the blue is sometimes too dark to read easily, but the rest of the colors that we have used so far usually read well. This is one reason that most users prefer the black or at least a dark background color.

Assigning a Color or a Linetype to an Object Instead of a Layer

You can also assign properties of layers, such as color, linetype, and lineweights, to objects. So, for example, think about the Roof layer. It is assigned the Dashed linetype. A line on the Roof layer can be assigned the Continuous linetype, even though all other lines on the Roof layer are dashed. The same is true for color and lineweights. Occasionally, this makes sense, especially for linetypes, but that is the exception, rather than the rule. To make such a change, select the line, open the Properties palette, and change the linetype from ByLayer to the linetype of your choice.

In this chapter, you have seen how to assign colors and linetypes to layers, in order to control the way objects on those layers appear. That is the rule to follow.

When objects are assigned properties that vary from those of their layer, the result can be confusing to someone working with your drawing file because the objects don't appear to be on their assigned layer. If the object's properties match those of another layer, you can mistakenly think the object is on that layer.

Making a Color or a Linetype Current

If you look at the Properties toolbar for a moment, you will see, to the right of the Layer Control drop-down list, more such lists. The first three are the Color, the Linetype, and the Lineweight controls. You use these tools to set a color, linetype, or lineweight to be current. When this is done, each object subsequently created will be assigned the current linetype, lineweight, and/or color, regardless of which linetype, lineweight, and color have been assigned to the current layer. If, for example, the Doors layer is set as the current layer, and the Dashed linetype and green color are also assigned as current, any lines drawn are dashed and green, but still on the Doors layer. This is not a good way to set up the system of layers, linetypes, and colors because of the obvious confusion it would create in your drawing, but beginners often accidentally do this.

The best way to keep all this straight is to keep the current linetype, lineweight, and color set to ByLayer, as they are by default. When you do this, colors and linetypes are controlled by the layers, and objects take on the color and linetype of the layers they are on. If this configuration is accidentally disturbed and objects are created with the wrong color or linetype, you can correct the situation without too much trouble. First, reset the current color, lineweight, and linetype to ByLayer by using the Property Control drop-down list on the Properties toolbar. Then click the Properties button to change the linetype, lineweight, or color of the problem objects to ByLayer. They will then take on the color, lineweight, and linetype of the layer to which they have been assigned.

If You Would Like More Practice...

All trades and professions that use AutoCAD will have their own standards for naming and organizing layers. The following suggestions urge you to apply this chapter's concepts to your individual use of the program.

Experiment with Linetypes and Linetype Scales

Choose Save As to save Cabin06b to a new file called Cabin06b_Linetype. Then experiment with the linetypes and linetype scales (Global and Object) to get a feel for how the linetypes look and how the scales work. You won't be using this practice file again, so feel free to draw new objects that will make it convenient for you to work with linetypes. Here are some suggestions for linetypes to experiment with:

▶ Dashed (.5×)

▶ Dashed (2×)

▶ Hidden (as compared to Dashed)

▶ Phantom

▶ DashDot

▶ Fenceline2

▶ HotWaterLine

Here is a summary of the steps to get a new linetype into your drawing:

1. Create a new layer or highlight an existing layer.

2. Click Continuous in the Linetype column for the chosen layer.

3. Click the Load button.

4. Highlight a linetype in the list and click OK.

5. Highlight the new linetype in the Linetype Manager dialog box and click OK.

6. Make the layer with the new linetype the Current layer, and then click OK to close the Layer Properties Manager dialog box.

7. Draw objects.

Once you have a few linetypes represented in the drawing, open the Linetype Manager dialog box and experiment with the global and object linetype scale factors.

Set Up Layers for Your Own Trade or Profession

Open a new drawing and set up approximately ten layers that you might use in your own profession. Assign them colors and linetypes. Most activities that use CAD have some layers in common, such as Centerline, Border or Titleblock, Drawing Symbols, Dimensions, Text or Lettering, and so on.

Are You Experienced?

Now you can...

☑ **create new layers and assign them a color and a linetype**

☑ **load a new linetype into your current drawing file**

☑ **move existing objects onto a new layer**

☑ **turn layers off and on**

☑ **make a layer current and create objects on the current layer**

☑ **reset the linetype scale factor to make noncontinuous lines visible**

☑ **use Polar Tracking to draw a diagonal line**

☑ **use the individual linetype scale factor to adjust the size of one dashed line**

CHAPTER 7

Grouping Objects into Blocks

▷ Creating and inserting blocks

▷ Using the Wblock command

▷ Detecting blocks in a drawing

▷ Working with AutoCAD's DesignCenter

▷ Controlling the appearance of palettes on your screen

Computer drafting gains much of its efficiency from a feature that makes it possible to group a collection of objects into an entity that behaves as one object. AutoCAD calls these grouped objects a *block*. The AutoCAD tools that work specifically with blocks make it possible to do the following:

- ▶ Create a block in your current drawing.

- ▶ Repeatedly place copies of a block in precise locations in your drawing.

- ▶ Share blocks between drawings.

- ▶ Create .dwg files either from blocks or from portions of your current drawing.

- ▶ Store blocks on a palette for easy reuse in any drawing.

In general, objects best suited to becoming part of a block are the components that are repeatedly used in your drawings. In architecture and construction, examples of these components are doors, windows, and fixtures or drawing symbols, such as a North arrow or labels for a section cut line (see Figure 7.1). In your cabin drawing, you will convert the doors with swings into blocks. You will then create a new block that you will use to place the windows in the cabin drawing. To accomplish these tasks, you need to learn two new commands.

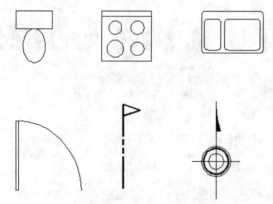

F I G U R E   7 . 1 :   Examples of blocks often used in architectural drawings

Making a Block for a Door

When making a block, you create a *block definition*. This is an invisible entity that is stored in the drawing file and consists of the following:

▶ The block name

▶ An insertion point to help you place the block in the drawing

▶ The objects to be grouped into the block

You specify each of these in the course of using the Make Block command. When the command is completed, the block definition is stored with the drawing file. You then insert the object (as a block) back into the drawing using the Insert Block command.

Before you create a block, you must consider the layers on which the objects to be blocked reside. When objects on the 0 layer are grouped into a block, they take on the color and linetype of the layer that is current when the block is inserted. Objects on other layers retain the properties of their original layers, regardless of which color or linetype has been assigned to the current layer. This characteristic distinguishes the 0 layer from all other layers.

As you define a block, you must decide which—if any—of the objects to be included in the block need to be on the 0 layer before they are blocked. If a block is always going to be on the same layer, the objects making up the block can remain on that layer. On the other hand, if a block might be inserted on several layers, the objects in the block need to be moved to the 0 layer before the block definition is created, so as to avoid confusion of colors and linetypes.

As you learn to make blocks for the doors, you will also see how layers work in the process of creating block definitions. We'll create a block for the exterior doors first, using the front door, and call it door3_0 to distinguish it from the smaller interior door. For the insertion point, you need to assign a point on or near the door that will facilitate its placement as a block in your drawing. The hinge point makes the best insertion point.

For this chapter, the Endpoint Osnap should be running most of the time, and Polar Tracking should be off. Follow these steps to set up your drawing:

1. If you are continuing from the last chapter, skip to step 2. If you are starting a new session, once AutoCAD is running, click the Open button on the Standard toolbar. In the Select File list, highlight Cabin06b and click Open. If this .dwg file is not in the list, click the arrow to the right of the Look In drop-down list at the top of the dialog box, navigate to your Training Data folder, and then select the file.

The objects that compose complex blocks can reside on more than one layer.

We are using the Freeze option for layers this time because we won't need to see the lines on the Roof and Headers layers for a while.

2. The Roof layer should be visible in the Layers drop-down list on the Object Properties toolbar. Click the list to open it, and then click Doors to make the Doors layer current. The list will close. Click the drop-down list again, and this time click the sun icons for the Roof and Headers layers to freeze them. The suns turn into snowflakes. Then click the Doors layer to close the list. The Doors layer is now current, and the headers and roof lines are no longer visible in the drawing (see Figure 7.2).

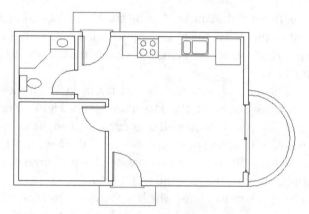

FIGURE 7.2: The floor plan with the Headers and Roof layers frozen

3. Check the status bar, and note whether the Osnap button is in the on position. Right-click the Osnap button and choose Settings from the shortcut menu.

4. In the Object Snap tab of the Drafting Settings dialog box, be sure the Endpoint check box is marked. Also, be sure Object Snap On is checked.

5. Click OK. In the status bar, click Polar off if it is on, and be sure only the Model and Osnap buttons are in the on position.

Now you're ready to make blocks.

You can also start the Block command by choosing Draw ➢ Block ➢ Make or by typing b↵.

1. Click the Make Block button on the Draw toolbar to open the Block Definition dialog box (see Figure 7.3). Notice the flashing cursor in the Name text box. Type **door3_0** but do not press ↵.

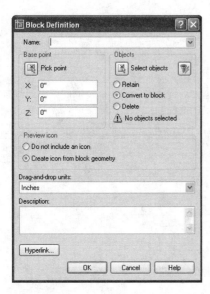

FIGURE 7.3: The Block Definition dialog box

2. Click the Pick Point button in the Base Point area. The dialog box momentarily closes, and you are returned to your drawing.

3. Zoom in to the front door area. In your drawing, click the Zoom Window button on the Standard toolbar, and make a window around the front door area. The area in the zoom window will fill the screen.

4. Move the cursor to the front door area, and position it near the hinge point of the door. When the square appears on the hinge point (see Figure 7.4a), click. This selects the insertion point for the door, and the Block Definition dialog box returns.

5. Click the Select Objects button in the Objects area. You are returned to the drawing again. The cursor changes to a pickbox, and the Command window displays the `Select objects:` prompt.

6. Select the door and swing, and then press ↵. You are returned to the Block Definition dialog box. At the bottom of the Objects area, the count of selected objects is displayed. Just above that are three radio buttons. Click the Delete radio button if it's not already selected.

7. Finally, in the middle of the dialog box, be sure Create Icon From Block Geometry is selected, and then click OK to close the dialog box. The door and swing disappear (see Figure 7.4b).

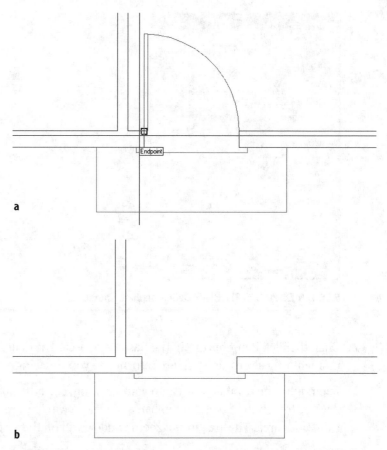

FIGURE 7.4: The front door opening when picking the hinge point as the insertion point (a), and after creating the door3_0 block and deleting the door and swing (b)

You have now created a block definition, called door3_0. Block definitions are stored electronically with the drawing file. You need to insert the door3_0 block (known formally as a *block reference*) into the front door opening to replace the door and swing that were just deleted when the block was created.

Inserting the Door Block

You will use the Insert Block command to place the door3_0 block back into the drawing.

1. On the Draw toolbar, click the Insert Block button to open the Insert dialog box (see Figure 7.5). At the top, the Name drop-down list

contains the names of the blocks in the drawing. In this case, there is only one so far, door3_0, so it is on top. Below the Name list are three areas with the Specify On-Screen option. These are used for the insertion procedure.

You can also start the Insert Block command by choosing Insert ➤ Block or by typing I↵.

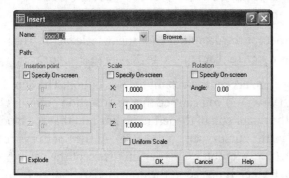

FIGURE 7.5: The Insert dialog box

2. Be sure the Specify On-Screen option is checked for all three areas. Also, make sure the Explode check box in the lower-left corner is unchecked.

3. Click OK. You are returned to your drawing, and the door3_0 block is now attached to the cursor, with the hinge point coinciding with the intersection of the crosshairs (see Figure 7.6). The Command window reads Specify insertion point or [Scale/X/Y/Z/Rotate/ PScale/PX/PY/PZ/PRotate]:.

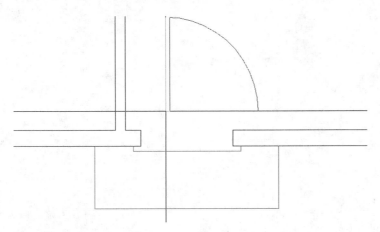

FIGURE 7.6: The door3_0 block attached to the cursor

4. With Endpoint Osnap running, move the cursor toward the upper end of the left jamb line in the front door opening. When a colored square appears at the jamb line's upper endpoint, click. The insertion point has been positioned, and the Command window now displays an additional prompt: Enter X scale factor, specify opposite corner, or [Corner/XYZ]<1>:.

5. Press ↵ to accept the default of 1 for the X scale factor. The prompt changes to Y scale factor <use X scale factor> :.

6. Press ↵ again to accept the default for this option. The door3_0 block comes into view, and you can see that its insertion point has been placed at the upper end of the left jamb line and that the block rotates as you move the cursor (see Figure 7.7a). At the Specify rotation angle <0.00>: prompt, press ↵ again to accept the default of 0.00. The door3_0 block is placed in the drawing (see Figure 7.7b).

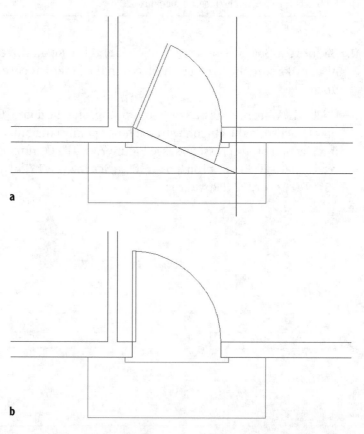

a

b

FIGURE 7.7: The rotation option (a), and the final placement (b)

Each time a block is inserted, you can specify the following on-screen or in the Insert dialog box:

► The location of the insertion point of the block

► The X and Y scale factors

► The Z factor in the dialog box (used for 3D drawings, in AutoCAD only)

► A rotation angle

After you insert blocks, you can stretch or flip them horizontally (the X scale factor) or vertically (the Y scale factor), or you can rotate them from their original orientation. Because you created the door3_0 block from the door and swing that occupied the front door opening, and the size was the same, inserting this block back into the front door opening required no rotation, so we followed the defaults. When you insert the same block into the back door opening, you will have to change the Y scale factor, because the door will be flipped vertically.

Flipping a Block While Inserting It

The X scale factor controls the horizontal size and orientation. The Y scale factor mimics the X scale factor unless you change it. For the next insertion, you will make such a change.

1. Click the Zoom Previous button on the Standard toolbar to zoom back out to a full view of the floor plan.

2. Click the Zoom Window button, and make a window around the back door area, including plenty of room inside and outside the opening so that you can see the door3_0 block as it is being inserted. You will be zoomed into a close view of the back door (see Figure 7.8).

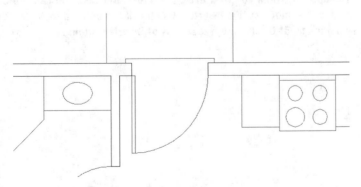

FIGURE 7.8: The result of the zoom

3. Use the Erase command to erase the door and swing from the back door opening.

4. Choose Insert ➤ Block. In the Insert dialog box, door3_0 should still be in the Name drop-down list.

5. Click OK. You are returned to your drawing, and the door3_0 block is attached to the cursor.

6. Move the cursor to the lower end of the left jamb line. When the colored square appears at that endpoint (see Figure 7.9a), click. The insertion point has been placed, and the prompt reads `Enter X scale factor, specify opposite corner, or [Corner/XYZ]<1>:`.

7. Press ↵ to accept the default X scale factor of 1. The prompt changes to read `Specify Y scale factor <use X scale factor:`. In order to flip the door down to the inside of the cabin, you need to give the Y scale factor a value of –1.

8. Type -1↵. Then press ↵ again to accept the default rotation angle of 0°. The Insert Block command ends, and the door3_0 block is placed in the back door opening (see Figure 7.9b).

   Figure 7.9b will look exactly like Figure 7.8.

9. Click the Zoom Previous button on the Object Properties toolbar to zoom back out to a full view of the floor plan.

Nothing has changed about the geometry of the door, but it is now a different kind of object. Before it was a rectangle and an arc; now it's a block reference made up of a rectangle and an arc.

N O T E   When inserting a block, giving a value of –1 to the X or Y scale factor has the effect of flipping the block, much like the Mirror command did in Chapter 4, when you first drew the doors. Because you can flip or rotate the door3_0 block as it is inserted, this block can be used to place a door and swing in any 3'-0" opening, regardless of its orientation.

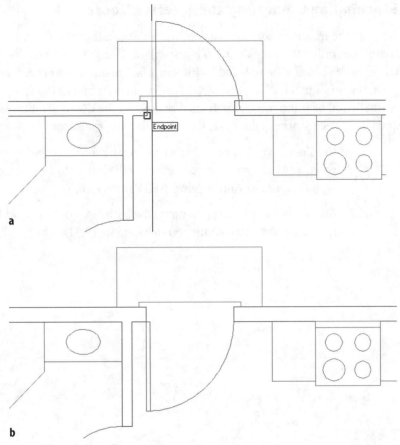

FIGURE 7.9: Placing the door3_0 insertion point (a), and the block after insertion (b)

Doors are traditionally sorted into four categories, depending on which side the hinges and doorknob are on and which way the door swings open. To be able to use one door block for all openings of the same size, you need to know the following:

► How the door and swing in the block are oriented

► Where the hinge point is to be in the next opening

► How the block has to be flipped and/or rotated during the insertion process to properly fit in the next doorway opening

Blocking and Inserting the Interior Doors

Because the interior doors are smaller, you will need to make a new block for them. We could insert the door3_0 block with a ⅚ scale factor, but the door thickness would also be reduced by the same factor, and we don't want that.

On the other hand, it's a good idea to orient all door blocks the same way, and the bath and bedroom doors are turned relative to the door3_0 block. We'll move and rotate the bathroom door and its swing like the front door.

1. Use Zoom Window to define a window that encloses both the bathroom and bedroom doors. The view will change to a close-up of the area enclosed in your window (see Figure 7.10a).

2. Use the Move command to move the bathroom door to the right, and then use the Rotate command to rotate it –90° (see Figure 7.10b).

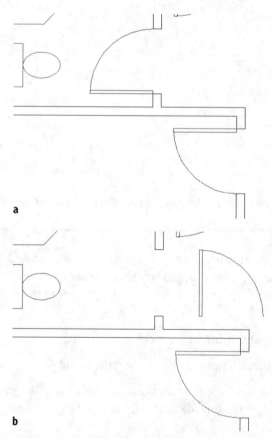

FIGURE 7.10: The result of a zoom window (a), the bathroom door moved and rotated (b)

3. Repeat a procedure similar to the one you used to make a block out of the front door and swing to make a block out of the bathroom door and swing. Here is a summary of the steps:

   A. Start the Block command. (Click the Make Block button on the Draw toolbar.)

   B. In the dialog box, type **door2_6** to name the new block. Don't press ↵.

   C. Click the Pick Point button, and pick the hinge point of the bathroom door.

   D. Click the Select Objects button and pick the door and swing. Then press ↵.

   E. In the Objects area, click the Delete radio button.

   F. Click OK. The door and swing disappear.

4. Insert the door2_6 block in the bathroom doorway opening. Follow the steps carefully. Here's a summary of the steps:

   A. Start the Insert Block command.

   B. Open the Name drop-down list, select door2_6, and then click OK.

   C. Pick the left end of the lower jamb line.

   D. Accept the default of 1 for the X scale factor.

   E. Accept the default of <use X> for the Y scale factor.

   F. Enter 90↵ for the rotation.

5. Erase the bedroom door, restart the Insert Block command, and insert the door2_6 block in the bedroom door opening. Here are the parameters:

   ▶ Check Specify On-Screen for Insertion Point, Scale, and Rotation.

   ▶ The insertion point will be at the left endpoint of the upper jamb line.

   ▶ The X scale factor will be –1.

   ▶ The Y scale factor will be 1.

   ▶ The rotation will be 90.

6. Zoom Previous (see Figure 7.11).

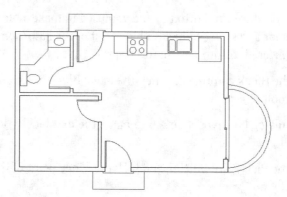

FIGURE 7.11: The floor plan with all swinging doors converted into blocks

 T I P   If you have trouble anticipating how a block such as the door block needs to be flipped or rotated during insertion, don't worry about it; just make sure to locate the insertion point accurately in the drawing. Then, after the block is inserted, you can flip or turn it by using the Mirror and Rotate commands.

THE FATE OF OBJECTS USED TO MAKE A BLOCK

The three radio buttons in the Objects area of the Block Definition dialog box represent the options you have for objects transformed into a block:

Retain   The objects remain unblocked. Use this if you want to make several similar blocks from the same set of objects.

Convert To Block   The objects become a block reference. Use this if the first use of the block has geometry identical to that of the set of objects it is replacing.

Delete   The objects are automatically erased after the block has been defined. Use this if the first use of the block will be at a different scale, orientation, or location from the set of objects it is replacing.

Note that when we made the first door block, we could have used the Convert To Block option because the door3_0 block replaced the front door and its swing. I decided not to use this option so that I could show you the insertion process with default X and Y scale factors and rotation.

This view looks the same as the view you started with at the beginning of this chapter; see Figure 7.2, shown earlier. Blocks look the same as other objects, and you can't detect them by sight. They're useful because you can use them over and over again in a drawing or in many drawings and because the block is a grouping of two or more (and sometimes many more) objects into a single object. The next section will go into how you can detect a block.

Finding Blocks in a Drawing

You can detect blocks in a drawing in at least three ways: by using grips, by using the List command, and by looking at the Properties palette.

Using Grips to Detect a Block

Grips appear on objects that are selected when no command is started. When an object that is not a block is selected, grips appear at strategic places. But if you select a block, by default, only one grip appears, and it's always located at the block's insertion point. Because of this, clicking an object when no command is started is a quick way to see if it is a block.

1. At the Command: prompt, click one of the door swings. The door and swing ghost, and a colored square appears at the hinge point.

2. Press Esc to clear the grip.

3. Choose Tools ➤ Options to open the Options dialog box, and then click the Selection tab. The Grips areas are on the right side. Enable Grips Within Blocks is unchecked by default. If this option is checked, grips appear on all objects in the block as if they weren't blocked when you click a block with no command running. Leave this setting unchecked.

4. Click OK to close the Options dialog box.

We'll look at grips in more detail in Chapter 11. You might need to know more about a block than just whether something is one. If that is the case, you will need to use the List command.

Using the List Command to Detect a Block

You can use the List command to learn more about a block.

1. Choose Tools ➤ Inquiry ➤ List.

2. Click the front door block, and then press ↵. The AutoCAD Text Window temporarily covers the drawing (see Figure 7.12). In the Text Window, you can see the words BLOCK REFERENCE Layer: DOORS, followed by eight lines of text. These nine lines describe the block you selected.

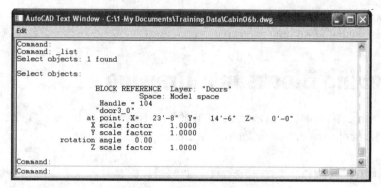

FIGURE 7.12: The AutoCAD Text Window

The information stored in the Text Window includes the following:

▶ What the object is (Block Reference)

▶ The layer the object is on (Doors layer)

▶ The name of the block (door3_0)

▶ The coordinates of the insertion point in the drawing

▶ The X and Y scale factors

▶ The rotation angle

3. Press F2. The drawing area returns.

4. Right-click and choose Repeat List from the shortcut menu.

5. At the Select objects: prompt, click one of the arcs that represents the balcony, click one of the wall lines, and press ↵.

6. The Text Window is displayed again, and you see information about the arc that you selected, followed by information about the selected wall line.

7. Press F2, and then slowly press it a few more times. As you switch back and forth between the Text Window and the drawing, notice that the last three lines in the Text Window are the three lines of text in the Command window of the drawing (see Figure 7.13). The Command window is displaying a strip of text from the Text Window, usually the last three lines.

8. Press F2 to display the drawing.

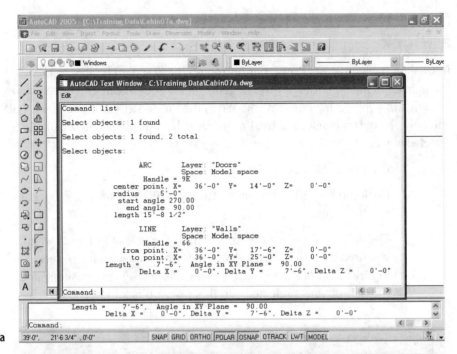

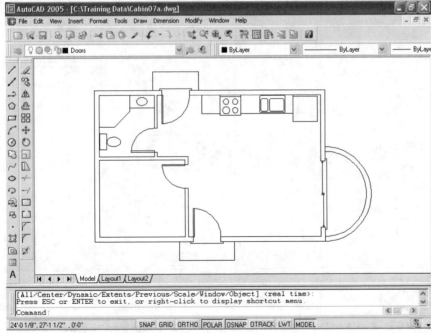

FIGURE 7.13: Toggling between the Text Window (a) and the drawing with its Command window (b)

Using the Properties Palette to Detect a Block

In Chapter 6, we used the Properties button on the Standard toolbar to change the individual linetype scale for the ridgeline of the roof. It can also be a tool for investigating objects in your drawing. When the Properties command is started, and only one object is selected, the Properties palette displays data specific to the selected object.

1. Click one of the door blocks.

2. Click the Properties button on the Standard toolbar. The Properties palette opens.

   The data displayed on the palette is similar to that displayed when you used the List command, but in slightly different form (see Figure 7.14). At the top of the dialog box, a drop-down list displays the type of object selected—in this case, a Block Reference.

> **Block insertion means the same thing as block reference, and both are casually called blocks.**

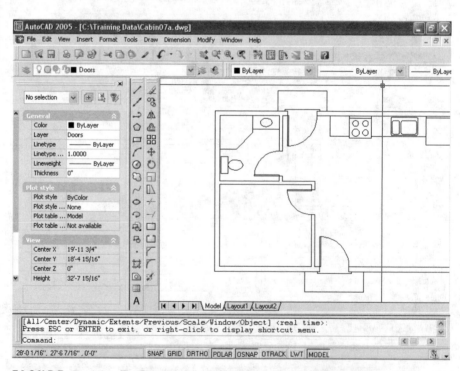

FIGURE 7.14: The Properties palette docked, with a door block selected

3. Close the Properties palette by clicking the X in the upper-right corner (upper-left corner if the palette is floating); then press Esc to remove the grip on the door block.

 TIP The *X* you need to click to close the Properties palette will be in the upper-left corner of the palette if it is floating, and in the upper-right corner if it is docked.

If you are ever working on a drawing that you did not draw, these tools for finding out about objects will be invaluable. The next exercise on working with blocks will involve placing windows in the walls of the cabin.

Creating a Window Block

You can create all the windows in the cabin floor plan from one block, even though they are four different sizes (see Figure 7.15). You'll create a window block and then go from room to room to insert the block into the walls.

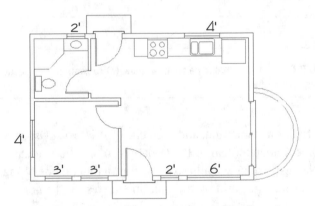

FIGURE 7.15: The cabin windows in the floor plan

1. Click the Layers list on the Object Properties toolbar to open the drop-down list, and click the 0 layer in the list to make it current.

2. Right-click the Osnap button on the status bar and choose Settings from the shortcut menu. Add check marks to Midpoint and Perpendicular Osnaps. Then click OK.

3. Zoom in to a horizontal section of wall where there are no jamb lines or intersections with other walls, by clicking the Zoom Window button on the Standard toolbar and picking two points to be opposite corners of the zoom window (see Figure 7.16). Because the widths of the windows in the cabin are multiples of 12", you can insert a block made from a 12"-wide window for each window, and you can apply an X scale factor to the block to make it the right width. The first step is to draw a 12"-wide window inside the wall lines.

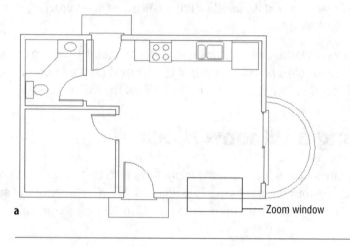

a   Zoom window

b

F I G U R E   7 . 1 6 :   Making a zoom window (a) to zoom in to a section of straight length of wall (b)

Use the Nearest Osnap tool when you want to locate a point somewhere on a line, but aren't concerned exactly where on the line the point is located.

4. Start the Line command, and then click the Nearest Osnap button on the Object Snap toolbar or the Osnap flyout on the Standard toolbar. The Nearest Osnap will allow you to start a line on one of the wall lines. It finds the point on the wall line nearest to the point you pick.

5. Move the cursor to the upper wall line, a little to the left of the center of the screen and, with the hourglass symbol displayed, click. A line begins on the upper wall line.

6. Move the cursor to the lower wall line. A colored perpendicular icon will appear directly below the point you previously picked. When it is displayed, click. The line is drawn between the wall lines. Press ↵ to end the Line command.

7. Start the Offset command. Type 12↵ to set the offset distance to 12". Pick the line you just drew, and then pick a point to the right of that line. The line is offset 12" to the right. Press ↵ to end the Offset command.

8. Start the Line command again. Move the cursor near the midpoint of the line you first drew. When the midpoint symbol appears, click. Move the cursor near the midpoint of the line that was just offset. When the Perpendicular or Midpoint symbol appears, click. Press ↵ to end the Line command. Your drawing should look like Figure 7.17.

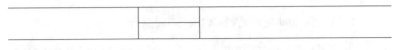

FIGURE 7.17: Completed lines for the window block

The three lines you've drawn will make up a window block. They represent the two jamb lines and the glass (usually called *glazing*). By varying the X scale factor from 2 to 6, you can create windows 2', 3', 4', and 6' wide.

Before you create the block, you need to decide the best place for the insertion point. For the doors, you chose the hinge point because you always know where it will be in the drawing. Locating a similar strategic point for the window is a little more difficult, but certainly possible. We know the insertion point can't be on the horizontal line representing the glazing, because it will always rest in the middle of the wall, and there is no guideline in the drawing for the middle of the wall. Windows are usually dimensioned to the midpoint of the glazing line rather than to either jamb line, so we don't want the insertion point to be at the endpoint of a jamb line. The insertion point will need to be positioned on a wall line but also lined up with the midpoint of the glazing line.

To locate this point, draw a guideline from the midpoint of the glazing line straight to one of the wall lines.

1. Press ↵ to restart the Line command. Move to a point near the midpoint of the glazing line. When the midpoint symbol appears, click.

2. Move to the bottom wall line. When the Perpendicular symbol appears, click. A guideline is drawn from the midpoint of the glazing line that is perpendicular to the lower wall line (see Figure 7.18). The lower endpoint of this line is the location of the window block insertion point. Press ↵ to end the Line command. Now you are ready to define the window block.

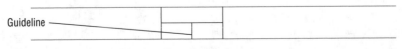

Guideline

FIGURE 7.18: The guideline is completed.

3. Type **b** ↵ to start the Block command. In the dialog box, type **win-1** for the block name and then click the Pick Point button.

4. Back in the drawing, with Endpoint, Midpoint, and Perpendicular Osnaps running, move the cursor to the lower end of the guideline you just drew. When the Endpoint symbol appears at that location, click.

If only the Perpendicular Osnap symbol appears, click Endpoint on the Object Snap toolbar, and then try again.

5. In the dialog box, click the Select Objects button.

6. Back in the drawing, select the two jamb lines and the glazing line, but don't select the guideline whose endpoint locates the insertion point. Press ↵.

7. Back in the dialog box, click the Delete radio button, and then click OK. The win-1 block has been defined, and the 12" window has been erased.

8. Erase the guideline using the Erase command.

9. Zoom Previous to zoom out to a view of the whole floor plan.

This completes the definition of the block that will represent the windows. The next task is to insert the win-1 block where the windows will be located.

Inserting the Window Block

Several factors come into play when deciding where to locate windows in a floor plan:

▶ The structure of the building

▶ The appearance of windows from outside the building

▶ The appearance of windows from inside a room

▶ The location of fixtures that might interfere with placement

▶ The sun angle and climate considerations

For this exercise, we will work on the windows for each room, starting with the bedroom.

Rotating a Block During Insertion

The bedroom has windows on two walls: two 3' windows centered in the front
wall 12" apart, and one 4' window centered in the left wall (see Figure 7.19).
You'll make the 4' window first.

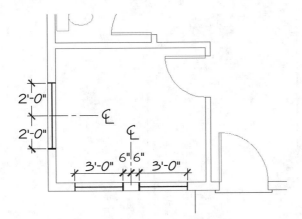

FIGURE 7.19: The bedroom windows

1. Use a zoom window to zoom in to a view of the bedroom similar to
   that in Figure 7.19. Click the Polar button on the status bar to turn
   on Polar Tracking. Polar, Osnap, and Model should now be in the on
   position.

2. Create a new layer by clicking the Layer button and then clicking the
   New button in the Layer Properties Manager dialog box. Layer1 will
   appear and be highlighted. Type **Windows**↵ to rename Layer1.

3. Click the color square in the Windows row to open the Select Color
   dialog box, with White highlighted in the Color text box. Type 30↵ to
   change the color to a bright orange. (If you don't have 256 colors
   available, choose any color.) The Select Color dialog box will close.

4. With Windows still highlighted in the Layers Properties Manager dialog box, click the Current button to make the Windows layer current.
   Then click OK. You are returned to your drawing, and Windows is the
   current layer.

5. Start the Insert Block command (it's on the Draw toolbar). Open the
   Name drop-down list in the Insert dialog box. In the list of blocks,
   click win-1. Be sure all three Specify On-Screen check boxes are
   selected, and then click OK.

6. In your drawing, the 12" window block is attached to the cursor at the insertion point (see Figure 7.20). Note that it is still in the same horizontal orientation that it was in when you defined the block. To fit into the left wall, you will need to rotate it as you insert it.

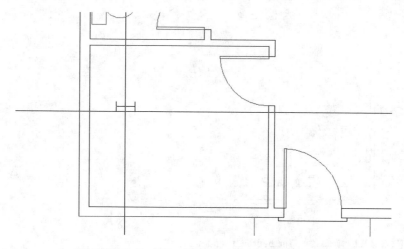

FIGURE 7.20: The win-1 block attached to the cursor

7. Move the cursor near the midpoint of the left inside wall line. When a colored triangle appears at the midpoint of that wall line, click.

8. You will be prompted for an X scale factor. This is a 4' window, so type 4↵. For the Y scale factor, type 1↵.

9. You are prompted for the rotation angle. The window block is now 4' wide and rotates with the movement of the cursor. Move the cursor so that it's directly to the right of the insertion point. The Polar tracking lines and tool tip appear (see Figure 7.21a). This will show you how the window will be positioned if the rotation stays at 0°. Obviously, you don't want this.

10. Move the cursor so that it is directly above the insertion point. Another tracking line and tool tip appear. This shows what position a 90° rotation will result in (see Figure 7.21b). The window fits nicely into the wall here.

11. With the tracking line and tool tip visible, click. The win-1 block is placed in the left wall. The Insert Block command ends (see Figure 7.21c).

> The Y scale factor will be 1 for all the win-1 blocks because all walls that have windows are 6" wide—the same width as the win-1 block.

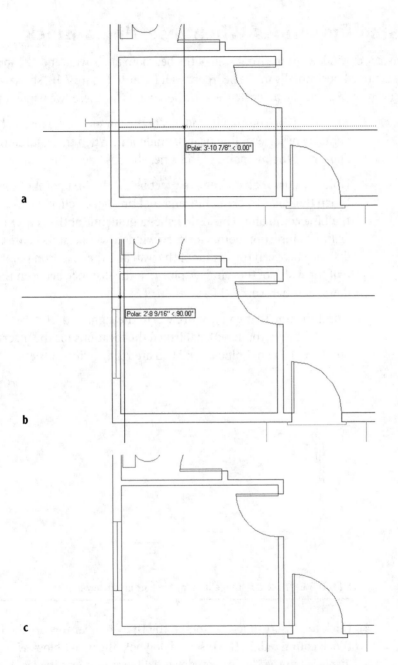

FIGURE 7.21: Rotating the win-1 block 0° (a), 90° (b), and the final position (c)

Using Guidelines When Inserting a Block

The pair of windows in the front wall of the bedroom are 3' wide and 12" apart and are centered horizontally in the bedroom wall (refer to Figure 7.19, shown earlier). You can use a guideline to locate the insertion points for these two windows.

1. Start the Line command, and locate the cursor on the inside, horizontal exterior wall line near its midpoint. When the colored triangle appears at the midpoint of this line, click. A line starts.

2. Hold the cursor at a point a few feet below the first point of the line. When the Polar tracking line and tool tip appear, click. Press ⏎ to end the Line command. This establishes a guideline at the center of the wall. The insertion points for each window will be at its center. The distance between the center of the wall and the insertion point will be half the width of the window, plus half the distance between the windows, in other words, 2 feet.

3. Offset the line that you just drew 2' to the right and left (see Figure 7.22). Now you have established the locations for the insertion points of the win-1 blocks, and you are ready to insert them.

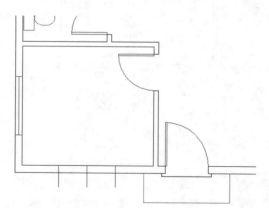

FIGURE 7.22: Guidelines for the pair of window blocks

4. Click the Insert Block button on the Draw toolbar to start the Insert Block command. In the Insert dialog box, the win-1 block will still be displayed in the Name drop-down list because it was the last block inserted. Click OK.

5. Back in the drawing, the win-1 block is again attached to the cursor. To locate the insertion point, you can choose the upper endpoint of one of the outer guidelines or the intersection of this guideline with

the exterior outside wall line. Which one would be better? The second choice requires no rotation of the block, so it's easier and faster to use that intersection.

6. Click the Intersection Osnap button on the Object Snap toolbar, and position the cursor on the outside wall without touching any other lines (see Figure 7.23a). A colored *x* appears with three dots to its right, along with a tool tip that says "Extended Intersection." Click.

Now hold the crosshair cursor on the lower portion of the leftmost offset guideline, again without touching any other lines. The *x* will appear, this time at the intersection of this guideline with the outside wall line, and without the three dots. The tool tip now says "Intersection" (see Figure 7.23b). Click again. The insertion point is set at the intersection of the guideline and the outside wall line.

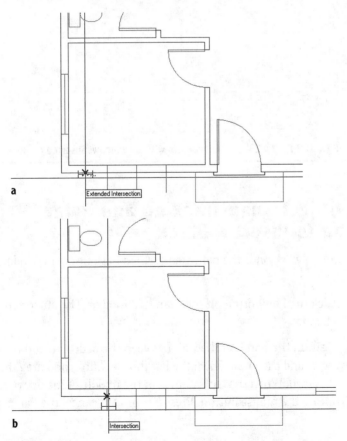

FIGURE 7.23: Selecting the first line (a) and the second (b)

7. Type 3↵ for the X scale factor, and then type 1↵ for the Y scale factor. At the rotation angle prompt, press ↵ to accept the default of 0°. The 3' window on the left is inserted in the front wall.

8. Repeat this procedure for the other 3' window.

9. Erase the three guidelines.

Because you chose to locate the insertion point on the lower of the two wall lines, the block needed no rotation. When finished, the bedroom will look like Figure 7.24.

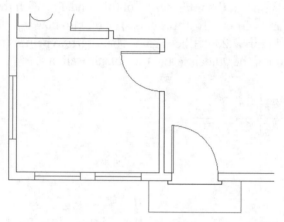

F I G U R E 7 . 2 4 : The bedroom with all windows inserted

Using Object Snap Tracking and Polar Tracking to Insert a Block

The next room to work on is the bathroom, which has one small window over the sink.

1. Click the Pan button on the Standard toolbar. The cursor changes to a hand.

2. Position the hand on the wall between the bedroom and the bath-room, and then hold down the left mouse button and drag the drawing down. When the bathroom is in the middle of the drawing area, release the mouse button. Press Esc or ↵ to cancel the Pan command.

LT users will not have the Otrack button on the status bar. Use the steps in the following "For LT Users" sidebars to achieve the same result.

You want to create one 2' window, centered over the sink. This time you'll insert the block without the use of guidelines. Be sure End-point and Midpoint Osnaps are running, and turn off Perpendicular Osnap. On the status bar, click the Otrack button to turn on Object Snap Tracking. Polar and Osnap should also be in the on position.

3. Start the Insert Block command. Be sure win-1 is in the Name drop-down list, and check that all Specify On-Screen check boxes are marked. Then click OK.

4. At the `Specify insertion point:` prompt, position the crosshair cursor near the midpoint of the line representing the front edge of the sink counter. When a colored triangle appears at the midpoint of that line, put the crosshair right on the triangle momentarily, with-out clicking. A small + will appear at the midpoint of the line (see Figure 7.25a). When it does, move the crosshair cursor up to the point where the right side of the shower meets the wall line. When the square box appears at the intersection, place the cursor on the box momentarily, again without clicking. Another + will appear there (see Figure 7.25b). You have set two temporary tracking points.

5. Move the cursor to the right, along the lower outside wall line, just in back of the sink. A horizontal tracking line appears and coincides with the wall line. When the crosshair reaches a point directly above the first tracking point, a vertical tracking line appears, and the tool tip identifies the intersection of the two tracking lines as `Endpoint: <0.00°, Midpoint: <90.00°` (see Figure 7.25c). When you see this tool tip, click. The insertion point has been placed on the inside wall line, centered over the sink.

6. At the X scale factor prompt, type 2⏎. Then, at the Y scale factor prompt, type 1⏎. Press ⏎ again to accept the default rotation angle of 0°. The 2' window is inserted into the wall behind the sink (see Fig-ure 7.26).

When Otrack is turned on and the + appears at the Object Snap symbol, a track-ing point has been *acquired*. It remains acquired until you place the cursor directly on the Object Snap symbol a sec-ond time or until that part of the command is over.

T I P When using Object Snap Tracking, you will inevitably acquire a tracking point that you don't need or want. To remove it, place the crosshair cursor on it momentarily. The tracking point will disappear.

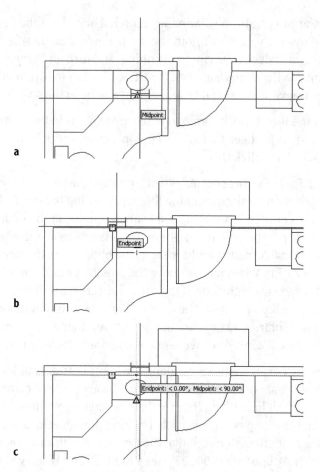

FIGURE 7.25: Setting a temporary tracking point (a), setting a second tracking point (b), and using the intersection of the two tracking lines to locate the insertion point (c)

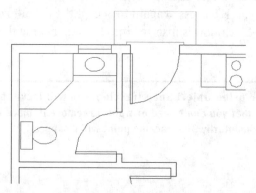

FIGURE 7.26: The 2' window after insertion

FOR LT USERS

LT users should follow these steps for the bathroom window:

1. Click the Pan button on the Standard toolbar. The cursor changes to a hand.

2. Position the hand on the wall between the bedroom and the bathroom, and then hold down the left mouse button and drag the drawing down. When the bathroom is in the middle of the drawing area, release the mouse button. Press Esc or ↵ to cancel the Pan command. You want to create one 2' window, centered over the sink. This time you'll insert the block without the use of guidelines. Endpoint and Midpoint Osnaps should be the only Osnaps set to be running. On the status bar, Polar and Osnap should be in the on position.

3. Start the Insert Block command. Be sure win-1 is in the Name drop-down list, and check that all Specify On-Screen check boxes are marked. Then click OK.

4. At the Specify insertion point: prompt, click the Tracking button at the top of the Object Snap toolbar, and then position the crosshair cursor near the midpoint of the line representing the front edge of the sink counter. When a colored triangle appears at the midpoint of that line, click.

5. Click the Perpendicular Osnap button on the Osnap toolbar, and then move the cursor up to the inside exterior wall line. When the Perpendicular Autosnap symbol appears, click. Now a line seems to begin on the wall line above the center of the sink. This is the location you want for the insertion point. Press ↵. The insertion point has been placed on the inside exterior wall line, centered over the sink.

6. At the X scale factor prompt, type **2**↵. Then, at the Y scale factor prompt, type **1**↵. Press ↵ again to accept the default rotation angle of 0°. The 2' window is inserted into the wall behind the sink (see Figure 7.26, shown earlier).

For LT users, this next series of steps duplicates the procedure used for the bathroom window. Apply the steps in the previous "For LT Users" sidebar to the kitchen window, using the midpoint of the lower edge of the sink and the upper-right corner of the stove as the points to click.

You're more than halfway done with the windows. Just three remain to be inserted: one in the kitchen and two in the living room. We'll use Object Snap Tracking again on the kitchen window.

1. Click the Pan button on the Standard toolbar. Then position the hand cursor on the back door swing. Hold down the left mouse button and drag the drawing over to the left until the kitchen is in the middle of the drawing area. Release the mouse button. Then press the Esc key or ↵ to cancel the Real Time Pan.

2. Zoom in to the sink area, leaving enough of the counter visible to see the line where the right edge of the counter meets the upper wall line.

3. You need to insert a 4' window in the back wall, centered behind the sink (see Figure 7.15, shown earlier). Start the Insert Block command to open the Insert dialog box, and then click OK. The win-1 block appears on the cursor.

4. At the Specify insertion point: prompt, move the cursor to the lower edge of the sink. When the midpoint triangle symbol appears, place the cursor directly on it until the + appears (see Figure 7.27a).

5. Move the cursor to the point where the right edge of the counter meets the wall line. When the Endpoint square symbol appears, place the cursor directly on the square until the + appears.

6. Move the cursor to the left, along the wall line. A tracking line will appear and coincide with the wall line. When the cursor reaches a point directly above the first tracking point, a vertical tracking line will appear and intersect the horizontal one, and the tool tip will read Midpoint: <90.00°, Endpoint: <180.00° (see Figure 7.27b). When this happens, click. The insertion point for the win-1 block has been established.

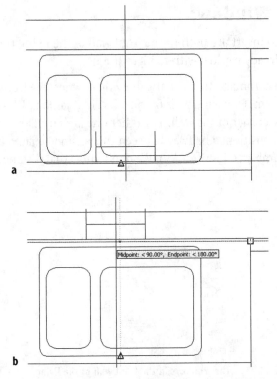

FIGURE 7.27: The first tracking point is established (a), and the intersection of the two tracking lines is the location of the insertion point (b)

7. Type 4↵ for the X scale factor. Then type 1↵ for the Y scale factor. For the rotation angle, press ↵ again to accept the default angle of 0°. The window is placed in the back wall, centered behind the sink.

8. Zoom Previous (see Figure 7.28).

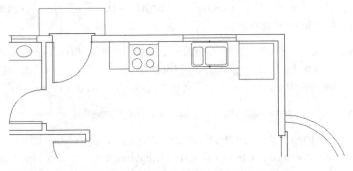

FIGURE 7.28: The inserted window behind the sink

Finishing the Windows

The last two windows to insert are both in the front wall of the living room. You will use skills you've already worked with to place them.

1. Use the Pan command to move the drawing down to the front wall of the living room. One window is 6' wide. Its right jamb is 12" to the left of the inside corner of the wall. The other one is a circular window, 2' in diameter, positioned halfway between the 6' window jamb and the front doorjamb (see Figure 7.29). We don't know that distance yet.

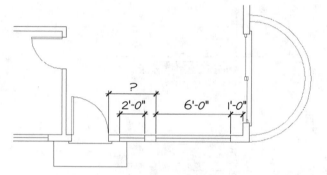

FIGURE 7.29: The windows in the front wall of the living room

2. Set the Osnaps so that only Endpoint is running. (To review how to do this, go back to the section in which you created the win-1 block.) Start the Insert Block command, and click OK in the Insert dialog box to select the win-1 block.

To turn Osnaps off, right-click Osnap in the status bar, choose Settings from the shortcut menu, uncheck any Osnaps that you want disabled, and then click OK.

3. Click the Temporary Tracking Point Osnap button. Then, with Endpoint Osnap running, pick the lower-right inside corner of the cabin. The insertion point will be positioned to the left of this corner at a distance of 12" in plus half the width of the 6' window, in other words, 4' from the corner.

4. Hold the crosshair cursor directly to the left of the point just picked. When the tracking path and tool tip appear, type 4'↵. This sets the insertion point 4' to the left of the corner, on the inside wall line.

5. For the scale factors, type 6↵, and then type 1↵.

6. For the rotation angle, hold the cursor directly to the right of the insertion point to see the position of the window at 0° rotation. Then hold the cursor directly above the insertion point to see how a 90° rotation

would look. Finally, hold the cursor directly to the left for a view of the effect of a 180° rotation. The 180° view is the one you want.

7. Type 180↵. The 6' window is placed in the front wall.

Finally, you need to locate the 2' circular window halfway between the left jamb of the 6' window and the right jamb of the front door opening. Use the Distance command to find out the distance between the two jambs. Then offset one of the jambs half that distance to establish the location of the insertion point on the wall lines. Of the two jamb lines, you must offset the doorjamb because the window jamb is part of the window block and can't be offset.

1. Type **di**↵ to start the Distance command. With Endpoint Osnap running, pick the upper end of the front doorjamb, and then pick the upper end of the left window jamb. In the Command window, the distance is displayed as 3'-10". You need to offset the doorjamb half that distance to locate the insertion point for the 2' window.

2. Start the Offset command, and then type 1'-11↵ to set the offset distance.

3. Pick the doorjamb and type **non**↵. Then pick a point to the right of the doorjamb. Press ↵ to end the Offset command.

4. Start the Insert Block command. Click OK to accept the win-1 block. Pick the bottom endpoint of the offset jamb line to establish the insertion point.

5. Type 2↵ for the X scale factor. Type 1↵ for the Y scale factor.

6. For the rotation angle, press ↵ to accept the default of 0°. The last window is inserted in the front wall, and the Insert Block command ends. Erase the offset jamb line (see Figure 7.30).

Typing non.↵ (none) cancels any running Osnaps for one pick.

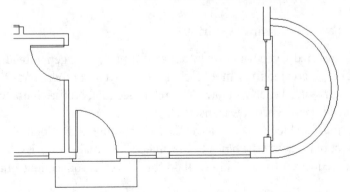

FIGURE 7.30: The two windows inserted in the front wall of the living room

**Zooming To Extents is
one of the zoom
options and is the
bottom button of the
Zoom flyout on the
Standard toolbar.**

7. Type z↵ e↵ to zoom out to the Extents view of the drawing. This changes the view to include all the visible lines. The view fills the drawing area.

8. Type z↵ .85x↵ to zoom out a little from the Extents view, so all objects are set in slightly from the edge of the drawing area (see Figure 7.31).

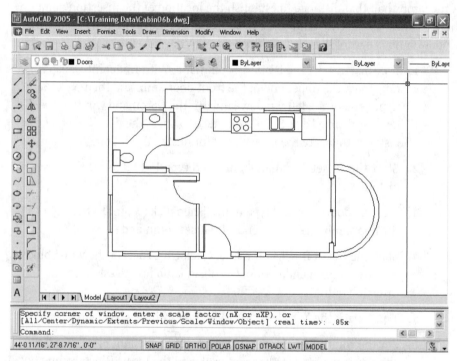

FIGURE 7.31: Zooming to .85x after zooming to Extents

9. Save this drawing as Cabin07a.

You have inserted seven windows into the floor plan, each generated from the win-1 block. You created the win-1 block on the 0 layer and then made the Windows layer current, so each window block reference took on the characteristics of the Windows layer when it was inserted.

You can ungroup blocks by using the Explode command. Exploding a block has the effect of reducing the block to the objects that make it up. Exploding the win-1 block reduces it to three lines, all on the 0 layer. If you explode one of the door blocks, it is reduced to a rectangle and an arc, with both objects on the Doors layer because these components of the door block were on the Doors layer when the block was defined.

Revising a Block

If you need to revise a block that has already been inserted in the drawing several times, explode one of these blocks and then modify it. You will need to choose a block whose parameters—the X and Y scale factors and the rotation—were all at the default values: 1 for the scale factors and 0 for the rotation. You inserted all the windows using different X and Y scale factors, so to revise the win-1 block, you'll need to insert that block one more time, this time using default scale factors and rotation. You can then make changes to the objects that make up the win-1 block reference. When finished with the changes, you can save the changes to the block definition. This redefines the block and updates all associated block references.

Let's say that the client who's building the cabin finds out that double glazing is required in all windows. You want the windows to show two lines for the glass. You can't make such a change in each window block because blocks can't be modified in this way, and you don't want to have to change seven windows separately. If you revise the win-1 block definition, the changes you make in one block reference will be made in all seven windows.

N O T E   Using standard commands, you can move, rotate, copy, erase, scale, and explode blocks. They can't be trimmed, extended, offset, or filleted, and you can't erase or move part of a block. All objects in a block are grouped together and behave as if they were one object.

1. Start the Insert Block command and click OK to accept the win-1 block to be inserted.

2. Pick a point in the middle of the living room. This establishes the insertion point location.

3. Press ↵ three times to accept the defaults for X and Y scale factors and the rotation angle. The win-1 block is inserted in the living room (see Figure 7.32).

LT users, you will use a slightly different procedure to achieve the same results. Follow the steps in the "Revising a Block with LT" sidebar.

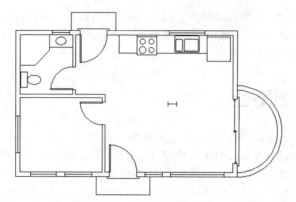

FIGURE 7.32: The win-1 block inserted into the living room

4. Choose Modify ➤ Xref And Block Editing ➤ Edit Reference In-Place.

5. Select the new block reference in the middle of the living room to open the Reference Edit dialog box. The win-1 block is identified, and a preview is displayed.

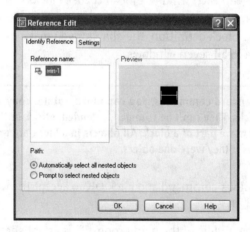

6. Click OK. In the drawing, the window block that you just inserted is now white (or black), the rest of the windows have disappeared, the other objects in the drawing have faded slightly, and the Refedit toolbar appears.

7. Zoom in to a closer view of the window you just inserted.

8. Use the Offset command to offset the glazing line 0.5" up and down. Then erase the original horizontal line (see Figure 7.33). This window block now has double glazing.

FIGURE 7.33: The result of the modifications to the win-1 block

9. On the right side of the Refedit toolbar, click the rightmost button, whose tool tip says "Save back changes to reference."

10. An AutoCAD warning window appears. Click OK. The window block changes back to orange, and the Refedit toolbar closes. The block definition has been revised.

11. Erase this block reference; we don't need it anymore.

12. Zoom Previous to view the entire drawing. All windows in the cabin now have double glazing.

13. Zoom in to a closer look at the bedroom in order to view some of the modified window block references (see Figure 7.34).

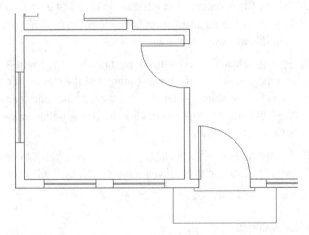

FIGURE 7.34: Zooming in to see the revised window blocks with double glazing

14. Zoom Previous to a view of the entire floor plan. Save this drawing as Cabin07b.

REVISING A BLOCK WITH LT

LT users should follow these steps to revise a block:

1. Start the Insert Block command, and click OK to accept the win-1 block to be inserted.

2. Pick a point in the middle of the living room. This establishes the insertion point location.

3. Press ↵ three times to accept the defaults for X and Y scale factors and the rotation angle. The win-1 block is inserted in the living room (see Figure 7.32, shown earlier).

4. Zoom in to a closer view of this window. Start the Line command. On the Object Snap toolbar, click the Snap To Insert button. (This button has a yellow rectangle and a circle.) Put the cursor anywhere in the window and click. A line is started from the insertion point of the block.

5. Pick another point a foot or so below the insertion point, and then end the Line command. This creates a marker for the insertion point. We will use it shortly.

6. Click the Explode button at the bottom of the Modify toolbar. Select the new block reference and press ↵. This de-blocks the window. It is now just three lines.

7. Use the Offset command to offset the glazing line 0.5" up and down. Then erase the original horizontal line (see Figure 7.33, shown earlier). This window now has double glazing.

8. Start the Make Block command. For the name, type **win-1**. For the insertion point, pick the upper endpoint of the marker line you just drew. For the objects, select the two glazing lines and the two jamb lines, but not the marker line. Click the Delete option in the Objects area, and then click OK.

9. A warning box will appear to tell you that a block by this name already exists and to ask if you want to redefine it. Click Yes.

10. Erase the marker line.

Continue with step 12.

Sharing Information between Drawings

You can transfer most of the information in a drawing to another drawing. You can do so in several ways, depending on the kind of information that needs to be transferred. You can drag blocks and lines from one open drawing to another when both drawings are visible on the screen. You can copy layers, blocks, and other *named objects* from a closed drawing into an open one using the DesignCenter. I'll demonstrate these two features—and touch on three others—as I finish this chapter.

Dragging and Dropping between Two Open Drawings

In AutoCAD, several drawings can be open at the same time, just like a word processing program. You can control which one is visible, or you can tile two or more to be visible simultaneously. When more than one drawing is visible, you can drag objects from one drawing to another.

1. With Cabin07b as the current drawing, click the QNew button on the Standard toolbar. If the Select Template dialog box opens, click the arrow next to the Open button, and then click the Open With No Template - Imperial option. If the Create New Drawing dialog box opens, be sure the Start From Scratch option is selected and click OK. These actions open a blank drawing.

2. Choose Window ➤ Tile Vertically. The new drawing (called Drawing1) appears alongside Cabin07b (see Figure 7.35).

Named objects are, quite simply, AutoCAD objects with names, such as blocks and layers. Lines, circles, and arcs don't have individual names, so they are not named objects.

Like most Windows-based programs, AutoCAD 2005 can have multiple drawing files open in a session. When you open the Window menu, the bottom of the menu contains a list of AutoCAD files currently open. Click the file that you want to be active.

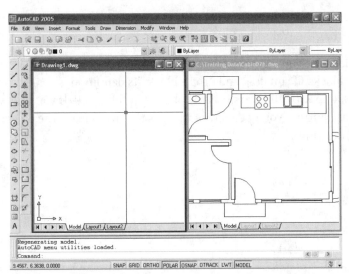

FIGURE 7.35: The user interface with two drawings tiled

Each drawing has a title bar, but only one drawing can be active at a time. At this time, Drawing1 should be active. If it is, its title bar will be dark blue or some other color, and the Cabin07b title bar will be grayed out. If your Cabin07b drawing is active instead, click once in Drawing1.

3. Choose Format ➤ Units. In the Drawing Units dialog box, change the type of units in the Length area to Architectural, and then click OK.

4. Click the Cabin07b drawing to make it the active drawing.

5. Zoom to Extents, and then use Realtime Zoom to zoom out a little.

6. Use the Layer Control drop-down list to turn off the Doors, Fixtures, Steps, and Windows layers and to make the Walls layer current. The walls and balcony should be the only lines visible.

7. Form a selection window to surround the cabin with its balcony. Grips will appear on all lines.

8. Place the cursor on one of the wall lines at a point where there are no grips, and then click and hold down the left mouse button. Drag the cursor across the drawing to the center of Drawing1, and then release the mouse button. Drawing1 is now active and contains the lines for the walls and balcony.

9. Zoom to Extents in Drawing1, use Realtime Zoom to zoom out a little, and then type ucsicon↵ off↵ (see Figure 7.36).

10. Open the Layer Control drop-down list and note that Drawing1 now has the Walls and Balcony layers.

In this fashion, you can drag any visible objects from one drawing into another, including blocks. If you drag and drop a block, its definition is copied to the new drawing, along with all layers used by objects in the block. If you drag with the right mouse button, you get a few options as to how to place the objects in the receiving drawing.

```
Copy Here
Paste as Block
Paste to Orig Coords
Cancel
```

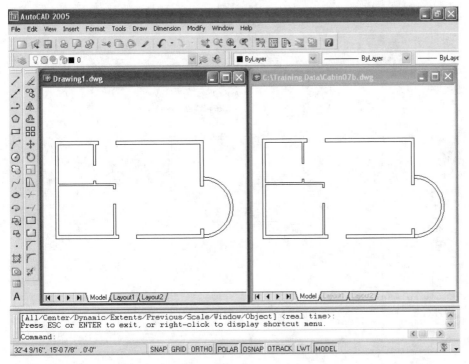

FIGURE 7.36: The result after dragging lines from one drawing to another

If you don't choose to have both open drawings visible at the same time, you can always use the Copy and Paste tools available in most Windows-based programs. Here's the general procedure:

1. Click the Maximize icon in the upper-right corner of the new drawing. The new drawing will fill the screen.

2. Click Window in the drop-down menu bar. When the menu opens, notice at the bottom that the open drawings are displayed with the active one checked (see Figure 7.37).

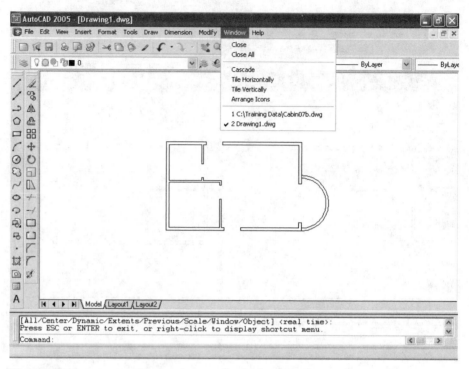

FIGURE 7.37: The Window menu with Drawing1 active

3. Click the Cabin07b drawing. It replaces the new drawing as the active drawing and fills the screen. Turn back on the layers that you turned off previously. Leave the Headers and Roof layers frozen.

4. Select the fixtures in the kitchen and bath from this drawing, using the selection tools you have learned, and then right-click and choose Copy With Base Point from the shortcut menu. You will be prompted to specify a base point in the Cabin07b drawing. Click the upper-left corner of the building with Endpoint Osnap. Click Esc to turn off the Grips.

5. Click Window in the drop-down menu bar. When the menu opens, click Drawing1 to make it active.

6. Click the Paste button on the Standard toolbar. Pick the upper-left corner of the building with Endpoint Osnap. The fixtures will be accurately positioned in the new drawing. If you check the layers, you will see that the new drawing now has a Fixtures layer, in addition to the Walls and Balcony layers.

Using AutoCAD's DesignCenter

DesignCenter is a tool for copying named objects (blocks, layers, text styles, and so on) to an opened drawing from an unopened one. You cannot copy lines, circles, and other unnamed objects unless they are part of a block. You'll see how this works by bringing some layers and a block into Drawing1 from Cabin07b.

1. Close Cabin07b. Do not save changes. Maximize the window for Drawing1 if it is not already maximized.

2. Click the DesignCenter button on the Standard toolbar. It's just to the right of the Properties button. The DesignCenter appears on the drawing area. It can be docked, floating, or, if floating, hidden (see Figure 7.38). Your screen may not look exactly like the samples shown here. The tree diagram of file folders on the left half may or may not be visible. Your DesignCenter may be wider or narrower.

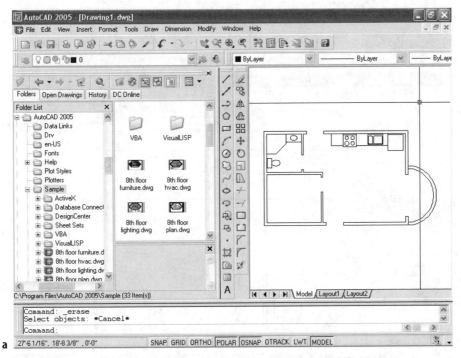

FIGURE 7.38: The DesignCenter docked (a), floating (b), and hidden (c)

continues

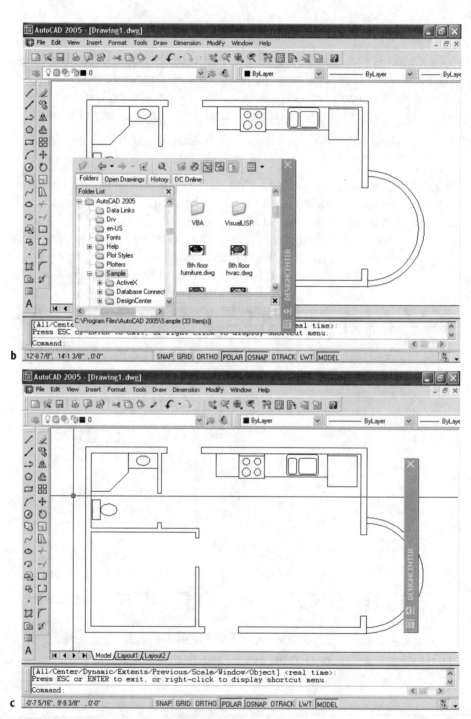

FIGURE 7.38 *continued:* The DesignCenter docked (a), floating (b), and hidden (c)

3. Click the Tree View Toggle at the top of the DesignCenter (the fourth button from the right) a few times to close and open the file folder tree diagram. You can resize the DesignCenter horizontally (and vertically as well, if it is floating), and you can resize the subpanels inside. If Auto-Hide is on, the Design Center hides behind the title bar until you put your cursor on it. Leave the tree view open.

4. On the left half of the DesignCenter window, use the same procedure you use in Windows Explorer to navigate to your Training Data folder.

5. When you find it, click the + symbol to the left of the Training Data folder to open it. Now the left side displays a list of your drawings in the Training Data folder. Highlight Cabin07b, and the right side shows the types of objects in Cabin07b that are available to be copied into the current drawing—in this case, Drawing1 (see Figure 7.39a).

6. On the left side once again, click the + symbol to the left of Cabin07b. The list of named objects that are on the right panel now appears below Cabin7b in the tree view on the left. Click the Layers icon on the left side. The list of layers in Cabin7b appears in the panel on the right (Figure 7.39b).

> To hide Design Center behind its title bar, right click its title bar and click Auto-Hide.

a
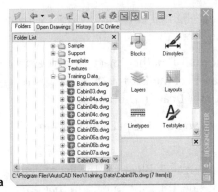

b
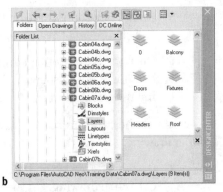

FIGURE 7.39: The DesignCenter displaying the files in the Training Data folder on the left and accessible objects on the right (a), and types of accessible objects on the left (b)

7. Click the Views button above the right window of the DesignCenter (the button on the far right). Choose List in the menu that opens. This changes the view of layers displayed into that of a list.

8. Use the Shift+ and Ctrl+ keys to help you select all the layers except 0, Balcony, Fixtures, and Walls (see Figure 7.40).

FIGURE 7.40: The DesignCenter with layers to grab highlighted

9. Right-click somewhere on the highlighted layers in the right window, and choose Add Layers from the shortcut menu.

10. Open the Layer Control drop-down list on the Object Properties toolbar. It will now display all the layers of the Cabin07b drawing, including those you just transferred to the Drawing1 drawing.

Now let's see how this process works when you want to get a block from another drawing.

1. On the left side of the DesignCenter, click Blocks in the list under the Cabin07b drawing. On the right side, the list of blocks in that drawing is displayed (see Figure 7.41a).

2. Click the Preview button at the top of the DesignCenter, and then click door3_0 in the right panel. A picture of the block is displayed in the lower-right corner of the DesignCenter (see Figure 7.41b). You can resize the preview picture window.

> If you prefer dragging and dropping, click and hold the left mouse button, drag the cursor onto the drawing, and then release.

> The next two figures show DesignCenter in floating mode, with its title bar on the right. Yours may be docked, or it may have its title bar on the left. These variations aren't significant.

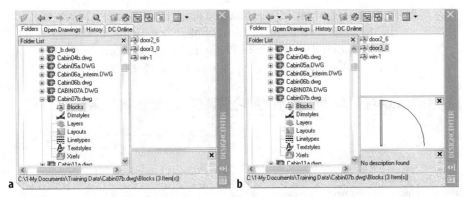

FIGURE 7.41: The DesignCenter with Blocks selected (a), and with the door3_0 block selected and Preview on (b)

3. Open the Layer Control list and make Doors the current layer.

4. Dock DesignCenter on the left side of the drawing area if it's not already there, and then zoom in to the front door area of the drawing (see Figure 7.42). Endpoint Osnap needs to be running.

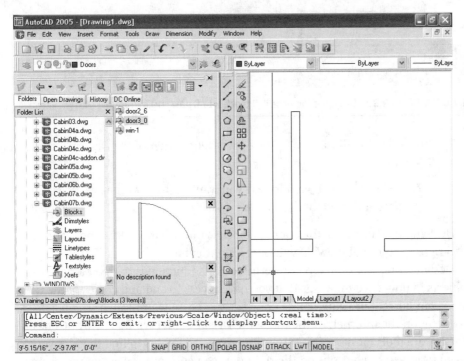

FIGURE 7.42: Zoomed in to the front door area with the DesignCenter docked

5. In the DesignCenter, left-click and drag door3_0 from the list over to the drawing. As the cursor comes onto the drawing, the door3_0 block appears. Use Endpoint Osnap to locate the block at the opening, as you did earlier in this chapter (see Figure 7.43).

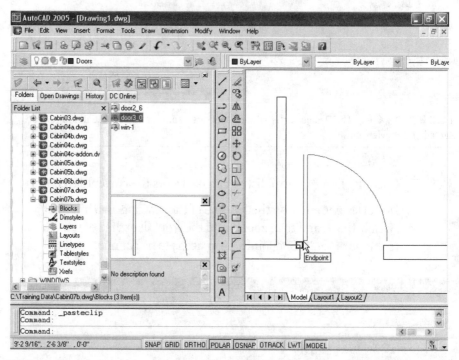

FIGURE 7.43: Dragging the door3_0 block into Drawing1 from the DesignCenter

6. Click the Close icon in the upper-right corner of the DesignCenter to close it.

7. Keep Drawing1 open in case you want to use it in the practice exercises at the end of this chapter. Otherwise, close it without saving it.

By doing this insertion, the door3_0 block is now a part of Drawing1, and you can reinsert it in that drawing without DesignCenter.

DesignCenter is a simple yet powerful tool. Its function is to find named objects in unopened drawings that you have access to and pull copies of them into your current drawing. These drawings can be on your hard drive, on a network, or on the Internet. At the top of the DesignCenter window, the buttons on the left are tools for navigating through drives and folders to find the files you need to access; the buttons on the right give you options for viewing the named objects in the window.

DesignCenter Options

Here's a brief description of the functions of the DesignCenter buttons, from left to right:

Load   Opens the Load dialog box, which you use to navigate to the drive, folder, or file from which you want to borrow named AutoCAD objects.

Left Arrow   Moves you one step back in your navigation procedure.

Right Arrow   Moves you one step forward in the navigation procedure that you have been using.

Up   Moves up one level in the folder/file/named objects tree.

Search   Opens a Search dialog box in which you can search for a file.

Favorites   Displays a list of files and folders that you have previously set up.

House Icon   Navigates to the DesignCenter folder in the AutoCAD program. This folder has subfolders of sample files that contain libraries of blocks and other named objects to import through DesignCenter.

Tree View Toggle   Opens or shuts the left panel that displays the logical tree of folders, files, and unnamed objects.

Preview   Opens a preview window at the bottom of the right palette window. When you highlight a drawing or block in the palette window, a preview is displayed. You can resize the preview window.

Description   Enables a previously written description of a block or drawing to be displayed. You can resize the description window.

Views   Controls how the items in the palette window are displayed. There are four choices. Clicking this button toggles from one type of view to another. Clicking the arrow to the right displays the list of four options.

Other Ways to Share Information between Drawings

You can transfer information between drawings in several other ways. We'll look at three of them. First, you can use the Wblock command to take a portion of a drawing and create a new drawing file from the selected objects. Second, you can insert any .dwg drawing file into any other drawing file. Finally, you can create *palettes* of blocks that can be accessed for any drawing.

Using the Wblock Command

To perform a Wblock operation, you create a new file and then tell AutoCAD which elements of the current drawing you want in the new file. Let's say you want to create a new .dwg file for the bathroom of the cabin. Here are the steps:

1. With Cabin07b as the current drawing, type w↵ to open the Write Block dialog box (see Figure 7.44).

FIGURE 7.44: The Write Block dialog box

2. At the top, under Source, click the Objects radio button.

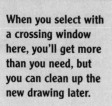

When you select with a crossing window here, you'll get more than you need, but you can clean up the new drawing later.

3. In the middle portion, the Base Point and Objects areas are similar to those for creating a block. For the Base Point, the default is 0,0. Click the Pick Point button, and in the drawing, pick a point just below and to the left of the area to be captured. For the Objects, click Select Objects, and use a crossing window to select everything near the part of the drawing you want. Click the Retain radio button in this area so that the selected material is not deleted from the current drawing.

4. In the Destination area, enter a filename for the new drawing, and choose a folder in which to save it.

5. In the Insert Units drop-down list, select Inches, in case the new drawing is used in a drawing that has units other than Architectural.

6. Click OK. The command ends, and the selected material is now a new drawing file located in the folder that you specified.

You can use the Wblock command in three ways. They are shown as radio buttons at the top of the Write Block dialog box. Here's a brief description of each.

Block   To make a drawing file out of a block that's defined in the current drawing, select the name of the block from the drop-down list at the top, and then follow the procedure in steps 4 through 6 in the previous exercise. When this procedure is followed, the objects in the new drawing are no longer in a block. Wblocking a block has the effect of unblocking it.

Entire Drawing   Click this button to *purge* a drawing of unwanted objects such as layers that have no objects on them and block definitions that have no references in the drawing. You are not prompted to select anything except the information called for in the previous steps 4 through 6. You can keep the same drawing name or type a new one. A preferable way to accomplish the same thing is to use the Purge command. Type **purge**↵ to open the Purge dialog box and select what to purge.

Objects   You select which objects to use to create a new file, as in the previous steps 1 through 6.

Inserting a Drawing into a Drawing

When you insert a drawing into another drawing, it comes in as a block. You use the same Insert Block command that you use to insert blocks, in a slightly different way. For example, say you have Wblocked a portion of Cabin07b.dwg and made a new file called Bath.dwg (see the previous section). Now you want to insert Bath.dwg into DrawingC.dwg. Use this procedure:

1. Make DrawingC current.

2. Start the Insert Block command.

3. In the Insert dialog box, click the Browse button, and then navigate to the folder containing Bath.dwg.

4. Open that folder, highlight Bath.dwg, and then click Open to return to the Insert dialog box. The drawing file that you selected is now displayed in the Name drop-down list. At this point, a copy of Bath.dwg has been converted to a block definition in DrawingC.

5. Set the insertion parameters, and then click OK.

6. Finish the insertion procedure as if you were inserting a block.

You transfer blocks between drawings by dragging and dropping or by using DesignCenter. You can also convert them into .dwg files by using the Wblock command, and you can insert them back into other .dwg files as blocks by using the Insert Block command. They become unblocked when they leave the drawing and reblocked when they enter another drawing.

A Look at AutoCAD's Palettes

AutoCAD provides a tool called *palettes* to make blocks and other features immediately accessible for any drawing. Let's take a brief look at the sample palettes that come with AutoCAD and see how to manage them on the screen.

1. Open the Cabin07b drawing, and Zoom it to Extents. Then use Realtime Zoom to zoom out a little.

2. If palettes are not already visible in the drawing area, choose Tools ➢ Tool Palettes Window to display the palettes (see Figure 7.45). They can be docked on either side of the drawing area, and the navigation bar can be on the left or right side.

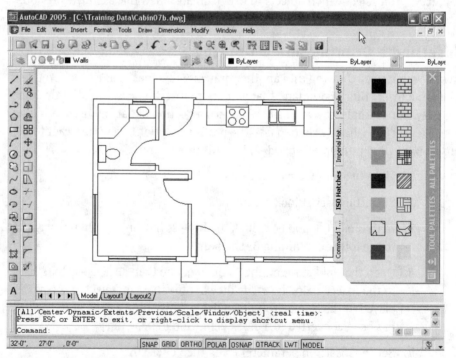

FIGURE 7.45: The palettes displayed on the screen

Your palettes may appear different from those shown in a couple of ways. The ones shown here are positioned on the right side but not docked there. Yours may be transparent, showing your drawing beneath it, or your palettes may be hidden and show only the title bar. In Figure 7.45, four tabs are on the left side, indicating the available palettes. On the right side is the palette title bar with control icons at the top and bottom.

On the palette itself is its content. The hatch sample palettes have hatch patterns and fills (to be discussed in Chapter 9), the Sample Office Project palette contains fills and furniture blocks, and the Command Tools palette has commands that have been copied from the various AutoCAD toolbars.

3. Click the Sample Office Project tab to display its content on the palette (see Figure 7.46).

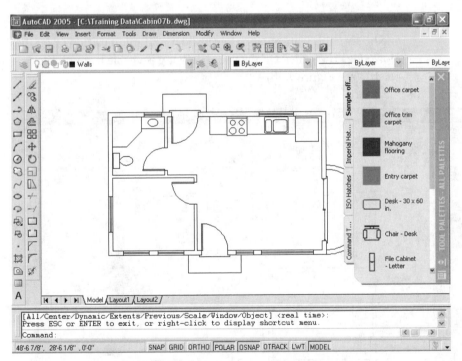

FIGURE 7.46: The palette for the Sample Office Project

Notice the scroll bar next to the title bar. This appears when there is more content than the palette can show. The palettes will eclipse part of the right side of the drawing. If you make the palettes transparent, you will be able to see the drawing underneath them.

4. Move the cursor to the title bar. Right-click and choose Transparency from the shortcut menu to open the Transparency dialog box (see Figure 7.47). Here you can toggle transparency on and off and adjust the degree of transparency for the palette.

FIGURE 7.47: The Transparency dialog box

5. Be sure the Turn Off Window Transparency check box is unchecked, and be sure the Transparency Level slider is at mid-position or on the More side. Then click OK. Now the drawing is visible through the palette (see Figure 7.48).

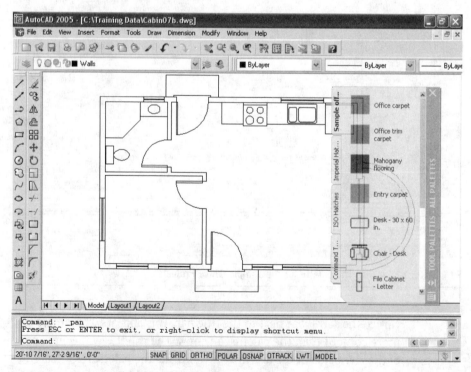

FIGURE 7.48: The palettes in transparent mode

6. Put the cursor back on the palette's title bar. Right-click and choose Transparency from the shortcut menu to open the Transparency dialog box again. Click the Turn Off Transparency check box, and then click OK.

7. Right-click the palette's title bar, and choose Auto-Hide from the shortcut menu. When the menu closes, move the cursor off the palettes. The palettes disappear except for the title bar (see Figure 7.49). When you move the cursor back onto the title bar, the palettes reappear—a handy feature.

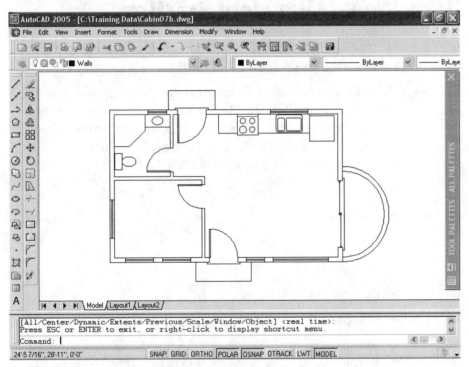

FIGURE 7.49: The palette title bar with Auto-Hide on

With both Transparency and Auto-Hide active, the palettes are less intrusive and take up less screen area, but remain easily accessible. In Chapter 9, you'll learn more about palettes and their properties and how to set up new palettes and change existing ones.

T I P   When they are in floating mode, the Properties palette and Design-Center also have the Auto-Hide option, but not the Transparency feature.

This chapter has outlined the procedure for setting up and using blocks, the Wblock command, and AutoCAD's DesignCenter. Blocks follow a set of complex rules, some of which are beyond the scope of this book. For a more in-depth discussion on blocks, see *Mastering AutoCAD 2005 and AutoCAD LT 2005* by George Omura (Sybex, 2004).

If You Would Like More Practice...

Here are some suggestions that will give you some practice in working with blocks, drag-and-drop procedures, and DesignCenter:

- ► Make blocks out of any of the fixtures in the bathroom or kitchen. Try to decide on the best location to use for the insertion point of each fixture. Then insert them back into the Cabin07b drawing in their original locations. Create them on the 0 layer, and then insert them on the Fixtures layer. Here's a list of the fixtures:

  - ► Shower

  - ► Bath sink

  - ► Toilet

  - ► Oven/range

  - ► Kitchen sink

  - ► Refrigerator

- ► At the end of Chapter 5, I suggested creating pieces of furniture for the kitchen, living room, and bedroom of the cabin. If you did that, it will be good practice to make blocks out of those pieces and insert them into the cabin floor plan. If you did not do that exercise, you could do that now and then convert the pieces of furniture into blocks.

- ► Drag some of the blocks on the Sample Office Palette into the Cabin07b drawing and experiment with ways in which the cabin might be set up as a small office.

▶ If you work in a profession or trade not directly concerned with architecture or construction, develop a few blocks that you can use in your own work.

  ▶ Electrical diagrams are made up many simple symbols, each of which can be a block.

  ▶ Cams and gears—or gear teeth—and other engine parts that have been made into blocks can be assembled into a mechanical drawing.

  ▶ Plumbing diagrams, like electrical ones, use a variety of symbols repetitively—valves, meters, pumps, joints. These can easily be made into blocks and then reassembled into the diagram.

In each of these examples, choosing the most useful location for the insertion point will determine whether the block that you create will be a handy tool or a big frustration.

Are You Experienced?

Now you can...

☑ **create blocks out of existing objects in your drawing**

☑ **insert blocks into your drawing**

☑ **vary the size and rotation of blocks as they are inserted**

☑ **detect blocks in a drawing**

☑ **use point filters to locate an insertion point**

☑ **revise a block**

☑ **drag and drop objects from one drawing to another**

☑ **use AutoCAD's DesignCenter**

☑ **use the Wblock command**

☑ **open palettes and control their appearance**

CHAPTER 8

Generating Elevations

- ▶ Drawing an exterior elevation from a floor plan
- ▶ Using grips to copy objects
- ▶ Setting up, naming, and saving a User Coordinate System and a new view
- ▶ Transferring height lines from one elevation to another
- ▶ Moving and rotating elevations

Now that you have created all the building components that will be in the floor plan, it's a good time to draw the exterior elevations. *Elevations* are horizontal views of the building, seen as if you were standing facing the building instead of looking down at it, as you do in the floor plan. An elevation view shows you how windows and doors fit into the walls and gives you an idea of how the building will look from the outside. In most architectural design projects, the drawings include at least four exterior elevations: front, back, and one from each side.

I'll go over how to create the front elevation first. Then I'll discuss some of the considerations necessary to complete the other elevations, and you'll have an opportunity to draw these on your own. Finally, we will look at how interior elevations are set up. They are similar to exterior elevations, but are usually of individual walls on the inside of a building to show how objects, such as doors, windows, cabinets, shelves, and finishes, will be placed on the walls.

In mechanical drawing, the item being drawn is often a machine part, or a gadget. The drafter uses orthographic projection to illustrate various views of the object and call them—instead of elevations and plans—front view, top view, side view, and so on. An exercise at the end of this chapter will give you practice with orthographic projection, but the procedure will be the same, whether you are drawing buildings or mechanical objects.

> *Orthographic projection* is a method for illustrating an object in views set at right angles to each other—hence, front, top, side, back, and so on.

Drawing the Front Elevation

You draw the front elevation using techniques similar to those used on a traditional drafting board. You will draw the front elevation view of the cabin directly below the floor plan by dropping lines down from key points on the floor plan and intersecting them with horizontal lines representing the heights of the corresponding components in the elevation. Those heights are shown in Figure 8.1.

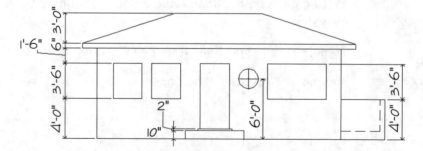

FIGURE 8.1: The front elevation with heights of components

1. Open Cabin07b.

2. Create a new layer called F-elev. Assign it color 42 and make it current. Here's a summary of the steps to do this:

   A. Click the Layer Properties Manager button, and then click New.

   B. Type **F-elev** and press ↵.

   C. Click the colored square for the F-elev layer. Type 42↵.

   D. Click the Set Current icon, and then click OK.

3. Use the Layer Control drop-down list to thaw the Roof and Headers layers. (They were frozen at the beginning of Chapter 7. We want the roof and headers to be visible again.) Then offset the bottom horizontal roofline 24' down. The offset line will be off the screen.

4. Click the Zoom Extents button on the Zoom flyout toolbar.

5. Use Realtime Zoom to zoom out just enough to bring the offset roofline up off the bottom edge of the drawing area.

6. Erase this offset line. Your drawing should look like Figure 8.2.

Objects on layers that are "frozen" are invisible. To make them visible again "thaw" their layers by clicking the layers' darkened sun icons on the Layer Control drop-down list.

FIGURE 8.2: The floor plan with space below it for the front elevation

Setting Up Lines for the Heights

You need to establish a base line to represent the ground. Then you can offset the other height lines from the base line or from other height lines.

1. Check the status bar to make sure that Polar, Osnap, and Model are in the on position while the other buttons are off. Draw a horizontal ground line across the bottom of the screen using the Line command. Make sure the line extends on the left to a few feet beyond a point directly below the outside edge of the roof, and on the right to a few feet beyond a point directly below the right edge of the balcony (see Figure 8.3).

FIGURE 8.3: The floor plan with the ground line

2. Offset the ground line 10" up to mark the height of the step. Then offset this new line 2" up to mark the top of the threshold.

3. Move back to the ground line and offset it 4' up to mark the top of the balcony wall and the bottom of the windows.

4. Offset the bottom line for the windows 3'-6" up to mark the top of the door and windows.

5. Offset the top line for the windows and door 1'-6" up to mark the soffit of the roof.

6. Offset the soffit line 6" up to mark the lower edge of the roof's top surface.

7. Offset this lower edge of the roof's top surface 3' up to mark the roof's ridge (see Figure 8.4).

8. Press ↵ to end the Offset command.

A *soffit* is the underside of the roof overhang that extends from the outside edge of the roof back to the wall.

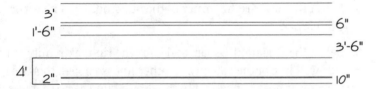

FIGURE 8.4: The horizontal height lines for the elevation in place

Each of these lines represents the height of one or more components of the cabin. Now you will drop lines down from the points in the floor plan that coincide with components that will be visible in the front elevation. The front elevation will consist of the balcony, front step, front door and windows, the front corners of the exterior walls, and parts of the roof.

Using Grips to Copy Lines

In the following steps, you will use grips to copy the dropped lines.

The Stretch command is a modifying tool that you use to lengthen or shorten lines and other objects. You'll have a chance to use it in Chapter 9.

Each of the commands that work with grips has a Copy option, which keeps the original object as is while you modify the copy. You can copy with grips in several ways that are not possible with the regular Copy command.

1. Start a line from the lower-left corner of the walls of the building. Select Perpendicular Osnap and click the ground line. Press ↵ to end the Line command (see Figure 8.5a).

2. At the Command: prompt, select the line you just drew. Small squares appear on the line's midpoint and endpoints (see Figure 8.5b). These are grips.

3. Click the grip on the upper endpoint. The grip changes color, and the prompt changes to Specify stretch point or [Base point/Copy/ Undo/eXit]:. This is the Stretch command, which is activated by grips. Any time you activate a grip, the Stretch command automatically starts.

4. Right-click, and choose Move from the shortcut menu. Right-click again, and choose Copy from the shortcut menu. This selects the Copy option. You'll use the Move command with its Copy option to copy the line that you just selected.

5. Select the lower-right corner of the building. The line is copied to this corner.

6. Select the Quadrant Osnap, and click the right extremity of the outside wall line of the balcony. Another line is copied, this time to the balcony. It does not extend to the ground line because it was directly copied and therefore is the same length as the other two lines. You will extend it later.

7. Type x↵ to end the Move command. Press Esc to remove the grips. Your drawing will resemble Figure 8.5c.

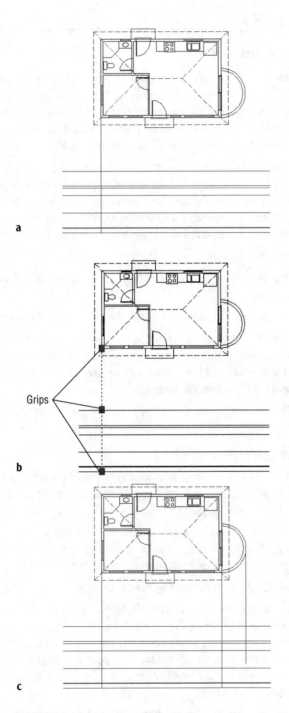

FIGURE 8.5: Dropping a line from the floor plan to the elevation (a), the dropped line with grips (b), and the copied lines (c)

GETTING A GRIP ON GRIPS

In Chapter 7, you saw how to use grips to detect whether an object is a block. They actually serve a larger function. The grips feature is a tool for editing objects quickly, using one or more of the following five commands: Stretch, Move, Rotate, Scale, or Mirror. These commands operate a little differently when using grips than when using them normally.

The commands can also do a few more things with the help of grips. Each command has a Copy option. So, for example, if you rotate an object with grips, you can keep the original object unchanged while you make multiple copies of the object in various angles of rotation. You can't do this by using the Rotate command in the normal way or by using the regular Copy command.

To use grips, follow these steps:

1. When no commands have been started, click an object that you want to modify.

2. Click the grip that will be the base point for the command's execution.

3. Right-click at this point and choose any of the five commands from the shortcut menu that opens on the drawing area. (You can also cycle through the five commands by pressing the spacebar and watching the command prompt.)

4. When you see the command you need, execute the necessary option.

5. Type **x**↵ when finished.

6. Press Esc to remove the grips.

The key to being able to use grips efficiently is knowing which grip to select to start the process. This requires a good understanding of the five commands that work with grips.

This book does not cover grips in depth, but will introduce you to the basics. You will get a chance to use the Move command with grips in this chapter, and we will use grips again when we get to Chapter 11.

Keep the following in mind when working with grips:

▶ Each of the five commands available for use with grips requires a base point. For Mirror, the base point is the first point of the mirror line. By default, the base point is the grip that you select to activate the process, but you can change base points. After selecting a grip, type **b**↵ and pick a different point to serve as a base point; then continue the command.

▶ When you use the Copy option with the Move command, you are essentially using the regular Copy command with the Multiple option.

Trimming Lines in the Elevation

The next task is to trim the appropriate lines in the elevation, but first you need to extend the line dropped from the balcony down to the ground line.

1. Click the line dropped from the balcony. Grips appear on the line. Click the bottom grip. Select Perpendicular Osnap, and then place the cursor on the ground line. When the perpendicular symbol appears on the ground line, click. Then press Esc to remove the grips.

2. Start the Trim command. Select the soffit line for a cutting edge for the two building lines, and then press ↵. The two lines to be trimmed are the ones that were dropped from the corners of the building. Pick them anywhere between the soffit line and the floor plan. The lines are trimmed (see Figure 8.6).

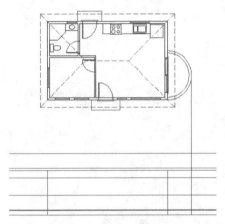

FIGURE 8.6: The building corner lines after being trimmed to the soffit line

3. Press ↵ twice to stop and restart the Trim command. You need to trim a horizontal height line and a vertical dropped line for the balcony. To select cutting edges, pick the line dropped from the balcony and the horizontal height line that represents the top of the balcony wall and the bottom of the windows (see Figure 8.7a). Press ↵.

4. To trim the lines properly, click the line dropped from the balcony anywhere above the balcony in the elevation. To trim the horizontal line representing the top of the balcony wall, pick this line anywhere to the right of the line dropped from the balcony (see Figure 8.7b). The lines are trimmed (see Figure 8.7c). Press ↵ to end the Trim command.

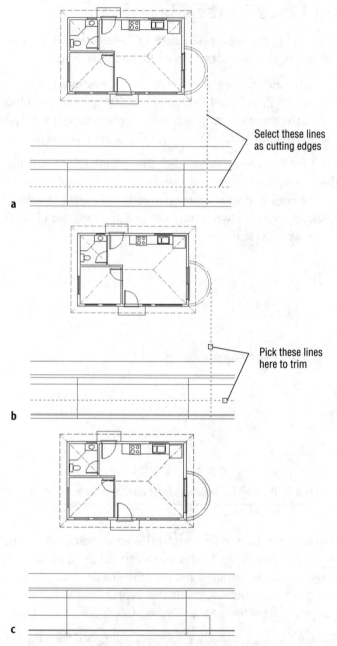

Select these lines
as cutting edges

a

Pick these lines
here to trim

b

c

F I G U R E   8 . 7 : Trimming the balcony lines: selecting cutting edges (a), picking lines to be trimmed (b), and the result (c)

This is the basic process for generating an elevation: Drop lines down from the floor plan, and trim the lines that need to be trimmed. The trick is to learn to see the picture you want somewhere in all the crossed lines and then to be able to use the Trim command accurately to cut the appropriate lines away.

TIPS FOR USING THE TRIM AND EXTEND COMMANDS

Trim and Extend are *sister* commands. Here are a few tips on how they work:

Basic Operation   Both commands involve two steps: selecting cutting edges (Trim) or boundary edges (Extend), and selecting the lines to be trimmed or extended. Select the cutting or boundary edges first, and then press ↵. Then pick lines to trim or extend. Press ↵ to end the commands.

Trimming and Extending in the Same Command   If you find that a cutting edge for trimming can also serve as a boundary edge, hold down the Shift key and click a line to extend it to the cutting edge. The opposite is true for the Extend command.

Correcting Errors   It's easy to make a mistake in selecting cutting or boundary edges or in trimming and extending. You can correct a mistake in two ways:

▶ If you select the wrong cutting or boundary edge, type **r**↵, and then rechoose the lines that were picked in error. They will unghost. If you need to keep selecting cutting or boundary edges, type **a**↵ and select new lines. When finished, press ↵ to move to the second part of the command.

▶ If you trim or extend a line incorrectly, click the Undo button on the Standard toolbar. This will undo the last trim. Click Undo again if you need to untrim or unextend more lines. When you have made all corrections, continue trimming or extending. Press ↵ to end the command.

If the command ended and you click the Undo button, all trimming or extending that was done in the last command will be undone.

Drawing the Roof in Elevation

To draw the roof in elevation, follow these steps:

1. Use the Line command to start a line from the right endpoint of the ridgeline of the roof. Then click the Snap To None Osnap button on the Object Snap toolbar. Draw the line straight down past the soffit line (see Figure 8.8a). End the Line command.

2. Click this line to activate grips. Select the grip at its upper endpoint. Press the spacebar once to access the Move command.

3. Type c↵, and then click the lower-right and lower-left corners of the roof and the left endpoint of the ridgeline. This copies the dropped line to these three locations (see Figure 8.8b).

> If the Osnaps that you have running get in the way of your trying to pick a point near to but not on an object, click the Snap To None Osnap. This will turn off any running Osnaps for the next pick. After that pick, the running Osnaps are reactivated.

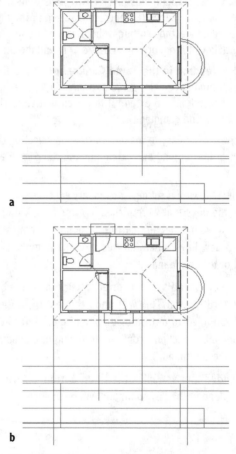

FIGURE 8.8: Dropping a line from the roof (a), and copying this line (b)

 N O T E   If you have difficulty picking the left end of the ridgeline, hold the cursor on the lower-left hip line, just above the midpoint. That should produce an Endpoint symbol where you want it.

4. Type x↵ to end the Move command, and then press Esc to remove the grips.

5. Start the Trim command, and select the two lines dropped from the ridgeline. Press ↵.

6. In the elevation, pick the ridgeline to the left and right of these dropped lines (see Figure 8.9a). The ridgeline is trimmed back to its correct length (see Figure 8.9b). Press ↵.

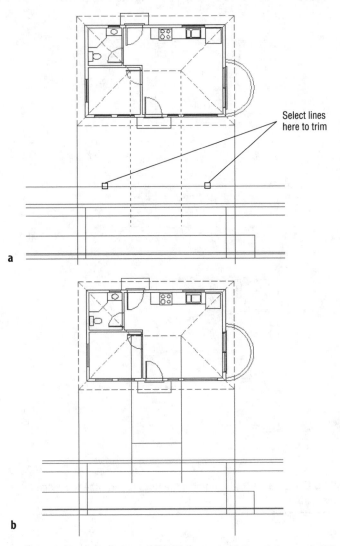

Select lines here to trim

a

b

FIGURE 8.9: Selecting the lines to trim (a), and the result (b)

7. Erase the two dropped lines that were just used as cutting edges.

8. Restart the Trim command. Select the two lines dropped from the corners of the roof, the horizontal soffit line, and the line 6" above the soffit line to be cutting edges—four lines in all. Press ↵.

9. To do the trim, click the dropped lines above and below the two horizontal cutting edges; then click the two selected horizontal lines to the left and right of the dropped lines—eight picks in all (see Figure 8.10a). Press ↵. The roof edge is complete (see Figure 8.10b).

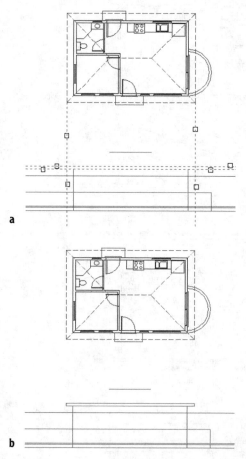

FIGURE 8.10: Trimming the lines to form the roof edge (a), and the result (b)

10. Use the Line command to draw the two hip lines from the roof edge to the ridgeline. Zoom in to do this if you need to; then Zoom Previous when you're finished to view the completed front elevation of the roof (see Figure 8.11).

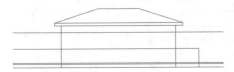

FIGURE 8.11:   The completed roof in elevation

Putting in the Door, the Step, and the Windows

To finish the front elevation, all we need to put in are the front door, the windows, the front step, and the threshold and a few finishing touches. We'll do the door and all the windows, except the round one, in one cycle. We'll save the step and threshold for later.

1. Use Zoom Window to zoom in to as close a view as possible that still displays as much of the drawing as you need. You will need to see the entire elevation, the front wall of the floor plan, and the lower half of the balcony, so make your zoom window large enough to enclose just those elements (see Figure 8.12a). I call this process *strategic zooming*.

2. Draw a line from the left end of the leftmost window in the front wall of the floor plan to the ground line, using Perpendicular Osnap for the second point. End the Line command.

3. Click the line to display its grips, and then click the upper grip on this line at the Command: prompt to activate it. Follow the same

process as you did in steps 2 and 3 of the "Drawing the Roof in Elevation" section to copy this line to the following:

▶ Each endpoint of the jamb line of each window in the front wall, except the 2' circular one to the right of the front door

▶ Each edge of the front door opening

Watch your Endpoint Osnap symbol carefully.

4. Type x↵ to end the Move command. Press Esc to remove the grips (see Figure 8.12b).

You can't zoom or pan while using grips. If you need to adjust your view, do so before displaying them.

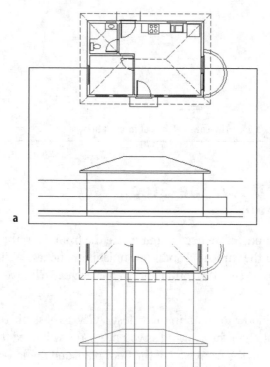

a

b

FIGURE 8.12: The window for zooming in closer (a), and dropping a line from a window and copying it to the edges of the windows and the front door (b)

Before we begin trimming all these lines, study the floor plan and elevation for a minute, and try to visualize the three windows and the door in the middle of all the crossing lines. We'll trim a few at a time, working from the top down.

5. Start the Trim command. For cutting edges, select the horizontal line representing the top of the windows and doors, and select the eight lines you just dropped from the floor plan. Press ↵.

6. To trim, pick the horizontal line at each segment between the windows and the door and near the endpoints of the line (five places). Then pick each selected dropped line above the tops of the windows and door (eight places). This makes 13 places to pick. Then press ↵. The results of the trim are shown in Figure 8.13.

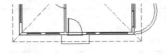

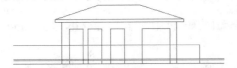

FIGURE 8.13: Trimming the top of the door and windows

Moving down, trim the lines that form the bottom of the windows.

7. Start the Trim command. Select the following as cutting edges:

   ▶ The horizontal line representing the bottom of the window and the top of the balcony wall

   ▶ The six vertical lines forming the sides of the windows

   ▶ The vertical line representing the right edge of the front wall

   Press ↵.

8. To trim, pick the horizontal line at the following places:

   ▶ At each segment between the windows (two picks)

   ▶ Between the right edge of the 6' window and the right edge of the building (one pick)

   ▶ Where it extends to the left of the leftmost window (one pick)

   Then pick the vertical lines that extend below the bottoms of the windows (six picks). This will be a total of 10 picks. Then press ↵. The results of the trim are shown in Figure 8.14.

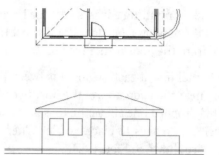

F I G U R E 8 . 1 4 : Trimming the bottom of the windows

 N O T E   It will be helpful if you zoom in to a closer view of the front elevation when you are picking lines to trim. After step 8, Zoom Previous.

Now we will draw the step and threshold, the bottom of the door, and the balcony floor.

1. Drop a line down from the left corner of the threshold to a point past the ground line. Use grips to copy this line to the other corner of the threshold and to the two corners of the step. End the grips (see Figure 8.15a).

2. Zoom in to a close view of the step and threshold. Use the Trim command to trim away the lines so that the result looks like Figure 8.15b. You'll probably have to stop and restart the command a couple of times in order to make all the trims you need. Here's one way to do it, in summary form:

   A. Create the step first. For cutting edges, select the two lower horizontal lines and the two outer vertical lines. To trim, pick each of these lines (except the ground line) in two places above and below or to the left and right of the step (6 picks).

   B. Create the threshold. For cutting edges, select the four lines that form the outside edges of the threshold. To trim, pick each of these lines (except the line that forms the top of the step) in two places above and below or to the left and right of the threshold (6 picks).

   C. Trim the left and right edges of the door up to the top of the threshold (see Figure 8.15b).

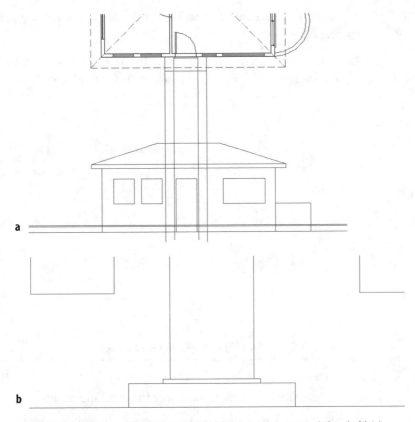

a

b

FIGURE 8.15: Dropped and copied lines for the step and threshold (a), and the finished step and threshold (b)

3. When finished, Zoom Previous to a view of the front elevation and the bottom of the floor plan.

The results show a nearly complete front elevation. To finish it, you need to put in the round window and complete the balcony. We'll then add some final touches. Take another look at Figure 8.1 (shown earlier), and note that the center of the round window is 6' above the ground line.

1. Offset the ground line 6' up.

2. Start the Line command; then click the Snap To Insert button on the Object Snap toolbar. Click the 2' window in the floor plan to start a line at the insertion point of this block reference. Draw the line down through the newly offset line. Then draw a circle, using the intersection of these two lines as the center, and give it a 12" radius.

3. Start the Trim command and select the circle as a cutting edge; then press ↵.

4. Pick the intersecting lines passing through the circle in four places outside the circle. The round window is finished (see Figure 8.16).

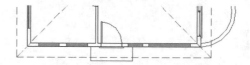

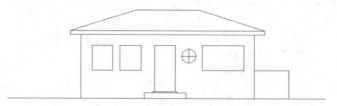

FIGURE 8.16: The completed round window

5. Make a zoom window around only the front elevation.

6. Offset the vertical line representing the balcony's right edge 6" to the left. Then offset the ground line up 10". These lines will serve to indicate the balcony's floor and inside wall.

7. Fillet these two lines at their intersection with a radius of zero. Then trim the balcony floor line back to the right wall line of the cabin.

8. Select these two new lines. Click the Properties button to open the Properties palette.

9. Click Linetype. Then open the Linetype list and click Dashed. Close the Properties palette and press the Esc key. The lines are changed to dashed lines to indicate that they are hidden in the elevation (see Figure 8.17).

10. Zoom Previous twice to a view of the completed front elevation with the entire floor plan. Save this drawing as Cabin08a.

This is a rare case in which we are assigning a line type to an object rather than to a layer. See the discussion at the end of this chapter.

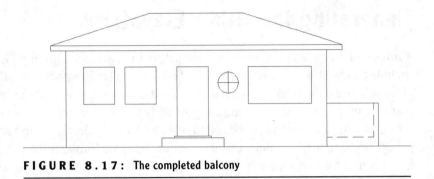

FIGURE 8.17: The completed balcony

Finishing Touches

You have gleaned all the information you can from the floor plan to help you with the front elevation. You might, however, want to add some detail to enhance the appearance of the elevation.

1. Try zooming in and adding detail to the windows and door, and place an extra step leading to the front step. Figure 8.18 shows an example. Yours can be different.

FIGURE 8.18: The front elevation with detail added

2. Zoom Previous to a full view of your drawing when finished.

3. Save this drawing as Cabin08b.

Generating the Other Elevations

A full set of drawings to be used by contractors to construct a building will include an elevation for each side of the building. In traditional drafting, the elevations are usually drawn on separate sheets. This requires transferring measurements from one drawing to another by taping drawings next to each other, turning the floor plan around to orient it to each elevation, and several other cumbersome techniques. You do about the same thing on the computer, but it is much easier to move the drawing around. You will be more accurate, and you can quickly borrow parts from one elevation to use in another.

Making the Rear Elevation

Because the rear elevation shares components and sizes with the front elevation, you can mirror the front elevation to the rear of the building and then make the necessary changes.

1. Open Cabin08a. You need to change the view to include space above the floor plan for the rear elevation.

2. Use Realtime Pan to move the floor plan to the middle of the screen. Then use Realtime Zoom to zoom out the view enough to include the front elevation.

3. Start the Mirror command. Use a window to select the front elevation and press ↵.

4. For the mirror line, select the Midpoint Osnap and pick the right edge line of the roof in the floor plan.

5. With Polar Tracking on, hold the crosshair cursor directly to the right of the point you just picked (see Figure 8.19a) and pick another point. At the Delete source objects?[Yes/No]<N> prompt, press ↵ to accept the default of No. The front elevation is mirrored to the rear of the cabin (see Figure 8.19b).

   You can now make the necessary changes to the rear elevation so that it correctly describes the rear of the cabin. But you might find it easier to work if the view is right side up.

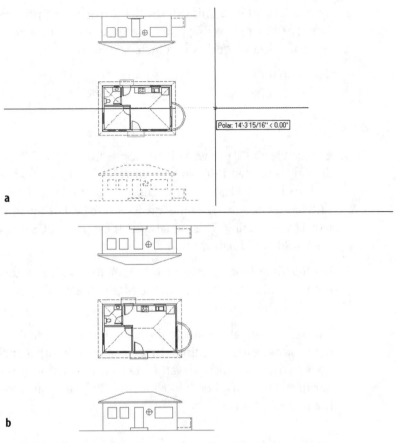

Polar: 14'-3 15/16" < 0.00°

a

b

F I G U R E 8 . 1 9 : Specifying a mirror line (a), and the result (b)

6. Choose View ➢ Display ➢ UCS Icon ➢ On to display the User Coordinate System icon. (We turned it off in Chapter 5.) Take a look at
the icon for a moment. The two arrows in the icon show the positive X and Y directions of the current user coordinate system, the
World Coordinate System, which is the default system for all Auto-
CAD drawings. We'll change the orientation of the icon to the
drawing and then change the orientation of the drawing to the
screen.

7. If your UCS icon is in the lower-left corner of the screen, go to step 8.
Otherwise, choose View ➢ Display ➢ UCS Icon ➢ Origin. This should
move the icon to the lower-left corner of the screen.

The User Coordinate
System (UCS) defines
the positive X and Y
directions relative to
your drawing. A draw-
ing can have several
UCSs but can use only
one at a time. The
World Coordinate
System (WCS) is the
default UCS for all
new drawings and
remains available in
all drawings.

When a check mark
is next to Origin in
the menu, the UCS
icon sits at the origin
(or the 0,0 point) of
the drawing. When
Origin is unchecked,
the icon sits in the
lower-left corner of
the screen.

8. Type ucs↵ z↵ 180↵. This will rotate the icon to an upside-down position. The square box disappears, meaning that you are no longer using the default World Coordinate System.

9. Choose View ➤ 3D Views ➤ Plan View ➤ Current UCS. The entire drawing is rotated 180°, and the mirrored front elevation, which will eventually be the back elevation, is now right side up. Note that the UCS icon is now oriented the way it used to be, but the square in the icon is still missing. This signals that the current UCS is no longer the World Coordinate System.

10. Use Realtime Zoom to zoom out enough to bring the outermost lines of the drawing slightly in from the edge of the drawing area. Then right-click and choose Zoom Window from the shortcut menu.

Move the cursor above and to the left of the floor plan; then click and hold down the mouse button. Drag open a window that encloses the floor plan and mirrored elevation. Release the mouse button. Press Esc to end Realtime Zoom (see Figure 8.20). Now you can work on the rear elevation.

> You used the UCS command to reorient the UCS icon relative to the drawing. You then used the Current option of the Plan command to reorient the drawing on the screen so that the positive X and Y directions of the current User Coordinate System are directed to the right and upward, respectively. This process is a little bit like turning your monitor upside down to get the correct orientation, but easier.

> When you access Zoom Window from the Realtime Zoom shortcut menu, it behaves differently from the regular Zoom Window. It requires a click-and-drag technique.

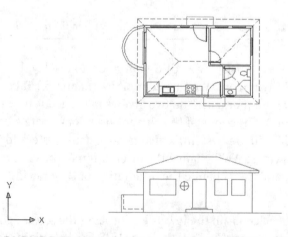

FIGURE 8.20: The cabin drawing rotated 180° and zoomed in

Revising the Rear Elevation

A brief inspection will tell us that the roof, balcony, and building wall lines need no changes. The windows and door need revisions, as do the step and threshold:

▶ The round window and one of the 3' windows need to be deleted.

▶ The two remaining windows need resizing and repositioning.

▶ The door, threshold, and step need repositioning.

▶ The step needs resizing.

These tasks can be accomplished quickly by using commands with which you are now familiar:

1. Erase the round window and one of the 3' windows.

2. Erase the sides of the remaining windows (see Figure 8.21a).

3. Drop lines down from the jambs of the two windows in the back wall of the floor plan, past the bottoms of the windows in elevation (see Figure 8.21b).

4. Extend the horizontal window lines that need to meet the dropped lines, and trim all lines that need to be trimmed. (You can use the Fillet command here instead of the Trim and Extend commands, but pick lines carefully.)

5. Use a similar strategy to relocate and resize the step. You can move the door and threshold into position by using any of several procedures, including dropping a guideline or using the Temporary Tracking Point Osnap—or for LT users, using the Tracking tool—with Polar Tracking. Use Zoom Window and Zoom Previous as needed. The finished rear elevation looks like Figure 8.21c.

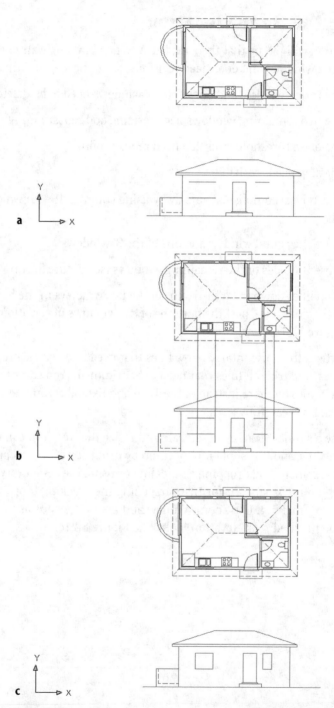

FIGURE 8.21: Erased lines (a), dropped lines (b), and the revised rear elevation (c)

6. You need to save the User Coordinate System (UCS) you used to work on this elevation so that you can quickly return to it in the future, from the World Coordinate System or from any other UCS you might be in. Type **ucs↵ s↵**. For the UCS name, type **rear_elev↵**. This will allow you to recall it if you need to work on this elevation again.

7. You can also save the view to be able to quickly recall it. Choose View ➤ Named Views to open the View dialog box. You can also start the View command by typing **v↵**.

8. Click New to open the New View dialog box.

9. In the New View text box, type **rear_elev**. Click the Current Display radio button and click OK. Back in the View dialog box, rear_elev appears in the list of views. Click OK again. Now you can restore the drawing to its original orientation with the front elevation below the floor plan and right side up.

10. Type **ucs↵↵** to restore the World Coordinate System as the current coordinate system.

11. Choose View ➤ 3D Views ➤ Plan View ➤ Current UCS. This zooms to Extents and displays a plan view of the drawing with the X and Y positive directions in their default orientation.

We created a new UCS as a tool to flip the drawing upside down without changing its orientation with respect to the World Coordinate System. You'll get a chance to use UCSs in another way in the Appendix. But for now, we'll use it again to create the right and left elevations.

Making the Left and Right Elevations

You can generate the left and right elevations using techniques similar to those you have been using for the front and back elevations. You need to be able to transfer the heights of building components from the front elevation to one of the side elevations. To do this, we'll make a copy of the front elevation, rotate it 90°, and then line it up so we can transfer the heights to the right elevation. It's really quite easy.

1. Use Realtime Zoom to zoom out slightly; then zoom in to a view of the floor plan and front elevation. Pan the drawing so that the floor plan and front elevation are on the left part of the drawing area. You need to transfer the height data from the front elevation to the right elevation. To ensure that the right elevation is the same distance

You can save any UCS in this way. The World Coordinate System is a permanent part of all drawings, so it never needs to be saved.

You can name and save any view of your drawing and then restore it later.

from the floor plan as the front elevation, we'll use a 45° line that extends down and to the right from the rightmost and lowermost lines in the floor plan.

Steps 2 through 6 are for AutoCAD only. LT users should follow steps 2 through 6 in the following "Steps 2 through 6 for LT Users" sidebar.

2. Turn on Polar Tracking, and be sure it's set to 45°. Also make sure that the Otrack button on the status bar is toggled on. Then set the Quadrant and Endpoint Osnaps to running, and be sure Midpoint Osnap is not running.

3. Start the Line command. Move the crosshair cursor to the right edge of the outside arc of the balcony in the floor plan. Hold it there for a moment. A cross will appear at the Quadrant point. Don't click yet.

4. Move the crosshair cursor to the lower-right corner of the step and hold it there until a cross appears at that point. Don't click yet.

5. Now move the crosshair cursor to a point directly to the right of the corner of the step and directly under the right quadrant point of the balcony (see Figure 8.22a). Vertical and horizontal tracking lines appear and intersect where the crosshair cursor is positioned, and a small *x* appears at the intersection. A tracking tool tip will also appear.

6. Click to start a line at this point.

STEPS 2 THROUGH 6 FOR LT USERS

LT users should follow these steps:

2. Turn on Polar Tracking and be sure it's set to 45°. Then set the Quadrant and Endpoint Osnaps to be running, and make sure Midpoint Osnap is not running.

3. Start the Line command, and then click the Tracking button on the Object Snap toolbar (it's the top button).

4. Move the cursor to the lower-right corner of the front step. When the Endpoint Osnap square appears there, click.

5. Move the cursor to the right edge of the outer arc of the balcony. When the Quadrant Osnap diamond appears there, click.

6. Press ↵. A line is begun at a point just below and to the right of the floor plan, in line with the lower edge of the front step and the right extremity of the balcony.

Now continue with step 7.

7. Move the crosshair cursor down, away from this point, and to the right at a negative 45° angle (or a positive 315° angle). When the 45° Polar tracking path appears, type 35'↵. Press ↵ again. The diagonal reference line is completed (see Figure 8.22b).

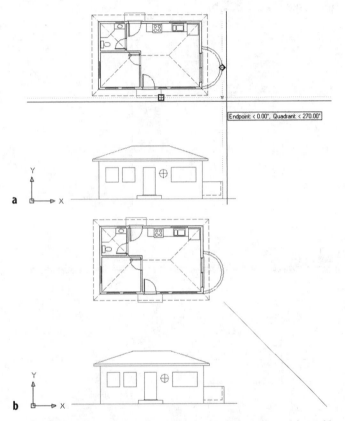

FIGURE 8.22: Starting a diagonal reference line with tracking points (a), and the completed diagonal line (b)

8. Turn off Quadrant as a running Osnap.

9. Start the Copy command, and select the entire front elevation and nothing else. Then press ↵.

10. For the base point, select the left endpoint of the ground line.

11. For the second point, pick the Intersection Osnap and place the cursor on the diagonal line. When the *x* symbol with three dots appears, click. Then move the cursor to any point on the ground line of the

front elevation. An *x* will appear on the diagonal line where the ground line would intersect it if it were longer (see Figure 8.23a).

12. When the *x* appears, click to locate the copy. Zoom out to include the copy; then Zoom Window to include the floor plan and front elevations (see Figure 8.23b).

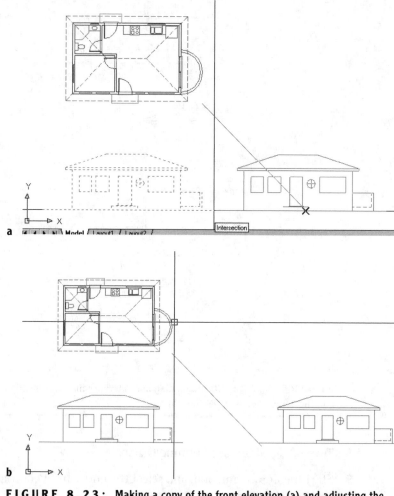

FIGURE 8.23: Making a copy of the front elevation (a) and adjusting the view (b)

13. Start the Rotate command and select this copy of the front elevation; then press ↵. Pick Intersection Osnap and click the intersection of

the diagonal line with the ground line. For the angle of rotation, type 90↵ (see Figure 8.24a).

14. Start the Move command, and when prompted to select objects, type p↵↵. The rotated front elevation will be selected. For the base point, click a point in a blank space to the right of the upper endpoint of the ground line of the rotated elevation. For the second point, move the cursor down using Polar Tracking until the top of the ground line is lower than the bottom line of the front step in the plan view. Then click.

15. Zoom out and Zoom Window to adjust the view (see Figure 8.24b).

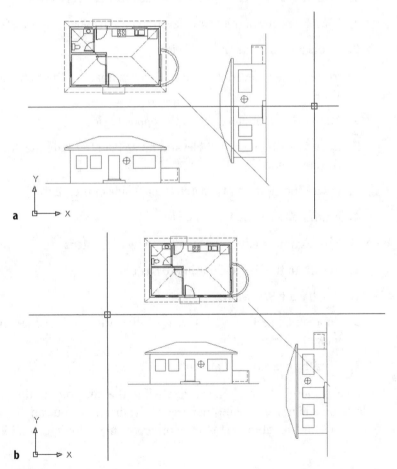

FIGURE 8.24: Rotating the copy of the front elevation (a) and the moved copy with the view adjusted

N O T E   If you're working on a small monitor, you might have to do some extra zooming in and out that isn't mentioned in these steps.

The rest of the process for creating the right elevation is straightforward and uses routines you have just learned. Here's a summary of the steps:

1. Set up a new UCS for the right elevation. (Type **ucs**↵ **z**↵ **90**↵.) Use the Plan command to rotate the drawing to the current UCS.

2. Drop lines from the floor plan across the height lines, which you will produce from the copied elevation.

3. Trim these lines as required and add any necessary lines.

4. Erase the copy of the front elevation and the diagonal transfer line.

5. Name and save the UCS and view.

You can create the left elevation from a mirrored image of the right elevation. Here are the steps:

1. Mirror the right elevation to the opposite side.

2. Set up a UCS for the left elevation. Use Plan to rotate the drawing to the current UCS.

3. Revise the elevation to match the left side of the cabin.

4. Name and save the UCS and view.

When you have completed all elevations, follow these steps:

1. Return to the World Coordinate System.

2. Display the Plan view.

3. Zoom out slightly for a full view of all elevations. The drawing will look like Figure 8.25a.

4. Save the drawing as Cabin08c.

Once an elevation is drawn, you can rotate it to the same orientation as the front elevation and move it to another area of the drawing. You can display the four elevations for the cabin next to each other, as shown in Figure 8.25b.

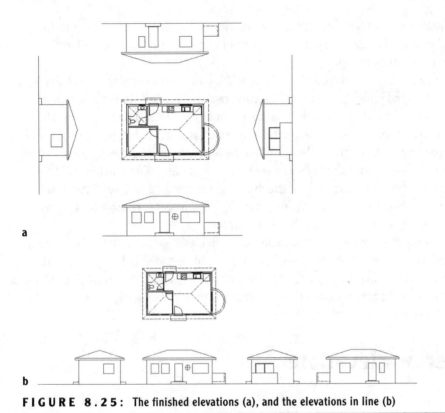

a

b

FIGURE 8.25: The finished elevations (a), and the elevations in line (b)

Drawing Scale Considerations

This last view raises several questions: How will these drawings best fit on a page? How many pages will it take to illustrate these drawings? What size sheet should be used? At what scale will the drawing be printed? In traditional hand drafting, the first line could not be drawn without answers to some of these questions. You have completed a great deal of the drawing on the computer without having to make decisions about scale and sheet size because in AutoCAD you draw in real-world scale or full-scale. This means that when you tell AutoCAD to draw a 10-foot line, it draws it 10 feet long. If you inquire how long the line is, AutoCAD will tell you that it is 10 feet long. Your current view of the line may be to a certain scale, but that changes every time you zoom in or out. The line is stored in the computer as 10 feet long.

You need to make decisions about scale when you are choosing the sheet size, putting text and dimensions on the drawing, or using hatch patterns and noncontinuous line types. Because we have a dashed line type in the drawing, we had to make a choice about scale in Chapter 6, when we assigned a linetype scale factor of 24 to the drawing. We chose that number because when the drawing consisted of only the floor plan and the view was zoomed as large as possible while still having all objects visible, the scale of the drawing was about ½" = 1'-0". That scale has a true ratio of 1:24, or a scale factor of 24. We will get further into scale factors and true ratios of scales in the next chapter.

If you look at your Cabin08c drawing with all elevations visible on the screen, the dashes in the dashed lines look like they might be too small, so you might need to increase the linetype scale factor. Don't worry about that now. Beginning with the next chapter, and right on through the end of this book, we will need to make decisions about scale each step of the way.

Interior Elevations

You construct interior elevations using the techniques you learned for constructing exterior elevations. You drop lines from a floor plan through offset height lines and then trim them away. Interior elevations usually include fixtures and built-in cabinets and shelves, and they show finishes. Each elevation will consist of one wall and can include a side view of items on an adjacent wall if the item extends into the corner. Not all walls are shown in an elevation—usually only those that require special treatment or illustrate special building components. You might use one elevation to show a wall that has a window and to describe how the window is treated or finished and then assume that all other windows in the building will be treated in the same way unless noted otherwise. A few examples of interior wall elevations are shown in Figure 8.26. Try to identify which walls of the cabin each one represents.

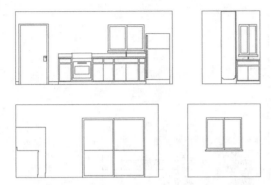

F I G U R E   8 . 2 6 : Samples of interior elevations of the cabin

In the next chapter, you will learn how to use hatch patterns and fills to enhance floor plans and elevations.

If You Would Like More Practice...

Here are three exercises for practicing the techniques you learned in this chapter. The last one will give you practice in basic orthogonal projection.

Exterior Elevations   Open Cabin08c and move the right, left, and rear elevations around so they fit in a line, as in Figure 8.25b (shown earlier).

Interior Elevations   For some practice with interior elevations, try drawing one or two elevations, using Figure 8.26 (shown earlier) as a guide. You can measure the heights and sizes of various fixtures in your own home or office as a guide. Save what you draw as Cabin8d.

Orthogonal Projection   Draw the three views of the block shown in Figure 8.27 using the procedures we used for the cabin elevations, except that, in this case, use the procedure that Mechanical drafters use; that is, draw the front view first and then develop the top and right side views from the front view.

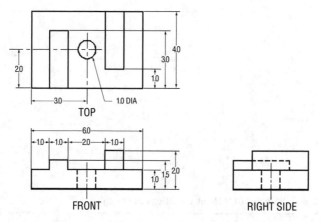

FIGURE 8.27: Front, top, and side views of a block

Are You Experienced?

Now you can...

- ☑ draw an exterior elevation from a floor plan

- ☑ use grips to copy objects

- ☑ add detail to an elevation

- ☑ set up, name, and save a User Coordinate System and a new view

- ☑ transfer height lines from one elevation to another

- ☑ copy, move, and rotate elevations

CHAPTER 9

Working with Hatches and Fills

▶ Selecting a predefined hatch pattern and applying it to a drawing

▶ Setting up and applying user-defined hatch patterns

▶ Modifying the scale and shape of a hatch pattern

▶ Specifying the origin of a hatch pattern

▶ Filling an enclosed area with a solid color

▶ Setting up and using palettes and palette tools

Hatches can be abstract patterns of lines, solid *fills*, or they can resemble the surfaces of various building materials. To give texture to an AutoCAD drawing, a drafter will hatch in areas or fill them in with a solid color. Solid fills in a drawing can give a shaded effect when printed using a half-screen, resulting in a look quite different from the solid appearance in the Auto-CAD drawing on the screen.

In an architectural floor plan, the inside of full-height walls are often hatched or filled to distinguish them from low walls. Wooden or tile floors can be hatched to a parquet or tile pattern. In a site plan, hatches are used to distinguish between areas with different ground covers, such as grass, gravel, or concrete. When working with elevations, almost any surface can be hatched to show shading and shadows, and realistic hatch patterns can be used to illustrate the surfaces of concrete, stucco, or shingles. Hatches and fills are widely used in mechanical, landscaping, civil, structural, and architectural details as a tool to aid in clear communication.

To learn how to hatch and fill areas, you will start with some of the visible surfaces in the front elevation of the cabin. You will then move to the floor plan and hatch the floors and put hatch patterns and fills in the walls. You'll use the *Hatch command* for all hatching and filling. It is a complex command with many options.

A key part of a hatch pattern is the boundary of the pattern. The area being hatched is defined through a complex procedure in which AutoCAD searches the drawing for lines or objects to serve as the hatch boundary.

Hatching the Front Elevation

Hatches and fills generally need to be on their own layers so they can be turned off without also making other objects invisible. We will begin the exercise by creating new layers for the hatches and assigning colors to them.

1. Open the Cabin08a drawing. It should contain the floor plan and front elevation only. Turn off any running Object Snaps and turn off the UCS icon.

T I P   To get the best visual effect from putting hatch patterns on the front elevation, change the background color for the drawing area to white. Choose Tools ➤ Options to open the Options dialog box and then click the Display tab. Click the Colors button and make the change.

2. Set up three new layers as follows:

Layer Name	Color
Hatch-elev-brown	42
Hatch-elev-gray	Gray (8)
Hatch-elev-black	Black (White) (7)

3. Make the Hatch-elev-gray layer current. Now any new objects you create will be assigned to this layer.

4. Click the Hatch icon on the Draw toolbar to open the Boundary Hatch And Fill dialog box (see Figure 9.1). You will use this dialog box to choose a pattern, set up the pattern's properties, and determine the method for specifying the boundary of the area to be hatched. The Hatch tab should be active. If it's not, click the tab. Predefined and ANSI31 should be displayed in the Type and Pattern drop-down lists, respectively. If not, open the lists and select those options.

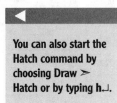

You can also start the Hatch command by choosing Draw ➢ Hatch or by typing h↵.

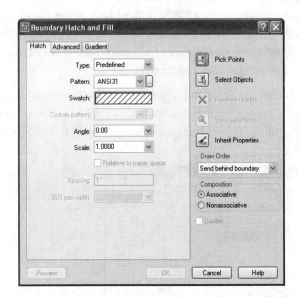

FIGURE 9.1: The Boundary Hatch And Fill dialog box

5. Move to the right of the Pattern drop-down list and click the Browse button to open the Hatch Pattern Palette dialog box (see Figure 9.2). Of the four tabs, ANSI will be active, and the ANSI31 pattern will be highlighted.

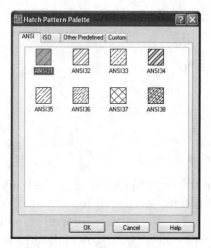

FIGURE 9.2: The Hatch Pattern Palette dialog box

6. Click the Other Predefined tab. Find the AR-RROOF pattern, click it, and then click OK. Back in the Boundary Hatch And Fill dialog box, note that AR-RROOF has replaced ANSI31 in the Pattern drop-down list. A new pattern is displayed in the Swatch preview box, which is below the Pattern list (see Figure 9.3).

You can change the Scale and Angle settings in their drop-down lists, which are below the Swatch preview box. In the Angle drop-down list, the preset angle of 0.00 is fine, but you need to adjust the Scale setting.

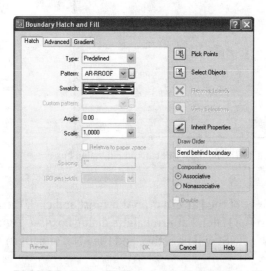

FIGURE 9.3: The Boundary Hatch dialog box with the AR-RROOF pattern chosen

7. In the Scale drop-down list, delete 1.0000 and type **6**. The Scale drop-down list contains preset scale factors that range from 0.2500 to 2.0000. To set the scale to 6, you have to type it. Once you do that, however, 6 is added to the drop-down list and is displayed as 6.0000 the next time you open the dialog box.

8. Move to the upper-right corner of the dialog box and click the Pick Points button. This returns you to the drawing.

9. In the elevation view, click the middle of the roof area. The lines that form the boundary of the roof area ghost, forming an outline of the area to be hatched (see Figure 9.4).

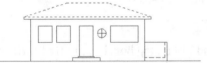

FIGURE 9.4: The roof's boundary is selected.

10. Right-click and choose Preview from the shortcut menu. In the preview drawing, take a look at how the hatch will appear. This hatch looks fine for now.

11. Right-click to accept this hatch. The hatch is now placed in the roof area (see Figure 9.5).

FIGURE 9.5: The finished hatch pattern in the roof area

12. Zoom in to a view of just the front elevation. Notice how the appearance of the hatch pattern changes with the new view.

Looking at Hatch Patterns

Let's take a short tour through the available patterns.

1. Start the Hatch command.

2. In the Boundary Hatch And Fill dialog box, be sure that the Hatch tab is active. Then click the Browse button that is next to the Pattern drop-down list to open the Hatch Pattern Palette dialog box.

3. Make the Other Predefined tab active if it is not already. Look at the display of hatch patterns. Eleven pattern names begin with *AR-*, including the one just used. These patterns have been designed to look like architectural and building materials; hence, the AR prefix. In addition to the roof pattern we just used, there are several masonry wall patterns, a couple of floor patterns, and one pattern each for concrete, shakes, and sand.

4. Scroll down the display and observe the other non-AR patterns. They are geometrical patterns, some of which use conventions to represent various materials.

5. Click the ANSI tab, and take a look at a few of the ANSI patterns. These are abstract line patterns developed by the American National

Standards Institute and are widely used by public and private design offices in the United States.

6. Click the ISO tab. These are also abstract line patterns developed by another organization, the International Organization for Standardization. The Custom tab will be empty unless custom hatch patterns have been loaded into AutoCAD.

7. Click Cancel in the Hatch Pattern Palette dialog box. Click Cancel again to close the Boundary Hatch And Fill dialog box.

As you work with hatch patterns, you will need to adjust the scale factor for each pattern so the patterns will look right when the drawing is printed. The AR patterns are drawn to be used with the scale factor set approximately to the default of one-to-one (displayed as 1.0000) and should need only minor adjustment. However, the pattern you just chose for the roof is an AR pattern, and its scale factor needed to be changed to 6.0000. The AR-RROOF pattern is somewhat anomalous compared with the rest of the AR patterns and requires this unusually large adjustment.

T I P   When using one of the AR patterns, leave the scale factor at 1.0000 until you preview the hatch; then you can make changes. This rule also applies to the 14 ISO patterns displayed on the ISO tab of the Hatch Pattern Palette dialog box.

For the rest of the patterns, you will need to assign a scale factor that imitates the true ratio of the scale at which you expect to print the drawing. Table 9.1 gives the true ratios of some of the standard scales used in architecture and construction.

T A B L E   9 . 1 : Standard Scales and Their Corresponding Ratios

Scale	True Scale Factor
1" = 1'-0"	12
½" = 1'-0"	24
¼" = 1'-0"	48
⅛" = 1'-0"	96
¹⁄₁₆" = 1'-0"	192

The scale is traditionally written by mixing inches with feet in the expression, which causes some confusion. For example, the third scale in the table, commonly called "quarter-inch scale," shows that a quarter inch equals one foot. A true ratio of this scale would have to express the relationship using the same units, as in ¼" = 1'-0". Simplifying this expression to have no fractions, you would translate it to, say, 1" = 48". This is how you arrive at the true scale factor of 48, or the true ratio of 1:48.

As you continue through this chapter, take special note of the various scale factors used for different hatch patterns.

Hatching the Rest of the Front Elevation

You will apply hatches to the foundation, front door, and front wall. We'll then work with some special effects.

Using a Concrete Hatch on the Foundation

For the foundation hatch, keep the Hatch-elev-gray layer current.

1. To represent the top of the foundation, draw lines from the upper-left and upper-right corners of the step to the edges of the building (see Figure 9.6a). Activate Osnaps as needed.

2. Start the Hatch command. Then click the Browse button next to the Pattern drop-down list in the Boundary Hatch And Fill dialog box.

3. Activate the Other Predefined tab. Find and select the AR-CONC pattern and click OK.

4. Open the Scale drop-down list and select 1.0000.

5. Click Pick Points. Then, in the drawing, click once in each rectangle representing the foundation. The borders of these areas will ghost.

6. Right-click, and then choose Preview. Then right-click again to accept the hatch. The concrete hatch pattern is applied to the foundation surfaces (see Figure 9.6b).

After you click the Pick Points button in the Boundary Hatch And Fill dialog box, pick a point in the area to be hatched. AutoCAD finds the boundary of that area and displays its ghosted form.

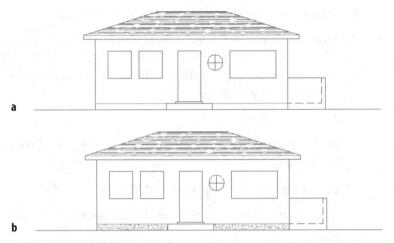

a

b

FIGURE 9.6: The front elevation with foundation lines drawn (a), and the resulting hatches in place (b)

Hatching the Front Door and Wall

For the front door, we'll use a standard hatch pattern, ANSI31. This is the default pattern when you first use the Hatch command, but now the default pattern is the last one used.

1. Start the Hatch command and click the Browse button.

2. Activate the ANSI tab. Select ANSI31 and click OK.

3. In the Scale text box, highlight 1.0000 and type 18. Then click Pick Points.

4. Click the middle of the door. The edges of the door and door sill ghost.

5. Right-click, and then choose Preview. Observe the preview, and then right-click again. The door is hatched (see Figure 9.7).

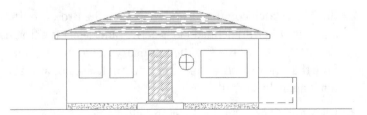

FIGURE 9.7: Hatching the door

6. Change the current layer to Hatch-elev-brown.

7. Start the Hatch command, and go through the same process to apply a hatch to the wall. This time you will use the AR-RSHKE pattern, which looks like wooden shingles (often called shakes). Here is a summary of the steps:

   A. Click the Browse button.

   B. Activate the Other Predefined tab, select the AR-RSHKE pattern, and click OK.

   C. Set the Scale to 1 and click Pick Points.

   D. Pick any place on the front wall that's not inside a window.

   E. Right-click, choose Preview, and then right-click again.

   The wall is hatched (see Figure 9.8).

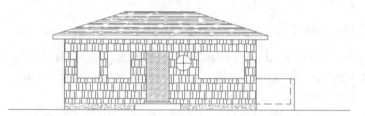

F I G U R E   9 . 8 : The hatching of the front wall is complete.

Using a Solid Fill Hatch

The windows will be hatched with a solid fill. You apply this hatch in the same way as the other hatches you have been using, except that you don't have a choice of scale or angle.

1. Make Hatch-elev-black the current layer.

2. Start the Hatch command, and then click the Browse button. Make sure the Other Predefined tab is active, and select the first pattern, SOLID. Click OK. Back in the Boundary Hatch And Fill dialog box, note that the text boxes for Scale and Angle are not available. These don't apply to solid fills.

3. Click Pick Points. In the drawing, select a point in the middle of each of the four windows. You will have to click the round window four times because of the mullions (the separators between the panes).

4. Right-click, choose Preview, and then right-click again. The windows have a solid black (or white) fill (see Figure 9.9).

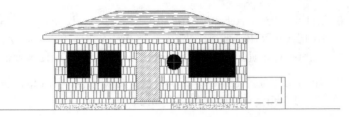

FIGURE 9.9: The windows with a solid fill hatch

Special Effects

To finish the front elevation, you need to show shading and work a little with a curved surface.

Applying Shading to a Surface

When shaded surfaces are illustrated on an exterior elevation, they give a three-dimensional quality to the surface. We'll put some additional hatching at the top portion of the wall to illustrate the shading caused by the roof overhang.

You need to hatch the top 2'-6" of the wall with the same hatch that was put on the front door. To determine the boundary line of the hatch, you need to turn off the layer that has the shake pattern. You will then create a guideline to serve as the lower boundary of the hatch.

1. Be sure the Hatch-elev-black layer is still current. Then turn off the Hatch-elev-brown layer.

2. Offset the soffit line of the roof down 2'-6" (see Figure 9.10a).

3. Start the Hatch command. In the Boundary Hatch And Fill dialog box, click the Inherit Properties button. You are returned to the drawing. The cursor is now a pickbox accompanied by a paintbrush, telling you that AutoCAD is in Select Hatch mode.

4. Click the hatch pattern on the door. The Command window displays the name, scale, and rotation of the hatch pattern you picked. Now the prompt is Select internal point:.

5. Pick a point on the wall above the offset line but not inside the door or windows. Click the door hatch above the offset line. The boundary lines ghost (see Figure 9.10b). Press ↵.

6. In the Boundary Hatch And Fill dialog box, change the scale from 18 to 16. Click the Preview button in the lower-left corner. After a look, right-click. The pattern is applied to the upper part of the wall.

7. Turn on the Hatch-elev-brown layer and erase the offset guideline. The drawing will look like Figure 9.10c.

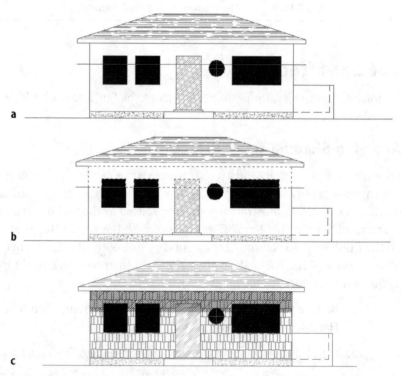

FIGURE 9.10: Applying a hatch to a shaded area: drawing a guideline (a), finding the hatch boundary (b), and the resulting effect (c)

You erased the offset guideline because there is no edge on the wall at the bottom of the shaded area. And you used the Inherit Properties button to set up a hatch pattern exactly like the one already present in the drawing. You can also use the List command on hatch patterns to find out the name, scale, and rotation of an existing pattern, as well as the layer that the hatch is on.

Indicating a Curved Surface

The curved outside wall of the balcony appears as a rectangle in the front elevation. You need to use a pattern that will increase in density in the X direction as
we move around the curve. Vertical straight lines will do the job if you space
them properly. You'll use the floor plan to help you to do that.

1. Make the Hatch-elev-brown current. Use Realtime Zoom and Zoom
Window to arrange a view similar to the one in Figure 9.11.

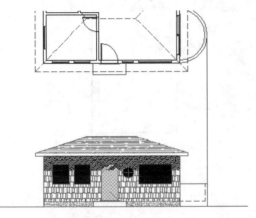

FIGURE 9.11: A line is dropped from the balcony in the floor plan to the
elevation.

2. Use the Line command with Quadrant Osnap to start a line from the
right extremity of the outside balcony wall. Use Endpoint Osnap to
end the line at the top-right corner of the balcony in the elevation.

3. Turn off the Headers, Roof, and Steps layers. Use Zoom Window to
zoom in to the lower half of the balcony in the floor plan. Set Endpoint Osnap to be running, and then use Center Osnap to draw a line
from the center point of the balcony arc down to the lower-right corner of the building (see Figure 9.12a).

When using the
Center Osnap, place
the cursor on the arc
or circle whose cen-
ter you are trying to
snap to. The Center
Osnap symbol
appears at the center
of the arc or circle.

If the arcs seem segmented after zooming in on them, choose View ➤ Regen to readjust the screen and make the arcs look like true arcs.

Here's the plan. If you create a series of equally spaced radii across the lower-right quadrant of the balcony, vertical lines dropped from these radii will give you a graduated spacing to indicate the curved surface of the balcony wall in elevation. The Polar Array tool helps you do that.

1. At the Command: prompt, click the Array button on the Modify toolbar to open the Array dialog box. At the top are two radio buttons. Click the Polar Array radio button.

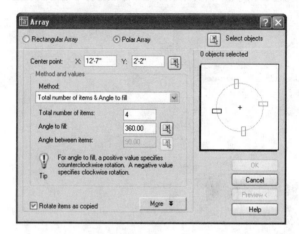

2. In the upper right of the Array dialog box, click the Select Objects button. Select the line that you just drew from the center of the balcony to the corner of the building, and then press ↵.

3. Just to the right of the Center Point X and Y coordinate text boxes, click the Pick Center Point button.

4. Back in the drawing, select the upper endpoint of the line that you just drew.

5. In the Array dialog box, note the Method drop-down list box. It should say Total Number Of Items & Angle To Fill. If it does, move to step 6. If not, open the drop-down list and select that option.

6. In the Total Number Of Items text box, enter **10**, but don't press ↵ yet.

7. In the Angle To Fill text box, enter **90** but don't press ↵ yet.

8. In the lower-left corner of the dialog box, make sure a check mark is in the Rotate Items As Copied box. Then click the Preview button. The preview should look like Figure 9.12b. If it does, click the Accept

button. The line is arrayed around the lower half of the balcony (see Figure 9.12b).

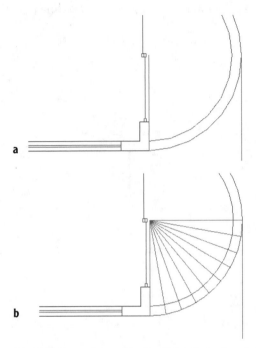

FIGURE 9.12 : The line drawn from the center of the balcony (a), and the results of the Polar array (b)

9. Set Endpoint Osnap to running, if it's not already. Then use grips again to copy/move the dropped line to the endpoint of each line that was just arrayed. Here is a summary of the steps:

   A. Click the dropped line to activate grips.

   B. Click the grip on the upper endpoint.

   C. Right-click and choose Move from the shortcut menu.

   D. Right-click again and choose Copy. This activates the Copy options for the Move command.

   E. Click each spoke line (like the spoke of a wheel) on its outer endpoint. Don't copy the line to the vertical spoke line you first drew.

   F. Type x↵, and then press Esc to remove the grips.

The results will look like Figure 9.13a. Now you have all the lines you need to complete the task. To finish, get rid of what you no longer need.

1. Erase all the spoke lines and the original dropped line (see Figure 9.13b).

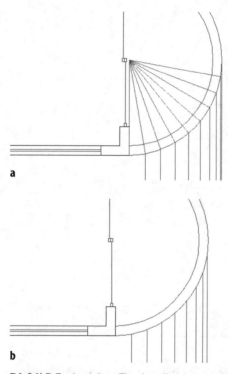

a

b

FIGURE 9.13: The drop line is copied to the ends of the spoke lines (a), and the spoke lines and first dropped line are erased (b).

2. Turn on the Headers, Roof, and Steps layers. Zoom Previous, and then zoom in close to the elevation of the balcony.

3. Erase the two dashed lines that represent the floor and inside wall of the balcony.

4. Start the Trim command, and select the line representing the top edge of the balcony wall and the ground line. Press ↵. Type f↵ to activate the Fence selection option.

5. Draw a horizontal line that crosses over the eight vertical lines extending above the balcony, and then press ↵. The eight lines are trimmed down to the balcony, and the Trim command is still running.

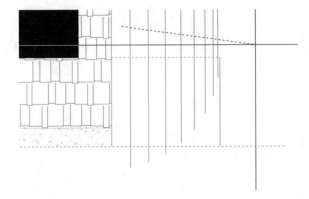

6. Click the three lines that extend below the ground line. Click them below the ground line. Press the Shift key and click the five lines that need to be extended to the ground line. Press ↵ to end the Trim command (see Figure 9.14).

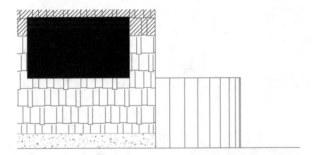

FIGURE 9.14: The balcony in elevation after erasing, extending, and trimming lines

Modifying a Hatch Pattern

You won't know for sure if the hatch patterns will look right until you print the drawing, but you can at least see how they look together now that you've finished hatching the elevation.

1. Zoom Previous, and use Realtime Pan to display both the floor plan and the elevation on the screen (see Figure 9.15a). The roof hatch could be a little denser. You can use the Modify Hatch command to change the hatch scale.

2. Double-click the roof's hatch pattern.

3. In the Hatch Edit dialog box, change the scale from 6.000 to 4.

4. Click OK. The roof hatch pattern is denser now (see Figure 9.15b).

> You can modify several kinds of objects by double-clicking them. This activates a dialog box in which you can edit them. I'll point out this feature along the way.

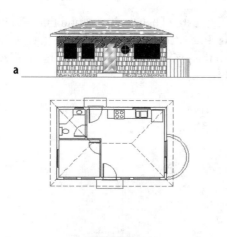

FIGURE 9.15: Full view of the drawing with the hatching completed for the front elevation (a), and the same view with the roof hatch modified (b)

5. Save this drawing as Cabin09a.

You can use the Modify Hatch command to change the pattern, scale, or angle of an existing hatch.

If you worked on putting more detail in the front elevation in the previous chapter and saved this drawing as Cabin08b, you can go through the exercise again with that drawing. You can then see how more detail and hatch patterns enhance the way the elevations appear. Figure 9.16 shows the front elevation with hatch patterns and more detail in the door and windows. If you have the time to do any hatching on this drawing, save your work as Cabin09b.

FIGURE 9.16: Cabin09b with the front elevation hatched

Using Hatches in the Floor Plan

In the floor plan, you can use hatches to fill in the walls or to indicate various kinds of floor surfaces. We'll start with the floors.

Hatching the Floors

So far you have used only predefined hatch patterns—the 69 patterns that come with AutoCAD. There is also a *user-defined pattern*, which is a series of parallel lines that you can set at any spacing and angle. If you want to illustrate square floor tile, select the Double option of the user-defined pattern, which uses two sets of parallel lines—one perpendicular to the other, resulting in a tiled effect.

The User-Defined Hatch Pattern

You'll use the user-defined pattern for a couple of rooms and then return to the predefined patterns.

1. With Cabin09a open, zoom in to the floor plan, and be sure the Headers and Doors layers are visible. You can use the header lines to help form a boundary line across an entryway to a room and to keep the hatch pattern from extending to another room.

2. With the floor plan in full view, zoom in to the bathroom and freeze the Roof layer. Even if the roof lines are dashed, they will still form a boundary to a hatch.

3. Create a new layer called Hatch-plan-floor. Assign it color 142 and make it current. (If you have only 16 colors, choose any color.)

4. Start the Hatch command. Be sure the Hatch tab is active.

5. Open the Type drop-down list and select User-defined. The list closes, and User-defined replaces Predefined as the current pattern type. The Pattern and Scale drop-down lists are not available, but the Spacing text box is.

6. In the Spacing text box, change 1" to 9". Below and to the right of that, click the Double check box to activate it. Then click Pick Points.

7. Back in the drawing, be sure no Osnaps are running. Then click a point in the bathroom floor, not touching the fixture lines or the door. Click the floor between the door swing and the door, being careful to not touch the door.

8. Right-click, and choose Preview from the shortcut menu. The tiled hatch pattern should fill the bathroom floor and stop at the header, while not going onto the door or fixtures. If the tile pattern looks OK, right-click again (see Figure 9.17).

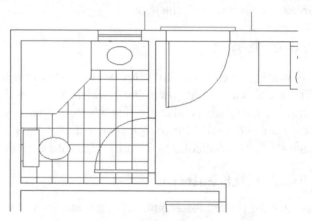

FIGURE 9.17: The tiled hatch pattern in place

Note that in the user-defined pattern, there is no scale factor to worry about. You simply set the distance between lines in the Spacing text box.

 W A R N I N G If you can't get the Hatch command to hatch the desired area, you might not have drawn some of the lines serving as the hatch boundary accurately. This can prevent AutoCAD from being able to find the boundary that you intend to use. Zoom in to the areas where objects meet and check to see that they really do meet where they should.

Controlling the Origin of the Hatch Pattern

Often a designer will want to lay out the tile pattern such that the pattern is centered in the room. To do this, the tiles are set to start in the center of the room and move out to the edges, where they are cut to fit. We'll use the Snapbase setting to set this up in the bedroom.

1. Use Realtime Pan to slide the drawing up until the bedroom occupies the screen. Use Realtime Zoom to zoom out if you need to.

2. Turn Otrack on (on the status bar), and set Midpoint Osnap to be running.

3. Type snapbase↵. Place the cursor at the midpoint of the inside wall line on the left. A cross (called a tracking point) will appear inside the triangular Midpoint Osnap symbol. Don't click.

   Move to the wall line at the upper part of the room and do the same thing. Then move the cursor straight down until it is positioned directly to the right of the first acquired tracking point. When the cursor is positioned properly, two tracking lines and a tool tip are displayed (see Figure 9.18a). Click. This sets the origin of any subsequently created hatch patterns at the center of the room.

Steps 2 and 3 are for AutoCAD users only. LT users should follow steps 2 and 3 in the following "For LT Users" sidebar.

FOR LT USERS

LT users should follow these steps:

2. Set Midpoint Osnap to be running.

3. Type **snapbase**↵. Click the Tracking button at the top of the Object Snap toolbar. Hold the cursor at the midpoint of the inside wall line on the left. When the Midpoint Osnap triangle appears, click.

   Move the cursor up to the upper wall line and do the same thing. Then press ↵. This sets the origin of any subsequently created hatch patterns at the center of the room.

4. Start the Hatch command. The User-defined pattern type is still current, and the spacing is set to 9".

5. Change the spacing to 12". Be sure Double is still checked, and then click Pick Points.

6. In the drawing, pick a point anywhere in the middle of the bedroom

and between the door swing and the door, similar to what you did in the bathroom. Right-click and choose Preview.

7. Inspect the drawing to see if the hatch looks all right, and then right-click again. The hatch of 12" tiles is placed in the bedroom (see Figure 9.18b). Note how the pattern is centered left to right and top to bottom.

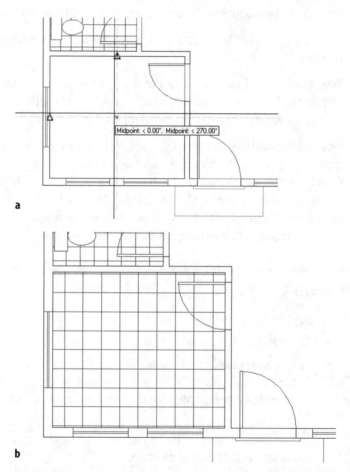

a

b

FIGURE 9.18: Hatching the bedroom: the two tracking lines (a), and the finished, centered hatch (b)

The default setting for Snapbase is 0,0, or the origin of the drawing. Each time you change this setting, all subsequent hatch patterns will use the new setting as their origin. For most hatches, the origin isn't important, but if you need to control the location of tiles or specific points of other hatch patterns, you can reset the Snapbase setting before you create the hatch.

Finishing the Hatches for the Floors

To finish hatching the floors, you'll use a parquet pattern from the set of predefined patterns in the living room and kitchen and another user-defined pattern on the balcony.

1. Use Realtime Pan and Zoom to adjust the view so it includes the living room, kitchen, and balcony.

2. Start the Hatch command and set the current pattern type to Predefined.

3. Click the Browse button and activate the Other Predefined tab. Select the AR-PARQ1 pattern. Set the scale to 1, and be sure the angle is set to zero. Then click Pick Points.

4. Click anywhere in the living room. Then click between each of the door swings and doors for the front and back doors. Check the ghosted boundary line to be sure that it follows the outline of the floor.

5. Right-click, and then choose Preview from the menu. The squares look a little small.

6. Press Esc to return to the Boundary Hatch And Fill dialog box. Reset the scale to 1.33.

7. Click Preview. This looks better. Right-click to accept it. The parquet pattern is placed in the living room and kitchen (see Figure 9.19).

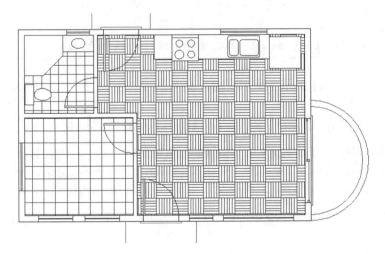

FIGURE 9.19: The parquet hatch in the living room and kitchen

8. Type **snapbase**↵. The Midpoint Osnap should still be running. Pick the threshold line that extends across the sliding glass door opening near its midpoint.

9. Restart the Hatch command, and set User-defined to be the pattern type.

10. Clear the Double check box. Set the spacing to 0'6". Click Pick Points.

11. Click anywhere on the balcony floor.

12. Right-click, and then choose Preview. Right-click again. The balcony floor is hatched with parallel lines that are 6" apart (see Figure 9.20).

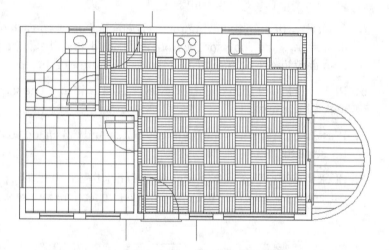

FIGURE 9.20: The user-defined hatch on the balcony floor

With the floors complete, the only components left to hatch are the walls.

Hatching the Walls in the Floor Plan

A solid fill is often used for full-height walls but not for low walls. The interior and exterior walls of the cabin are all full height and will be hatched with a solid fill. You'll then use a regular predefined pattern for the low balcony wall.

1. Zoom and pan to a full view of the floor plan.

2. Create a new layer called Hatch-plan-wall. Assign it the same color that you are using for the Walls layer, and make this new layer current.

3. Start the Hatch command. Set the type to Predefined. Open the Pattern drop-down list, and select Solid from the list.

4. Click Pick Points. In the drawing, click the 10 areas inside the wall and between the door and window jamb lines.

5. Right-click, choose Preview, and look at the drawing. The fill will look a little odd because the blue boundaries of the wall line are ghosted. Check to be sure all 10 areas in the wall are properly filled, and then right-click again. The walls now have a solid fill.

6. Restart the Hatch command and click Pattern.

7. Select ANSI31 for the pattern, and enter a scale of 24.

8. Click Pick Points, and pick a point between the two balcony arcs.

9. Right-click, choose Preview, right-click again, and then click OK. A diagonal crosshatch pattern is placed on the balcony wall (see Figure 9.21).

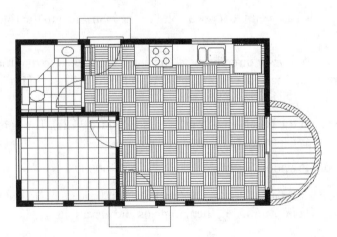

FIGURE 9.21: The hatched balcony wall

This completes the exercises for setting up and placing hatch patterns.

Modifying the Shape of Hatch Patterns

The next exercise will demonstrate how hatches are *associative*. An associative hatch pattern automatically updates when you modify the part of a drawing that is serving as the *boundary* for the pattern. You will be changing the current drawing, so before you begin making those changes, save the drawing as it is.

1. Zoom out and pan to get the floor plan and front elevation in the view. Thaw the Roof layer.

2. Save this drawing as Cabin09c. You'll use the Stretch command to modify this drawing.

3. Turn off the Hatch-elev-gray layer. Zoom in to the front elevation. Turn Polar Tracking on.

4. Click the Stretch button on the Modify toolbar.

5. Pick a point above and to the right of the ridge of the roof in elevation. Drag a window down and to the left until a crossing selection window encloses the ridgeline of the roof (see Figure 9.22a). Click to complete the window. Then press ↵ to finish the selection process.

6. For the base point, choose a point in the blank area to the right of the elevation.

7. Hold the cursor directly above the point you picked so that the Polar Tracking line and tool tip appear; then type 3'↵. The roof is now steeper (see Figure 9.22b).

8. Turn on the Hatch-elev-gray layer (see Figure 9.22c). The hatch pattern has expanded to fill the new roof area.

9. Zoom Previous. Save this drawing as Cabin09d.

Hatches are a necessary part of many drawings. You have seen a few of the possibilities AutoCAD offers for using them in plans and elevations.

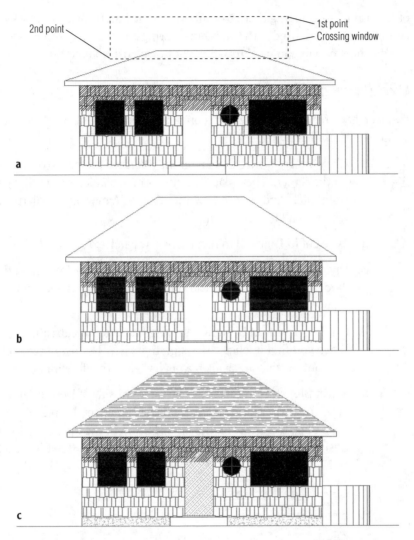

FIGURE 9.22: The crossing selection window (a), the modified roof (b), and the adjusted hatch pattern (c)

Creating and Managing Tool Palettes

If you find yourself using particular hatch patterns over and over in various drawings, make them available at a moment's notice instead of setting them up each time. AutoCAD's tool palettes let you do just that. You looked at this feature briefly in Chapter 7, but now we'll go through the process of setting up a couple of them and customizing them to contain specific hatch patterns, blocks, and commands that are used with the cabin drawings. From this exercise, you will get the information you need to set up your own custom palettes.

Creating a New Tool Palette

You'll create a new tool palette and then populate it with the blocks we've used so far in the cabin drawing.

1. Click the Tool Palettes icon on the Standard toolbar to display palettes on the screen. Then place the cursor on a blank space on the palettes, right-click, and choose New Tool Palette. A new blank palette displays with a small text box on it.

2. Type **Cabin Blocks**↵ to name the new palette.

3. Open DesignCenter by clicking the DesignCenter button on the Standard toolbar. If it isn't already docked, dock it on the left side of the drawing area.

4. On the left side of DesignCenter, navigate to the Cabin09c drawing. When you find it, click the + sign to its left. The list of types of drawing content that are available opens below the drawing.

5. Select Blocks from this list. Now the right side of DesignCenter displays the three blocks in Cabin09c, either as small images or by name only. Click the arrow on the Views button in the upper-right corner of DesignCenter, and choose List as the view option (see Figure 9.23).

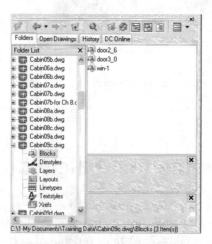

FIGURE 9.23: DesignCenter with the List view option

6. Select door2_6, then hold down the Shift key and click win-1 to select all three blocks. Then left-click and drag the three blocks over to the new palette. Small images of the blocks are displayed on the Cabin Blocks palette (see Figure 9.24), and they are now available for any drawing. Simply drag a block off the palette onto the drawing. You can then fine-tune its location, rotate it, and so forth. Any layers used by the block will also be brought into the drawing.

FIGURE 9.24: The new Cabin Blocks tool palette

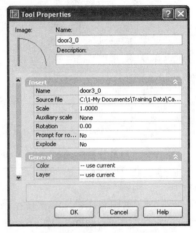

FIGURE 9.25: The Tool Properties dialog box

7. Place the cursor on door3_0 on the new palette, right-click, and then select Properties to open the Tool Properties dialog box. It displays information about door3_0 (see Figure 9.25).

8. Close the Tool Properties dialog box.

Setting Up a Palette for Hatches

To create a palette for hatches, you create and name a new palette using the same procedure as in the previous section, but the hatches get onto the palette in a different way.

1. Right-click in a blank space on the Cabin Blocks palette, choose New Tool Palette, and then type **Cabin Hatches**⏎ in the text box.

2. Zoom in on the front elevation of the cabin, and click the roof hatch to display a grip.

3. Move the cursor to a portion of the roof hatch that is not close to the grip, then left-click and drag the hatch pattern over to the new palette (see Figure 9.26).

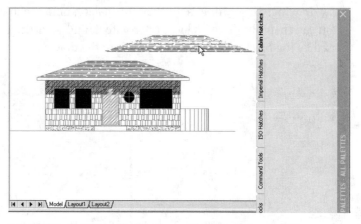

FIGURE 9.26: Moving the roof hatch to the new palette

4. When the cursor is over the palette and a horizontal line appears there, release the mouse button. The roof hatch is now positioned on the palette and available for use in any drawing. Simply drag it off the palette and into the enclosed area in your drawing that you desire to hatch with that pattern.

5. Place the cursor on the new swatch of AR-RROOF, right-click, and choose Properties. The Tool Properties dialog box opens.

6. Change the name from AR-RROOF to Cabin Roof. Enter a description of what the hatch represents, such as Composition Roofing. Notice that the hatch has the angle and scale that were used on the roof and that it's also on the Hatch-elev-gray layer. Use the slider at the left to view all the properties. Click OK to close the dialog box and update the palette is (see Figure 9.27).

FIGURE 9.27: The Cabin Hatches palette after being renamed

By using the Properties palette, you can also give hatches color. All the hatches that you've used for the cabin so far can be placed on the palette in the same manner. They retain the properties that they had in the original drawing, but by using the Properties dialog box, you can change those properties.

Creating a Palette for Commands

Take a moment to look at some of the sample palettes that come with AutoCAD, and check the properties of some of the items that you see. In addition to blocks and hatches, there are also command icons. These are placed on the palette in a slightly different way from blocks and hatches.

1. Right-click the Cabin Hatches palette in a blank area, and choose New Tool Palette from the shortcut menu.

2. Name the new palette **Commands**.

3. Right-click the new palette, and choose Customize to open the Customize dialog box. Be sure Commands is the active tab (see Figure 9.28).

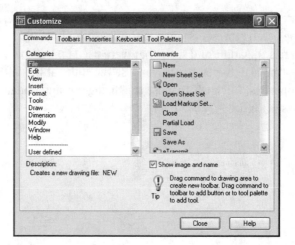

FIGURE 9.28: The Commands tab in the Customize dialog box

4. In the list of categories on the left, highlight Draw. Then scroll down the commands list on the right and drag Arc Start Center Angle over to the palette, just as you dragged the hatches in the previous section.

5. Drag Circle Center Radius to the palette. Then select the Modify category, scroll down the commands list again, and drag Copy Object and Stretch over to the Commands palette (see Figure 9.29).

FIGURE 9.29: The Commands palette with four command icons

When you need to use one of these commands, simply click the icon on the palette.

If you set the palettes to Auto-hide, they fold under the palette title bar. When you put your cursor on the bar, the palettes display and then hide a moment after your cursor moves off the palettes. To activate Auto-hide, right-click the palette title bar and choose Auto-hide from the shortcut menu.

This has been a brief introduction to the palette feature. I encourage you to experiment with the various options to become familiar with them, so you can use them as you find the need. Try right-clicking a blank portion of the palette and investigating the commands available on the resulting shortcut menu. You can delete any palette, and you can copy tools from one palette to another.

If You Would Like More Practice...

If you would like to practice what you've learned in this chapter, here are a couple of extra exercises.

Create a Hatch Pattern for the Roof in Plan View

To create your hatch pattern for the roof, make these changes and additions:

1. Make the Roof layer current, and change its linetype from Dashed to Continuous. Turn off all other layers.

2. Put a chimney in the roof approximately as shown in Figure 9.30a. Here are the dimensions:

   ▶ The rectangle is 2'-8" by 3'-0".

   ▶ The circle has an 8" radius. It is centered horizontally, and its lower quadrant point is set 4" up from the lower edge of the rectangle.

3. Create a new layer called Hatch-plan-roof. Assign it the same color you are using for the Roof layer. Make this new layer current.

4. Apply the AR-RSHKE pattern to each quadrant of the roof, changing the rotation angle by 90° for each adjacent area. Use a scale of 1.0000. When you pick the quadrant with the chimney, pick a point in the quadrant that is outside the chimney rectangle. The result should look like Figure 9.30b.

5. Double-click the hatch in the quadrant that contains the chimney. In the Hatch Edit dialog box, click the Advanced tab to make it active. In the Island Detection area, select the Outer option. Click the Hatch tab, and then click OK. Now the hatch pattern does not appear in the circle.

6. Move the chimney rectangle and circle to a different location in the quadrant and see the results (see Figure 9.30c). The hatch adjusts. What happens if you move the circle and rectangle that make up the chimney to a different quadrant or to a location completely off the roof? Try it.

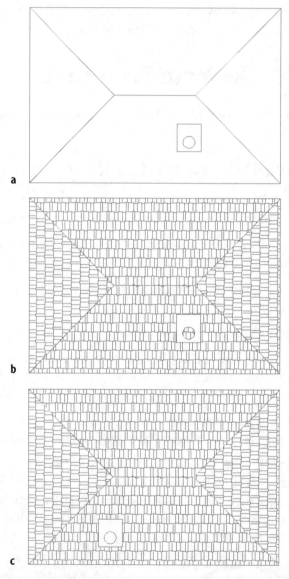

FIGURE 9.30: The roof with continuous lines and with a chimney (a), the new hatch for the roof (b), and the roof hatch with Island Detection adjusted and chimney moved (c)

Create Your Hatch Palette

It is true that any hatch pattern can be used to represent anything you want it to, but most trades and professions follow some sort of standard, even if loosely. The ANSI31 pattern of parallel lines is probably the most widely used pattern. Though it "officially" represents, according to the ANSI standard, Iron, Brick, and Stone Masonry, it is universally accepted as representing any cross-section view of any material, that is, the part of the object that was actually "sliced" through to make the view.

Create a new palette of hatches that you might use in your work. Use the same method that I demonstrated in the previous section of this chapter:

1. Open DesignCenter, and find the `acad.pat` file in the `UserData-Cache\Support` subfolder of the `AutoCAD 2005` or `AutoCAD LT 2005` folder. Open that file.

2. Use the Large Icon view to view the patterns on the right side of DesignCenter.

3. Scroll through and highlight any patterns you might use by holding down the Ctrl key as you select them. Do include the eight ANSI patterns.

4. When finished, right-click and choose Create New Tool Palette from the shortcut menu.

5. Close DesignCenter, and name the new palette.

6. Hold the cursor briefly over the name of each hatch to display a tool tip that describes the purpose of the hatch.

7. If you have brought any patterns to the palette that you don't want there after all, right-click each of them and choose Delete from the shortcut menu. Don't worry about changing any of the properties such as scale or rotation. That will come later, as you begin to use these hatches in your own work.

8. Check out the tools on the sample palettes: ISO Hatches, Imperial Hatches, and Sample Office Project. Right-click some of the hatches, fills, or blocks, and note how the rotation and scales vary for hatches that look the same on the palette. One hatch, such as ANSI31, might be repeated several times on the same palette, with each occurrence having a different scale or rotation. Note that the names of the hatches and fills have been removed from two of the sample palettes. Can you figure out how to do this or how to store the names?

Are You Experienced?

Now you can...

☑ create a predefined hatch pattern and apply it to a drawing

☑ set up and apply user-defined hatch patterns

☑ create a polar array of a line

☑ use lines to indicate a curved surface

☑ modify the scale of a hatch pattern

☑ modify the shape of a hatch pattern

☑ control the origin of a hatch pattern

☑ create and populate a tool palette for blocks, hatches, or commands

CHAPTER 10

Controlling Text in a Drawing

▶ Setting up text styles

▶ Placing new text in the drawing

▶ Modifying text in a drawing

▶ Working with grid lines

▶ Managing single-line and multiline text

▶ Creating a table

Y ou will have many uses for text in your drawings, including titles of views, notes, and dimensions. Each of these may require a different height, orientation, and style of lettering. To control the text, you will need to learn three basic operations:

▶ Determine how the text will look by setting up text styles.

▶ Specify where the text will be and enter it into the drawing.

▶ Modify the text already in your drawing.

AutoCAD offers two types of text objects: single-line and multiline. Single-line text makes a distinct object of each line of text, whether the line is one letter or many words. This type of text is useful for titles of drawings, titles of views within a drawing, room labels, and schedules. Dimensions, tables, and longer notes are done with multiline text. AutoCAD treats a whole body of multiline text as one object, whether the text consists of one letter or many paragraphs.

The two types of text share the same text styles, but each has its own command for placing text in the drawing. When you modify text, you can use the same commands for either type of text, but the commands operate differently for multiline than for single-line text. Any text used in *dimensioning*—a process by which you indicate the sizes of various components in your drawing—is handled slightly differently from other text and will be covered in Chapter 11.

We will progress through this chapter by first looking at the process of setting up text styles. We will then start placing and modifying single-line text in the cabin drawing. Finally, we'll look at the methods for creating and controlling multiline text as it is used for notes and tables. If you work in a non-AEC profession or trade, be assured that the features presented in this chapter will apply directly to your work. The basic principles of working with text in AutoCAD and AutoCAD LT "cross the curriculum" (an educational metaphor) and apply universally.

Setting Up Text Styles

In AutoCAD, a text style consists of a combination of a style name, a text font, a height, a width factor, an oblique angle, and a few other, mostly static settings. You specify these text style properties with the help of a dialog box that opens when you start the Style command. You will begin by setting up two text styles—one for labeling the rooms in the floor plan and the other for putting titles on the two views. You will need a new layer for text.

1. Open the Cabin09c drawing.

2. Create a new layer named Text1. Assign it a color, and make it current.

3. Freeze the Hatch-plan-floor and Hatch-plan-wall layers. Be sure all other layers are thawed and turned on. Your drawing should look like Figure 10.1.

FIGURE 10.1: The Cabin09c drawing with the Hatch-plan-floor and Hatch-plan-wall layers frozen

Text and Drawing Scale

When you set up text styles for a drawing, you have to determine the height of the text letters. To make this determination, you first need to decide the scale at which the final drawing will be printed.

In traditional drafting, you can ignore the drawing scale and set the actual height of each kind of text. This is possible because, while the drawing is to a scale, the text doesn't have to conform to that scale and is drawn full size.

In AutoCAD, a feature called *layouts* makes it possible to set the height of text in the same way—that is, at the height at which it will be printed. You will learn about using layouts in Chapter 13. In that chapter, you'll place text on layouts; in this chapter, I'll demonstrate how text is used without layouts. You'll place text in the cabin drawing. The drawing is actual size, but the text has to be much larger than actual size because both the drawing and its text will be scaled down by the same factor in the process of printing the drawing.

In this drawing, we will use a final scale of ⅛" = 1'-0". This scale has a true ratio of 1:96 and a scale factor of 96. (See Table 9.1 in Chapter 9.) If you want text to be ⅛" high when you print the drawing at ⅛-inch scale, multiply ⅛" by the scale factor

A *layout* is a drawing environment that has been overlaid on the drawing of your project. The layout and the drawing are part of the same file.

of 96 to get 12" for the text height. You can check that calculated text height by studying the floor plan for a moment and noting the sizes of the building components represented in the drawing. You can estimate that the room label text should be about half as high as the front step is deep, or 1 foot high.

Defining a Text Style for Room Labels

Now that you have a good idea of the required text height, it's time to define a new text style. Each new AutoCAD .dwg file comes with one predefined text style named Standard. You will add two more.

1. Type st↵ to start the Style command and open the Text Style dialog box (see Figure 10.2). In the Style Name area, you will see the default Standard text style.

You can also start the Style command by choosing Format ➤ Text Style.

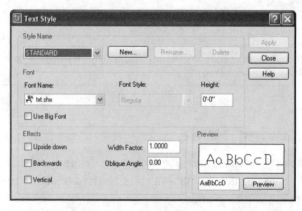

FIGURE 10.2:   The Text Style dialog box, in which text styles are set up

2. Click New to open the New Text Style dialog box. There is a Style Name text box with style1 in it, highlighted. When you enter a new style name, it will replace style1.

3. Type Label↵. The New Text Style dialog box closes, and in the Text Style dialog box, Label appears in the Style Name drop-down list. You have created a new text style named Label. It has settings identical to those of the Standard text style, and it is now the current text style. Now you will change some of the settings for this new style.

By default, all new .dwg files have the Standard text style as the current text style.

4. Move down to the Font area and click the Font Name drop-down list to open it. A list of fonts appears; the number of choices depends on what software is installed on your computer.

5. Scroll through the list until you find romans.shx, and then click it. The list closes, and in the Font Name text box, the romans.shx font replaces the txt.shx font that was previously there. In the Preview area in the lower-right corner, a sample of the romans.shx font replaces that of the txt.shx font.

6. Press the Tab key to jump to the next text box. The Height setting is highlighted at the default of 0'-0".

7. Type 12, and then press Tab again. A height of 1'-0" replaces the default height.

8. You won't need to change any of the other parameters that define the new text style. They can all stay at their default settings.

9. Click Apply in the upper-right corner of the dialog box. The Label text style is saved with the current drawing and becomes the current text style.

A *font* is a collection of text characters and symbols that all share a characteristic style of design and proportion.

N O T E   The current text style is similar to the current layer. All text created while a text style is current will follow the parameters or settings of that text style.

When you define a new text style, you first name the new style. This has the effect of making a copy of the current text style settings, giving them the new name, and making the new text style current. You then change the settings for this new style and save the changes by clicking Apply.

Defining a Second Text Style

Before you close the dialog box, define another text style.

1. Click New.

2. In the New Text Style dialog box, type **Title** and click OK. A new text style called Title has been created and is now the current text style. Its font, height, and other settings are a copy of the Label text style. Now you will make changes to these settings to define the Title text style.

Romans.shx and romand.shx are frequently used fonts in AutoCAD. Romans (formally named roman simplex) is usually applied to notes in the drawing. Romand (duplex) is a boldface version of romans and can be used for titles of views, titles of details, and dimensioning. Two more fonts in the roman font family—romanc and romant—are used for larger text.

3. Click the current font, romans.shx. The drop-down list of fonts opens. Scroll up one font and click romand.shx. The list closes, and romand.shx is displayed as the chosen font.

4. Press Tab once to move to the Height text box, type 18, and then press Tab once more. The height is converted to 1'-6".

T I P   If you press ↵ after typing the height, the new style is automatically applied, meaning it is saved and made the current text style. Don't do this if you need to change other settings for the style.

5. Click Apply, and then click Close.

Of the many fonts available in AutoCAD, you will use only a few for your drawings. Some are set up for foreign languages or mapping symbols. Others would appear out of place on architectural or technical drawings, but might be just right for an advertising brochure or a flier. Later in this chapter, you'll have a chance to experiment with the available fonts.

Look back at Figure 10.2 for a moment, and note that the Standard text style has a height of 0'-0". When the current text style has a height set to 0, you are prompted to enter a height each time you begin to place single-line text in the drawing. The default height will be ³⁄₁₆" (or 0.20 for decimal units and 2.5 for metric). Multiline text will use the default height of ³⁄₁₆" unless you change it.

Now that you have two new text styles, you can start working with single-line text.

Using Single-Line Text

Your first task is to put titles in for the floor plan and front elevation, using the new Title text style.

Placing Titles of Views in the Drawing

The titles need to be centered approximately under each view. If you establish a vertical guideline through the middle of the drawing, you can use it to position the text.

1. Pan the drawing up to create a little more room under the front elevation.

2. Set up your Osnaps and status bar such that Polar and Osnap are on and Endpoint and Midpoint Osnaps are running. Drop a line from the midpoint of the ridgeline in the floor plan, down through the front elevation, to a point near the bottom of the screen.

3. Offset the bottom line of the front step in the floor plan down 4'.

4. Choose Draw ≻ Text ≻ Single Line Text to start the Dtext command—the command used for single-line text.

5. The bottom line of text in the Command window reads Specify start point of text or [Justify/Style]:. The line above it displays the name of the current text style and the style's height setting. The bottom line is the actual prompt, with three options. By default, the justification point is set to the lower-left corner of the text. You need to change it to the middle of the text to be able to center it on the guideline.

6. Type j↵. All the possible justification points appear in the prompt.

7. Type c↵ to choose Center as the justification.

8. Hold down the Shift key and right-click to open a menu of Osnap options next to where the cursor had just been positioned.

Temporary track point
From
Mid Between 2 Points
Point Filters   ▸

Endpoint
Midpoint
Intersection
Apparent Intersect
Extension

Center
Quadrant
Tangent

Perpendicular
Parallel
Node
Insert
Nearest
None

Osnap Settings…

9. Choose Intersection and pick the intersection of the guideline and the offset line.

10. For the rotation, press ↵ to accept the default angle of 0°. An I cursor will be positioned at the intersection (see Figure 10.3).

You can also start the Dtext command by typing dt↵.

The *justification point* for the text functions like the insertion point for blocks.

The Osnap Cursor menu (Shift+right-click) contains all the Object Snap tools, access to the Osnap Settings dialog box to allow you to set running Osnaps, and a Point Filters menu.

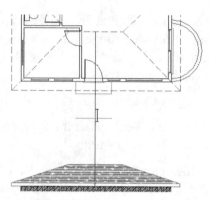

FIGURE 10.3: The text cursor sits on the guidelines.

11. With Caps Lock on, type **floor plan**⏎. The text is at the intersection as you type it (but not centered yet), and the cursor jumps down to allow you to type another line (see Figure 10.4a).

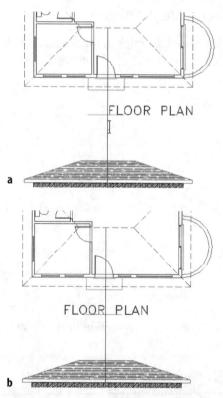

FIGURE 10.4: The first line of text is entered (a) and placed (b).

12. Press ↵ again to end the Dtext command. The text is centered relative to the vertical guideline and sits on the offset line (see Figure 10.4b).

13. Offset the ground line of the elevation down 4'. Start the Dtext command again, and repeat steps 4 through 12, this time entering **front elevation** (again with Caps Lock on). When finished, erase the offset lines and the vertical guideline. Your drawing will look like Figure 10.5.

FLOOR PLAN

FRONT ELEVATION

FIGURE 10.5: The drawing with the titles complete

You specified a location for the text in two steps: first, you set the justification point of each line of text to be centered horizontally; then you used the Intersection Osnap to position the justification point at the intersection of the two guidelines. I'll discuss justification in more depth a little later in this chapter.

Next you will move to the interior of the cabin floor plan and place the room labels in their respective rooms.

Placing Room Labels in the Floor Plan

Text for the room labels will use the Label text style, so you need to make that style current before you start placing text. You can accomplish this from within the Dtext command by using the Style option.

1. Pan down the drawing and zoom in to the floor plan. Click the Polar and Osnap buttons on the status bar to turn off these features.

2. Start the Dtext command. At the prompt, type s↵ to choose the Style option. The prompt reads Enter style name or [?] <Title>:.

3. Type ?↵↵ to see a list of defined text styles. In the text screen, you see Label, Standard, and Title listed along with information about the parameters of each style (see Figure 10.6). At the bottom of the text screen, you can see the Dtext prompt again.

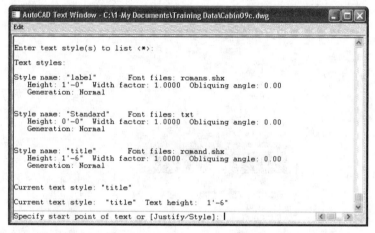

FIGURE 10.6: The text screen listing the defined text styles

4. Type s↵ again. Then type label↵ to make Label the current text style.

5. Press F2 to close the text screen and return to the drawing.

6. Pick a point in the kitchen a couple of feet below and to the left of the oven.

7. Press ↵ at the Rotation prompt. The text cursor appears at the point you picked.

8. With Caps Lock on, type kitchen↵ living room↵ bedroom↵ bath↵↵. The Dtext command ends. You will have four lines of text in the kitchen and living room area (see Figure 10.7).

FLOOR PLAN

FIGURE 10.7: The four room labels placed in the cabin

For this text, you used the default Left justification, and each line of text was positioned directly below the previous line at a spacing set by AutoCAD. In many cases, it is more efficient to type a list of words or phrases first and then move the text to its appropriate location. That's what we are doing for this text.

Moving Text

We will eyeball the final position of this text because it doesn't have to be exactly centered or lined up precisely with anything. It should just sit in the rooms in such a way that it is easily readable.

1. Click anywhere on the BATH text. One grip appears, at the justification point of the text.

2. Click the grip to activate it. The BATH text is attached to the cursor and moves with it (see Figure 10.8a). The Stretch command automatically starts. Because text can't be stretched, the Stretch command functions like the Move command.

3. Be sure that Ortho, Polar, Osnap (and, for AutoCAD only, Otrack) are turned off. Move the cursor to the bathroom, and click a location to place the word in such a way that the letters—while they may be on top of the door swing and the roof line—don't touch any fixtures or walls.

4. Press Esc to remove the grip (see Figure 10.8b). Then select the BED-ROOM text.

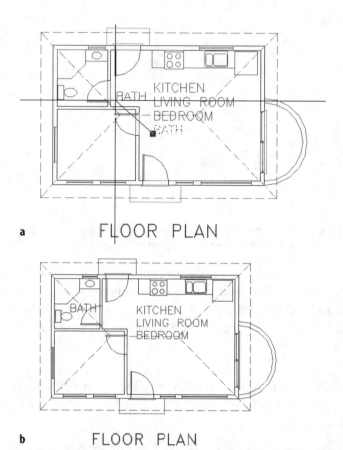

a FLOOR PLAN

b FLOOR PLAN

FIGURE 10.8: Moving the BATH text (a), and its new location (b)

5. Click the grip for the newly selected text.

6. Pick a point in the bedroom so that the BEDROOM text is positioned approximately at the center of the bedroom and crossing only the roof line. Press Esc to remove the grip.

7. Repeat this process to move the LIVING ROOM and KITCHEN text into their appropriate locations (see Figure 10.9). You may not have to move the KITCHEN text.

> When you move text in this way, you are actually using the Stretch command. Because text can't be stretched, it just moves with the cursor.

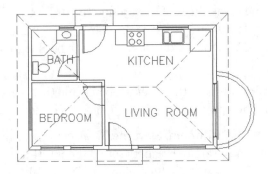

FLOOR PLAN

FIGURE 10.9: The BEDROOM, LIVING ROOM, and KITCHEN text moved to their positions

As you have seen, you can easily move text around the drawing. Often, however, you will be unable to position it without it sitting on top of a line or other object. In the cabin, three of the room labels are crossing the roof line, and BATH is crossing a door swing. You need to erase parts of these lines around the text. To do this, you'll use the Break command.

Breaking Lines

The Break command chops a line into two lines. When working with text that is sitting on a line, you will usually want a gap between the lines after the break. The Break command provides this option as well as others.

1. Be sure no Osnaps are running, and then click the Break button on the Modify toolbar.

2. Move the cursor near the roof line that crosses through the LIVING ROOM text. Place the pickbox on the roof line just above the text and click. The line ghosts, and the cursor changes to the crosshair cursor.

3. Put the crosshair cursor on the roof line just below the text and pick that point. The line is broken around the text, and the Break command ends.

4. Press ↵ to restart the Break command, and do the same operation on the roof line that crosses the BEDROOM text.

You can also start the **Break command by choosing Modify ➤ Break or by typing br↵.**

Chapter 10 • Controlling Text in a Drawing

5. Press ↵ again, and break the roof line around the BATH text. The arc representing the door swing is part of the door2_6 block and, as such, cannot be broken. You must explode the block to be able to break the arc.

 6. Click the Explode button on the Modify toolbar, and then select the bathroom door. Then press ↵. The door2_6 block is exploded.

7. Zoom in closer to the bathroom. Start the Break command, and select two points on the arc to break it around the BATH text. Zoom Previous to get a full view of the floor plan (see Figure 10.10).

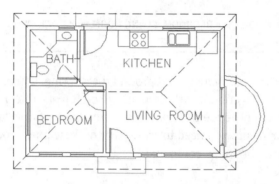

FLOOR PLAN

FIGURE 10.10: Lines are broken around the room labels.

A CLOSER LOOK AT THE BREAK COMMAND

Use your own judgment to determine how far from the text a line has to be broken back. You have to strike a balance between making the text easy to read and keeping what the broken line represents clear. In the bathroom, you were directed to keep the text away from any fixtures because if any lines of the fixtures had to be broken to accommodate the text, this might have made it difficult for a viewer to recognize that those lines represent a shower or a toilet.

Continued on next page

Here are some other options for the Break command:

▶ Normally, when you select a line to be broken, the point where you pick the line becomes the beginning of the break. If the point where the break needs to start is at the intersection of two lines, you must select the line to be broken somewhere other than at a break point. Otherwise, AutoCAD won't know which line you want to break. In that case, after selecting the line to break, type **f⏎**. You will be prompted to pick the first point of the break, and the command continues. Now that AutoCAD knows which line you want to break, you can use Intersection Osnap to pick the intersection of two lines.

▶ To break a line into two segments without leaving a gap, click the Break At Point button, which is just above the Break button. You might want to do this to place one part of a line on a different layer from the rest of the line. To break the line this way, start the command, select the line to break, and then pick the point on the line where the break is to occur, using an Osnap if necessary. AutoCAD will make the break and end the command.

▶ When you create a gap in a line for text, the line will have a gap in it even when the text layer is turned off. This will be a problem for the bath door swing and the roof line. We'll attend to this issue in the last few chapters of this book.

Using Text in a Grid

AutoCAD provides a grid of dots, which you worked with in Chapter 3. The grid is a tool for visualizing the size of the drawing area and for drawing lines whose geometry conforms to the spacing of the dots. Many floor plans have a separate *structural* grid, created specifically for the project and made up of lines running vertically and horizontally through key structural parts of the building. At one end of each grid line, a circle or a hexagon is placed, and a letter or number is centered in the shape to identify it. This kind of grid is usually reserved for large, complex drawings, but we will put a small grid on the cabin floor plan to learn the basic method for laying one out.

1. Create a new layer called Grid. Assign it a color, and make it current.

2. Type z↵ .6x↵ to make more room around the floor plan.

3. Offset the upper roof line up 10'. Offset the left roof line 10' to the left. Offset the lower roof line down 2'. Offset the right roof line to the right 4'. Pan and zoom as necessary.

4. Set Endpoint and Perpendicular Osnaps to be running, and then start the Line command.

5. Draw lines from the upper-left and upper-right corners of the exterior walls up to the horizontal offset line. Then draw lines from the left upper and lower corners of the exterior walls to the vertical offset line on the left (see Figure 10.11).

FIGURE 10.11: The first grid lines

6. Now you need to draw grid lines through the middle of the interior walls. Zoom in to the bathroom area, and draw a short guideline across the interior wall between the bathroom and bedroom, where this wall meets the exterior wall (see Figure 10.12).

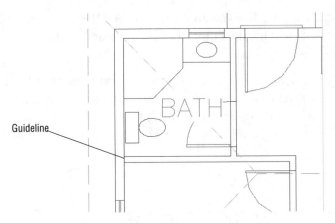

FIGURE 10.12: A guideline for drawing a grid line through one of the interior walls

7. Use Realtime Zoom and Pan to set up the view so that it contains the bathroom and the offset roof lines above and to the left of the floor plan.

8. Draw two vertical lines and one horizontal line from the middle of the interior walls out to the offset roof lines. Use Midpoint Osnap and pick one of the jamb lines or the guideline to start each line from the middle of a wall (see Figure 10.13).

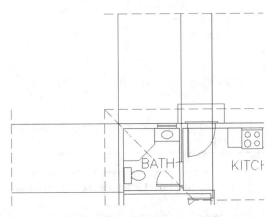

FIGURE 10.13: Drawing the grid lines

  T I P   If Midpoint Osnap were running, it would be difficult to pick the midpoint of the little guideline because Endpoint would have been running too. When you select Midpoint from the Object Snap toolbar, you cancel all running Osnaps for the next pick.

9. Erase the guideline you drew in step 6, and then zoom out to a view that includes the floor plan, the grid lines, and all the offset roof lines (see Figure 10.14a).

10. Use the Extend command to extend the seven grid lines to the right or down, and use the offset roof lines on those sides of the floor plan as boundary edges (see Figure 10.14b).

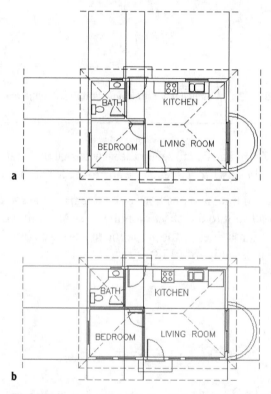

FIGURE 10.14: The zoomed view for completing the grid lines (a), and the completed grid lines (b)

 T I P   When erasing the guideline, select it with a regular selection window.

This completes the grid lines. To finish the grid, you need to add a circle with a letter or a number in it to the left or upper end of the lines. We'll use letters across the top and numbers running down the side.

1. Erase the four offset roof lines. Zoom out a little.

2. Choose Draw ➤ Circle ➤ 2 Points, and then pick the upper end of the leftmost vertical grid line.

3. Type @2'<90⏎. A circle 2' in diameter is placed at the top of the grid line (see Figure 10.15a).

4. Click the KITCHEN text. A grip will appear.

5. Click the grip and type c, for copy, and press ⏎.

6. Select the Center Osnap and click the circle on the grid. The KITCHEN text is placed on the circle with the lower-left corner of the text at the center of the circle (see Figure 10.15b). Press Esc twice, once to end the Stretch command and again to clear the grip.

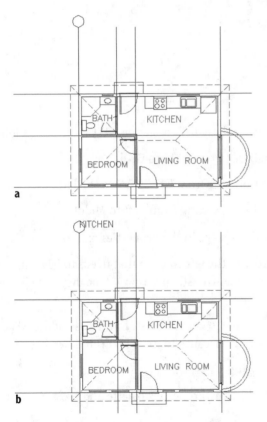

FIGURE 10.15: The circle on the grid line (a), and the KITCHEN text copied to the circle (b)

7. Click the copy of the KITCHEN text that is now on the grid, and then click the Properties button on the Standard Properties toolbar to open the Properties palette. Text is displayed on the drop-down list at the top, telling you that you have selected a text object.

► This may seem like a roundabout way to generate letters for the grid symbols, but this exercise is meant to show you how easy it is to use text from one part of the drawing for a completely different text purpose. It's a handy technique, as long as you want to use a font that has been chosen for a previously defined text style. A faster way to do this is to use the Single Line Text command with the justification set to Middle, use Center Osnap to place the text cursor at the center of the circle, and then type A.↵↵.

8. Use the Properties palette to change the KITCHEN text as follows:

   A. Change the Layer from Text1 to Grid.

   B. Change the Contents from KITCHEN to the letter *A*.

   C. Change the Justify setting from Left to Middle.

For each change, follow these steps in the Properties palette:

1. Click the category in the left column that needs to be changed. If the setting is on a drop-down list, an arrow will be displayed in the right column.

2. Click the Down arrow to open the list. In the case of the KITCHEN text, just highlight it, because there is no drop-down list.

3. Click the new setting, or type it.

4. When finished, close the Properties palette and press Esc to remove the grip.

The KITCHEN text changes to the letter *A*, is centered in the grid circle, and moves to the Grid layer (see Figure 10.16).

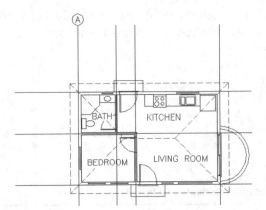

FIGURE 10.16: The grid circle with the letter *A*

You used the Center Osnap on the KITCHEN text to position its justification point at the center of the circle. You then modified the justification point from the Left position (which is actually short for Lower Left) to the Middle position (short for Center Middle). The Middle position is the middle of the line of text, horizontally and vertically. So what we did had the effect of centering the text in the circle. Let's look at Text Justification briefly.

Text Justification

Each line of single-line text is an object. It has a justification point, which is similar to the insertion points on blocks. When drawing, you can use the Insert Osnap to precisely locate the justification point of text (or the insertion point of blocks) and thereby control the text's position on the drawing. When you use the Dtext command, the default justification point is the lower-left corner of the line of text. At the Dtext prompt (`Specify start point of text or [Justify/Style]:`), if you type j↵, you get the prompt `Enter an option [Align/Fit/Center/ Middle/Right/TL/TC/TR/ML/MC/MR/BL/BC/BR]:`. These are your justification options.

Most of these options are represented in Figure 10.17. The dots are in three columns—left, center, and right—and four rows—top, middle, lower, and base. The names of the justification locations are based on these columns and rows. For example, you have TL for Top Left, MR for Middle Right, and so on. The third row down doesn't use the name Lower. It simply goes by Left, Center, and Right. Left is the default justification position, so it's not in the list of options. The Middle position will sometimes coincide with the Middle Center position, but not always. For example, if a line of text has *descenders*—lowercase letters that drop below the base line—the Middle position will drop below the Middle Center position. Finally, the lowest row, the *Base row*, sits just below the letters at the lowest point of any descenders.

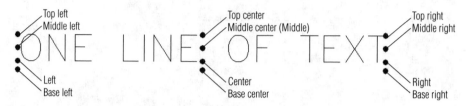

FIGURE 10.17: The justification points on a line of text

Finishing the Grid

To finish the grid, you need to copy the grid circle with its text to each grid line and then change the text.

1. Be sure Endpoint Osnap is still running. Then, at the Command: prompt, select the letter *A*, and then click the circle. Grips appear.

2. Click the grip at the bottom of the circle to activate it.

3. Right-click and choose Move; then right-click again and choose Copy to activate the copy option.

4. Pick the top end of each vertical grid line; then right-click and choose Enter (see Figure 10.18).

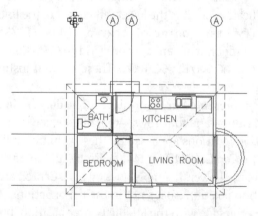

FIGURE 10.18: The grid circle and letter are copied to the top of all three vertical lines.

5. Move back to the original grid circle, and select the grip on the right side of the circle to activate it.

6. Repeat steps 3 and 4 to copy the original grid circle and letter to the left end of each horizontal grid line.

7. Press Esc to remove the grips. Now you'll use the Text Edit command to change the text in each circle.

8. Be sure Caps Lock is on. Type ed↵. Select the letter *A* in the second grid circle from the left on the top row to open the Edit Text dialog box.

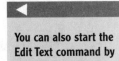

You can also start the Edit Text command by choosing Modify ➢ Object ➢ Text ➢ Edit or by double-clicking the text that you want to modify.

9. With Caps Lock on, type b↵. The *A* changes to *B*.

10. Click the *A* in the next circle to the right, and then type c↵. The *A* changes to *C*.

11. Repeat this process for the remaining four grid circle letters, changing them to *D*, *1*, *2*, and *3*. Press ↵ to end the Edit Text command. The letters and numbers are all in place, and the grid is complete (see Figure 10.19).

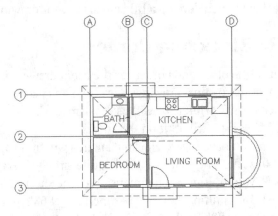

FIGURE 10.19: The completed grid

12. Zoom to Extents, and then zoom out a little to get a view of the entire drawing with the grid completed (see Figure 10.20).

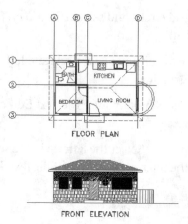

FIGURE 10.20: The Cabin10a drawing

13. Save this drawing as Cabin10a.

Often it is easier to copy existing text and modify it than to create new text, and grips are a handy way to copy text. Using the Edit Text command (technically called Ddedit) is a quick way to modify the wording of short lines of text, those that consist of a word or a few letters. The Properties palette is useful for changing all aspects of a line of text.

For the next exercise with text, you get a chance to set up some more new text styles, place text precisely, and use the Ddedit command again to modify text content. This will all be done as you develop a title block for your drawing.

Creating a Title Block and Border

The first step in creating a title block and border for the cabin drawing is deciding on a sheet size for printing the final drawing. Because many people have access to an 8.5 × 11-inch format printer, we will use that sheet size. If you print the drawing at a scale of ⅛" = 1'-0", will it fit on the sheet?

To answer that question, you have to ask, How big an area will fit on an 8.5 × 11-inch sheet at ⅛" = 1'-0" scale? The answer is really quite simple: if every inch on the sheet represents 8', you multiply each dimension of the sheet in inches by 8' per inch. For this sheet, you multiply 8.5" × 8' per inch to get 68'. And you multiply 11" × 8' per inch to get 88'. So the 8.5 × 11-inch sheet represents a rectangle with dimensions of 68' × 88' at a scale of 1" = 8'-0" (usually called *eighth-inch scale*). That should be plenty of room for your cabin drawing. This is the information that you need to start creating the title block.

Drawing the Border

The border of the drawing will be set in from the edge of the sheet.

1. Create a new layer called Tblk1. Leave the default color assigned, and make this layer current.

2. Start the Rectangle command (used in Chapter 4 to make the doors).

3. At the prompt, type 0,0↵. Then type 68',88'↵. A rectangle is drawn that extends off the top of the screen (see Figure 10.21a).

4. Use Realtime Zoom to zoom out until the entire rectangle is visible in the drawing area (see Figure 10.21b). You need to fit the drawing into the rectangle as if you were fitting it on a sheet of paper—the easiest and safest way to do this is to move the rectangle over to enclose the drawing.

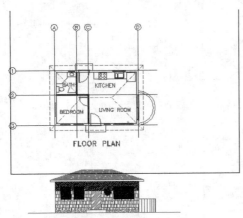

FLOOR PLAN

FRONT ELEVATION

a

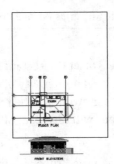

b

FIGURE 10.21: Creating the rectangle (a), and zooming out to include the entire rectangle (b)

5. At the Command: prompt, click the rectangle to turn on the grips. Grips appear at the corners of the rectangle.

6. Click the lower-left grip. Press the spacebar once. Then move the rectangle over the drawing (see Figure 10.22a).

7. When the rectangle is approximately in the position shown in Figure 10.22b, click. Then press Esc to turn off the grips. The rectangle is positioned around the drawing and represents the edge of the sheet.

> **Once you activate a grip and the Stretch command begins, pressing the spacebar toggles through the other four commands in this order: Move, Rotate, Scale, Mirror.**

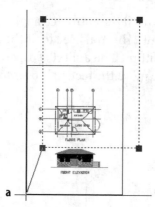

a

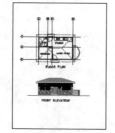

b

FIGURE 10.22: Moving the rectangle with grips (a), and the results (b)

8. You need a border set in from the edge. Offset the rectangle 3' to the inside. (With a scale of 1" = 8'-0", which is another way of expressing the scale of ⅛" = 1'-0", each 1'-0" on the drawing will be represented by ⅛" on the sheet. So a 3' offset distance will create an offset of ⅜" on the printed sheet.)

9. Double-click the inside rectangle to open the Properties palette.

10. In the list of Geometry settings, change the Global Width from 0" to 3". Close the Properties palette, and press Esc to remove the grips.

11. Zoom to Extents, and then zoom out a little to create a view in which the drawing with its border nearly fills the screen (see Figure 10.23). The outer rectangle represents the edge of the sheet of paper, while the thicker, inner rectangle is the drawing's border.

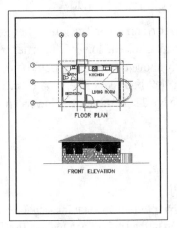

FIGURE 10.23: The drawing with its border

Constructing a Title Block

The *title block* is a box that contains general information about a drawing, such as the name of the project, the design company, and the date of the drawing. It will be set up in the lower-right corner of the border and will use the same special line—the *polyline*—that was used in the Rectangle command.

We first used the Rectangle command in Chapter 4 for drawing the doors. At that time, I mentioned that rectangles created with the Rectangle command are made up of a polyline whose four segments are grouped as one object. In step 10 of the previous section, you saw that these segments could have varying widths.

The *Polyline command*, nicknamed the Pline command, allows you to draw continuous straight and curved line segments of varying widths, with all segments behaving as if they were one object.

When you explode a polyline using the Explode command, the segments lose any width they have and become independent lines. The ability of a polyline to have a width makes it useful in constructing title blocks. We'll use the Pline command to draw the various lines that make up the title block, and then we'll fill in the text.

1. Zoom in to a view of the lower third of your drawing, including the bottom of the border. Be sure Endpoint and Perpendicular Osnaps are running.

2. Click the Polyline icon on the Draw toolbar. The `Specify start point:` prompt appears in the Command window.

3. Click Polar on the status bar to turn on Polar Tracking. Then select the Temporary Tracking Point Osnap. Click the lower-left corner of the border, and hold the cursor directly above that point. When the vertical tracking path appears along the left boundary line, type 12'↵. This starts a polyline on the left side of the border 12' above the lower-left corner.

You can also start the Polyline command by typing pl↵ or by choosing Draw ➢ Polyline.

If you're using LT, see the following "For LT Users" sidebar for a way to complete this step.

FOR LT USERS

LT users should follow this step:

3. Click Polar on the status bar to turn on Polar Tracking. Then click the Tracking button at the top of the Object Snap toolbar. Use Endpoint Osnap to click the lower-left corner of the border, hold the cursor directly above that point, and type **12'↵**. This starts a polyline on the left side of the border 12' above the lower-left corner.

Now continue with step 4.

4. Notice the bottom two lines in the Command window. The upper one tells you the current width set for polylines. The lower one displays the options for the Polyline command, with the default option being to pick a second point. This is the time to set the line width.

5. Type w↵, and then type 3↵↵. This sets the starting and ending width of polyline segments to 3". The original Polyline command prompt returns, and you can pick a point to define the line segment (see Figure 10.24a).

6. Hold the crosshair cursor on the right side of the border. When the perpendicular icon appears on the border line, click. Then press ↵. The first polyline segment is drawn (see Figure 10.24b). The 3" width setting will stay until you change it and will be saved with the drawing file.

7. Restart the Polyline command. Choose the Midpoint Osnap, and start a new segment at the midpoint of the line you just drew.

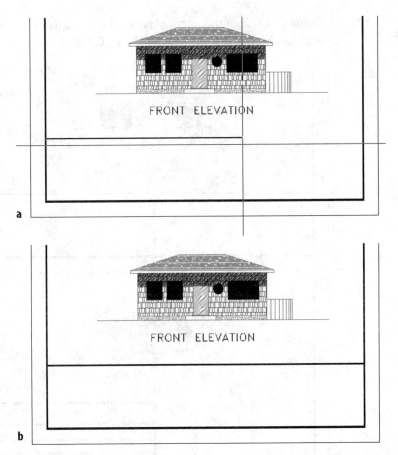

FIGURE 10.24: Drawing a polyline: setting the width (a), and completing the segment (b)

8. Move to the bottom of the border near its midpoint. When the running Perpendicular Osnap is activated, click. The left edge of the title block is drawn (see Figure 10.25a). Press ↵ to end the Polyline, or Pline, command.

9. Trim the left half of the first pline drawn back to the pline just drawn.

10. Offset the horizontal pline down 4', offset this new line down 3', and then offset this new line down 2'-6" (see Figure 10.25b).

11. Start the Pline command. Using Midpoint Osnap, start a pline at the midpoint of the third horizontal line down. Then end the segment at the bottom of the border, taking advantage of the running Perpendicular Osnap. Press ↵ to end the Pline command.

12. Trim the right side of the line just above the bottom of the border, back to the line you just drew (see Figure 10.25c).

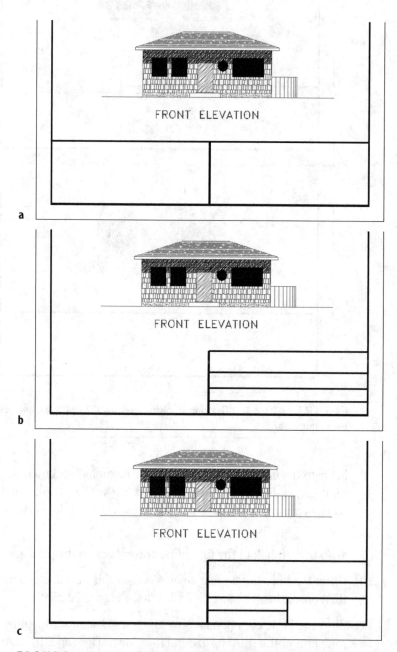

FIGURE 10.25: Building the title block: the left edge (a), the horizontal lines (b), and the last line trimmed (c)

The lines for the title block are almost done. Some of the plines may look wider than others. This almost certainly is caused by the monitor distorting the picture at the current view. By zooming in, you can assure yourself that everything is correct.

1. Zoom in to a close view of the title block. Notice that the intersection of the outer lines in the upper-left corner doesn't seem clean.

2. Zoom in to that corner using a zoom window (see Figure 10.26a). The lines don't intersect in a clean corner. They need to be joined.

3. Type pe↵ to start the Polyline Edit (Pedit) command, and select one of the two lines. You must place the pickbox on the edge of the polyline to select it, not in the middle of it.

4. Type j↵ to activate the Join option, and then select the other pline and press ↵. The corner is corrected (see Figure 10.26b). Type x↵ to end the Pedit command.

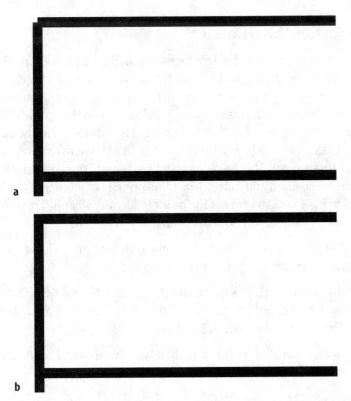

FIGURE 10.26: Zoomed in to the upper-left corner (a), and the corner corrected (b)

5. Zoom Previous once. Then use Realtime Zoom to zoom out just enough to see the FRONT ELEVATION text at the top of the screen (see Figure 10.27).

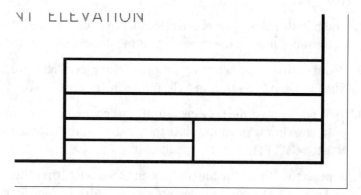

FIGURE 10.27: The completed lines of the title block after zooming out

Putting Text in the Title Block

The title block has five boxes that will each contain distinct pieces of information. The large one at the top will contain the name of the project. Below that will be the name of the company producing the drawing—your company. (If you don't have a company name, make one up.) Below that on the left will be the initials of the person—you—who drew this drawing and, below that, the date. In the lower-right corner will be the sheet number, in case more than one sheet is required for this project. This follows a standard format. Most title block layouts contain this information and more, depending on the complexity of the job.

You need to put labels in some of the boxes to identify what information will be shown there. For this, you need to set up a new text style.

1. Choose Format ➤ Text Style to open the Text Style dialog box. The Label text style should still be current.

2. Click New, type **Tblk-label**, and then click OK. Leave the font set to romans.shx, but change the height to 8". Then click Apply & Close. Tblk-label is the current text style.

3. Be sure Caps Lock is on, and then type dt↵ to start the Dtext command. Click the Snap To None Osnap button. Then pick a point in the

If you press ↵ after changing the height, the Apply button ghosts. Pressing ↵ at this point has the same effect as clicking the Apply button.

upper-left corner of the upper box of the title block. It doesn't have to be the perfect location now; you can fix it after you see the text.

4. Press ↵ at the rotation prompt. Type project:↵↵. PROJECT: will be placed in the upper box (see Figure 10.28a).

5. If necessary, move this text to the upper-left corner, as far as possible, while still allowing it to be readable. It will help if Polar and Osnap are temporarily turned off.

T I P   If you have running Osnaps and need to have them off for one pick, you can click the Snap To None Osnap button. This cancels all running Osnaps for the next pick. If you need running Osnaps turned off for several picks, click the Osnap button on the status bar. Click it again when you want the running Osnaps to become active.

The closer you zoom in, the more precisely you will be able to fine-tune the location of the text. You then need to zoom out to check how it looks.

6. Use the Copy command to copy this text to the bottom two boxes on the left, using the Multiple option and the endpoint of the horizontal lines above each of the boxes as the base and displacement points. This will keep each piece of text in the same position relative to the upper-left corner of each box.

7. Type ed↵ to start the Ddedit command. Then click the upper of the two copies of text. The Edit Text dialog box appears with PROJECT: highlighted.

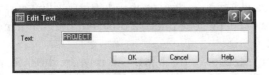

8. Type drawn by: and click OK. Pick the lower copy of text. The Edit Text dialog box returns.

9. Type date: and click OK. Press↵ to end the Ddedit command. The text is changed and three of the boxes have their proper label (see Figure 10.28b).

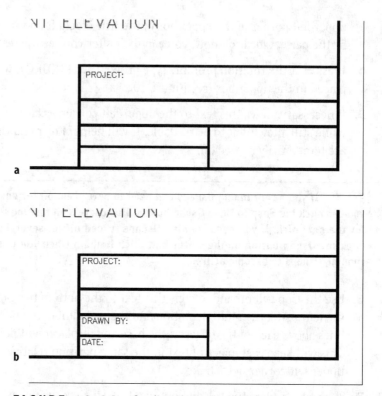

FIGURE 10.28: One line of text placed (a), and the text changed to the correct wording (b)

Using the Ddedit command is a quick way to change the wording of text and correct spelling. You have to change one line at a time, but the command keeps running until you stop it.

The next area to work on is the lower-right box. This is where the sheet number is located, and it is usually displayed in such a way that the person reading the drawing can tell not only the page number of the current sheet, but also the number of sheets being used for the project. We will create a new text style for this box.

1. Start the Style command. In the Text Style dialog box, click New.

2. Type Sheet_No and click OK. For the font, select romand.shx. Change the height to 1'-3". Click Apply, and then click Close. Sheet_No is now the current text style.

3. You will need to center the text horizontally in the box. This will require breaking the horizontal line running across the top of this box at the upper-left corner of the box. To do this, click the Break At

Point button on the Modify toolbar. Then select the line to break at a point where no other lines are touching it.

4. Use the Endpoint running Osnap to pick the upper-left corner of the box. AutoCAD breaks the line at that point without leaving a gap and ends the command.

5. Start the Dtext command and type j↵. Then type tc↵. Select Midpoint Osnap, and pick a point on the line across the top of the box.

6. Press ↵ at the rotation prompt. With Caps Lock on, type **sheet no.:**↵ 1 of 1↵↵. (When you get to the *of,* turn off Caps Lock.) For clarity, leave an extra space after the first *1* and before the second *1.* The text is inserted into the box and is centered horizontally (see Figure 10.29a).

7. With Polar Tracking on, use the Move command to move the text down and center it vertically in the box (see Figure 10.29b). Remember, when you select the text to move it, you have to pick each line because they are two separate objects.

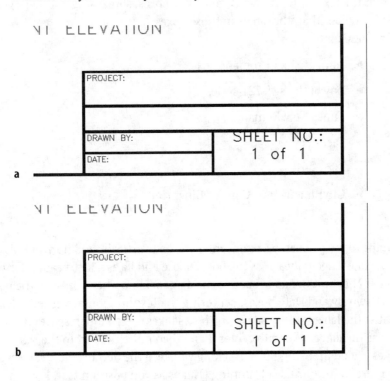

FIGURE 10.29: The text after being inserted (a), and after centering vertically (b)

Now it's time for you to experiment. Use the techniques you just went through to fill in the text for the other four boxes. Feel free to try other fonts, but you will have to adjust the height for each text style so that the text fits in its box. Some guidelines for height follow.

Box	Recommended Height of Text
Project:	2'-6"
Company:	1'-3"
Drawn By:	1'-0"
Date:	1'-0"

You will have to set up a new style for each new font or height you choose unless you set up a style with a height of 0'-0". In that case, you will be prompted for the height each time you start to place text in the drawing. This is the recommended way to operate for the top two boxes because it will give consistency to the text even when heights vary. You might try several fonts and then come back to this technique at the end. I also recommend that you use a relatively simple font for the text in the Drawn By and Date boxes, something a little larger and possibly bolder than the labels in those boxes.

Try these fonts:

- ▶ romant.shx or romanc.shx
- ▶ Any of the swis721 series
- ▶ Times New Roman
- ▶ Technic
- ▶ SansSerif
- ▶ CityBlueprint or CountryBlueprint
- ▶ Arial

In the top two boxes, you can center the text vertically and horizontally if you draw a line diagonally across the box, choose Middle as a justification for the text, and use Midpoint Osnap to snap to the diagonal line when you start the text. For the Drawn By and Date boxes, centering the text horizontally is not advisable because the label text already in the boxes takes up too much space. However, you can use the diagonal line to center it and then move the text to the right until it makes a good fit. Using Polar Tracking will keep the new text vertically centered.

Be careful in your use of running Osnaps as you position text. If you are eyeballing the final location, it is best to have no running Osnaps. On the other hand, if you are precisely locating justification points by snapping to lines and other objects, you might try having the following Osnaps running: Endpoint, Intersection, Perpendicular, and Insertion, with Midpoint optional.

When you finish, your title block should look something like Figure 10.30. In this sample, romant.shx font was used for a style that was set to zero height and then applied to the top two boxes at the recommended heights. The romand.shx font was used for the Drawn By and Date boxes, also at the recommended height.

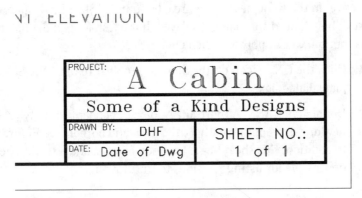

FIGURE 10.30: The completed title block

If you are going to design your own company title block, be ready to spend a little time setting it up and deciding which fonts will give the look that best reflects the image you want to project. You can then use this title block on all your subsequent projects.

Zoom to Extents, and then zoom out a little to view the entire drawing. Save this drawing as Cabin10b (see Figure 10.31).

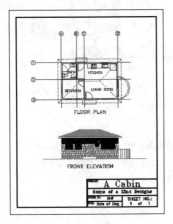

FIGURE 10.31: The latest version of the cabin drawing

A Look at AutoCAD's Title Blocks

Now that you've created a title block and a border, let's take a brief look at the title blocks and borders that AutoCAD provides in its template files and see how you can use these files to set up a new drawing. To follow the steps, set up Auto-CAD so that it does not display a Start Up dialog box when you create a new drawing. Choose Tools ➤ Options to open the Options dialog box. Make the System tab active. In the General Options area, be sure the Start Up drop-down list has Do Not Show A Start Up Dialog displayed. If it doesn't, open the list and select that option. Click Apply and then click OK.

1. Click the QNew icon on the Standard toolbar to open the Select Template dialog box.

2. Double-click ANSI A (portrait) - Color Dependent Plot Styles. The new drawing appears with a title block and border (see Figure 10.32). In addition, this sheet has extra lines, arrows, and a section near the upper edge for listing revisions to the drawing.

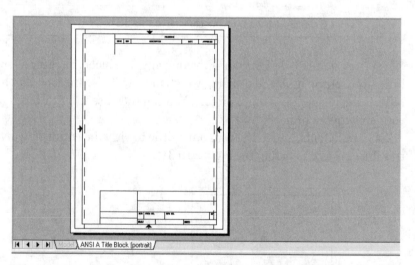

FIGURE 10.32: A new drawing made from the ANSI A (portrait) template

3. Zoom in to the title block on the lower part of the drawing. Notice that it has spaces for the scale and sheet number, among other information, and that some areas are left blank.

4. Close this drawing, and click the QNew button again to look at some of the other template files on the list. Don't worry about the part of the template name that identifies plot style types. That will be covered in Chapter 14. The background for the template files is gray because they use *layouts*, which are introduced in Chapter 13.

When you open a new drawing by selecting a template file, AutoCAD uses the template file as the basis of your new drawing. It copies the information in the template file onto the new drawing file and names the new drawing `Drawing 1`, `Drawing 2`, and so on. You can convert any drawing into a template file. Simply choose File ➤ Save As, and in the Files Of Type drop-down list at the bottom of the Save Drawing As dialog box, select AutoCAD Drawing Template (*.dwt). The new file will have the `.dwt` extension. It can be stored in AutoCAD's Template folder or any folder you choose. When you click Save, the Template Description dialog box opens, giving you the option of writing a description of the new template file and choosing whether the template will use metric or English units (see Figure 10.33).

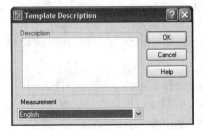

FIGURE 10.33: The Template Description dialog box

The final part of this chapter introduces you to multiline text, which you will also work with as you learn about dimensions in the next chapter, and tables.

Using Multiline Text

Multiline text (often referred to as *Mtext*) is a more complex form of text than single-line text. It can be used the same way single-line text has been used in this chapter, and it can do more. If you have several lines of text, or if you need certain words within a line of text to appear differently than the adjacent words, multiline text is the best thing to use.

A paragraph of multiline text is a single entity. The text wraps around, and you can easily modify the length of a line after you place the text in the drawing. Within the multiline text entity, all text can be edited and behaves as if it were in a word processor. You can give a special word or letter of the text its own text style or color. Everything you learned about defining a new text style applies to multiline text, because both kinds of text use the same text styles. Just as polylines become lines when exploded, multiline text is reduced to single-line text when exploded.

Dimensions use multiline text, and any text that is imported into an AutoCAD drawing from a word-processing document or text editor will become multiline text in the drawing. In this section, you will learn how to place a paragraph of multiline text in the cabin drawing and then modify it. In Chapter 11, you will work with dimension text and text with leader lines, both of which use multiline text.

We will start by adding a note in the lower-left corner of the drawing, using the Multiline Text command.

> Use the Explode command to turn multiline text into single-line text, to unblock objects in a block reference, and to convert a polyline into regular lines. Click the Explode button on the Modify toolbar to start the command.

1. Click the Make Object's Layer Current button just to the right of the drop-down Layer Control list on the Layers toolbar. Then click the FRONT ELEVATION text to make the Text1 layer current. Zoom in to the blank area to the left of the title block in the lower-left corner of the cabin drawing.

2. Click the Osnap button on the status bar to the off position. This will temporarily disable any running Osnaps. Then click the Multiline Text button on the Draw toolbar. The Command window displays the name of the current text style and height and prompts you to specify a first corner.

> You can also start the Multiline Text command by typing t↵ or by choosing Draw ➢ Text ➢ Multiline Text.

3. Select a point near the left borderline in line with the top of the title block. The prompt now reads Specify opposite corner or [Height/Justify/Line spacing/Rotation/Style/Width]:. These are all the options for the Multiline Text command.

4. If the current style is Label, go on to step 5. Otherwise type s↵ for the Style option and type label↵.

5. Drag open a window that fills the space between the left border and the left side of the title block. This defines the line length for the multiline text (see Figure 10.34). Click to finish the window.

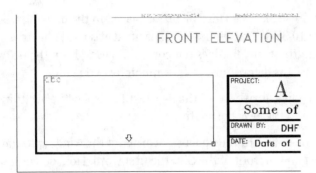

FIGURE 10.34: Making a Multiline Text window

6. The Text Formatting toolbar appears, and below it, the Multiline Text Editor opens where you made the window in step 5. This is where you will type the text. In the drop-down lists on the toolbar above, you can see the current text style and its font and height.

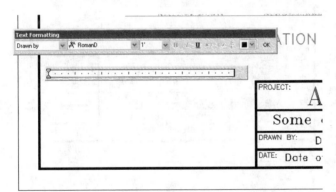

7. Open the drop-down list on the left and select Label. Type the following text, using single spacing and pressing Enter only at the end of the first line and at the end of each note.

   GENERAL NOTES:

1. All work shall be in accordance with the 2000 Ed. Uniform Building Code and all local ordinances.

2. Roof can be built to be steeper for climates with heavy snowfall.

3. Solar panels available for installation on roof.

4. All windows to be double-paned.

You can expand the Multiline Text Editor typing area to the right and down to accommodate more lines of text and greater line length.

When finished, click OK. The text is placed in the drawing (see Figure 10.35a). The window you specified was used only to define the line length. Its height does not control how far down the text will come; that is determined by how much text you enter.

8. Double-click anywhere on the new text to display the Multiline Text Editor and the Text Formatting toolbar.

9. Move the cursor to the upper-left corner of the window containing the text and in front of the *G* in the first word. Hold down the left mouse button and drag to the right and down until all the text is highlighted. Release the mouse button.

   In the rightmost drop-down list on the Text Formatting toolbar, change the Text Height from 1' to 9" and click OK. The text is redrawn smaller and now makes a better fit within the space available (see Figure 10.35b).

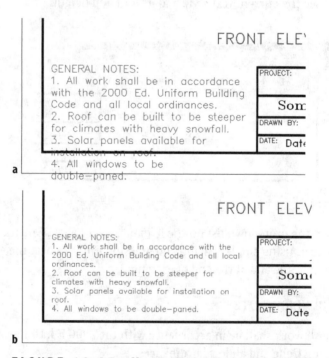

FIGURE 10.35: Mtext in the drawing (a), and modified to be smaller (b)

10. Double-click the Mtext again. The Multiline Text Editor opens and displays the text you just clicked.

11. Highlight all the text again. In the middle drop-down list on the Text Formatting toolbar, select SansSerif as the current font. The selected text changes to the new font.

12. Click OK. The Mtext in the drawing has become more compact, and there is room for more notes (see Figure 10.36).

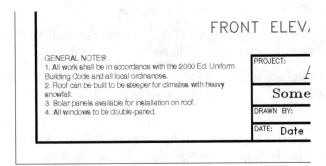

FIGURE 10.36: The results of a font modification

SansSerif is a TrueType font supported by Windows. When used in AutoCAD drawings, it can be italic or boldface. To see how to change individual words within the text, we will underline and boldface the Uniform Building Code text.

1. Double-click the Mtext again to open the Multiline Text Editor dialog box.

2. Use the same technique as earlier to highlight just the Uniform Building Code text. Then click the Bold (B) and Underline (U) buttons on the Text Formatting toolbar. The selected text is underlined and boldfaced.

3. Click OK. The text is redrawn with the changes (see Figure 10.37).

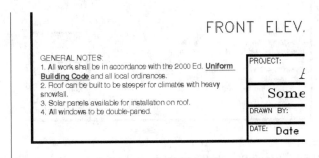

FIGURE 10.37: The Mtext with individual words modified

You can also italicize individual words and give them a different color or height from the rest of the Mtext by using the other tools on the Text Formatting toolbar. I encourage you to experiment with all these tools to become familiar with them.

You can easily alter the length of a line to make the Mtext fit more conveniently on the drawing. Let's say you've decided to put your company logo to the left of the title block. You need to squeeze the text into a narrower space. You have some extra room at the bottom, so you should be able to do it.

1. At the Command: prompt, click the Mtext to select it. Four grips appear at the corners of the body of Mtext.

2. On the status bar, be sure Polar is on and Osnap is off. (For AutoCAD users only, Otrack should also be off.) Then click the upper-right grip to activate it.

3. Slowly move the cursor to the left. When the bottom line of text gets close to the bottom line of the border, you will have moved about a third of the way to the left borderline (see Figure 10.38a).

4. Click the mouse, and then press Esc. The text is squeezed into a narrower space but still fits on the page (see Figure 10.38b).

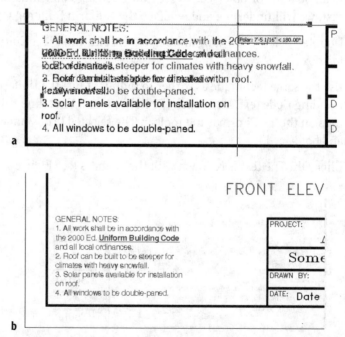

FIGURE 10.38: Modifying the Mtext line length with grips (a), and the results (b)

The ruler at the top of the Mtext Editor window has two sliding indicators for setting indentions. The top indicator is for the first line, in case it is a title. The bottom indicator is for the rest of the text. We set that one in a little to make the note numbers stand out.

1. Double-click the text one last time.

2. In the Mtext Editor window, highlight the four notes.

3. Use the mouse to slide the bottom indicator on the ruler two notches to the right (see Figure 10.39a).

4. Click OK. The list of notes is now more readable (see Figure 10.39b).

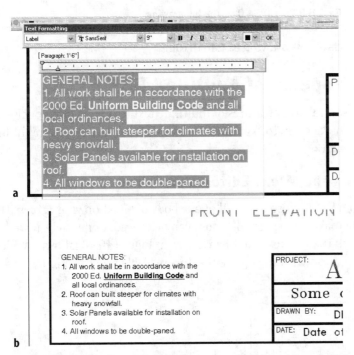

FIGURE 10.39: Adjusting the paragraph slider on the ruler (a), and the results (b)

5. Zoom to Extents, and then zoom out a little to a view of the whole drawing (see Figure 10.40). You won't be able to read the Mtext at this magnification, but it will look fine when you print your drawing.

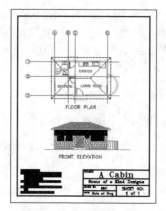

FIGURE 10.40: The full drawing

6. Save this drawing as `Cabin10c`.

Other Aspects of Multiline Text

There are several other features of multiline text that I can only touch on in this book. I encourage you to experiment with any features that you might find useful to your work.

Adjusting the Mtext Editor Size

If you zoom in too close to see all of one body of Mtext on your screen, the Mtext Editor will make the text smaller so it can be viewed. Conversely, if you zoom out so much that the text can't be read, as in Figure 10.40 (shown previously), the Mtext Editor will scale up the text to a readable size (see Figure 10.41).

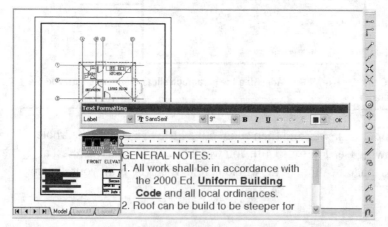

FIGURE 10.41: The Mtext Editor with the text enlarged to a readable size

Justification Points

Mtext has justification points similar to those of single-line text, and they behave the same way. The default justification point for Mtext, however, is the upper-left corner of the body of text, and the available options are for nine points distributed around the perimeter of the body of text and at the center (see Figure 10.42).

GENERAL NOTES:
1. All work shall be in accordance with the 2000 Ed. **Uniform Building Code** and all local ordinances.
2. Roof can be built to be steeper for climates with heavy snowfall.
3. Solar panels available for installation on roof.
4. All windows to be double-paned.

FIGURE 10.42: Justification points for Mtext

When you need to modify the justification of Mtext, open the Mtext Editor, place the cursor in the Editing window, and right-click to display a shortcut menu that contains several commands for modifying Mtext, including Justification. I'll describe the other items on this menu in the upcoming "Tools for Modifying Multiline Text" sidebar.

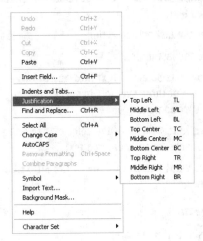

Special Characters

With Mtext, you can add special characters—the degree symbol, the diameter symbol, and so on—that are not included in most font character packages. You will have a chance to do this in the next chapter.

If you want to play around with the Mtext in the cabin drawing, make a copy of it and place it outside the drawing. Double-click it and see what you can learn about the Multiline Text Editor, the Text Formatting toolbar, and the Mtext shortcut menu. Features of the last two are summarized in the following sidebar.

TOOLS FOR MODIFYING MULTILINE TEXT

Here's a brief summary of the various features of the Text Formatting toolbar and the Mtext shortcut menu:

The Text Formatting Toolbar

The features of the Text Formatting toolbar are:

Style Drop-Down List   Contains a list of all existing text styles in the drawing file.

Font Drop-Down List   Sets the font for the selected text or sets the font for subsequently entered text.

Height Drop-Down Text Box   Sets the height for selected text or sets the height for subsequently entered text.

Bold, Italic, and Underline Buttons   Changes selected text or sets up for subsequently entered text.

Undo Button   Undoes the last editing action.

Redo Button   Redoes the last undo.

Fraction Button   Converts selected text into any of three styles of stacked fractions. Use one of three symbols to specify the fraction bar: horizontal (/), slanted (#), and none (^).

Text Color Drop-Down List   Changes the color of a selected portion of text or sets a color for subsequently entered text.

OK Button   Executes what has been done in the Mtext Editor and returns you to your drawing.

The Mtext Shortcut Menu

The features of the Mtext shortcut menu are:

Undo, Redo, Cut, Copy, and Paste   These commands are self-explanatory and appear on most AutoCAD shortcut menus.

Continued on next page

Insert Field   Opens the Field dialog box, which you use to insert a field into the selected text. If you select text containing a field, this menu item changes to three menu items: Edit Field, Update Field, and Convert Field To Text.

Indents And Tabs   Opens the Indents And Tabs dialog box. It has settings for indenting the first line and subsequent paragraphs of Mtext (similar to what the sliders do on the ruler above the Mtext Editor window) and tab stop positions.

Justification   Opens a flyout menu that contains the nine justification points for Mtext, illustrated earlier in Figure 10.42. Use this to change the justification of selected text or to set up justification for new text.

Find And Replace   Opens the Replace dialog box, in which you search for a word or a series of words (text string) and replace them with text that you specify.

Select All   Highlights all the selected text.

Change Case   Changes the case of all highlighted text to uppercase or lowercase.

AutoCAPS   When checked, capitalizes all text.

Remove Formatting   Removes formatting, such as bold, underline, and so on, from highlighted text.

Combine Paragraphs   Joins highlighted individual paragraphs into one paragraph.

Symbol   Imports symbols (such as diameter, degree, and so on) that are not available in the font you are using.

Import Text   Used to import a word-processing or text file into an AutoCAD drawing. The maximum size allowed is 16KB, so the smallest Word document possible is too large; you can, however, use files in Text Only or RTF formats. Clicking the Import Text button opens the Select File dialog box that displays only files having the `.txt` and `.rtf` extensions. You can bring in text files with other extensions if you enter the full filename with its extension and if they are not larger than 16KB. Text comes in as Mtext and uses the current text style, height setting, and layer. The imported file may not retain complex code fields for such things as tabs, multiple margin indents, and so on.

Background Mask   Opens the Background Mask dialog box in which you specify color for and activate a background mask to go behind the selected Mtext object.

Help   Opens a help page on Multiline text.

Character Set   Opens a menu of several languages. When applicable, the codes of the selected language will be applied to selected text.

Creating a Table

All professions that use AutoCAD use tables to consolidate and display data in organized formats. Architectural construction documents usually include at least three basic tables: door, window, and room finish schedules. These are usually drawn in table form and display the various construction and material specifications for each door or window type or for each room. To illustrate the tools AutoCAD offers for creating tables, we'll construct a simple door schedule for the cabin.

You create tables in AutoCAD by first creating a table style and then creating a table using that style—it's a process similar to that of defining a text style and then inserting text in a drawing using that style.

Defining a Table Style

Table styles are more complex than text styles. They include parameters for width and height of rows and columns and, among other things, at least one text style.

1. Make Cabin10c the current drawing. We'll make a new file by saving this file to the new file's name.

2. Choose File ➤ Save As, and in the Save Drawing As dialog box, rename this file as Cabin10c-Sheet2 and click Save.

3. Make sure all layers are thawed and turned on, and then erase everything in the drawing except the border and the title block. This drawing still has all the layers, blocks, and text styles that the Cabin10c drawing had.

4. In the title block, change the sheet number from "1 of 1" to "2 of 2."

5. Create a new layer called Tables, assign it color number 7, and make it the current layer. Choose Format ➤ Table Style to open the Table Style dialog box (see Figure 10.43). On the left is the Styles list box. It displays all defined table styles. To the right of that is a preview window that displays the current table style—in this case, the Standard style because it's the only one defined so far. Below the Styles list box is a drop-down list called List that gives you options for which table styles to display. To the right of the Preview Of window are four buttons.

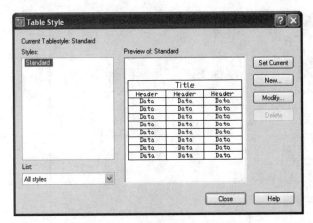

FIGURE 10.43: The Table Style dialog box

6. Click the New button to open the Create New Table Style dialog box (see Figure 10.44). In the New Style Name text box, Copy of Standard is highlighted.

FIGURE 10.44: The Create New Table Style dialog box

7. Type **Door Schedule** to create a new table style name and click Continue. The New Table Style dialog box opens with Door Schedule in the title bar (see Figure 10.45). The new style we are defining will be like the Standard style with the changes we make here. Notice the three tabs at the top: Data, Column Heads, and Title. They refer to the three parts of the sample table that's displayed in the preview window to the right. You can specify text and line characteristics for each of the three parts. Be sure the Data tab is active and on top.

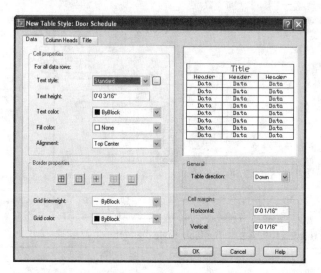

FIGURE 10.45: The New Table Style dialog box

8. Click the Browse button to the right of the Text Style drop-down list to open the Text Style dialog box. We want a new text style for the door schedule.

9. Define a new style called Table, and use the Arial font and 0 height. Click Apply and then click Close. Then open the Text Style drop-down list and select the new text style you created, Table.

10. Set the Text Height to 9". Leave Text Color and Fill Color at their default settings. Change Alignment to Middle Center.

11. Click the Column Heads tab in the New Table Style dialog box and make it active. Choose the same text style (Table) and set the height to 12".

12. Click the Title tab in the New Table Style dialog box, select the Table text style again, and set the height to 15".

We'll leave the Border properties at their default settings. These control the visibility of the horizontal and vertical lines of the table, their lineweight, and color. Your individual professions may have their own standards for these parameters.

13. Leave Table Direction set to Down. In the Cell Margins area, change the Horizontal and Vertical settings to 6". Click OK.

14. Back in the Table Style dialog box, in the Styles list, click Door Schedule to highlight it, and then click the Set Current button to make it the current table style (see Figure 10. 46). Then click Close.

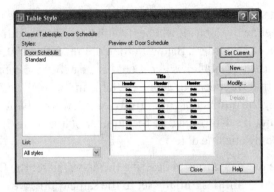

FIGURE 10.46: The Table Style dialog box with Door Schedule as the current table style

Now let's look at the geometry of the new table.

Designing a Table

The height of the rows has been set by the parameters in the Door Schedule table style. We now need to determine the width of the columns and figure out how many columns and rows we need for the door schedule. This is done as we insert a new table. Remember that Door Schedule is the current table style.

 1. Zoom in to the upper portion of the drawing. Near the bottom of the Draw toolbar, click the Table icon to open the Insert Table dialog box (see Figure 10.47). In the Table Style Settings area, the Door Schedule is displayed in the Table Style Name drop-down list because it is now the current table style. An abstract version of the table is displayed below in the preview window.

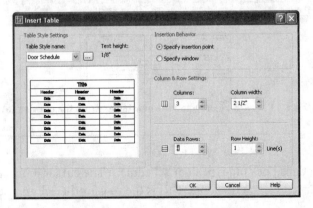

FIGURE 10.47: The Insert Table dialog box

2. On the right side, click the Specify Window radio button. We'll make a window to define the table. It will be the full horizontal width of the drawing inside the borders. Below, in the Column & Row Settings area, Column Width and Data Rows ghost out because they are defined by the window that we specify to define the table in the drawing. We need to define only the number of columns. We won't worry about the row height for now. It's determined by the number of lines of text, and we're using only one line of text.

3. We will have five categories to describe the doors, so set the Columns box to 5. Each column is initially set to the same width. We can adjust it later. Click OK.

4. Back in the drawing, turn off Osnap and Polar on the status bar. Then click a point near the upper-left corner of the border, just inside it. This establishes the upper-left corner of the new table.

5. Drag the cursor across the drawing and down until the screen displays a table that spans the drawing and has a title bar and six rows below (see Figure 10.48a). When that is displayed, release the mouse button. The new table is displayed inside the drawing's border (see Figure 10.48b). Its title bar has a flashing cursor, and above the drawing, the Text Formatting toolbar floats.

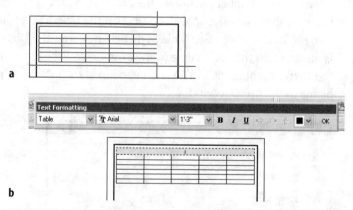

FIGURE 10.48: Dragging the new table across the drawing (a) and the results (b)

6. With Caps Lock on, type **door schedule**↵. The cursor jumps to the upper-left cell on the table. This is the row for the column heads.

7. With Caps Lock on, type **sym.** and press the Tab key. Then, moving across the header row, type (in caps) **name**, press the Tab key, type **width & height**, press the Tab key, type **type**, press the Tab key, and then type **material**.↵. This completes the row of column heads (see Figure 10.49a).

8. Now you can fill in the data for the door schedule that's shown in Figure 10.49b in the same manner. Pressing the Tab key instead of ↵ moves the activated cell left to right across each row and then down to the next row. Pressing ↵ moves the activated cell down each column and then ends the command. Double-click in a cell to activate that cell and display the Text Formatting toolbar again.

9. When finished, click OK on the Text Formatting toolbar (see Figure 10.49b). Some of the cells have increased in size vertically to accommodate the long text. You can adjust the width of some columns to make more room in others.

a

DOOR SCHEDULE				
SYM.	NAME	WIDTH & HEIGHT	TYPE	MATERIAL

b

DOOR SCHEDULE				
SYM.	NAME	WIDTH & HEIGHT	TYPE	MATERIAL
1	FRONT	3'-0" x 6'-8"	SWINGING	WOOD-SOLID CORE
2	BEDROOM	2'-6" x 6'-8"	SWINGING	WOOD - HOLLOW CORE
3	BATH	2'-6" x 6'-8"	SWINGING	WOOD - HOLLOW CORE
4	BACK	3'-0" x 6'-8"	SWINGING	WOOD - SOLID CORE
5	BALCONY	7'-0" x 6'-8"	SLIDING GLASS	GLASS - ALUMINUM FRAME

FIGURE 10.49: The table with its title and column heads (a), and the table completely filled in (b)

10. Click any line in the table. Grips appear, and the lines and text in the table ghost (see Figure 10.50a).

11. Click the grip at the top right of the SYM. column, and then drag it to the left to narrow that column. Click the other grips at the top of the

columns to drag them and narrow or widen them. The This should give you a result similar to Figure 10.50b. The boxes of data are not all the same size vertically.

12. Click on the table again to bring back the grips. Click the grip in the lower-right corner. Turn off Running Osnaps but keep Polar on, then move the cursor straight up above the selected grip until the cells appear to have the same vertical height. Click and then press Esc to remove the grips (see Figure 10.50c).

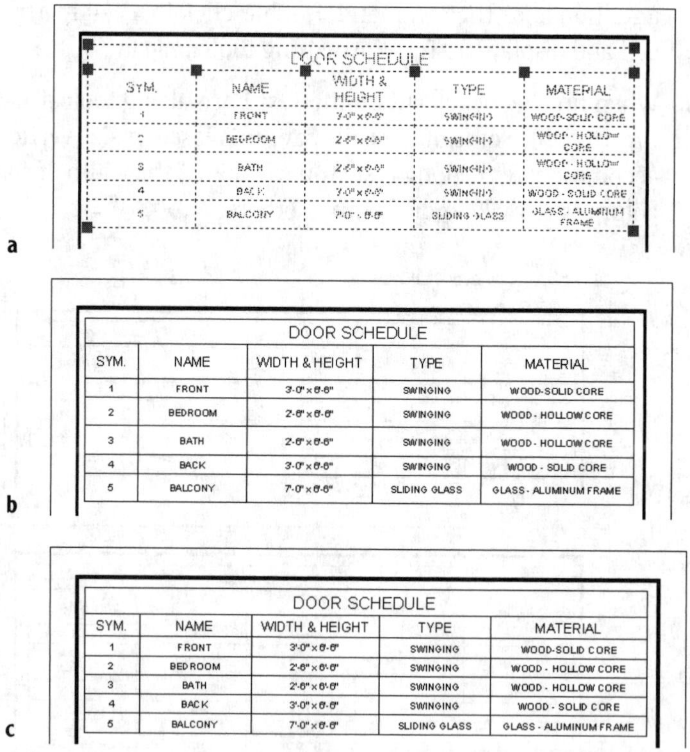

FIGURE 10.50: The table after being selected (a), the table with column width adjusted (b), and the table after final adjustment (c)

13. Save this drawing. It's already been named Cabin10c_Sheet2.

This concludes the chapter on text. In the next chapter, we look at the dimensioning features of AutoCAD. You create and manage dimensions using techniques similar to the ones you learned to work with text and tables.

If You Would Like More Practice...

Trades and other professions outside the area of architecture and construction will use text with AutoCAD and AutoCAD LT in exactly the same way as demonstrated in this chapter.

For more practice using single-line text, follow these steps:

1. Close all drawings, and then open Cabin04c-addon.dwg.

2. Using DesignCenter, bring in the Title and Label text styles from the Cabin10a drawing while it is closed.

3. Add labels to the features that were added.

   ▶ Use the Title text style to identify the addition as GARAGE.

   ▶ Use the Label text style to give the features the following names: WALKWAY, STORAGE, OFFICE, and CAR.

For more practice using Mtext, follow these steps:

1. Open Cabin10c, and zoom in to the blank space between the structural grid and the top border.

2. Create a new text style called Description that uses the Times New Roman font and a height of 12".

3. Start Mtext, and specify a rectangle for the text that covers the width of the sheet between the borders and occupies the space above the structural grid.

4. Enter the following text exactly as shown here, spelling errors and all:

   This is a design for a small vaction cabin. It contains approximately 380 square feet of living space and includes one bedrooms and one bath. It can be adopted to provide shelter in all climates and can be modified to allow constuction that uses local building materials. Please sund all inquiries to the manufacturer.

5. Double-click the new text and make these changes:

   ▶ Correct all spelling errors.

   ▶ Change "square feet" to "sq. ft."

▶ Boldface the following : "one bedroom," "one bath," "all climates," and "local building materials."

▶ Italicize the last sentence.

▶ See if you can modify the shape of the defining rectangle so that the text fits in the space in the upper-left corner.

Are You Experienced?

Now you can...

☑ **set up text styles**

☑ **place single-line text in a drawing for titles and room labels**

☑ **create a grid for a drawing**

☑ **modify single-line text**

☑ **construct a title block and place text in it**

☑ **use AutoCAD template files**

☑ **place Mtext in a drawing**

☑ **modify Mtext in several ways**

☑ **set up a table style and create a table**

CHAPTER 11

Dimensioning a Drawing

- ▶ Setting up a dimension style
- ▶ Dimensioning the floor plan of the cabin
- ▶ Modifying existing dimensions
- ▶ Modifying existing dimension styles

D imensions are the final ingredient to be added to your drawing. To introduce you to dimensioning, I'm going to follow a pattern similar to the one I used in the previous chapter on text.

Dimension Styles

Dimension styles are similar to text styles, but are more complex. You set them up in the same way, but many parameters control the various parts of dimensions, including the dimension text.

Before you start setting up a dimension style, you need to make a few changes to your drawing to prepare it for dimensioning.

1. Open Cabin10c and zoom in to the upper half of the drawing.

2. Create a new layer called Dim1. Assign it a color and make it current.

3. Freeze the Grid layer.

4. Set Endpoint Osnap to be running.

5. Set the status bar so that only the Osnap and Model buttons are in the on position.

6. Right-click any button on any toolbar on the screen to display the toolbar menu. Click Dimension to open the Dimension toolbar on the drawing area in the form of a floating toolbar.

7. Move the Dimension toolbar to the top center of the drawing area, being careful to avoid docking it. (You learned about moving toolbars around on the screen in Chapter 1.) Your drawing will look like Figure 11.1.

Making a New Dimension Style

Each dimension has several components: the dimension line, arrows or tick marks, extension lines, and the dimension text (see Figure 11.2). An extensive set of variables that is stored with each drawing file controls the appearance and location of these components. You will work with these variables through a series of dialog boxes that have been designed to make setting up a dimension style as easy and trouble free as possible. Remember that AutoCAD is designed to be used by drafters from many trades and professions, each of which has its own standards for drafting. To satisfy these folks' widely varied needs, AutoCAD dimensioning features have many options and settings for controlling the appearance and placement of dimensions in drawings.

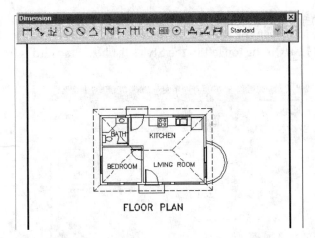

FIGURE 11.1: The floor plan of Cabin10c with the Dimension toolbar centered at the top of the drawing area

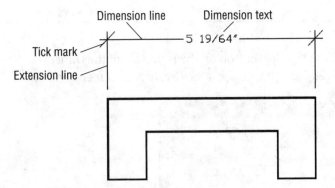

FIGURE 11.2: The parts of a dimension

Naming a Dimension Style

Every dimension variable has a default setting, and these as a group constitute the default Standard dimension style. As in defining text styles, the procedure is to copy the Standard dimension style and rename the copy—in effect, making a new style that is a copy of the default style. You then make changes to this new style so it has the settings you need to dimension your drawing.

1. Click the Dimension Style button on the right end of the Dimension toolbar to open the Dimension Style Manager dialog box (see Figure 11.3). On the top left in the Styles list box, Standard is listed.

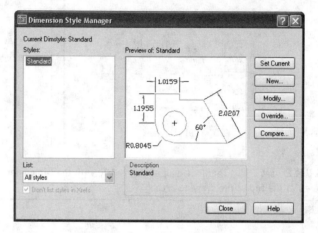

FIGURE 11.3:   The Dimension Style Manager dialog box

2. Click the New button on the right side of the Dimension Style Manager dialog box to open the Create New Dimension Style dialog box.

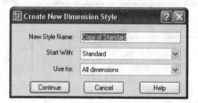

3. In the New Style Name text box, Copy Of Standard is highlighted. Type **DimPlan** but don't press ↵ yet. Notice that Standard is in the Start With drop-down list just below. Because it is the current and only dimension style in this drawing, the new dimension style you are about to define will begin as a copy of the Standard style. This is similar to the way in which new text styles are defined (as you saw in Chapter 10). The Use For drop-down list allows you to choose the kinds of dimensions to which the new style will be applied. In this case, it's all dimensions, so we don't need to change this.

4. Click the Continue button. The Create New Dimension Style dialog box is replaced by the New Dimension Style: DimPlan dialog box (see Figure 11.4). It has six tabs. You have created a new dimension style that is a copy of the Standard style, and now you will make the changes necessary to set up DimPlan to work as the main dimension style for the floor plan of the cabin.

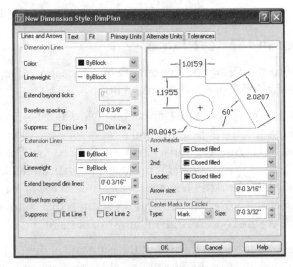

FIGURE 11.4: The New Dimension Style dialog box with DimPlan as the current style and Lines And Arrows as the active tab

5. Be sure the Lines And Arrows tab is active (on top). If it's not, click it.

Using the Lines And Arrows Tab

You will use the Lines And Arrows tab to control the appearance of the dimension and extension lines, the arrowheads, and the center marks.

1. In the Arrowheads area, click the down arrow in the first drop-down list to open the list of arrowheads.

2. Click Architectural Tick. The drop-down list closes with Architectural Tick displayed in the first and second drop-down lists. In the preview window above the Arrowheads area, a graphic displays the new arrowhead type. It doesn't display the actual thickness that the tick mark line will have in your drawing.

3. In the Arrow Size spin box, highlight the default setting and change it to ⅛.

Tick marks are used almost exclusively by the architecture profession. This list contains options for several kinds of arrowheads, dots, and so on.

4. Move to the Dimension Lines area. Change the Extend Beyond Ticks setting from 0" to ³⁄₃₂" by highlighting the 0 and typing ³⁄₃₂. This will extend the dimension line past the tick mark a short distance.

5. In the Extension Lines area, highlight the Extend Beyond Dim Lines setting and change it to ⅛. This controls how far the extension line will extend beyond the dimension line.

Before saving these changes, make some more modifications to the DimPlan style.

Making Changes in the Text Tab

The settings in the Text tab control the appearance of dimension text and how it is located relative to the dimension and extension lines.

1. Click the Text tab in the New Dimension Style dialog box. Settings in three areas affect the appearance and location of dimension text. Look ahead to Figure 11.5 for a graphic of the Text tab. The preview window appears in all tabs and is updated automatically as settings are modified. Move to the Text Appearance area in the upper-left corner of the dialog box where there are six settings that control how the text looks. We are concerned about only two of them.

2. Click the Browse button that sits at the right end of the Text Style drop-down list to open the Text Style dialog box. Set up a new text style called Dim that has the following parameters:

   ▶ Romand.shx font

   ▶ 0'-0" height

   ▶ 0.8000 width factor

   ▶ All other settings at their default

   If you need a reminder on creating text styles, refer to Chapter 10. Apply this text style to make it current, and then close the Text Style dialog box.

3. Back in the Text tab, open the Text Style drop-down list and select the new Dim style from the list.

4. Change the Text Height setting to ³⁄₃₂".

5. Move down to the Text Placement area. These settings determine where the text is located, vertically and horizontally, relative to the dimension line. There are two settings to change here.

6. Open the Vertical drop-down list and select Above. At this setting, the text will sit above the dimension line and not break the line into two segments. Set the Offset From Dim Line setting to ⅓₂".

7. Now move to the Text Alignment area. Two radio buttons control whether dimension text is aligned horizontally or with the direction of the dimension line. The ISO Standard option aligns text depending on whether the text can fit between the extension lines. Only one of the buttons can be active at a time. Horizontal should already be active. Click the Aligned With Dimension Line button. Notice how the appearance and location of the text has changed in the preview window. This finishes our work in this tab. The settings should look like Figure 11.5.

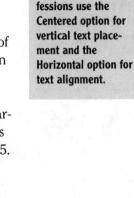

Many trades and professions use the Centered option for vertical text placement and the Horizontal option for text alignment.

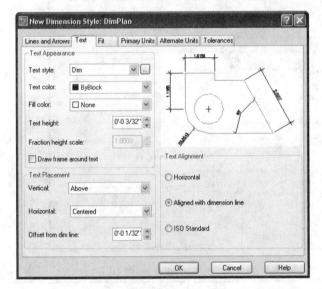

FIGURE 11.5: The Text tab with settings for the DimPlan style

There are four more tabs with settings, but we'll be making changes in only two of them: Fit and Primary Units.

Working with Settings in the Fit Tab

The settings in the Fit tab control the overall scale factor of the dimension style and how the text and arrowheads are placed when the extension lines are too close together for both text and arrows to fit.

1. Click the Fit tab in the New Dimension Style dialog box. Look ahead to Figure 11.6 to see a graphic of the Fit tab.

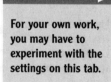

2. In the upper-left corner, in the Fit Options area, click the Text radio button.

3. In the Text Placement area, click the Over The Dimension Line, Without A Leader radio button.

4. Make no changes in the Fine Tuning area for now. Move to the Scale For Dimension Features area. Be sure the Use Overall Scale Of radio button is active. Set the scale to 96. (Use the highlight-and-type method described in step 4 of the earlier section, "Using the Lines And Arrows Tab.") The settings in the Fit tab should look like Figure 11.6.

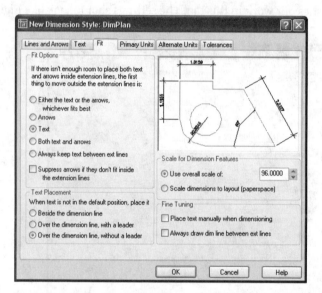

FIGURE 11.6: The new settings in the Fit tab

Setting Up the Primary Units Tab

In the preview window, you may have noticed that the numbers in the dimension text maintained a decimal format with four decimal places, rather than the feet and inches format of the current Architectural units. Dimensions have their own units setting, independent of the basic units for the drawing as a whole. In the Primary Units tab, you will set the dimension units.

1. Click the Primary Units tab and take a peek ahead at Figure 11.7 to see how it's organized. There are two areas: Linear and Angular Dimensions. Within each of these areas are a few settings and one or two nested areas.

2. In the Linear Dimensions area, starting at the top, make the following changes:

   A. Change the Unit Format setting from Decimal to Architectural.

   B. Change the Fraction Format setting to Diagonal.

   C. In the Zero Suppression area, uncheck 0 Inches.

N O T E Zero Suppression controls (a) whether the zero is shown for feet when the dimensioned distance is less than one foot and (b) whether the zero is shown for inches when the distance is a whole number of feet. For the cabin drawing, we will suppress the zero for feet, but we will show the zero for inches. So 9" will be shown as 9", and 3' will be shown as 3'-0".

3. In the Angular Dimensions area, leave Decimal Degrees as the Units Format, and change Precision to two decimal places, as you did for the basic drawing units in Chapter 3. For now, leave the Zero Suppression area as it is. After these changes, the Primary Units tab will look like Figure 11.7.

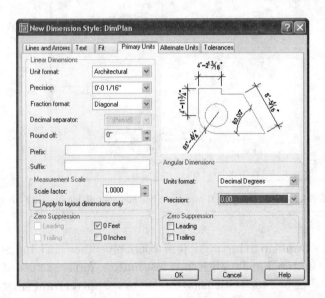

FIGURE 1 1 . 7 : The Primary Units tab after changes have been made

Of the last two tabs, Alternate Units can be used by any industry involved in global projects, and Tolerances are used mostly by the mechanical engineering trades and professions. We won't need to make any changes to these tabs for this tutorial, but we'll take a brief look at those tabs before we start dimensioning the cabin.

It's time to save these setting changes to the new DimPlan dimension style and begin dimensioning the cabin.

1. Click the OK button at the bottom of the New Dimension Style dialog box. You will be returned to the Dimension Style Manager dialog box (see Figure 11.8).

   DimPlan is displayed with a gray swatch in the Styles list box, along with Standard. In the lower-right corner of the dialog box, in the Description area, the following information is presented about the new style: the name of the original style that the new style is based on and the changes that were made to the original style to create the new style. Unfortunately, the area is much too small to display all the changes we've made, so use the chart later in this section as a reference.

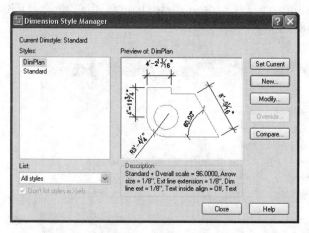

FIGURE 11.8: The Dimension Style Manager dialog box with DimPlan listed

2. Click DimPlan to highlight it in a dark blue; then click the Set Current button. Finally, click the Close button. You are returned to your drawing, and the Dimension toolbar now displays DimPlan in the Dim Style Control drop-down list. This indicates that DimPlan is now the current dimension style.

You have made changes to 17 settings that control dimensions. This is not too many, considering that there are more than 50 dimension settings. Here is a summary of the changes you've made to make the dimensions work with the cabin drawing:

Tab	Setting	Default Setting	DimPlan
Lines And Arrows	Arrowheads	Closed Filled	Architectural Tick
	Arrowhead Size	$^3/_{16}$"	$^1/_8$"
	Dim Line Extension	0"	$^3/_{32}$"
	Ext. Line Extension	$^3/_{16}$"	$^1/_8$"
Text	Text Style	Standard	DimPlan
	Text Height	$^3/_{16}$"	$^3/_{32}$"
	Text Vertical Justification	Centered	Above
	Offset From Dim Line	$^3/_{32}$"	$^3/_{32}$"
	Text Alignment	Horizontal	Aligned With Dimension Line
Fit	Fit Options	Either—whichever is best	Text
	Text Placement	Beside The Dimension Line	Over the Dimension Line, Without A Leader
	Overall Scale	1.0000	96.0000
Primary Units	Unit Format	Decimal	Architectural
	Fraction Format	Horizontal	Diagonal
	Zero Suppression	Feet, Inches	Feet only
	Angular Precision	No decimal places	Two decimal places

[handwritten note: SCALE TO PAPER SPACE]

You will change a few more settings throughout the rest of this chapter as you begin to dimension the cabin in the next set of exercises. Let's look briefly at the Alternate Units and Tolerances tabs.

The Alternate Units Tab

If your work requires your dimensions to display both Metric and Architectural units, use the Alternate Units tab in the New Dimension Style dialog box. In the example shown here, the primary units are Architectural and were set in the previous section. Now we'll set up the alternate units.

1. Click the Dimension Style button on the Dimension toolbar.

2. Highlight DimPlan if it's not already highlighted.

3. Click the Modify button.

4. Click the Alternate Units tab. When we're finished here, it will look like Figure 11.9. There are only three or four changes to be made on this tab.

5. In the upper-left corner of the tab, click to put a check mark in the Display Alternate Units check box. This will make the rest of the settings on the tab available to us for making changes.

6. If Decimal is not displayed in the Unit Format drop-down list, open it and select Decimal.

7. If the precision is not set to 0, open that drop-down list and select that level of precision.

8. Set Multiplier For Alt Units to 25.4. This will make millimeters the alternate units.

9. Finally, in the lower-right quarter of the tab, in the Placement area, select Below Primary Value. This will have the effect of placing the alternate units below the primary units. The tab should look like Figure 11.9a, and the resulting dimensions for the upper portion of the floor plan should look like Figure 11.9b.

10. Don't save this setting. We won't be using alternate units when we dimension the cabin.

> If you want centimeters to be the alternate units, change the Multiplier For Alt Units setting to 2.54 and set the precision to 0.00.

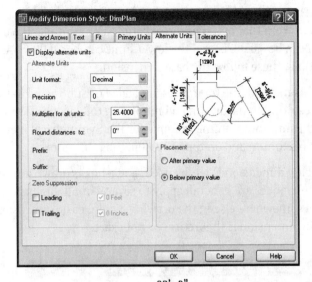

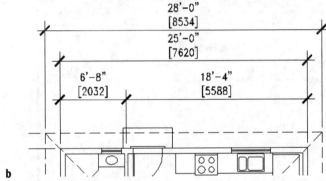

FIGURE 11.9: The Alternate Units tab after being set up for millimeters (a) and the resulting horizontal dimensions (b)

The Tolerances Tab

AutoCAD offers features whose options help you create several kinds of tolerances. In the Tolerances tab, you have four methods for doing what is called *lateral tolerances*, the traditional kind of tolerance that most draftspeople are familiar with. This is the *plus or minus* kind of tolerance. Take a look at the choices in the Method drop-down list shown in Figure 11.10. Each of these is a method for displaying a plus/minus type of tolerance:

Symmetrical   This method is for a single plus-or-minus expression after the base dimension; used when the upper allowable limit of deviation is identical to that for the lower limit, as in 1.0625 ± 0.0025.

Deviation   This method is for the instance in which the upper allowable deviation is different from that of the lower deviation. For example, the upper limit of the deviation can be +0.0025, and the lower limit can be –0.0005. As in the Symmetrical method, these follow the base dimension.

Limits   In this method, the tolerances are added or subtracted to the base dimension, resulting in maximum and minimum total values. The maximum is placed over the minimum. In the example for the Symmetrical method, 1.0650 would be the maximum and on top of 1.0600, the minimum.

Basic   The base dimension is left by itself, and a box is drawn around it, indicating that the tolerances are general, apply to several or all dimensions in boxes, and are noted somewhere else in the drawing. Often, basic dimensions are shown when a dimension is theoretical or not exact.

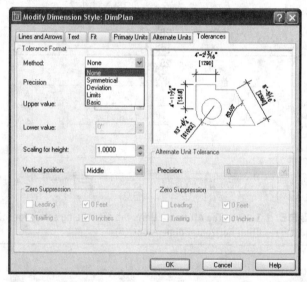

FIGURE 11.10:   The top of the Tolerances tab, showing the Method drop-down list options

When you select one of these options, the settings in the tab become available. If you select Deviation, all settings become available.

Precision   Controls the overall precision of the tolerances.

Upper Value and Lower Value   The actual values of the tolerances.

Scaling For Height   The height of the tolerance text. A value of 1 here sets the tolerance text to match that of the base dimension. A value of greater than 1

makes the tolerance text greater than the base dimension text, and a value of less than 1 makes it smaller than the base dimension text.

Vertical Position   Where the base dimension is placed vertically relative to the tolerances. It can be in line with the upper or lower tolerance or in the middle.

The Zero Suppression areas at the bottom, when checked, suppress extra zeros that occur before or after the decimal point. If you set up the Tolerances tab as shown in Figure 11.11a, a dimension looks like the one shown in Figure 11.11b.

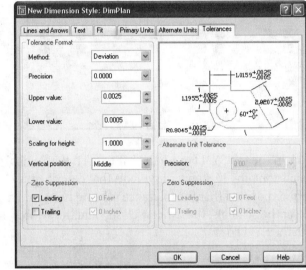

a

b

FIGURE 11.11: The Tolerances tab with some settings changed (a), and a dimension with deviation tolerances (b)

A more complex family of tolerances is available through the Dimension toolbar. It's called *geometric tolerancing* and involves setting up a series of boxes that contain symbols and numbers that describe tolerance parameters for forms, positions, and other geometric features. Usually there are two to six boxes in a row with the possibility of multiple rows. These all constitute the *feature control frame*, which eventually is inserted in the drawing and attached in some way to the relevant dimension.

1. Click the Tolerance button on the Dimension toolbar to open the Geometric Tolerance dialog box, in which you set up the feature control frame. The black squares will contain symbols, and the white rectangles are for tolerance or datum values or for reference numbers.

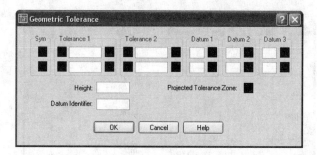

2. Click in the top SYM box on the left to open the Symbol window, which contains 14 standard symbols that describe the characteristic form or position that the tolerance is being used for. When you select one of the symbols, the window closes, and the symbol is inserted into the SYM box.

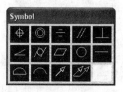

3. Click the first black square of Tolerance 1. A diameter symbol is inserted.

4. Now click the last black square of Tolerance 1. The Material Condition window opens and displays the three material condition options. When you click one, it is inserted.

You can insert any of these three symbols in Tolerance 2 and Datum 1, 2, or 3, if you need them.

5. Now you can fill in the actual tolerance value(s) and datum references in the white boxes.

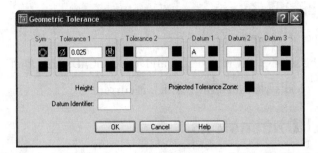

6. When you are finished, click OK. The feature control frame can be inserted into your drawing like a block and can be referenced to a part or a dimension.

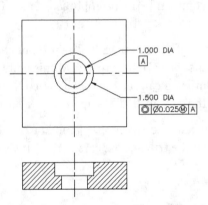

This exercise is intended solely to show you the tools that AutoCAD provides for setting up the most commonly used lateral and geometric tolerances when you use the Tolerances tab in the Dimension Style Dialog box and the Tolerance button on the Dimension toolbar. My intention here is not to explain the methodology of geometric tolerances or the meanings of the various symbols, numbers, and letters used in them. That is a subject beyond the scope of this book.

Placing Dimensions on the Drawing

Upon returning to your drawing, it should still look almost exactly like Figure 11.1 (shown earlier), and it should have the following:

▶ A new layer called Dim1, which is current

▶ A new dimension style called DimPlan, which is current and is now displayed in the drop-down list on the Dimension toolbar

▶ The Grid layer frozen

▶ Endpoint Osnap running

▶ On the status bar:Ortho, Polar, and for AutoCAD, Otrack off

▶ A new text style called Dim, which is current

Horizontal Dimensions

First, you will dimension across the top of the plan, from the corner of the building to the center of the interior wall, then to the other corner. You'll then dimension the roof.

1. Click the Linear button at the left end of the Dimension toolbar to activate the Dimlinear command. The prompt reads Specify first extension line origin or <select object>:.

2. Pick the upper-left corner of the cabin walls. The prompt changes to Specify second extension line origin:. At this point, zoom in to the bathroom area until you can see the wall between the bathroom and kitchen, as well as the back wall, close up.

3. Activate Midpoint Osnap and click the upper jamb line of the bathroom door opening when the triangle appears at the jamb's midpoint (see Figure 11.12).

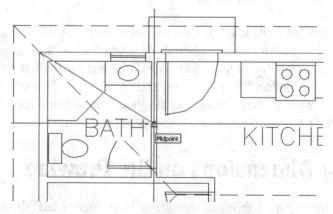

FIGURE 11.12: Selecting the jamb with Midpoint Osnap

4. Use Realtime Pan to pan the drawing down until there's room above the roof line to place the dimension. Notice how the dimension appears in ghosted form attached to, and moving with, the cursor (see Figure 11.13a). Notice that the right extension line starts just above the midpoint of the jamb you just picked.

5. Move the cursor until the dimension line is about 3' above the back step. Click to place it.

6. Click anywhere on the new dimension. Five grips appear. Click the grip at the bottom of the right extension line. Select Perpendicular Osnap and move the cursor up to the exterior wall line. When the Osnap symbol appears, click. The right extension line has been adjusted. Press Esc to remove the grips (see Figure 11.13b).

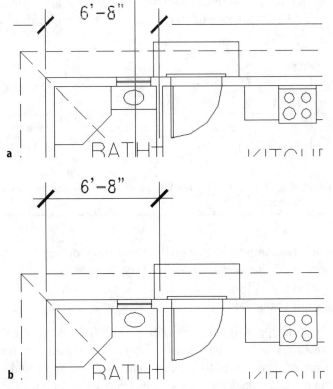

FIGURE 11.13: The dimension attached to the cursor (a), and adjusted after placement (b)

Your first dimension is completed.

When dimensioning walls, you usually dimension to the outside of the exterior ones and to the center of the interior ones. The next dimension will run from the right side of the first dimension to the right corner.

N O T E   Studs are the vertical 2" × 4" or 2" × 6" members in the framing of a wall. When dimensioning buildings that have stud walls, architects usually dimension to the face of the stud for the outside walls, but I am not able to go into that level of detail in this book.

The Continue Command

AutoCAD has an automatic way of placing adjacent dimensions in line—the Continue command.

1. Zoom out and pan until you have a view of the upper wall and roof line, with space above them for dimensions (see Figure 11.14).

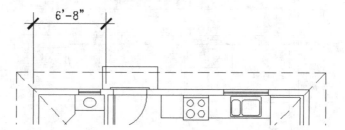

F I G U R E   1 1 . 1 4 :   The result of zooming and panning for a view of the top of the floor plan

2. Click the Continue button on the Dimension toolbar. The prompt reads Specify a second extension line origin or [Undo/Select] <Select>:. All you need to do here is pick a point for the right end of the dimension—in this case, the upper-right corner of the walls.

3. Click the upper-right corner of the house. The second dimension is drawn in line with the first (see Figure 11.15). Note that the same prompt has returned to the Command window. You could keep picking points to place the next adjacent dimension in line, if there was need of one. Press Esc to cancel the Continue command.

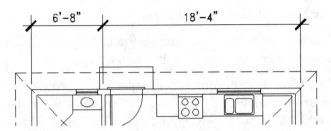

FIGURE 11.15: The completion of the Continue command

With the Continue command, you can dimension along a wall of a building quickly, just by picking points. AutoCAD assumes that the last extension line specified for the previous dimension will coincide with the first extension line of the next dimension. If the extension line you need to continue from is not the last one specified, press ↵ at the prompt, pick the extension line you want to continue from, and continue the command.

Another automatic routine that can be used with linear dimensions is called Baseline.

The Baseline Command

The Baseline command gets its name from a style of dimensioning called baseline, in which all dimensions begin at the same point (see Figure 11.16). Each dimension is stacked above the previous one. Because of the automatic stacking, you can use the Baseline command for overall dimensions. AutoCAD will stack the overall dimension a set height above the incremental dimensions.

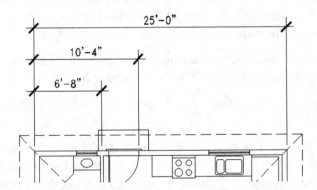

FIGURE 11.16: An example of baseline dimensions

1. Click the Baseline button on the Dimension toolbar. The prompt reads `Specify a second extension line origin or [Undo/Select] <Select>:`, just like the first prompt for the Continue command.

2. Press ↵ to choose the Select option.

3. Pick the extension line that extends from the upper-left corner—the first extension line of the first dimension.

4. Pick the upper-right corner of the walls, and then press Esc to cancel the Baseline command. The overall dimension is drawn above the first two dimensions (see Figure 11.17). (The Baseline command will keep running until you cancel it, just like the Continue command.)

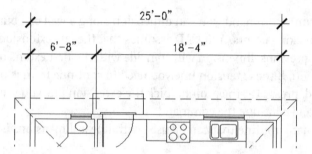

FIGURE 11.17: The completion of the overall dimension with the Baseline command

The Baseline command assumes the baseline is the first extension line of the last dimension. For the cabin, that would be the extension line that extends to the center of the interior wall. You want the baseline to be the extension line above the upper-left corner of the walls, so press ↵ to select that extension line.

It would be nice to have a dimension for the roof spaced the same distance above the overall dimension as the overall dimension is spaced above the incremental dimensions. The Baseline command can help you do this.

1. Start the Baseline command again. This time, don't press ↵. We'll use the first extension line of the last dimension for our baseline.

2. Pick the extension line for the upper-left corner of the walls as the baseline.

3. Pick the upper-right corner of the roof. A dimension is placed above the overall dimension (see Figure 11.18a). Press Esc to cancel the Baseline command. To finish it, you need to move the left extension line of this last dimension to the upper-left corner of the roof.

4. Click the text of the roof dimension. Grips appear in five places on the dimension, and the dimension ghosts (see Figure 11.18b).

5. Click the grip at the bottom of the left extension line to activate it.

6. Click the upper-left corner of the roof, and then press Esc. The extension line moves, and the dimension text is updated to display the full length of the roof (see Figure 11.18c).

This completes the horizontal dimensions for the back wall.

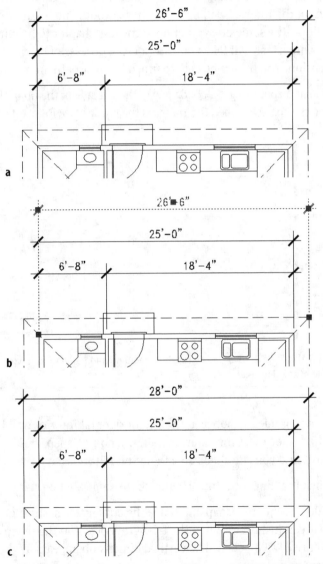

FIGURE 11.18: The result of the second use of the Baseline command (a), starting grips to modify the dimension (b), and the result (c)

Vertical Dimensions

Because the Linear command can be used for vertical and horizontal dimensions, you can follow the steps in the previous exercise to do the vertical dimensions on the left side of the floor plan. The only difference from the horizontal dimensioning is that there is no jamb line whose midpoint can be used to establish the center of the interior wall between the bedroom and bathroom. You will draw a guideline—the same one you drew in the last chapter to help make the grid. The following steps will take you through the process of placing the first vertical dimension. You'll then be able to finish the rest of them by yourself.

1. Pan and zoom to get a good view of the left side of the floor plan, including the space between the roof and the border (see Figure 11.19).

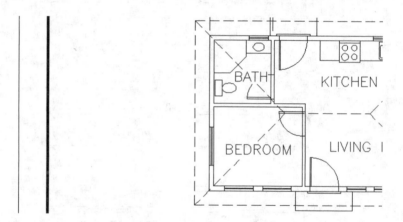

FIGURE 11.19: The result of zooming and panning for a view of the left side of the floor plan

You drew the same guideline in Chapter 10 when you drew the structural grid.

2. Draw a guideline between the two horizontal interior wall lines where they meet the exterior wall. Endpoint Osnap should be running, and you should be able to do this without having to zoom in.

3. Click the Linear button. Then pick the upper-left corner of the walls.

4. Select Midpoint Osnap and move the cursor to the short guideline that you just drew. When the triangle appears on the line (see Figure 11.20a), click. The vertical dimension appears in ghosted form, attached to the cursor.

5. Move the dimension line to a point about 3' to the left of the roof line and click. The first vertical dimension is drawn (see Figure 11.20b).

6. Erase the short guideline from between the interior walls.

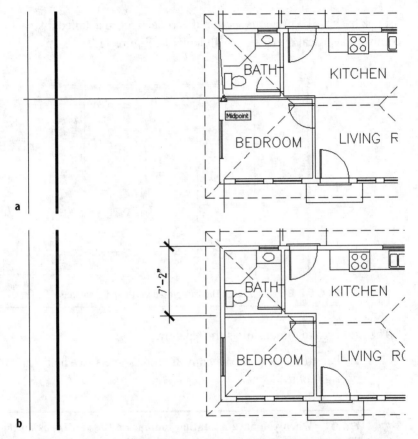

FIGURE 11.20: A guideline is drawn to help find the center of an interior wall (a), and the first vertical dimension is placed (b).

Finishing the Vertical Dimensions

You place the rest of the vertical dimensions using the procedure you used to complete the horizontal dimensions. Here is a summary of the steps:

1. Use the Continue command to dimension the bedroom.

2. Use the Baseline command to place an overall dimension.

3. Use the Baseline command to place a roof dimension to the left of the overall dimension.

4. Use grips to move the first extension line of the roof dimension to its corner.

Look back at the previous section if you need more detailed instructions. The completed vertical dimensions will look like Figure 11.21.

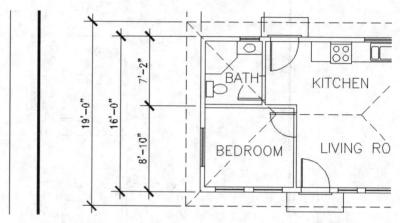

FIGURE 11.21: The completed vertical dimensions

The next area to dimension is the balcony.

1. Pan to a view of the balcony. Include some space below and to the right of it.

T I P When you have a floating toolbar on the screen, using the Zoom Window command doesn't take into account the area that the floating toolbar takes up. When you can, it's better to use Realtime Pan and Zoom to adjust your view in this situation.

2. Start the Linear command, and pick the lower-right corner of the building walls.

3. Use Quadrant Osnap, and pick near the rightmost edge of the outside balcony wall.

4. When the dimension appears, move it a couple of feet below the bottom roof line and place it there (see Figure 11.22).

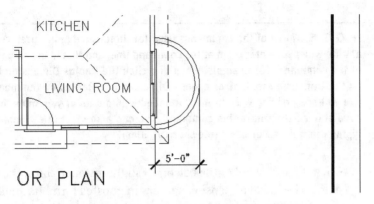

FIGURE 11.22: The horizontal balcony dimension

This will be enough on vertical and horizontal linear dimensions for now. Let's take a look at some other kinds of dimensions.

Other Types of Dimensions

AutoCAD provides tools for placing radial and angular dimensions on the drawing and for placing linear dimensions that are neither vertical nor horizontal. You'll use the Radial command to dimension the inside radius of the balcony.

Radial Dimensions

On the Dimension toolbar are icons for radial and diameter dimensions. They both operate the same way and are controlled by the same settings.

     T I P   The icons on the toolbars don't really look like buttons until you move the pointer cursor onto them. In this book, I refer to them as both icons and buttons.

1. Click the Osnap button on the status bar to temporarily disable any running Osnaps.

2. Click the Radius Dimension button to start the Dimradius command.

N O T E   Most of the commands used for dimensioning are prefaced with a "dim" when you enter them at the command line, and that is the actual name of the command. For example, when you click the Radius Dimension button on the Dimension toolbar or choose Dimension ➤ Radius on the menu bar, you will see _dimradius in the Command window to let you know that you have started the Dimradius command. You can also start this command by typing **dimradius**↵ or **dra**↵ (the shortcut alias).

3. Click the inside arc of the balcony a slight distance above the midpoint. The radial dimension appears in ghosted form. Its angle of orientation is determined by where you pick the arc. The dimension text then stays attached to the cursor (see Figure 11.23).

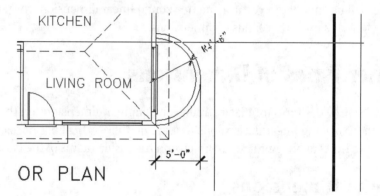

FIGURE 11.23: The radial dimension initially positioned in the arc

4. Notice that the tick mark used for linear dimensions is used here also. We must have an arrowhead for the radial dimension. Press Esc to cancel the command.

We will have to alter the dimension style to specify an arrowhead for radial dimensions.

Parent and Child Dimensioning Styles

The DimPlan dimension style that you set up at the beginning of this chapter applies to all dimensions and is called the *parent* dimension style. But you can change settings in this dimension style for particular types of dimensions, such as the radial type, for example. This makes a *child* dimension style. The child version is based on the parent version, but has a few settings that are different.

In this way, all your dimensions will be made using the DimPlan dimension style, but radial dimensions will use a child version of the style. Once you create a child dimension style from the parent style, you refer to both styles by the same name, and you call them a dimension style *family*.

1. Click the Dimension Style button on the Dimension toolbar to open the Dimension Style Manager dialog box. It will look like Figure 11.24.

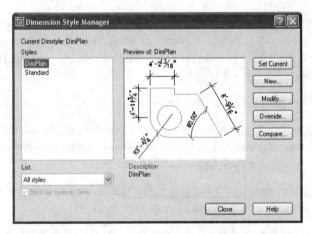

FIGURE 11.24: The Dimension Style Manager dialog box with DimPlan current

2. Be sure DimPlan is highlighted in the Styles list, and then click the New button to open the Create New Dimension Style dialog box.

3. Open the Use For drop-down list and select Radius Dimensions. Then click the Continue button. The New Dimension Style dialog box opens and has the six tabs you worked with earlier. Its title bar now includes Radial, and the preview window shows a radial dimension.

4. Activate the Lines And Arrows tab. Then move to the Arrowheads area and open the second Arrowhead drop-down list.

5. Select Right-Angle. Notice how the preview window now illustrates a radial dimension with a right-angle arrowhead.

6. Click the Text tab.

7. In the Text Placement area, open the Vertical drop-down list and select Centered.

8. Click OK to close the New Dimension Style: DimPlan: Radial dialog box.

9. In the Dimension Style Manager dialog box, notice the Styles list. Radial is now a substyle of DimPlan. Radial is referred to as a "child" style of the "parent" style DimPlan. Click Close to close the Dimension Style Manager dialog box.

10. Click the Radius button on the Dimension toolbar.

11. Click the inside arc of the balcony at a point about 15° above the right quadrant point. The radius dimension appears in ghosted form, and it now has an arrow instead of a tick mark.

12. Move the cursor to the outside of the balcony, and place the dimension text so that it looks similar to Figure 11.25.

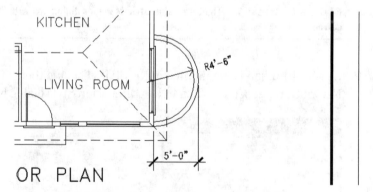

FIGURE 11.25: The radius dimension for the balcony

When placing the radial dimension, you have control over the angle of the dimension line (by where you pick the arc) and the location of the dimension text (by where you pick the second point).

The balcony also needs to be given a name in the drawing, like the other rooms.

Leader Lines

Use the Leader command to draw an arrow to the balcony and place the text outside the arcs. Before you do that, you need to adjust a few dimension style settings for the leader dimension.

1. Click the Dimension Style button on the Dimension toolbar.

2. With DimPlan highlighted, click New.

3. In the Create New Dimension Style dialog box, open the Use For drop-down list and click Leaders And Tolerances. Then click Continue.

4. Activate the Lines And Arrows tab, move to the Arrowheads area, and open the Leader drop-down list. Click Right-Angle.

5. Click the Text tab. In the Text Placement area, change Above to Centered. Then click OK.

T I P   If you want the Balcony label text in the same text style as the room labels, you can change the Text Style in the Text Appearance area of the Text tab to the Label text style.

6. Notice how Leader is now a child style, along with Radial, in the Styles list. Click Close. Another child DimPlan dimension style is created that is identical to the regular DimPlan style except for the two settings that you just changed.

7. Click Close to close the Dimension Style Manager, and then click the Quick Leader button on the Dimension toolbar.

8. Click the Osnap button in the status bar to temporarily disable running Osnaps, if it's not already in the off position.

9. Pick a point inside the balcony just below the radial dimension line.

10. Drag the line to the outside of the balcony, making the line approximately parallel to the radial dimension line, and pick a point (see Figure 11.26a).

11. Press ↵. Then, at the Specify text width <0">: prompt, press ↵ again. At the next prompt, with Caps Lock on, type **balcony**↵. The prompt changes to read Enter next line of annotation text:. Now you can enter multiple lines of text for the leader. Press ↵. The leader is completed, and the word *BALCONY* is placed at the end of the leader line (see Figure 11.26b).

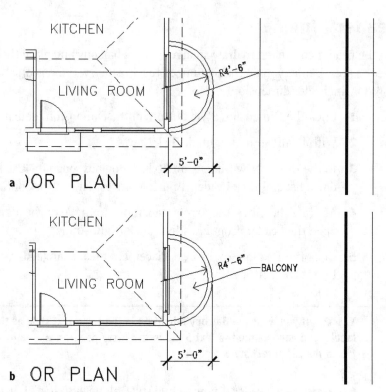

FIGURE 11.26: The leader line being drawn (a), and the completed leader (b)

 N O T E   If the angle of the leader line is steeper than 15°, a short horizontal line called a *dogleg* or *hook line* is added between the leader line and the text.

12. Zoom to Extents, and then zoom out a little and pan to view the whole drawing with dimensions.

13. Save this drawing as Cabin11a.

This exercise got you started using the Leader command. Later in this chapter, in the section on modifying dimensions, you will get another chance to work with leader lines and their text. Next, I will introduce you to two more types of dimensions.

Angular and Aligned Dimensions

To get familiar with the aligned and angular dimension types, play around with the two commands, using the roof lines to experiment. Here's how to set up Cabin11a to work with aligned and angular dimensions:

1. Type **undo↵**, and then type **m↵**.

2. Make the Roof layer current.

3. Turn off all other layers by following these steps:

   A. Click the Layers button.

   B. In the Layer Properties Manager dialog box, place the cursor any- where on the list of layer names and right-click to open a small menu.

   C. Choose Select All But Current on the menu. Then click one of the light bulbs for any highlighted layer in the On column.

   D. The light bulbs for all selected layers turn off, indicating that those layers have been turned off.

   E. Click OK to close the dialog box and return to the drawing. Every- thing has disappeared except the roof lines.

4. Pan and zoom to get a closer view of the roof.

5. Create a new layer called Dim2. Accept the color that is assigned to it, and make Dim2 current.

6. Set Endpoint Osnap to be running. Now you are ready to dimension.

Aligned Dimensions

Aligned dimensions are linear dimensions that are not horizontal or vertical. You place them in the same way that you place horizontal or vertical dimensions with the Linear command. You can also use the Baseline and Continue com- mands with aligned dimensions.

Use the Aligned command to dimension a hip line of the roof. Try it on your own. Follow the prompts. It works just like the Dimlinear command, except that the dimension is not displayed on the drawing until you finish the command.

Start the Aligned command by clicking the Align button on the Dimension toolbar. Look ahead to Figure 11.27 to see the results you should get.

Angular Dimensions

The angular dimension is the only basic dimension type that uses angles in the dimension text instead of linear measurements. Generally, tick marks are not used with angular dimensions, so you need to create another child dimension style for this type of dimension. Follow the steps given earlier in this chapter for setting up the Radial and Leader child styles. The only change you need to make is on the Lines And Arrows tab: replace the Architectural tick with the Right-Angle arrowhead.

Try making an angular dimension on your own. You can start the Angular command by clicking the Angular button on the Dimension toolbar. Follow the prompts and see if you can figure out how this command works.

Figure 11.27 illustrates angular and aligned dimensions on the roof.

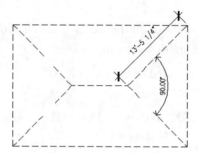

FIGURE 11.27: The roof with angular and aligned dimensions

Don't save your drawing as is. Instead, type **undo**↵, and then type **b**↵. This will undo the angular and aligned dimensions you just created and the Dim2 dimension style and leave your drawing at the state it was in when you last saved it as Cabin 11a.

When you change settings for a dimension style, dimensions created when that style was current will be automatically updated to reflect the changes. You'll modify more dimensions in the next section.

You have been introduced to the basic types of dimensions—linear, radial, leader, and angular—and some auxiliary dimensions—baseline, continue, and aligned—that are special cases of the linear type. The baseline and continue dimensions can also be used with angular dimensions.

Ordinate Dimensions

Ordinate dimensions are widely used by the mechanical and civil engineering professions and related trades. They differ from the kind of dimensioning we have been doing so far in this chapter in that ordinate dimensioning specifies X and Y coordinate values for specific points in a drawing based on an absolute or relative Cartesian coordinate system, rather than on a distance between two points. This method is used to dimension centers of holes in sheet metal or machine parts and to locate surveying points on an area map.

We don't need ordinate dimensions in our cabin project, so we will go through a quick exercise in setting them up to dimension the holes in a plate. This will give you a glimpse of the tools that AutoCAD provides for working with them. If you are not interested in ordinate dimensioning, move on to the next section on modifying the dimensions we've already created for the cabin.

1. Open a new drawing, and leave the units at the default of Decimal with a precision of four decimal places. Set Polar Tracking to be on.

2. Set up a new text style called Arial; select Arial as the font and 0.125 as the height. Click Apply & Close to make it the current text style.

3. Draw a rectangle using 0,0 as the first point and 6,–4 as the second.

4. Zoom to Extents, and then zoom to .5x. Turn off the UCS icon.

5. Draw a circle somewhere in the upper-left quadrant of the rectangle with a radius of 0.35 units; then, using Polar Tracking, copy that circle once directly to the right and once directly below the original and to two other locations not aligned with any other circle, so the configuration looks something like Figure 11.28a.

6. Set Endpoint and Center Osnaps to be running.

   What we care about with ordinate dimensioning is not how far apart the holes are from each other, but how far the X and Y coordinates of the centers of the holes are away from some reference point on the plate. We'll use the upper-left corner of the plate as our reference point, or *datum point,* because it is positioned at the origin of the drawing, or at the 0,0 point.

7. Click the Ordinate button on the Dimension toolbar.

8. Click the upper-left corner of the rectangular plate, and then move the cursor straight up above the point you picked. When you are about an inch above the plate, click again. This sets the first ordinate dimension (see Figure 11.28a).

9. Repeat step 8 for the four circles near the middle or upper portions of the plate, using their centers as points to snap to and aligning the ordinate dimensions by eye. The lower circle is in vertical alignment with the one above it, so it needs no horizontal dimension. Place an

ordinate dimension on the upper-right corner of the plate to finish up. The result will look like Figure 11.28b. Note that one of the extension lines has a jog in it for spacing. You will see that this is an option for each ordinate dimension you place.

10. Repeat this procedure for the *y* ordinate dimensions. Once again, ignore any circles that are in vertical alignment, but include the upper- and lower-left corners of the plate (see Figure 11.28c).

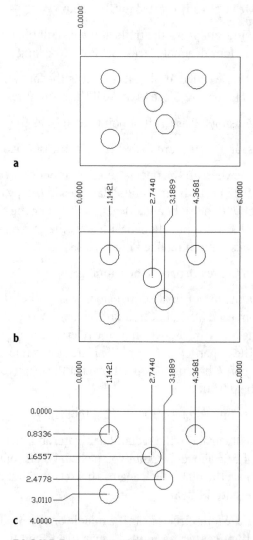

FIGURE 11.28: Placing the first ordinate dimension (a), finishing up the X coordinate dimensions (b), and placing the Y coordinate dimensions (c)

In civil engineering, ordinate dimensions are used almost the same way, but displayed differently. A datum reference point is used, but the dimensions are displayed at each point. This is because the points are a set of surveying points spread randomly over a large area, and the datum or reference point may be miles away (see Figure 11.29).

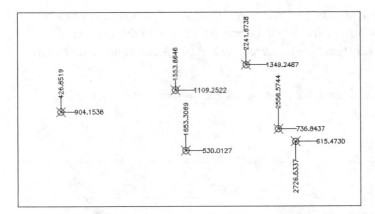

FIGURE 11.29: A sample surveyor's datum points with ordinate dimensions

The final part of this chapter will be devoted to teaching you a few techniques for modifying dimensions.

Modifying Dimensions

You can use several commands and grips to modify dimensions, depending on the desired change. You can:

- ▶ Change the dimension text content.
- ▶ Move the dimension text relative to the dimension line.
- ▶ Move the dimension or extension lines.
- ▶ Change the dimension style settings for a dimension or a group of dimensions.
- ▶ Revise a dimension style.

The best way to understand how to modify dimensions is to try a few.

Modifying Dimension Text

You can modify any aspect of the dimension text. We'll look at how to change the content first.

Editing Dimension Text Content

To change the content of text for one dimension, or to add text before or after the actual dimension, use the Ddedit command. (You used this command in Chapter 10 to modify text.) We'll change the text in the horizontal dimensions for the roof and walls.

1. Zoom and pan until your view of the floor plan is similar to Figure 11.30.

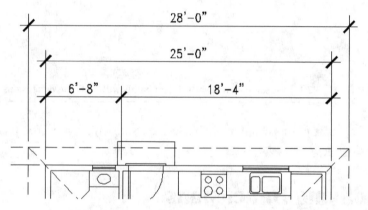

FIGURE 11.30: A modified view of the floor plan

2. Type ddedit↵. Then select the horizontal roof dimension at the top of the drawing. The Multiline Text Editor window and the Text Formatting toolbar appear. The angle brackets in the editing window represent the existing text in the dimension, 28'-0". You can highlight the brackets and enter a new dimension or enter new text before or after the brackets.

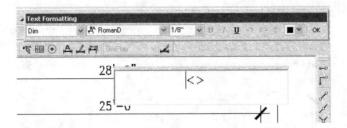

3. Click to the right of the brackets, press the spacebar to create a space, type **verify in field**, and click OK on the right end of the toolbar. The phrase is added to the dimension (see Figure 11.31a). The prompt tells you that you can select another object to edit.

4. Click the dimension just below the roof dimension.

5. In the Multiline Text Editor window, click to the right of the angle brackets again. Then right-click, and choose Symbol from the short-cut menu to open a flyout.

6. Select Plus/Minus. The ± symbol is now in the edit window.

7. Click OK. The dimension now has a ± after it (see Figure 11.31b). Press ↵ to end the Ddedit command.

If you need to change the text of several dimensions at once, use the Dimedit command.

1. Click the Dimension Edit button on the Dimension toolbar.

2. At the `Enter type of dimension editing [Home/New/Rotate/Oblique] <Home>:` prompt, type n↵ to replace the existing text or to add to it.

3. In the Multiline Text Editor dialog box, highlight the angle brackets.

4. Type **Unknown** and click OK.

5. In the drawing, click the 6'-8" and 18'-4" dimensions. Then press ↵.

6. The two dimensions now read Unknown (see Figure 11.31c).

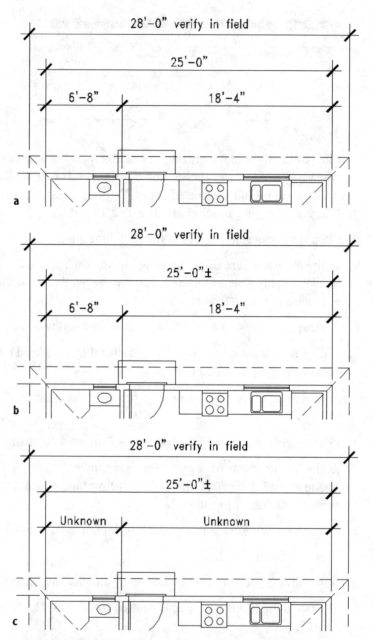

FIGURE 11.31: Adding a phrase to dimension text (a), adding a special character (b), and editing more than one dimension text at a time (c)

Next, you'll learn about moving a dimension.

Moving Dimensions

You can use grips to move dimensions. We used grips to move the extension line of the roof dimension when we were putting on the vertical and horizontal dimensions. This time we'll move the dimension line and the text.

1. Zoom in to a view of the right side of the floor plan until you have a view that includes the entire balcony and its three dimensions, as well as the entire right cabin wall.

2. At the Command: prompt, click the 5'-0" dimension. Grips appear.

3. Click the grip on the right tick mark to activate it.

4. Move the cursor up until the dimension text is above the balcony. Then click again to fix it there. Click the grip that's on the text, and with Polar Tracking on, move the text slightly to the right to clear it from the roof line. Then press Esc (see Figure 11.32a). The dimension, line, and text move to a new position, and the extension lines are redrawn to the new position.

5. Click the leader line. Then click the word *BALCONY*. Two grips appear on the leader line, and one appears on the text.

6. Hold down the Shift key and click the two grips near the text. Then release the Shift key.

7. Click one of the two activated grips. Move the cursor down to reposition the leader and text slightly below the Quadrant point of the balcony arcs. Then click to fasten them there. Press Esc (see Figure 11.32b).

8. Be sure Osnap is turned off, and then click the 4'-6" radial dimension. Three grips appear.

9. Click the grip at the arrowhead.

10. Move the cursor to the inside arc and below the just-relocated leader line until the Radial dimension line and its text display in a clear space. Pick that point.

11. Press Esc (see Figure 11.32c).

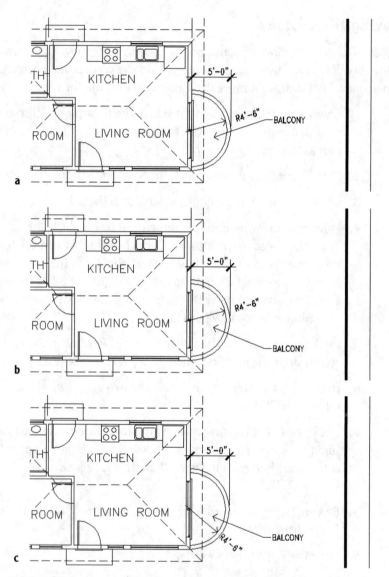

FIGURE 11.32: Moving the balcony dimensions with grips: the Linear dimension (a), the leader (b), and the Radial dimension (c)

To finish the changes to the balcony, you need to suppress the left extension line of the 5'-0" dimension because it overlaps the wall and header lines.

Dimension Overrides

You suppress the left extension line with the Properties command, which allows you to change a setting in the dimension style for one dimension without altering the style settings.

1. Turn off the Headers layer.

2. Click the Properties button on the Standard toolbar. If necessary, drag the Dimensioning toolbar far enough to the right to clear the Properties palette.

3. Click the 5'-0" dimension.

4. In the Properties palette, move to the Lines And Arrows heading. If this section is not open, click the double arrows to the right.

5. Scroll down the list of settings in this section and click Ext Line 1. Then click the down arrow in the right column to open the drop-down list. Click Off. The left extension line on the linear balcony dimension is suppressed.

6. Close the Properties palette. Press Esc to remove the grips (see Figure 11.33).

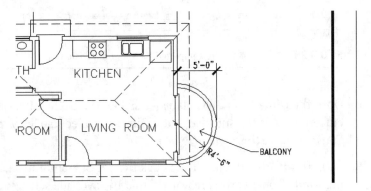

FIGURE 11.33: The 5'-0" dimension with the left extension line suppressed

The bedroom needs a horizontal dimension. Because space outside the floor plan is tight, you'll place the dimension inside the bedroom and suppress both extension lines with an override to the current dimension style.

1. Pan the drawing over until the bedroom is fully in view.

2. Open the Dimension Style Manager dialog box and click the Override button.

3. Activate the Lines And Arrows tab. In the Extension Lines area, move to the bottom where it says Suppress, and put a check mark in the Ext Line 1 and Ext Line 2 check boxes. Then click OK.

4. In the Dimension Style Manager dialog box, click Close.

5. Click the Linear button on the Dimension toolbar.

6. Activate running Osnaps. In the bedroom, pick the lower-left inside corner, and then pick the lower-right inside corner. The dimension appears in ghosted form, attached to the cursor.

7. Suppress the running Osnaps for one pick. Then move the dimension up to a position below the BEDROOM text and above the lower wall, and click to fix it there. The dimension is placed, and both extension lines are suppressed (see Figure 11.34).

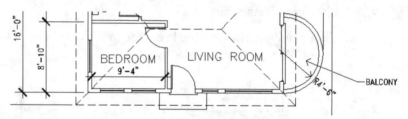

FIGURE 11.34: The completed bedroom dimension

8. Open the Dimension Style Manager dialog box. In the Styles list, the current style is the substyle under DimPlan called <style overrides>. You can delete this style now, as it is no longer needed.

9. Click DimPlan in the list. Then click the Set Current button. A warning window opens. You are warned that the override settings will be deleted if you make DimPlan the current dimension style. Click OK. The style overrides are deleted.

10. Click Close to close the dialog box.

 T I P   If you set a style override that you later decide should be incorporated into the parent dimension style, highlight Style Overrides in the Styles list, right-click, and then choose Save To Current Style from the shortcut menu.

To illustrate how dimension style overrides work, we suppressed extension lines in two dimensions without having to alter the dimension style. Extension lines are usually the thinnest lines in a drawing. It is usually not critical that they be suppressed if they coincide with other lines because the other lines will overwrite them in a print. In the bedroom, for example, if the extension lines are not suppressed, they are overwritten by the wall lines.

However, in the first example, the left extension line of the 5'-0" dimension for the balcony coincides with the line representing a header. If the Headers layer is turned off, you would have to suppress or move the extension line of this dimension so it would not be visible spanning the sliding door opening. Also, if you dimension to a noncontinuous line, such as a center line, suppress the extension line that coincides with that line. In the practice exercises at the end of this chapter, you'll get a chance to learn how to dimension to center lines.

Dimensioning Short Distances

When you have to dimension distances so short that both the text and arrows (or tick marks) can't fit between the extension line, a dimension style setting determines where they are placed. To see how this works, you'll redo the horizontal dimensions above the floor plan, this time dimensioning the distance between the roof line and wall line, as well as the thickness of the interior wall. The setting changes that we made in the Fit tab when we set up the DimPlan dimension style will help us now.

1. Zoom and pan to a view of the upper portion of the floor plan so that the horizontal dimensions above the floor plan are visible (see Figure 11.35).

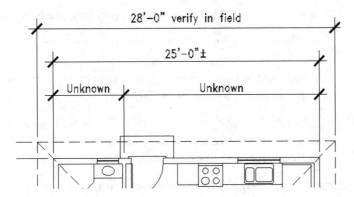

FIGURE 11.35: The new view of the upper floor plan and its dimensions

2. Use the Erase command to erase the four dimensions that are above the floor plan. Each dimension is a single object, so you can select the four dimensions with four picks or one crossing window.

3. Activate the running Osnaps, click the Linear button, and pick the upper-left corner of the roof. Then pick the upper-left corner of the wall lines. Place the dimension line about 3' above the upper roof line (see Figure 11.36a).

4. Click the Continue button. Click the upper end of each interior wall line, click the upper-right corner of the wall lines, and finally click the upper-right corner of the roof (see Figure 11.36b). Press Esc to cancel the Continue command.

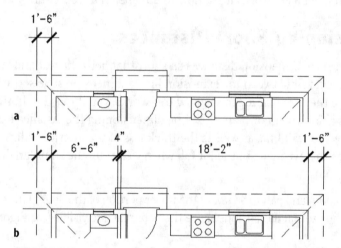

FIGURE 11.36: The first dimension is placed (a), and the other dimensions (b)

5. Click the Baseline button. Press ↵ and then pick the left extension line of the 1'-6" dimension on the left end.

6. Click the upper-right corner of the roof. The overall dimension is placed a preset distance above the lower dimensions (see Figure 11.37a). Press Esc to cancel the Baseline command.

Because some of the dimension text in the lower dimensions was placed higher than normal, the overall dimension needs to be raised a little.

1. Click the overall dimension. Grips appear. Click the grip at the intersection of the right extension line and the dimension line to activate it.

2. Click the Snap To None Osnap button, move the cursor up until the dimension line clears the higher text of the lower dimensions, and click. Press Esc. The text of the two 1'-6" dimensions crosses over the outer extension lines (see Figure 11.37b).

3. You can move dimension text with grips. Click the right 1'-6" dimension. Grips appear. Click the grip right in the middle of the text. Turn on Polar, and turn off Osnap. Then move the text to the left until it clears the extension line, and click to place it.

4. Click the 1'-6" dimension on the left and repeat step 3, this time moving the text to the right.

5. When the text is where you want it, press Esc twice to clear the grips (see Figure 11.37c).

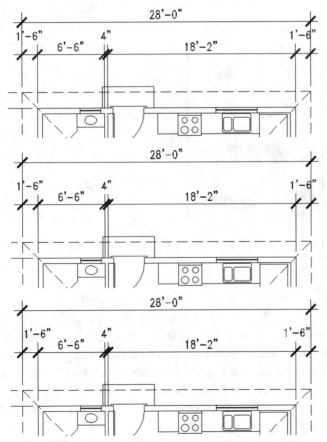

FIGURE 11.37: The overall dimension is placed using Baseline (a), raised using grips (b), and the 1'-6" dimensions are moved to clear the extension lines (c).

This concludes the exercises for dimensions in this chapter. The current drawing won't be used in future chapters, so feel free to experiment with the dimensioning commands that you just learned. When you finish a drawing session, before you save, it is a good habit to Zoom to Extents and then zoom out a little so all visible objects are on the screen. This way, the next time you open this drawing, you will have a full view of it at the beginning of your session.

1. Click the X in the upper-right corner of the Dimension toolbar to close it.

2. Zoom to Extents, and then zoom out a little to a full view of the cabin (see Figure 11.38).

3. Save this drawing to your training folder as `Cabin11b`.

4. Take a break. You deserve one!

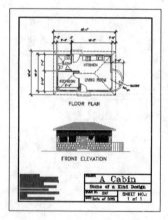

FIGURE 11.38: The full view of the cabin drawing with dimensions complete

Working successfully with dimensions in your drawing requires an investment of time to become familiar with the commands and settings that control how dimensions appear, how they are placed in the drawing, and how they are modified. The exercises in this chapter have led you through the basics of the dimensioning process. For a more in-depth discussion of dimensions, refer to *Mastering AutoCAD 2005 and AutoCAD LT 2005* by George Omura (Sybex, 2004).

The next chapter will introduce you to external references, a tool for viewing a drawing from within another drawing.

If You Would Like More Practice...

In the first exercise, you will get a chance to practice the dimensioning tools that you just learned. After that, there is a short exercise that shows a technique for incorporating center lines into dimensions.

Exercise 1: Dimensioning the Garage Addition

Try dimensioning the garage addition to the cabin that was shown at the end of Chapter 4 (Cabin04b-addon.dwg). Use the same techniques and standards of dimensioning that you used in this chapter to dimension the cabin.

1. Dimension to the outside edges of exterior walls and to center lines of interior walls.

2. Use the DimPlan dimension style that you set up and used in this chapter. Close all files that you used in this chapter, and open Cabin04b-addon. Then use DesignCenter to bring over the Dim-Plan dimension style, the Dim text style, and the Dim1 layer.

3. If you added text to this drawing and saved it in the practice exercise in Chapter 10, use this drawing (see Figure 11.39).

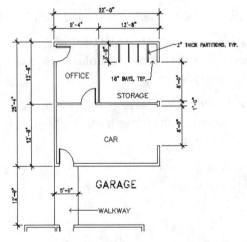

FIGURE 11.39: The walkway and garage dimensioned

4. When finished, save this drawing as Cabin11b-addon.

Exercise 2: Dimensioning to a Center Line

This exercise will take you through a series of steps to show you how to use center lines as replacements for extension lines in dimensions. I'll use as many of the default settings for AutoCAD as I can to give you a look at what "out of the box" or "vanilla" AutoCAD looks like, that is, how drawings look if you use the default settings for text styles, dimension styles, units, and so forth. The drawing that you will make will be similar to the one made in Chapter 2, but you know so much more now.

1. Choose File ➢ New ➢ Select Start From Scratch to start a new drawing. (If the Select Template dialog box opens, click the down arrow next to Open, and select Open With No Template - Imperial.)

2. Start the Rectangle command, and click a point in the lower-left quadrant of the drawing area. For the second point, type **6,2↵**.

3. Turn off the UCS icon, zoom to Extents, and then zoom to .5x. Pan to move the new rectangle down a little.

4. Create a new layer called Center. Assign it to be the current linetype. Leave its color as White, but click Continuous in the Linetype column. In the Select Layer dialog box, click Load, scroll down in the Load Or Reload Linetypes dialog box to find the Center linetype, select it, and click OK.

5. Back in the Select Linetype dialog box, highlight Center and click OK.

6. Back in the Layer Properties Manager dialog box, the Center linetype should be assigned to the new Center layer, and it should be the current layer. Click OK to return to the drawing.

7. Draw a line from the midpoint of the lower horizontal line of the rectangle upward to a point about 2" above the upper horizontal line of the rectangle. End the Line command.

8. Click that new line, and then drag the lower grip down a little past the lower horizontal line of the rectangle (see Figure 11.40).

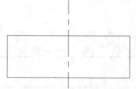

FIGURE 11.40: The rectangle and the center line

We want to dimension from the upper-left corner of the rectangle to the center line and then to the upper-right corner. We will select the Dimension command from the menu bar and use the default dimension settings.

1. Create a new layer called Dim, accept the White color, and make Dim current. Set Endpoint and Intersection Osnaps to be running, and then choose Dimension ➤ Linear. Click the upper-left corner of the rectangle, and then click the intersection of the center line with the upper horizontal line of the rectangle. Drag the dimension line up to a point near the upper endpoint of the center line and click. The first dimension is placed.

2. Choose Dimension ➤ Continue to start the Continue Dimension command, and select the upper-right corner of the rectangle. This places the second dimension. Press Esc to end the Continue Dimension command. Now we need to use an Override dimension to suppress the second extension line of the first dimension and the first extension line of the second dimension.

3. Click the text of the first dimension, and then use the Properties palette to change the Ext Line 2 setting to Off. Press Esc to delete the grips, select the second dimension, and in the Properties palette, change the Ext Line 1 setting to Off. Close the Properties palette, and press Esc to delete the grips. The characteristic breaks of the center line should now be visible throughout its length.

As a final touch, we'll put a center line symbol at the top of the center line, using the MText command.

1. Start the MText command, and make a small defining rectangle somewhere in a blank portion of the drawing area.

2. Right-click in the MText Editor and select Symbol. In the menu that displays, select Center Line. A center line symbol is now in the MText Editor. Highlight it and change its height from 0.2000 to 0.4000. Right-click again in the MText Editor, click Justification, and then click Bottom Center. Then click OK in the MText toolbar to execute the changes.

3. Click the center line symbol to activate the grips. Click the lower middle grip, and then click the upper end of the center line. This locates the symbol.

4. Press Esc to delete the grips, and then click the center line. Click the upper grip, and with Osnaps turned off for one click, move the upper

endpoint of the center line down slightly to create a small space between it and the center line symbol (see Figure 11.41).

This completes the exercise.

FIGURE 11.41: The center line symbol and a center line used as part of two dimensions

Other Exercises

Use the skills you've learned in this chapter to do the following:

▶ Set up a dimension style for your own use.

▶ Dimension a drawing as you would in your own profession or trade.

▶ Dimension any of the other drawings offered in previous chapters, such as the screw, the gasket, or the parking lot.

Are You Experienced?

Now you can...

☑ **create a new dimension style**

☑ **place vertical and horizontal dimensions in a drawing**

☑ **use radial, aligned, and angular dimensions**

☑ **create leader lines for notes**

☑ **modify dimension text**

☑ **override a dimension style**

☑ **modify a dimension style**

CHAPTER 12

Managing External References

▶ Understanding external references

▶ Creating external references

▶ Modifying external references

▶ Converting external references into blocks

The floor plan of a complex building project may actually be a composite of several AutoCAD files that are linked together as external references to the current drawing. This enables parts of a drawing to be worked on at different workstations (or in different offices) while remaining linked to a central host file. In mechanical engineering, a drawing may similarly be a composite of the various subparts that make up an assembly.

External references are .dwg files that have been temporarily connected to the current drawing and are used as reference information. The externally referenced drawing is visible in the current drawing. You can manipulate its layers, colors, linetypes, and visibility, and you can modify its objects, but it is not a permanent part of the current drawing.

External references are similar to blocks in that they behave as single objects and are inserted into a drawing in the same way. But blocks are part of the current drawing file, and external references are not.

Blocks can be exploded back to their component parts, but external references cannot; however, external references can be converted into blocks and become a permanent part of the current drawing. In Chapter 7, you were able to modify the window block, and in so doing, update all instances of the window block in the drawing without having to explode the block. With an external reference—usually called an *Xref*—the same mechanism can be applied. To manage external references, you need to learn how to set up an Xref, manipulate its appearance in the host drawing, and update it.

Before you set up the Xref, you will create a site plan for the cabin. You will then Xref the cabin drawing into the site drawing. In Figure 12.1, the lines of the cabin floor plan constitute the Xref, and the rest of the objects are part of the host drawing. After these exercises, we will look at a few ways that design offices use external references.

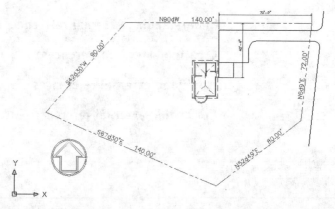

FIGURE 12.1: The site plan with the cabin as an external reference

Drawing a Site Plan

The site plan you will use has been simplified so that you can draw it with a minimum of steps and get on with the external referencing. The following are essential elements:

- ▶ Property lines
- ▶ Access road to the site
- ▶ North arrow
- ▶ Indication of where the building is located on the site

The first step is to draw in the property lines.

Using Surveyor Units

You draw property lines using Surveyor units for angles and decimal feet for Linear units. In laying out the property lines, you will use relative polar coordinates, so you will enter coordinates in the format @*distance<angle*, in which the distance is in feet and hundredths of a foot, and the angle is in Surveyor units to the nearest minute.

Surveyor Units

Surveyor units, called *bearings* in civil engineering, describe the direction of a line from its beginning point. The direction (bearing), described as a deviation from the north or south toward the east or west, is given as an angular measurement in degrees, minutes, and seconds. The angles used in a bearing can never be greater than 90°, so bearing lines must be headed in one of the four directional quadrants: northeasterly, northwesterly, southeasterly, or southwesterly. If north is set to be at the top of a plot plan, south is down, east is to the right, and west is to the left. Thus, when a line from its beginning goes up and to the right, it is headed in a northeasterly direction. And when a line from its beginning goes down and to the left, it is headed in a southwesterly direction, and so on. A line that is headed in a northeasterly direction with a deviation from true north of 30 degrees and 30 minutes is shown as N30d30' E in AutoCAD notation.

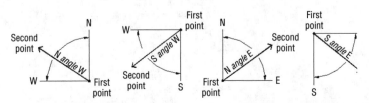

With the Surveyor unit system, a sloping line that has an up-and-to-the-left direction would have a down-and-to-the-right direction if you started from the opposite end. So in laying out property lines, it is important to move in the same direction (clockwise or counterclockwise) as you progress from one segment to the next.

Laying Out the Property Lines

You will set up a new drawing and then start at the upper-right corner of the property lines and work your way around counterclockwise.

1. Open Cabin11a from your training folder. Choose File ➤ Save As, and save the drawing as Cabin12a.

2. Click the QNew button on the Standard toolbar to open the Create New Drawing dialog box. Click Start From Scratch, and then click OK. (If the Select Template dialog box opens instead of the Create New Drawing dialog box, open the Open drop-down list and select Open With No Template - Imperial.)

3. From the menu bar, choose Format ➤ Units to open the Drawing Units dialog box, and change the precision in the Length area to two decimal places (0.00).

4. In the Angle area, open the Type drop-down list and select Surveyor's Units. Then change the precision to the nearest minute (N0d00' E). Click OK. You will need an area of about 250' × 150' for the site plan.

5. Open the Format menu again and choose Drawing Limits. Press ↵ to accept the default 0.00,0.00 for the lower-left corner. Type 250,150↵. Don't use the foot sign.

6. Right-click the Snap button on the status bar, and then choose Settings. Change Snap Spacing to 10.00, and change Grid to 0.00. Then click the Grid check box to turn on the grid, but leave Snap off. Click OK.

7. In the drawing, type z↵ a↵. Then zoom to .85x to see a blank space around the grid (see Figure 12.2).

> We are using Decimal linear units in such a way that 1 decimal unit represents 1 foot. The foot symbol (') is used only with Architectural and Engineering units.

FIGURE 12.2: The site drawing with the grid on

8. Create a new layer called Prop_line. Assign it a color and make it current.

9. Start the Line command. For the first point, type 220,130↵. This will start a line near the upper-right corner of the grid.

10. Be sure Snap is turned off. Then type:

    @140<n90dw↵

    @90<s42d30'w↵

    @140<s67d30'e↵

    @80<n52d49'e↵

    c↵

The property lines are completed (see Figure 12.3).

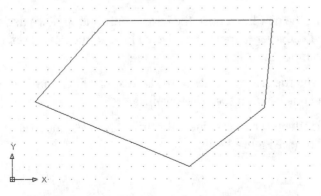

FIGURE 12.3: The property lines on the site drawing

Drawing the Driveway

The driveway is 8' wide and set 5' from the horizontal property line. The access road is 8' from the parallel property line. The intersection of the access road line and the driveway lines forms corners, each with a 3' radius. The driveway extends 70' in from the upper-right corner of the property.

Let's lay this out now.

1. Choose Format ➤ Units from the menu bar. Change the units to Architectural and the angular units to Decimal degrees. Then set the length precision to 1/16" and the angular precision to 0.00. Click OK. Because of the way AutoCAD translates decimal units to inches, your drawing is now only ¹⁄₁₂th the size it needs to be. (Use the Distance command to check it.) You will have to scale it up.

2. Click the Scale button on the Modify toolbar.

3. Type all↵↵. For the base point, type 0,0↵.

4. At the `Specify scale factor or [Reference]:` prompt, type 12↵. Then click Grid on the status bar to turn off the grid.

5. Zoom to Extents, and then zoom out a little. The drawing looks the same, but now it's the correct size. Check it with the Distance command, which you encountered in Chapter 7.

6. Offset the upper, horizontal property line 5' down. Offset this new line 8' down.

7. Offset the rightmost property line 8' to the right (see Figure 12.4a).

8. Create a new layer called Road. Assign it the color White, and make the Road layer current.

9. Click the new lines, open the Layer Control drop-down list, and click the Road layer to move the selected lines to the Road layer. Press Esc to remove the grips.

10. Extend the driveway lines to the access road line. Trim the access road line between the driveway lines.

11. Fillet the two corners where the driveway meets the road, using a 3' radius (see Figure 12.4b).

> You can also start the Scale command by choosing Modify ➤ Scale from the menu bar or by typing sc↵.

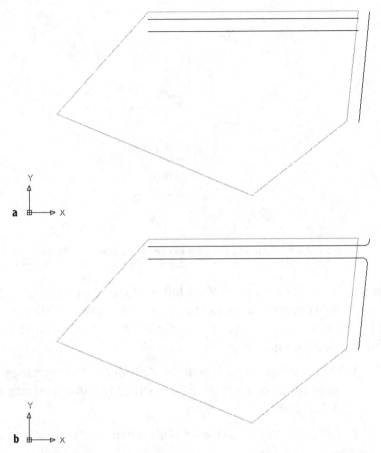

FIGURE 12.4: Offset property lines (a), and the completed intersection of the driveway and access road (b)

Finishing the Driveway

A key element of any site plan is information that shows how the building is positioned on the site relative to the property lines. Property lines are staked out by surveyors. The building contractor then takes measurements off the stakes to locate one or two corners of the building. In this site, you need only one corner because we are assuming the cabin is facing due west. A close look at Figure 12.1, shown earlier in this chapter, shows that the end of the driveway lines up with the outer edge of the back step of the cabin. Below the driveway is a square patio, and its bottom edge lines up with the bottom edge of the back step. So the bottom corner of the back step coincides with the lower-left corner of the patio. This locates the cabin on the site (see Figure 12.5).

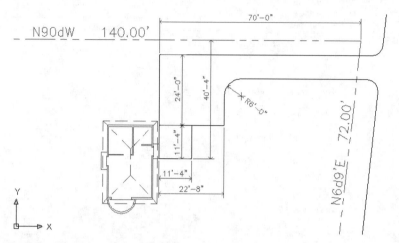

FIGURE 12.5: The driveway and patio lined up with the cabin

Imagine the site being on a bluff of a hill overlooking land that falls away to the south and west, providing a spectacular view in that direction. To accommodate this view, we will want to change the orientation of the cabin when we Xref it into the site drawing.

1. On the status bar, turn on Polar. Then draw a line from the upper-right corner of the property lines straight up to a point near the top of the screen.

2. Offset this line 70' to the left. This will mark the end of the driveway.

3. Draw a line from the lower endpoint of this offset line down a distance of 40'-4". Then, using Polar Tracking, continue this line 11'-4" to the right.

4. Offset the 40'-4" line 11'-4" to the right. Offset the newly created line 11'-4" to the right as well.

5. Offset the upper driveway line 24' down. These are all the lines you need to finish the site plan (see Figure 12.6a).

6. Finish the driveway and patio by using the Trim, Fillet, and Erase commands as you have in previous chapters. The radius of the corner to fillet is 6' (see Figure 12.6b).

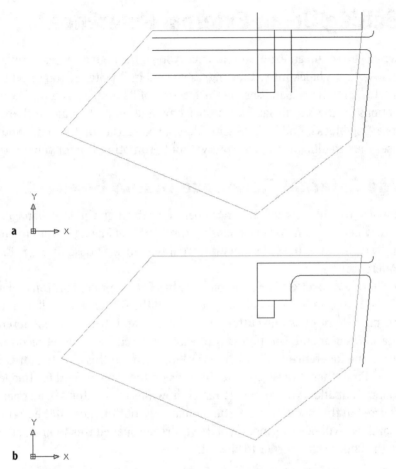

FIGURE 12.6: The offset lines (a), and the finished driveway and patio (b)

7. Make the 0 layer current, draw a north arrow, and place it in the lower-left corner.

8. Open the Layer Properties Manager dialog box, and change the linetype for the Prop_line layer to Phantom. (You will have to load it; see Chapter 6.)

9. Type **ltscale↵**, and then type **100↵**. You will see the phantom linetype for the property lines.

10. Save this drawing in your training folder as Site12a.

This completes the site plan. The next step is to attach the cabin drawing as an external reference into the site plan.

Setting Up an External Reference

When you set up an external reference, you go through a process similar to that of inserting a block into a drawing, as you did in Chapter 7. You select the drawing to be referenced and specify the location of its insertion point. There are options for the X scale factor, Y scale factor, and rotation angle, as there are for inserting blocks. And here, as with blocks, you can set up the command so that it uses the defaults for these options without prompting you for your approval.

The External Reference Dialog Box

You can run all external reference operations through the Xref Manager dialog box, which you can open by choosing Insert ➤ Xref Manager from the menu bar or by typing xr↵. To set up a new external reference, choose Insert ➤ External Reference.

There is also a Reference toolbar that has five command buttons related to Xrefs. You open it the same way you opened the Dimension toolbar in the last chapter: Right-click any button on the screen, and then choose Reference from the shortcut menu. But unless you're an advanced user, I don't recommend using the Reference toolbar while working through this chapter, for two reasons. First, there are seven other buttons on the toolbar used for Image commands that allow you to import raster drawings into AutoCAD, an operation not covered in this book. Second, the toolbar does not include all the Xref commands we will be covering. If you have already opened this toolbar, click the X in the upper-right corner to close it.

1. With Site12a as the current drawing, create a new layer called Cabin. Use the default color of White/Black and make the Cabin layer current.

2. Choose Insert ➤ External Reference to open the Select Reference File dialog box.

3. Locate the Training Data folder (or the folder that your training files are stored in) and select Cabin12a.dwg. Then click Open to open the External Reference dialog box.

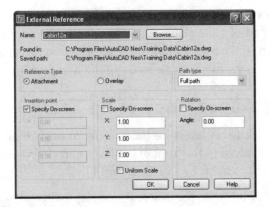

The file being referenced, Cabin12a, is displayed in the drop-down list at the top of the dialog box, with the full path of the file's location just below. The bottom half contains three options for the insertion process, which are like those in the Insert dialog box that you used for inserting blocks in Chapter 7. Note that only the insertion point is specified on-screen. The Scale and Rotation options should be set to use their default settings. If they are not, click the appropriate check boxes so that this dialog box matches that in the previous graphic.

1. Be sure Attachment is selected in the Reference Type area, and then click OK. A technical AutoCAD message may appear that doesn't concern us right now.

2. If the message appears, click OK to close it. You return to your drawing, and the cabin drawing appears and moves with the crosshair cursor.

3. Pick any point within the property line and to the left of the patio to be the insertion point. The Xref drawing is attached and appears in the site plan (see Figure 12.7).

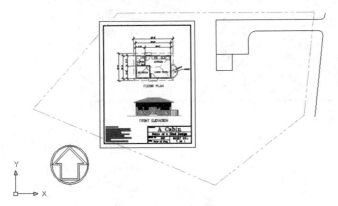

FIGURE 12.7: The Cabin12a drawing attached to the Site12a drawing

The attached Xref appears exactly as it did when it was the current drawing. When we use this file as part of a site plan, we don't want all the information in Cabin12a to be visible. In fact, we want most of the information invisible. We will accomplish this by freezing many of the layers in the Xref drawing.

Controlling the Appearance of an Xref

Xref layers will be part of the list of layers for the current, or host, drawing. But the name of the Xref file is added to the front of the layer's previous name, separated from the layer's previous name by a vertical bar (|).

1. Click the Layer button on the Object Properties toolbar to open the Layer Properties Manager dialog box. Right-click the Name heading at the top of the column of layer names, and then choose Maximize Column from the shortcut menu that opens. Layers from the Xref drawing all have *Cabin12a* and a vertical bar before the name of the layer, as in Cabin12a|Balcony. Before changing any aspect of the layers, we want to save the layer's state as it is now.

2. Click the Layer States Manager button near the upper-left corner to open the Layer States Manager dialog box.

3. Click New to open the New Layer State To Save dialog box.

4. In the New Layer State Name text box, type **as is** but don't press ↵ yet. Enter a description of the layer state you are saving, such as, " State of layers just after attaching Cabin 12a." Then press ↵ or click OK to return to the Layer States Manager dialog box.

5. In the Layer Settings To Restore area, be sure check marks are in the On/Off, Frozen/Thawed, Locked/Unlocked, Color, and Linetype check boxes. Don't concern yourself with the other boxes.

6. Click Close. Now we can make a few changes in the Layer Properties Manager dialog box.

7. Freeze all layers beginning with Cabin12a *except:*

▶ Cabin12a|Balcony

▶ Cabin12a|Roof

▶ Cabin12a|Steps

▶ Cabin12a|Walls

Here's how to do this:

A. Click the Cabin12a|Dim1 layer.

B. Hold down the Shift key and click the Cabin12a|Windows layer.

C. Hold down the Ctrl key and click the last three layers listed earlier to deselect them. The Cabin12a|Balcony layer was not originally selected.

D. Click one of the sun icons for a highlighted layer.

8. Click OK to close the dialog box and view the drawing (see Figure 12.8).

> We are freezing layers here rather than turning them off because we don't expect them to be made visible again for quite a while.

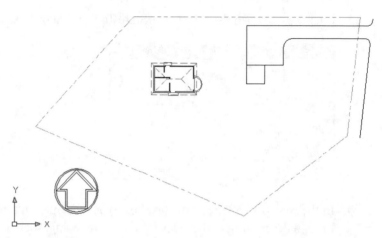

FIGURE 12.8: The site plan with most of the cabin layers frozen

You can resize the Layer Properties Manager dialog box to display more layers at a time. Depending on the size of your screen and your screen resolution, you might be able to view all Xref layers at once.

Using Layer Filters

On the left side of the Layer Properties Manager dialog box, take a look at the Layer Filter Tree View box. Here's where you control which layers are displayed in the Layer List on the right.

1. Click the plus sign (+) next to Xref. Cabin12a is displayed.

2. Click Cabin12a. Now only the Xreffed layers are shown in the layer list. The 0, Defpoints, Prop_line, and Road layers are not shown.

3. In the lower-left corner of the dialog box, click the Invert Filter check box. This reverses the effect of the Cabin12a filter and displays all layers except the Cabin12a Xreffed layers.

4. Uncheck the Invert Filter check box; then click the New Property Filter button in the upper-left corner of the dialog box. This displays the Layer Filter Properties dialog box (see Figure 12.9) in which you can set up and manage your own filters.

> **The Defpoints layer holds information about dimensions and is always part of the host file layers.**

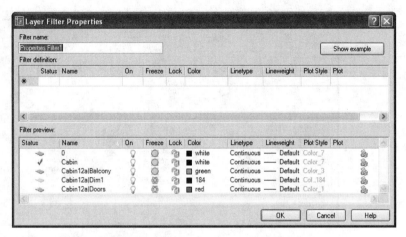

FIGURE 12.9: The Layer Filter Properties dialog box

Let's set up a filter for the four layers in the Xref that we are going to keep visible in the site drawing.

5. In the Filter Name text box, type **Cabin visible**, but don't press ↵ yet. In the Filter Definition area, the various properties of layers are the headers of the columns. We can define our new filter by describing the part of the filters' names that the four layers have in common and by specifying that the filters need to be thawed. The Filter Preview area will show the list of layers that qualify to pass through the filter as we define it.

6. Click in the box below Name in the Filter Definition area. A cursor appears in the box followed by an asterisk.

7. Type **Cabin12a|** but don't press ↵ yet. In the Filter Preview area, only the Xref layers are visible.

8. Click in the box below Freeze, click the down arrow, and then click the sun. In the Filter Preview area, only the four visible Xref layers are listed (see Figure 12.10).

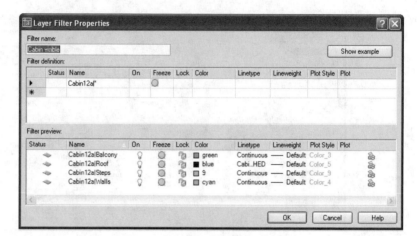

FIGURE 12.10: The new Cabin Visible filter in the Layer Filter Properties dialog box

9. Click OK. In the Layer Properties Manager dialog box, Cabin visible is now displayed in the list of layers in the Layer Filters Tree View box on the left.

10. Click All in that list. All layers are listed. Then click Cabin visible. Only the four layers we didn't freeze are listed (see Figure 12.11).

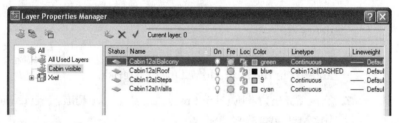

FIGURE 12.11: The result of the Cabin Visible filter in the Layer Properties Manager dialog box

USING THE GROUP FILTERS OPTION

In the Layer Properties Manager dialog box, in the upper-left corner, the second of the three buttons is the New Group Filter button. Click this button to create a filter made up of layers that have some characteristic in common, such as those layers containing any kind of text. For example, to filter out all layers that don't have text on them, click the New Group Filter button, and rename the filter to, for example, Text Layers. You can then add layers to the new filter in two ways:

▶ Click All, and then drag layers that have text in them onto the new filter's name in the Layer Filter Tree View box.

▶ Right-click the new filter and then choose Select Layers ➤ Add from the shortcut menu. In the drawing, click on objects whose layers you want in the filter. When finished, right-click again.

After the filter is set up, it behaves just like the Properties filters.

We have one more change to make to these four layers. Because we want the visible parts of the cabin to read as a unit, we will assign the same color to all the thawed cabin layers. Let's make those changes now.

1. Right-click one of the four layers, and then choose Select All from the shortcut menu. Change the color of one of the selected layers to a dark green. The rest of the selected layers will also change to a dark green. Click All in the Layer Filters Tree View box. This is a new layer state, so let's save it as we did the previous layer state.

2. Click the Layer States Manager button near the upper-right corner to open the Layer States Manager dialog box.

3. Click New to open the New Layer State To Save dialog box.

4. In the New Layer State Name text box, type **Xref** but don't press ↵ yet. Enter a description of the layer state you are saving, such as, " State of Cabin layers for Xref." Then press ↵ or click OK to return to the Layer States Manager dialog box.

5. In the Layer Settings To Restore area, be sure check marks are in the On/Off, Frozen/Thawed, Locked/Unlocked, Color, and Linetype check boxes. Don't concern yourself with the other boxes.

6. Click Close. The cabin is now all one color.

Moving and Rotating an Xref

Now you need to move the cabin and rotated it to its position next to the patio.

1. Zoom in to a view where the cabin and the left side of the patio are visible.

2. Start the Rotate command and click the cabin. The entire cabin is selected. Press ↵.

3. To specify a location for the base point, click anywhere near the middle of the cabin, and then type –90↵. The cabin is rotated to the correct orientation (see Figure 12.12a).

4. Be sure Endpoint Osnap is running. Then use the Move command to move the lower-right corner of the back step to the lower-left corner of the patio (see Figure 12.12b).

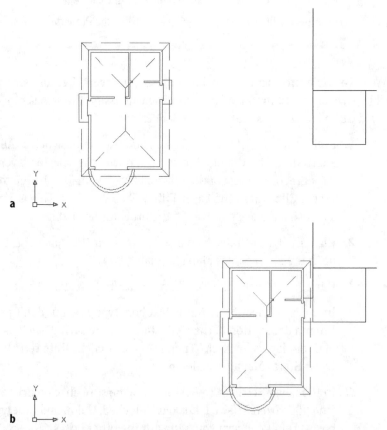

a

b

FIGURE 12.12: The cabin rotated (a), and positioned next to the patio (b).

5. Zoom Previous to a view of the whole site. The cabin is oriented correctly on the site (see Figure 12.13). This is the same view as in Figure 12.1 (shown earlier).

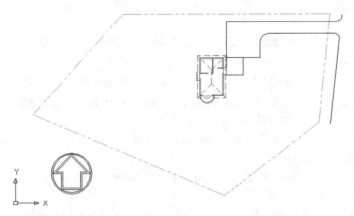

FIGURE 12.13: The cabin Xref is located on the site drawing.

You have established Cabin12a as an external reference in this drawing and
modified the appearance of some of the Xref's layers. The next step is to make
some revisions to Cabin12a and see how this affects the Xref.

USING THE LAYER STATES MANAGER

You use the Layer States Manager tool to save the current setup of various
properties and *states* of layers in the current drawing. You can activate it by
clicking the Layer States Manager button in the Layer Properties Manager
dialog box. All the operations for controlling the Layer States Manager are
performed through this dialog box. Here's how to work your way through it.

To set up a new layer state, follow these steps:

1. In the Layer Properties Manager dialog box, set up the layer properties and states as you want them to be saved, and then click the
Layer States Manager button.

2. In the Layer States Manager dialog box, enter a name for the new
layer state.

Continued on next page

3. In the Layer Settings To Restore area, check the layer settings you want to save as part of the new layer state. (You will learn about Plot/No Plot, Current VP Frozen/Thawed, Lineweight, Plot Style, and New VP Frozen/Thawed in Chapters 13 and 14.)

4. Click Close to save the new layer state.

You also use the Layer States Manager dialog box to manage existing layer states. Here are its features:

Layer States List Box   Displays a list of previously set up layer states.

Restore Button   Restores the layer state that is highlighted in the Layer States list box.

Delete Button   Deletes a layer state. This does not affect the current layer setup.

Import Button   Imports a .las file as a new layer state in the current drawing.

Export   Exports the chosen saved layer state to be saved as a .las file.

To modify a layer state, restore it to be the current layer state, and then change it. To rename a layer state, highlight it, click its name, and type the new name.

Modifying an Xref Drawing

You can modify an Xref drawing by making it the current drawing, making the modification, saving the changes, making the host drawing current, and reloading the Xref. AutoCAD users can also modify an Xref by using a special modification command while the host drawing is current. We'll start by opening Cabin12a and making an addition to it. Then we'll make Site12a current again and use Auto-CAD to modify Cabin12a as an Xref.

Before we do anything, however, we need to change a setting so that the new layer states and the changes we have made to the layers of the Xref are saved with the host file.

1. Type visretain↵. If the value in the angle brackets is set to 1, press ↵. Otherwise, type 1↵ to set the value to 1. This will allow you to save the layer settings of the Xref layers and the new layer states with the current file.

2. Choose File ≻ Save As and save the current file as Site12b.

3. Click Window on the menu bar. At the bottom of the menu, Cabin12a should be displayed next to 1.

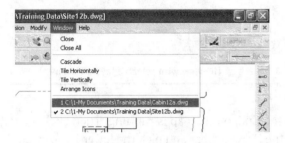

4. Select Cabin12a.dwg to make it the current drawing. Notice that the wall, roof, balcony, and steps in the floor plan of this drawing retain their original colors and are not dark green, and notice that most of the other layers in the drawing are visible.

Modifying an Xref by Making It the Current Drawing

Because we found such a spectacular site for the cabin, we want to add a deck around what was originally the front door and is now the west-facing entrance.

1. Zoom in to the area that includes the floor plan and the area between it and the front elevation.

2. Create a new layer called Deck. Assign it a color and make it current. Next, adjust the drawing's layers to give yourself some room to make this revision.

3. Turn off the following layers:

   ▶ Dim1

   ▶ F-elev

   ▶ Tblk1

   ▶ Text1

   ▶ Any Hatch layers that aren't already frozen

4. The drawing will look like Figure 12.14. Use the Pline command to draw a deck across the front of the cabin that extends down 10'. (The Polyline command was introduced in Chapter 10.)

FIGURE 12.14: The view with selected layers frozen

The Command window shows the polyline width currently set to 3", from when you drew the border and title block in Chapter 10.

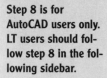

Step 8 is for AutoCAD users only. LT users should follow step 8 in the following sidebar.

5. Make sure the Endpoint Osnap is running. Then click the Polyline button on the Draw toolbar and pick the lower-left corner of the cabin walls to start the Pline.

6. Type w↵. Then type 0↵↵ to reset the Pline width to zero.

7. Be sure Polar is clicked on. Then hold the crosshair cursor straight down below the first point picked and type 10'↵.

8. Click the Otrack button on the status bar to turn on Otrack mode. Hold the crosshair cursor on the lower-right corner of the cabin walls for a moment, until a cross appears. When it does, begin moving the crosshair cursor directly down, while staying on the tracking path. A small *x* will appear at the intersection of the vertical tracking path and the horizontal polar tracking line, as well as a Polar & Endpoint tool tip (see Figure 12.15a). When you see the small *x* and tool tip, click once to establish the second line segment. A horizontal line is drawn that parallels the front wall of the cabin and is 10' below it.

STEP 8 FOR LT USERS

LT users should follow this step:

8. Click the Tracking button at the top of the Osnap toolbar, and then put the cursor on the lower-right corner of the cabin walls. When the square appears, click. Move the cursor to the bottom end of the 10' polyline segment you just drew. When the square appears, click. Press ↵. A horizontal line is drawn that parallels the front wall of the cabin and is 10' below it.

Now continue with step 9.

9. Finally, pick the lower-right corner of the cabin walls to complete the outline of the deck. Press ↵ to end the Pline command.

10. Offset this polyline 6" to the inside (see Figure 12.15b). When a polyline is offset, all segments are automatically offset together and filleted to clean up the corners. (The fillet radius is zero for this operation, even if it's currently set to a nonzero value.)

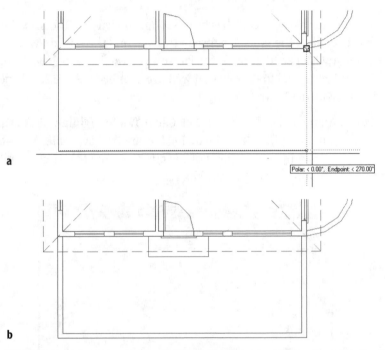

a

b

FIGURE 12.15: The vertical tracking path (a), and the offset deck line (b)

This concludes the modifications we will make to the Cabin12a drawing in this exercise, though we will make some more later. Now we can return to the Site12b drawing.

11. It is important to save the file at this point. Keep the name as Cabin12a; otherwise the Xref in the Site12b drawing will not be updated to include the deck. This is a revision to the Cabin12a drawing that has

been externally referenced into the Site12b drawing. Save Cabin12a, and then choose Window ➤ Site12b to switch back to the site drawing. If you are using AutoCAD, a balloon message will appear in the lower-right corner to tell you that an external reference file has changed and that it might need reloading.

12. On the drop-down menus, choose Insert ➤ Xref Manager to open the Xref Manager dialog box.

Once an external reference has been set up, you will use the Xref Manager dialog box to control the linkage between the Xref and the host drawing. When the host drawing is opened, it reads the latest saved version of a drawing that is externally referenced to it. Now that we have changed Cabin12a, we need to update the Cabin12a Xref to reflect those changes.

1. In the list of Xref files, click Cabin12a to highlight it. All the buttons on the right side of the dialog box are now available, and—in Auto-CAD only—when you put the cursor on the Needs... text in the Status column, a tool tip–like box reads "Needs reloading."

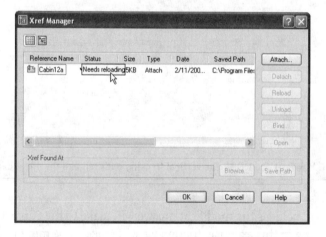

2. Click the Reload button, and then click OK. You are returned to the Site12a drawing; the new deck has been added (see Figure 12.16).

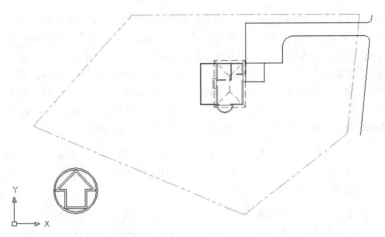

FIGURE 12.16: The Site12b drawing with the revised Xref of the cabin

3. Save this drawing. It's still called Site12b.

In this exercise, you have seen how a host drawing is updated when the drawing that is externally referenced is made current, modified and saved, and then updated as an Xref. You also saw how you can control the appearance of objects in the Xref drawing from the host drawing by working with the Xref layers. This is a good example of the power of layers. You can set them up one way in the actual drawing and another way in the Xref of that drawing in a host file. In fact, you can Xref the same drawing into any number of host files; have the layer characteristics of visibility, color, and linetype be different in each host file; and save them as such with each host file. Xref is a powerful feature of AutoCAD, and you will learn more about the possible applications of this tool toward the end of this chapter.

Modifying an Xref from within the Host Drawing

In Chapter 7, we used the In-Place Xref And Block Edit command to update the window block. You can use the same tool here for editing an Xref while the host drawing is the current drawing. You can't create a new layer with this tool, but many of the regular editing commands are available when you use it. We'll make a few modifications related to the new deck to illustrate this feature.

AutoCAD LT 2005 doesn't have the In-Place Xref And Block Edit feature. To keep your drawing current with the book, read through the following section to see what changes we are making, and then use the technique for modifying Cabin12a that we used in the previous section to draw the new deck. That is, make Cabin12a current, make the modifications described in the following exercise, save the changes, make Site12b current, and use the Xref Manager to reload Cabin12a. Then continue with step 9 in the following exercise.

1. Use the Window menu to switch to Cabin12a, and then close this file. (Choose File ➤ Close.) Site12b will return to the drawing area. Make the 0 layer current.

2. Zoom in to the cabin floor plan on the site plan (see Figure 12.17a). We need to erase the old front step and fill in the roof lines that were broken out to make room for the room label text.

3. On the drop-down menus, choose Modify ➤ Xref And Block Editing ➤ Edit Reference In-Place. You are prompted to select the Xref to edit.

4. Click anywhere on the cabin; it's all one object for now. The Reference Edit dialog box opens. On the Identify Reference tab, Cabin12a is listed as the selected Xref, and a preview window illustrates the Xref drawing. At the bottom, select the Prompt To Select Nested Objects radio button.

5. Click OK. At the Select nested objects: prompt, click the six roof hip lines that need repair, the roof ridge line, and the three lines that make up what was formerly the front step. Then press ↵. The Command: prompt returns to the command window. The Refedit toolbar appears.

You are now free to use many of the Draw and Modify commands on the lines that we just selected. They are displayed in a slightly darker color than the unselected lines.

6. Use the Erase command to erase the three lines of the front step and the three broken roof line segments that connect to the ridgeline.

7. Use the Fillet command with a radius of zero to extend the three remaining broken roof line segments to the ridgeline (see Figure 12.17b).

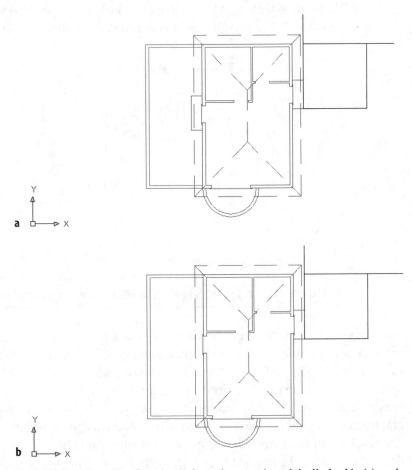

FIGURE 12.17: Zooming in for a close-up view of the Xref cabin (a), and the Xref cabin with the step erased and the roof lines filled in

TIP The correct fillet will require you to use the ridgeline as one of the lines to fillet, rather than the unbroken hip line, because the latter line was not selected to be part of the Xref edit in step 5.

8. Move to the Refedit toolbar. On the far right end, click the Save Back Changes To Reference button. When the warning dialog box opens, click OK.

9. Zoom to Extents, and then zoom out a little to a view of the whole site (see Figure 12.18). Save this drawing. It is still named Site12b.

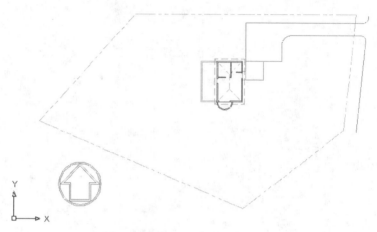

FIGURE 12.18: The Site12b drawing with the revised Xref of the cabin

In this exercise, you have seen how a host drawing is updated when its external reference is changed and how the appearance of objects in the Xref drawing can be controlled from the host drawing by working with the Xref layers. You also saw how you can modify objects in the Xref from the host drawing by using the In-Place Xref Edit tool. A drawing can serve as an external reference in several host drawings at the same time and have a different appearance in each one. The results of in-place Xref editing, however, must be saved back to the original drawing in order to be viewed in the Xref. So in this case, when you open Cabin12a, the front step will be missing. Also, the roof hip lines will be drawn over the room label text, as they were before they were broken in Chapter 10. In-place Xref editing is usually done only when the results are meant to be permanent changes in the original source drawing. We used it in this case only to show you how the feature works.

Applications for Xrefs

There are many different uses for external references. I will describe two common applications to illustrate their range.

Let's suppose you are working on a project as an interior designer and a subcontractor to the lead architect. The architect can give you a drawing of a floor plan that is still undergoing changes. You load this file onto your hard disk, in a specially designated folder, and then Xref it into your drawing as a background—a drawing to be used as a reference to draw over. You can now proceed to lay out furniture, partitions, and so on, while the architect is still refining the floor plan.

At an agreed-on time, the architect will give you a revised version of the floor plan. You will overwrite the one that you have on your computer with the latest version. You can then reload the Xref into your furniture layout drawing, and the newer version of the floor plan will now be the background. In this example, the lead architect might also be sending the same versions of the floor plan to the structural and mechanical engineers and the landscape architect, all of whom are working on the project and using the architect's floor plan as an Xref in their respective host drawings (see Figure 12.19).

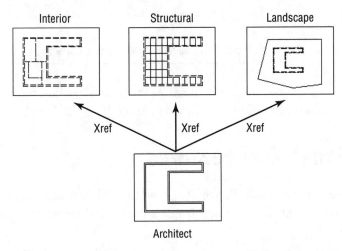

FIGURE 12.19: A single floor plan as an Xref to three subcontractors

Xrefs are often used when parts of a job are being done in an office where a network is in place. Suppose a project involves work on several buildings that are all on the same site. By using Xrefs, each building can be externally referenced to the site plan. This keeps the site plan drawing file from getting too large and allows the project work to be divided among different workstations, while the project manager can open the host site plan and keep track of progress on the whole project (see Figure 12.20).

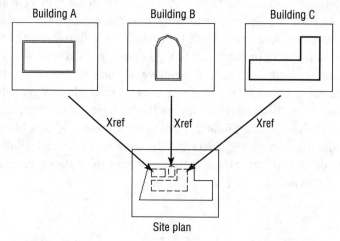

FIGURE 12.20: Three buildings as Xrefs to a single site plan

These two applications for setting up Xrefs in relation to a host file are applicable to almost any profession or trade using AutoCAD.

Additional Xref Features

You have seen how you can change the properties of layers in an Xref and how you can modify an Xref. A few other features of external references deserve mention.

The Xref Path

When you attach an Xref to the host drawing, AutoCAD stores the name of the Xref and its path.

N O T E   The path of a drawing file is the name of the drive, folder, and subfolder where a file is stored, followed by the name of the drawing. `C:\ 1-My Documents\Training Data\Site12b.dwg` **is the path of the current drawing file.**

Each time you open the host drawing, AutoCAD searches for any Xrefs saved with the host file and displays them in the host drawing. If the Xref drawing is moved to a new folder after the Xref has been attached, AutoCAD won't be able to find the Xref and can't display it. To avoid that situation, you must update the host drawing with the new path to the Xref file. We'll go through a quick exercise to illustrate how this works.

1. Close the `Site12b` drawing momentarily.

2. Use My Computer or Windows Explorer to create a new subfolder called Xref within the Training folder you previously set up. Move `Cabin12a` to this folder.

3. Return to AutoCAD, and open `Site12b` again. The Xref does not show up, but there's a little line of information in the host drawing where the insertion point of the Xref was located. If you zoom in a couple of times, you will be able to read the information. It says "Xref `C:\1-My Documents\Training Data\Cabin12a.dwg`." This is the original path of the Xref.

4. Press F2 to switch to the AutoCAD text screen for a moment, and note the line that says "`C:\1-My Documents\Training Data\Cabin12a.dwg` cannot be found." AutoCAD is unable to find the Xref because the path has changed. Press F2 again.

5. Open the Xref Manager dialog box (choose Insert ➤ Xref Manager). In the large box where Xrefs are listed, the path is displayed for each Xref under the heading Saved Path. You can slide the scroll bar to the right to see the full path. Notice also that the Status column for this Xref reads "Not Found."

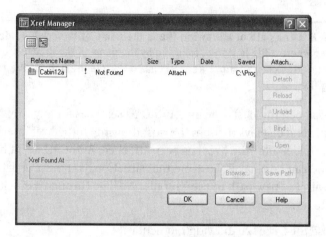

6. Click the Cabin12a Xref to highlight it.

7. Next to the Xref Found At text box, click Browse. Find Cabin12a in the new Xref folder. Highlight it and click Open.

8. Back in the Xref Manager dialog box, the path has been updated for Cabin12a. Click OK. Zoom Previous one or two times. The Xref is restored in your drawing.

 W A R N I N G When you're working with a lot of Xrefs, be careful where you store files that are acting as Xrefs to other files.

Binding Xrefs

On occasion, you will want to permanently attach an Xref to the host drawing. If you send your drawing files to a printing service to be plotted, including a set of Xref files can complicate things. Also, for archiving finished work, it's better to reduce the number of files. There may also be occasions when the Xref has been revised for the last time and no longer needs to be a separate file. In all these situations, you will use the Bind command to convert an external reference into a block that will be stored permanently in the host drawing.

1. Open the Xref Manager dialog box and highlight the Cabin12a Xref.

2. Click the Bind button to open the Bind Xrefs dialog box.

The two options in the Bind Type area have to do with how layers are treated when an Xref is bound to the host drawing. The default is Bind. It sets the Xref layers to be maintained as unique layers in the host drawing. With the Insert option, layers that have the same name in the two drawings will be combined into one layer. None of the layers in Cabin12a have the same name as any layers in Site12b. Let's use the Insert option.

3. Change the Bind Type to Insert and click OK. The Xref disappears from the list of Xrefs.

4. Click OK. Your drawing looks unchanged.

5. Click the cabin, and then type li↵. The text window shows that the cabin is now a block reference.

6. Press F2 and click the Layer button on the Object Properties toolbar. The cabin's layers have all become layers in the Site12b drawing and no longer have the Cabin12al prefix.

7. Click OK, and then choose Insert ➤ Block. In the Insert dialog box, open the Name drop-down list. Cabin12a is listed here as a block, along with the window and two door blocks that you created in Chapter 7. One or two additional blocks may be on the list. These blocks are used by the dimensions in the drawing.

8. Close the drop-down list by clicking a blank portion of the dialog box. Then click Cancel to return to your drawing. The cabin is now a permanent part of the Site12b drawing. If you need to make changes to the cabin part of the drawing, you can explode it and use the Modify commands to make those changes. Or, if you're running AutoCAD, you can use the In-Place Xref and Block Edit tools that you used previously in Chapter 7 to modify the window block and, again in this chapter, to modify the roof lines and erase the front step.

9. Save this drawing as Site12c.

This has been a quick tour of the basic operations that are used to set up and control external references. There are more features and commands for working with Xrefs than I've covered here, but you now know enough to start working with them.

Other Features of Xrefs

What follows are a few additional operations and features that you may find useful when you delve more deeply into external references. Play around a little and see what you can do.

▶ Externally referenced drawings can have drawings externally referenced to them. These are called *nested* Xrefs. There is no practical limit to the number of levels of nested Xrefs that a drawing can have.

▶ You can't explode an Xref, but you can detach it from the host. The Detach command is a button on the Xref Manager dialog box.

▶ Large, complex drawings that are Xreferenced often have their insertion points coordinated in such a way that all Xrefs are attached at the 0,0 point of the host drawing. This helps keep drawings aligned properly. By default, any drawing that is Xreferenced into a host drawing uses 0,0 as its insertion point. But you can change the coordinates of the insertion point with the Base command. With the drawing you want to change current, type **base.** and enter the coordinates for the new insertion point.

▶ You can limit which layers and, to some degree, which objects in a drawing are Xreferenced in the host drawing by using Indexing and Demand Loading.

▶ A host drawing can be Xreferenced into the drawing that has been Xreferenced into the host. This is called an *overlay* and is an option in the Attach Xref dialog box. Overlays ignore nested Xreferences.

▶ If you freeze the layer that was current when an Xref was attached, the entire Xref is frozen. Turning off this same layer has no effect on the visibility of the Xref.

▶ The Unload button in the External Reference dialog box lets you deactivate Xrefs without detaching them from the host file. They stay on the list of Xrefs and can be reloaded at any time with the Reload button. This can be useful when working with complex drawings that have many Xrefs.

If You Would Like More Practice...

In this chapter, you Xreferenced the cabin drawing into the site drawing, as a landscape architect who was designing the development plan for the site might have done. If you were the lead architect, you might want to Xref the landscape architect's site plan into your cabin drawing. Try doing this.

1. Open Cabin07b. Create a new layer called Xref, assign it a color number, and make it current. Freeze all layers except 0, Balcony, Roof, Steps, and Walls.

2. Attach Site12a to Cabin07b as an Xref. Zoom to Extents, and then rotate the site 90°. Move the Site12a Xref to a position such that the patio meets the back step in the same way that it did earlier in this chapter. Pan and zoom in and out as needed.

3. Change the Site12a layers to a dark green.

4. Rotate the UCS 90° around the z-axis (as you did in Chapter 8).

5. Use the Plan command to position the drawing correctly, and then zoom out a little.

6. Change Ltscale to 100. Your drawing should look similar to that in Figure 12.13, shown earlier in this chapter.

7. Use In-Place Reference Editing to widen the patio 3' to the east, and change the radius of the driveway to 10' in the Xref.

8. Do not save the changes back to the Site12a drawing file.

Are You Experienced?

Now you can...

- ☑ draw a basic site plan

- ☑ use Surveyor units to lay out property lines

- ☑ attach an external reference

- ☑ control the appearance of an external reference by modifying layers

- ☑ use Visretain to save Xref layer changes

- ☑ revise a drawing that is externally referenced

- ☑ modify an Xref from the host drawing

- ☑ update an Xref path

- ☑ bind an Xref to a host file

- ☑ set up layer filters

CHAPTER 13

Using Layouts to Set Up a Print

▶ Putting a title block in a layout

▶ Setting up viewports in a layout

▶ Aligning viewports

▶ Controlling visibility in viewports

▶ Setting up a text style for a layout

▶ Adding text in a layout

I n the previous chapter, I introduced external references, which are useful and powerful tools. Although the commands for Xrefs are a little tricky, the overall concept is fairly straightforward—in effect, you are viewing another drawing from within the current drawing. In contrast, the concept of the Layout display mode is a little difficult to understand, but the commands are fairly simple. External references help you combine several drawings into a composite; layouts allow you to set up and print several views of the same file. The layout is a view of your drawing as it will sit on a sheet of paper when printed. (The Layouts feature was added to AutoCAD with version 2000.)

Each layout has a designated printer and paper size for the print. You adjust the positioning of the drawing and the scale of the print. The part that is difficult to understand is the way two scales are juxtaposed in the same file: the scale of the drawing on the printed paper (usually a standard scale used by architects, such as ¼" = 1'-0") and the scale of the layout, which is almost always 1:1, or the actual size. Other professions, such as mechanical or civil engineering, set up their drawings the same way. They may use a different set of standard scales for the drawing on the printed paper, but the layout almost always remains 1:1.

One way to visualize how a layout works is to think of it as a second drawing, or a specialized layer, that has been laid over the top of your current drawing. Each layout that you create will have one or more *viewports*—special windows through which you will view your project at a scale to be printed. The layouts are usually at a scale of 1:1 (actual size) and contain some of the information that you originally included with the building lines, such as the border and title block, notes, the scale, north arrow, and so on.

Think for a moment about drawing the floor plan of a building on a traditional drafting table. You draw the building to a scale such as ⅛" = 1'-0". Then, on the same sheet of paper, you print a note using letters that are, say, ⅛" high. If you look at those letters as being on the same scale as the building, they would measure 1' high, and that's what we've been doing on the cabin drawing so far. But in traditional drafting, you don't think that way; instead, you work with two scales in the drawing without thinking about it. So a letter is ⅛" high (actual size), and a part of the building that measures ⅛" on the paper is thought of as being 1' long (at a scale of ⅛" = 1'-0"). Layouts are designed to let you juggle two or more scales in a drawing in the same way, in order to set up the drawing to be printed.

Setting Up Layouts

We will begin working with Cabin11a, the drawing we used for basic dimensioning in Chapter 11. This drawing is essentially complete and ready to print. You will print it in the next chapter, just as it is (see Figure 13.1), without using layouts.

For now, you will modify this drawing and create a layout for it to get a basic understanding of what layouts are and how they are activated and set up. Then, in the next chapter, you'll print this same drawing twice, both with and without a layout.

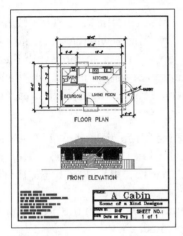

FIGURE 13.1: Cabin11a **ready to print**

In setting up a new layout, we will use an 8.5" × 11" sheet.

1. Open Cabin11a. Notice the border of the drawing and the rectangle just outside the border that represents the edge of the sheet of paper on which the print will be made. You will recall from Chapter 10 that when you constructed the border and title block for this drawing, you had to calculate the size of the border for a scale of ⅛" = 1'-0". This was based on a rectangle 68' wide by 88' high, which you then offset 3' to make the border. With layouts, you don't have to make this kind of calculation; you draw the border actual size.

2. Create a new layer called Tblk-L1. Assign it a color and make it current. Before creating a new layout, choose Tools ➢ Options to open the Options dialog box, and click the Display tab. In the Layout Elements area (lower-left corner), be sure all the check boxes are checked, and then click OK.

   Each layout has settings that spell out which plotting device is to be used to print the layout and how that print will appear. You specify these settings through a *page setup* that becomes associated with the layout.

3. Look at the lower-left corner of the drawing area. Next to the Model tab, you will see two Layout tabs.

Click the Layout1 tab. After a moment, the Page Setup Manager dialog box opens (see Figure 13.2a). This is where you create a new page setup—or assign an existing one—to be associated with the new layout. The example shows an Epson Stylus Photo 890 for the Device Name and Plotter in the Selected Page Setup Details area, but yours may be different.

4. Click New to open the New Page Setup dialog box. In the New Page Setup Name text box, type **Cabin11a-L1** and click OK. This opens the Page Setup dialog box, which has Layout1 added to the title bar (see Figure 13.2b). There are ten areas in the dialog box containing settings that control how the drawing will fit on the printed page and what part of the drawing is printed.

> I designed this chapter so that you can follow along even if you don't have a printer hooked up to your computer or if your printer isn't the one referred to in the text.

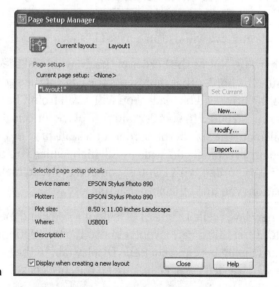

a

FIGURE 13.2: The Page Setup Manager dialog box (a), and the Page Setup dialog box with Layout1 added to the title (b)

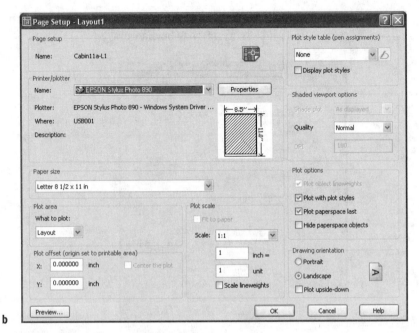

b

FIGURE 13.2: (continued)

5. In the Paper Size area, be sure the drop-down list is set to Letter. In the Printer/Plotter area, Epson Stylus Photo 890 is the selected printer, but yours may be different. If your computer is linked to more than one printer, make sure you choose a printer that takes 8.5" × 11" paper.

Click the Properties button next to the Name drop-down list to open the Plotter Configuration Editor dialog box. Click the Device And Document Settings tab. In the upper area, highlight Modify Standard Paper Sizes (Printable Area). In the area below (now called Modify Standard Paper Sizes), scroll down the list to the Letter size and highlight it. At the bottom of this area are displays of data about the Letter sheet size, including, in the example, Printable Area: 8.2" × 10.27". This shows the maximum area that your printer can print on an 8.5" × 11" sheet of paper and thus gives you an idea of how close to the edge of the paper the printer will print. Jot down the printable area. In this example, it's 8.20 × 10.27 inches. Yours may be different.

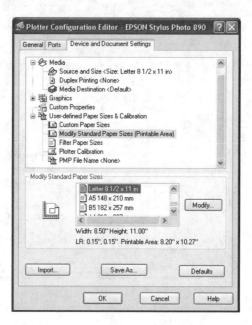

Click Cancel to close this dialog box.

N O T E   The terms *print* and *plot* are used interchangeably in this book, as are *printer* and *plotter*. In the past, *plot* and *plotter* referred to large-format devices and media, but that's not necessarily true today. *Print* and *printing* are more widely used now because of changes in the technology of the large-format devices.

6. Back in the Page Setup dialog box, move to the Drawing Orientation (lower-right corner) area and select Portrait.

7. The Plot Area area contains a drop-down list with three options for selecting what is to be plotted. Be sure that Layout is selected.

8. In the Plot Scale area, the scale to be used is 1:1. If it's not already selected, open the Scale drop-down list and select 1:1 from the 33 preset scale choices.

9. In the Page Setup area (upper-left corner), Cabin11a-L1 is displayed as the current page setup. We'll ignore the other areas of this dialog box for now.

10. Click OK. You are returned to the Page Setup Manager dialog box. Cabin11a-L1 is now on the Page Setups list.

11. Highlight Cabin11a-L1, click Set Current, and then click Close to close the Page Setup Manager dialog box. You are returned to your drawing, and Layout1 is displayed (see Figure 13.3).

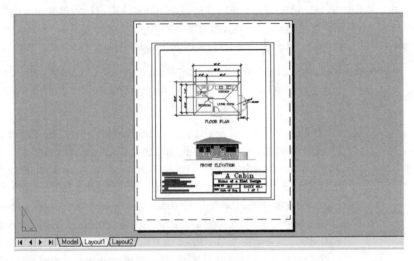

FIGURE 13.3: Layout1 for Cabin11a

With the way I have set up AutoCAD for this book, the drawing area now displays a white sheet of paper resting on a gray background. The drawing of the cabin is centered on the paper with its border and outer rectangle. We'll be changing these two elements in a moment. Outside this rectangle is another rectangle. This is a *viewport*, and it was automatically created when you set up Layout1. The viewport creates a hole, or a window, in the layout so that you can see through the layout to the drawing of the building. You can think of the building as residing "underneath" the layout. Finally, near the outer edge of the white rectangle is a rectangle of dashed lines. This represents the 8.20" × 10.27" printable area of our printer.

Look to the lower-left corner of the drawing area at the Model and Layout tabs. Note that the Layout1 tab is now active.

1. Click the Model tab. A view of Cabin11a, without Layout1, appears.

2. Click the Layout1 tab. The layout returns.

So far in this book, you have been drawing in the Model tab (sometimes called *Model Space*). You have put some information—some of the text, the title block, and the border—on the Model tab that is usually put on the layout if you're using the Layouts feature. Notice the triangle in the lower-left corner of the drawing area. This icon indicates that your cursor is currently residing on the active layout. In this setup, you cannot select any part of the cabin to work on, and any new objects that you create will be on the layout.

To work on the cabin itself, you need to move the cursor to Model Space. You can do this in two ways. One is to click the Model tab. This temporarily removes the layout and leaves you with just the drawing, or *model*. The other way is to switch to Model Space while a layout is active. We'll try this latter method now.

As the term *Model Space* implies, the lines and other AutoCAD objects that make up the components of the cabin are often referred to as a *model*. This distinguishes them from other AutoCAD objects, such as the title block and border, that often reside on a layout.

1. Move the crosshair cursor around, and notice that it can be placed at any point in the drawing area. You can move the cursor over the cabin, but you can't select any part of the cabin drawing.

2. On the far right end of the status bar, click Paper. The Paper button changes to become the Model button. Continue moving the cursor around the drawing area. The cursor becomes a crosshair only when it is placed inside the viewport surrounding the cabin drawing (see Figure 13.4). Otherwise the cursor changes to a pointer arrow, as it does when it is placed on the toolbars and menus. When the cursor is within the viewport, the lines of the crosshair extend only to the edge of the viewport. This is the boundary of where you can pick points to draw when working on the cabin.

When you activate Model Space while a layout is active, it is like opening a window and reaching through the opening to touch the drawing of the building behind the window.

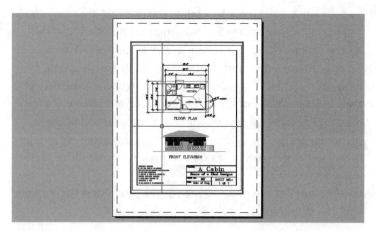

FIGURE 13.4: The crosshair cursor in Model Space with the layout

N O T E   If the lines of your crosshair cursor don't normally extend to the edges of the drawing area, choose Tools ➢ Options to open the Options dialog box and click the Display tab. In the lower-left corner, where it says Crosshair Size, move the slider all the way to the right and click Apply. The new setting will be 100, and the crosshair lines extend to the drawing area edges.

Once layouts are set up, you will find it practical to click the Model tab when making major changes to the drawing. This will temporarily disable the layout and make it invisible. To make minor changes to the cabin (or to your widget or to whatever objects make up your drawing), leave the Layout tab active, and click the Paper button on the status bar to make Model Space active while the layout is still visible.

You need to transfer the title block and border from Model Space to the layout. We'll start by drawing a new border on the layout.

Drawing a Border on a Layout

You draw the border for a layout at the actual size that it will be when it is printed, because the layout is the actual size of the paper to be used, in this case, 8.5" × 11".

1. Click the Model button on the status bar. This moves the crosshair cursor back to the layout.

2. Start the Rectangle command and type 0,0↵. Then type the printable area number that you jotted down in step 5 in the previous exercise. For the example here, type 8.2,10.27↵. A rectangle is drawn that coincides with the dashed lines representing the printable area of the sheet (see Figure 13.5).

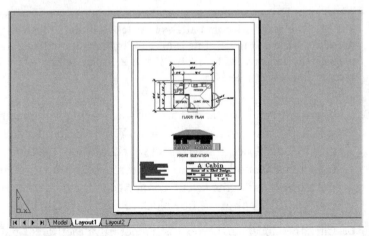

F I G U R E   1 3 . 5 : Layout1 with a rectangle drawn on the boundary of the printable area

3. We want the border to be set in from the rectangle that you just drew by about ⅛". Offset the new rectangle ⅛" to the inside.

4. Erase the outer rectangle. The dashed lines become visible again. The border should be a line ¹⁄₃₂" wide.

5. Click the new rectangle, and then activate the Properties palette. Change Global Width from 0 to ¹⁄₃₂. Close the Properties palette, and press Esc to clear the grips. The lines of the offset rectangle are now ¹⁄₃₂" wide and will serve as the new border (see Figure 13.6).

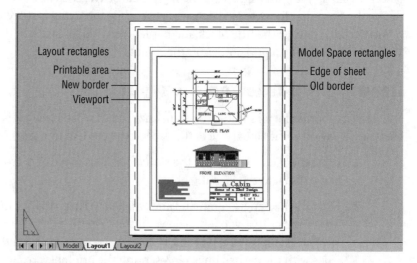

FIGURE 13.6: The new border in the layout, among a lot of rectangles

T I P   You may notice that after you enter ¹⁄₃₂ in the Properties palette, AutoCAD changes it to ¹⁄₁₆". This is because in the units settings, we set the precision for Linear units to ¹⁄₁₆". But that is a display setting—AutoCAD still records Global Width as ¹⁄₃₂".

There are a lot of rectangles around the drawing of the cabin, but you will be removing some of them soon. You have a border and a rectangle in Model Space, the second of which indicates the edge of the sheet of paper. Both of these will be removed. But first you need to put a title block in the layout, connected to the border that you just created. Let's look at the title block you've already drawn.

6. Click the Model tab. Layout1 is temporarily deactivated, and you are back in Model Space. Take note of the title block.

Designing a Title Block for a Layout

The original title block was drawn to a size that could be plotted at ⅛" scale, so its dimensions are quite large (see Figure 13.7a). You will need to make the size of the new title block much smaller to make it fit on the border that you just drew. How much smaller? The dimensions of the new title block drawn at actual size are shown in Figure 13.7b.

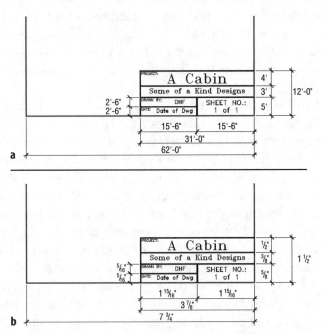

FIGURE 13.7: The original dimensions of the cabin title block (a), and the new, actual-size dimensions in the layout (b)

The text, too, has to be made smaller to fit into the new title block. The following is a chart showing the heights of the various text used in the two title blocks:

Text	Original Title Block	Layout1 Title Block
A Cabin	2'-6"	$\frac{5}{16}$"
Some of a Kind Design	1'-3"	$\frac{5}{32}$"
DHF	1'-0"	$\frac{1}{8}$"
Date of Dwg	1'-0"	$\frac{1}{8}$"
SHEET NO.: 1 of 1	1'-3"	$\frac{5}{32}$"
PROJ.:, DRAWN BY:, DATE:	8"	$\frac{1}{12}$"

This may seem complicated at first, but think about the discussion near the beginning of this chapter in which I talked about using two scales in the same drawing. Traditional drafting uses a scale for the lines that represent the building. The text, title block, and border are drawn at actual size. In CAD drafting without layouts, you have the convenience of being able to draw the building at full size, but you have to draw the text, title block, and border larger than they will eventually be in the finished plot because there is only one scale for the drawing. With layouts, you can return to the method used by traditional drafters. The layout is the part of the drawing where you put everything that relates to the actual size of the sheet, and Model Space is where the building lines and objects representing building components reside. You'll see shortly how the two spaces work together to make a complete drawing.

Let's get back to this title block and finish making one on the layout. You need to look at the change of size of the title block and text from the original title block to the new one. Because Cabin11a is set up to be printed at a scale of ⅛" = 1'-0", the text, border, and title block have all been drawn larger than their actual size by the scale factor of ⅛" scale. And what is the scale factor of ⅛" scale? It's the true ratio of the scale and is found by dividing the smaller number on one side of the equation into the larger number on the other side of the equation. If you divide ⅛" into 1'-0" (or 12"), you will get the scale factor, 96. We did this in Chapter 10. The text, border, and title block are all 96 times larger in the original than they need to be in the layout, where they will be actual size.

After scaling the original title block down by a factor of 96, you will have a new title block that will be actual size. You will then need to put it in the layout and attach it to the border. You can easily do the scaling and the moving after using AutoCAD's cut-and-paste tools.

Cutting and Pasting in AutoCAD

When you use the Windows cut-and-paste tools that have been customized to work with AutoCAD, the objects that are cut (or copied) can have an insertion point and can be inserted as a block back into the drawing or into another drawing. With Layout1 deactivated, the Cabin11a drawing is visible on the screen.

1. Right-click anywhere on the screen, and choose Copy With Base Point from the shortcut menu. Use the Endpoint Osnap and pick the lower-left corner of the title block as the base point. Use a regular selection window to select the title block and all its text, but not the border. (Selection windows were described in Chapter 6, when you

were selecting the kitchen and bathroom fixtures to move them onto the Fixtures layer.) Press ↵.

2. Click the Layout1 tab again, click the Paper button on the status bar, and then erase the original border and title block and the outer rectangle representing the edge of the sheet—all of which were created in the original Cabin11a drawing. The two rectangles and the original title block disappear (see Figure 13.8a).

3. Click the Model button (on the status bar) to move the cursor back to Layout1.

4. Right-click the screen, and choose Paste As Block from the shortcut menu. Part of the image of the title block appears in the drawing, attached to the cursor. It's huge; you can see only the end of one line. Remember that we drew the original title block and border in a scaled-up fashion so that they would match the drawing's scale. The original scale factor we used to scale it up was 96 for ⅛" scale, so we'll use the reciprocal of that to scale it down.

5. Use the Nearest Osnap and pick a point anywhere on the left half of the bottom borderline as the insertion point. Now we'll use the Scale command to scale down the title block.

6. Start the Scale command. Select the large polyline by clicking its edge, and then press ↵. At the `Specify base point:` prompt, move the cursor to the center of the bottom edge of the polyline. When the Endpoint Osnap symbol appears there, click. Then type **1/96**↵ (see Figure 13.8b). The title block is now the correct size.

7. Start the Move command. Be sure Polar is on. Using the Endpoint and Perpendicular Osnaps, move the title block to the right until the right end of the top line in the title block (Endpoint) meets the right side of the border (Perpendicular). This will position the title block correctly on the border (see Figure 13.8c).

8. Use the Explode command to explode the title block. Then click the Properties button to move the title block lines and its text to the Tblk-L1 layer. This completes the transfer of the title block from Model Space to Layout1.

Polylines that have a nonzero width need to be picked at their side edges to be selected, but their Midpoint and Endpoint Osnap points lie on a line that runs down the polyline's center. Therefore, the Endpoint Osnap points lie at the center of the ends of each polyline segment.

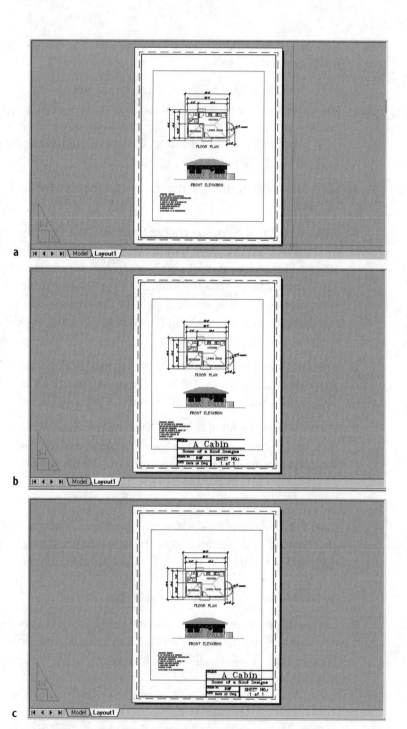

FIGURE 13.8: Removing the title block and border rectangles (a), pasting the title block into Layout1 (b), and positioning it correctly (c)

Adjusting a Viewport

The last step in using the Layouts feature to set up Cabin11a to print is to adjust the size of the default viewport to more closely fit into the border and to set the scale of the cabin drawing to ⅛" = 1'-0".

1. The button at the right end of the status bar should still read Paper. Click the viewport's boundary to select the viewport. Grips appear. Click the Osnap and Polar buttons on the status bar to temporarily deactivate them.

2. Click the upper-right grip to activate it.

3. Move the cursor to a point near the upper-right corner of the border, but still inside it, and then click.

4. Click the lower-left grip. Then move, as in step 3, to a point close to the lower-left corner of the border and click to set it.

5. Press Esc to remove the grips. The viewport is now about as large as it can be on the page (see Figure 13.9). To complete the last step, you need to adjust the scale of the cabin drawing to be ⅛" = 1'-0" and make the viewport border invisible.

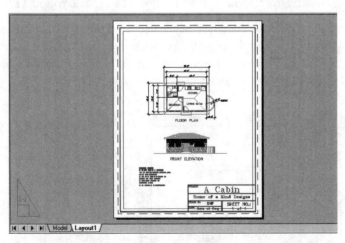

FIGURE 13.9: Layout1 of the Cabin11a drawing with the viewport enlarged to nearly the size of the border

6. Create a new layer called Vports-L1. Assign it a color that really stands out, such as purple. Don't make this new layer current.

T I P   It's useful to assign a color to the Vports-L1 layer that will stand out in your drawing, so you are reminded that the viewports, while an essential part of the drawing, are usually designed to be invisible.

7. Click the viewport's boundary to select the viewport. Then open the Layer Control drop-down list and select Vports-L1. The viewport is now on the Vports-L1 layer. Don't press Esc yet.

8. Right-click any toolbar button and open the Viewports toolbar. Then open the Scale drop-down list, and select ⅛" = 1'. Close the Viewports toolbar. Press Esc to turn off grips.

9. Click Paper on the status bar to move to Model Space.

10. Use Realtime Pan to pan the drawing so it fits properly within the new viewport.

11. Click Model on the status bar to return to Paper Space.

Locking a viewport is an important step and will be discussed in the next section.

12. Click the viewport's boundary to select the viewport again. Right-click and choose Display Locked from the shortcut menu. Choose Yes on the little flyout menu to place a check mark next to it if there isn't one already. This locks the viewport at the scale you just set.

13. Tblk-L1 should be current. Freeze the Vports-L1 layer (see Figure 13.10). The drawing looks much like the original Cabin11a before layouts were introduced, but we now have the title block and border on a layout at 1:1 scale.

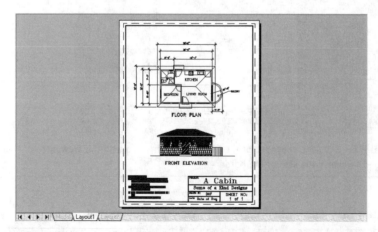

F I G U R E   1 3 . 1 0 :   Cabin11b with the title block and border on Layout1

Switching between Model Space and a Layout

Let's look at our drawing for a moment to see what happens when you switch from Model Space to a layout. Currently, Layout1 is active, and on the status bar, the Model/Paper button says Paper.

1. Start the Erase command and pick the top dimension to erase. Try to select something on the front elevation. You will find that you cannot pick anything in the cabin drawing. The only objects you can select are the title block and the borderlines, which are on Layout1. When Layout1 is current, only objects on the layout can be chosen. The triangle icon in the lower-left corner of the drawing area is visible when a layout is current. Press Esc to cancel the Erase command.

2. Click Paper on the status bar. Paper changes to Model, and the triangular Paper Space icon disappears.

 N O T E   When a layout is active, the Paper/Model button on the status bar controls whether the current layout or Model Space portion of the drawing is active, that is, accessible. If Model Space is active, the status bar always displays the Model button. If you click the Model button when Model Space is active, the last current layout becomes active, and the button on the status bar changes to the Paper button.

3. Restart the Erase command and try to select objects in the cabin drawing again. This time you are able to choose anything within the viewport except the title block and its text.

 N O T E   The crosshair cursor always resides in the active portion of the drawing. Work can be done in only one of the two portions (Model Space or a layout) at any given time.

4. Try to select the viewport boundary line, the border, or the title block. You can't choose anything on the layout when Model Space is current. Cancel the Erase command.

N O T E   The viewports in layouts are called *floating* viewports because they can be moved around. They always reside in the layout portion of the drawing. There is another kind of viewport in AutoCAD called a *tiled* viewport, which is fixed and exists only in Model Space. For brevity, in this chapter, we will refer to floating viewports as viewports.

5. Click the Model tab. The layout disappears, and you now view your drawing without a title block or border. We transferred them to Layout1, so they are no longer visible when the Model tab is active.

6. Zoom in to the front door of the elevation, and then click the Model button on the status bar. Layout1 returns with the previous view of the cabin that you had when Layout1 was most recently active.

7. Click the Model tab again. Zoom to Extents. Click the Layout1 tab.

8. Click Paper in the status bar. Now use Zoom Window to zoom in to the front door again. Because the viewport is locked for scale, AutoCAD switches to the viewport (or to Paper Space) to make the zoom and then switches back to Model Space. Press F2 and note the last few lines on the command sequence.

9. Press F2 again, Zoom Previous, click the Model button on the status bar, and then save this drawing as Cabin13a.

N O T E   When a Layout tab is active, the situation is sometimes referred to as being "in Paper Space." Conversely, when the Model tab is active, the situation is called being "in Model Space." When a layout is active (that is, when you are in Paper Space), you can switch to Model Space, while keeping the layout visible, by clicking the Paper button on the status bar. The button will change to the Model button, and you can work on the portion of your drawing that is visible in the viewport. You can then click the Model button and switch back to the layout (or Paper Space).

Picturing your drawing as two drawings in one is still a useful way to understand layouts and will help you to understand how layouts and Model Space work together.

Once you have set up a title block, border, and viewport in a layout, you can deactivate the layout and work on your drawing from within Model Space. Then, when you are ready to plot it out, reactivate the layout. The orientation and magnification of your drawing relative to the layout border will be preserved. You can also work on your drawing while the layout is active by clicking the Paper button. However, once you select a scale for Model Space within the viewport, you don't want to zoom while in Model Space because that changes the relationship between Model Space and the layout that you set up when you selected a scale in the Scale drop-down list on the Viewport toolbar. That scale must be preserved so that the drawing plots at the correct scale.

This is why it was important to lock the viewport, as you did in step 12 in the earlier section, "Adjusting a Viewport." If you want to zoom in to your drawing while a layout is visible and when you are in Model Space, lock the viewport. AutoCAD will automatically switch to the layout to zoom and then switch back to Model Space. That way, the Model Space scale won't be affected.

 N O T E   When a layout is active, you can also switch back and forth between the layout and Model Space by typing ps.⌐ or ms.⌐.

This may seem like too much work to be worth the effort for a small drawing such as this one, but be patient. As you start working on larger drawings, you will see what layouts can do for you.

Working with Multiple Viewports in a Layout

The previous exercises introduced you to layouts and taught you how they work. I used the example of a single viewport within a border and title block, all of which were on Layout1. This is the way layouts are used much of the time, even in large projects or on large sheets. A title block is developed for a project. Each sheet in a set of drawings is a .dwg file with a title block on a layout and one viewport, which encompasses most of the area inside the border, where you view the building components in Model Space. But this is certainly not the only way layouts are used. At times, more than one viewport will be used within a border, or a drawing file will have more than one viewport. The rest of the exercises in this chapter will lead you through an exploration of the advantages and techniques of using multiple viewports and layouts.

Setting Up Multiple Viewports

You'll start by creating a new layout with two viewports using the Layout Wizard. You'll then adjust the views of the cabin on the layout sheet. To give ourselves room to work, we'll use a sheet of 11" × 17" paper.

1. Using Cabin13a, create a new layer called Tblk-L2, assign it a color, and make it current. If you have a Layout2 tab in the lower-left corner of the drawing area, right-click it and choose Delete from the shortcut menu. Then, with Layout1 enabled and active, go to the drop-down menus and choose Insert ➣ Layout ➣ Create Layout Wizard. The Create Layout dialog box opens, and Begin is in the title bar (see Figure 13.11a). On the left side, a list of the steps for creating a new Layout is displayed, and an arrow points at Begin. In a text box on the bottom right of the dialog box, Layout2 is highlighted as the name of the new layout.

2. Leave Layout2 in the box and click Next. The dialog box now displays a list of printers on the right. The pointer on the left is now at Printer (see Figure 13.11b). If you have DWF6 ePlot .pc3 in the list of printers or any printer that takes an 11" × 17" sheet of paper, highlight it and click Next again.

3. As the pointer indicates, the next step is to specify paper size. Be sure Inches are selected in the Drawing Units area, and then open the drop-down list near the upper-right corner and select ANSI B (17.00 × 11.00 Inches). Then click Next again.

4. In the Orientation step, select Landscape, if it isn't already selected. Click Next again.

5. The next step is to choose a predrawn title block or to choose None and make your own. Click a few choices to see how they look in the preview port. We will make our own, so when you're finished browsing, highlight None. Then click Next.

6. Now you will set up viewports in the new layout (see Figure 13.11c). Open the Viewport Scale drop-down list and select ⅛" = 1'-0". (Don't select 1:8.) In the Viewport Setup area are four choices. Because we want two viewports side by side, we'll use the Array option. Click Array. The Array specification boxes become enabled below the Viewport Setup area. Change the number of rows to 1, and leave the other three boxes as they are. Then click Next.

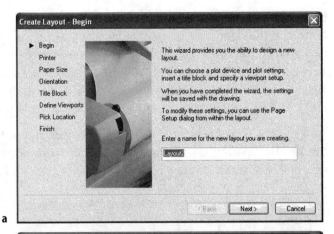

a

b

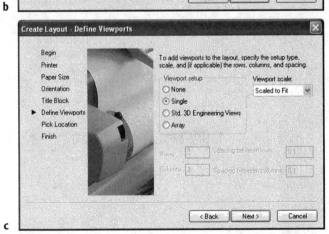

c

FIGURE 13.11: Three screens in the Layout Wizard: Begin (a), Printer (b), and Define Viewports (c)

7. Now the pointer is indicating Pick Location. Click the Select Location button on the right. You are returned to the drawing, and Layout2 is displayed at the correct orientation. You are prompted to Specify first corner. This means that you need to create a window in the layout that will encompass the area to be taken up with the new viewports. Make a window similar to the one in Figure 13.12a.

8. Back in the Create Layout dialog box, click Finish. In the drawing, two identical viewports are drawn with the cabin drawing in each one, both displayed at a scale of ⅛" = 1'-0" (see Figure 13.12b).

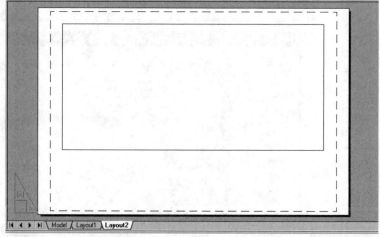

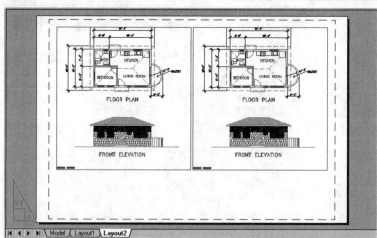

FIGURE 13.12: Windowing the viewport area in Layout2 (a), and the new viewports (b)

We'll work on the viewports in a moment, but first we need to create a border and title block for Layout2.

1. Right-click the Layout2 tab and choose Page Setup Manager from the shortcut menu. In the Page Setup Manager dialog box, click New to open the New Page Setup dialog box.

2. In the New Page Setup Name text box, type **Cabin13a-L2** and click OK.

3. In the Page Setup dialog box, check the Paper Size area to be sure ANSI B (17.00 × 11.00 Inches) is displayed, and then move to the Printer/Plotter area and click Properties.

4. As you did when setting up Layout1, click Modify Standard Size (Printable Area) in the upper window of the Plotter Configuration Editor dialog box. In the Modify Standard Paper Sizes area, find and highlight the paper size we are using and jot down the Printable Area data that is displayed below the list of sizes. (It's 16.54 × 9.60 inches in this example.) Click Cancel. Back in the Page Setup dialog box, click OK.

5. In the Page Setup Manager dialog box, click Cabin 13a-L2 and click Set Current. Then click Close to return to the drawing and view the new layout.

6. Start the Rectangle command. Type 0,0↵. Then enter as coordinates the two numbers that define the printable area. For example, if the printable area is 16.54" × 9.60", type **16.54,9.60**↵. A rectangle will be drawn over the dashed line that represents the printable area on the layout.

7. As you did for Layout1, offset this rectangle ⅛" to the inside. Erase the outer rectangle. Open the Properties palette and change the width of the polyline of the new rectangle to ¹⁄₃₂" (see Figure 13.13a).

8. Click the Layout1 tab to switch to Layout1. Be sure the Model/Paper button on the status bar is displaying Paper. If it's not, click the button to change it. Then right-click and choose Copy With Base Point.

9. Click the Osnap button on the status bar to the on position to activate the running Osnaps. Use the Endpoint Osnap to pick the lower-right corner of the border as the base point.

10. Use a regular selection window to select the title block without the border. Press ↵.

11. Click the Layout2 tab to switch back to Layout2. Choose Edit ➤ Paste and pick the lower-right corner of Layout2's border as the insertion point. The title block has been copied from Layout1 to Layout2 (see Figure 13.13b).

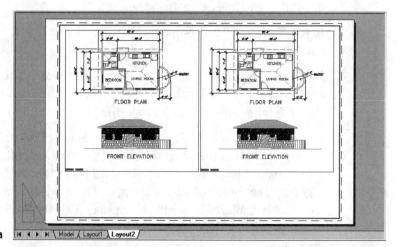

a

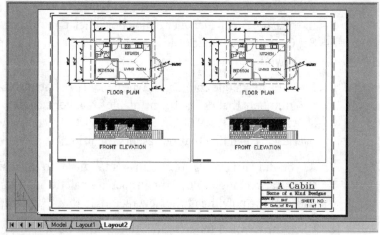

b

FIGURE 13.13: The new border for Layout2 (a), and the copied title block from Layout1 (b)

12. Reselect the title block and use the Layer Control drop-down menu to move the title block objects onto the Tblk-L2 layer.

Now we're ready to work on the viewports.

Aligning Viewports

We want the floor plan to be displayed in the left viewport and the front elevation to be displayed in the right viewport. We also want the titles of these two views to line up with each other horizontally. To accomplish this, we will need to perform some steps in Model Space and some on the layout, so we'll be switching back and forth while keeping Layout2 visible.

1. Click Paper on the status bar to switch to Model Space. Then move the cursor onto the viewports. The one that is active is the one where the crosshair cursor is visible.

T I P   When Model Space is active, only one viewport can be active at a time. This is the one with the crosshair cursor. The active viewport's border is also highlighted. You can manipulate objects in the active viewport. To make a viewport active, place the arrow cursor in the viewport and click.

2. Click Polar to turn it on, and then click in the right viewport to make it active. Use Realtime Pan to pan the drawing so that the front elevation is positioned halfway between the top and bottom of the 11" × 17" sheet.

   Also, if necessary, continue panning the view so the drawing is centered horizontally in the viewport. End the Realtime Pan command. Check the left viewport. If the drawing also needs centering horizontally, make it current and pan it to center it. End the Realtime Pan command again. Make the right viewport current again.

3. Type mvsetup↵. Then type a↵ to select the Align option.

4. Type h↵ to select the Horizontal option.

5. At the Specify basepoint: prompt, click the Insert Osnap. Then click the FRONT ELEVATION text.

6. At the next prompt, click the Insert Osnap again. Click the left viewport to make it active, and then click the FLOOR PLAN text. The floor plan in the left viewport is panned down so that its title is aligned with the title of the front elevation in the right viewport (see Figure 13.14). Press Esc to end the Mvsetup command.

◄

LT users can skip to the "Aligning Viewports for LT" section (following step 6) for an alternate series of steps.

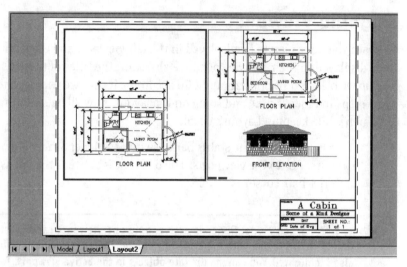

F I G U R E   1 3 . 1 4 : The text in the two viewports is aligned.

Aligning Viewports for LT

 Continuing from step 2 in the previous section, LT users should follow these steps:

3. Turn on Polar Tracking. Click the Model button on the status bar to switch to Paper Space.

4. Use Insert Osnap to draw a line from the insertion point of the FRONT ELEVATION text in the right viewport across the left viewport.

5. Switch back to Model Space and make the left viewport active.

6. Type -p↵. Click Insert Osnap and click the FLOOR PLAN text.

7. Move the cursor straight down until the horizontal crosshair of the cursor lines up with the horizontal line you just drew, as best you can eyeball, and then click.

8. End the Line command, switch to Paper Space, and erase the horizontal line.

Now you have the result as in Figure 13.14 (shown earlier).
There are one or two more things to do to finish the layout.

Finishing the 11" × 17" Drawing

We want to make the floor plan in the right viewport invisible, and we want to add the Mtext that was in the lower-left corner of the original drawing (Cabin11a) to the lower-left corner of Layout2. We'll use grips to adjust the right viewport.

1. Click the Model button on the status bar to move the cursor back to Paper Space. (LT users should already be in Paper Space.)

2. Click the boundary of the right viewport to select the viewport. Grips will appear at its corners.

3. Turn off the running Osnaps. Click the upper-right grip to activate it.

4. Move the crosshair cursor down along the right edge of the right viewport until the horizontal line of the crosshair sits between the floor plan and the elevation, and then click. The viewport now only extends to just above the elevation.

5. Click the lower-right grip. Move it up slightly so that the top of the note text in the lower-left corner of the viewport is no longer visible, and then click. Press Esc. Now the right viewport displays only the front elevation (see Figure 13.15).

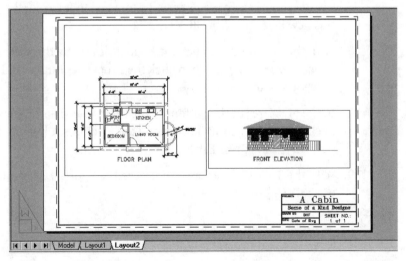

FIGURE 13.15: The right viewport showing only the front elevation after adjustments

6. If necessary, select the left viewport and adjust it in the same way so that only the floor plan is visible.

To finish this drawing, you need to place the note text in the lower-left corner. You can accomplish this by creating a third viewport.

1. Choose View ➢ Viewports ➢ 1 Viewport.

2. Pick two points in the lower-left corner to create a square viewport. The Model Space drawing appears in the viewport (see Figure 13.16a).

3. Open the Viewports toolbar, click the new viewport's border, and change the scale to ⅛" = 1' on the toolbar. Then close the Viewports toolbar. Click the Paper button to switch to Model Space.

4. Be sure the new viewport is active. If not, click in it, and then pan the drawing in the new viewport until the note text is in the viewport and near the lower-left corner of the 11" × 17" sheet's border. Press Esc to cancel Realtime Pan.

5. If necessary, click the Model button to switch back to Paper Space; then use grips to resize the viewport and to move it.

6. Click the Model button to switch to Paper Space, if you haven't already (see Figure 13.16b).

7. Create a new layer called Vports-L2 and assign it a color. Don't make this new layer current. Click OK.

8. With the layout active, click the boundaries of the three viewports to select these viewports. Then click the Properties button and move the viewports onto the Vports-L2 layer.

9. In the Misc area at the bottom of the Properties palette, click Display Locked. Open the drop-down menu and click Yes. Close the Properties palette and press Esc to remove the grips.

10. With the Tblk-L2 layer current, freeze the Vports-L2 layer (see Figure 13.17).

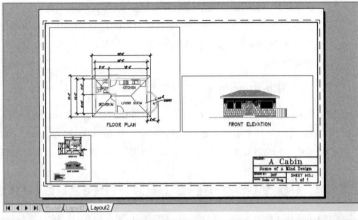

b

FIGURE 13.16: A third viewport is created (a), and the results of panning and zooming the view (b)

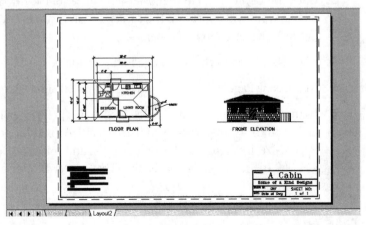

FIGURE 13.17: The completed 11" × 17" drawing within Layout2

11. Click the Layout1 tab to view the smaller layout sheet. Click the Model tab to view the original drawing without its border and title block. Click the Layout2 tab again. All three views are of the same drawing.

12. Save this drawing to your training folder as Cabin13b.

Now you have two prints set up in layouts, both based on the same drawing in Model Space. There is room for more views in the larger of the two, possibly another elevation or a detail, but we're going to move on to a larger drawing.

Setting Up Viewports in Different Scales

In the next set of exercises, you will create a new layout for a 30" × 42" sheet for the site plan you created in Chapter 12. You will then create several viewports that have drawings of different scales. Because the site plan has the cabin drawing Xreferenced into it, you will also have a chance to see how external references are handled in a drawing that is using layouts.

Setting Up a Layout for a 30" × 42" Drawing

To set up a 30" × 42" layout, you will use almost the same procedure you used earlier. The title block will be different, but you won't take the time to fill in a complete title block; you'll just indicate its location in the drawing.

1. Close Cabin13b, and then open Site12b.

2. Create new layers called Tblk-L1 and Vports-L1. Assign colors to them. Then make the Tblk-L1 layer current.

3. Click the Layout1 tab in the lower-left corner of the drawing area. A blank layout will appear on the screen for an instant. Then the Page Setup Manager dialog box opens.

4. Click New to open the New Page Setup dialog box.

5. In the New Page Setup Name text box, type **Site12b-L1** and click OK.

6. In the Page Setup Manager dialog box, go to the Printer/Plotter area and open the Name drop-down list. Select DWF6 ePlot.pc3. In the Paper Size area, open that drop-down list and select ARCH E1 (30.00 × 42.00 Inches). Then move back to the Printer/Plotter area and click Properties.

7. As you did when setting up Layout1, click Modify Standard Size (Printable Area) in the upper window of the Plotter Configuration Editor dialog box. In the Modify Standard Paper Sizes area, find and highlight the paper size we are using and jot down the Printable Area data that is displayed below the list of sizes. (It's 40.60 × 29.54 inches in this example.) Click Cancel. Back in the Page Setup dialog box, click OK.

8. In the Page Setup Manager dialog box, click Site12b-L1 and click Set Current. Then click Close to return to the drawing and view the new layout.

There is a viewport whose boundary is set in from the edge of the sheet. Site12b is zoomed to Extents within the viewport (see Figure 13.18).

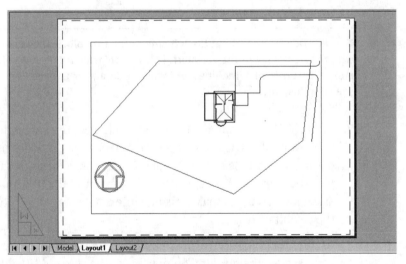

FIGURE 13.18: Site12b within Layout1

9. Use the Rectangle command to draw a rectangle from 0,0 to the point you jotted down in step 7 (in the example, 40.60,29.54).

10. Offset the rectangle ⅛" to the inside. Zoom in to a corner, erase the outer rectangle, and Zoom Previous to a full view of the layout (see Figure 13.19a).

11. Click the border rectangle to turn on the grips. Hold down the Shift key and select the two grips on the left side to activate them. Be sure Polar is on and the running Osnaps are off. Click one of the two active grips. Hold the cursor directly to the right of the selected grips and type 1↵. The left side of the border is moved 1" to the right, leaving room for a binding on the left edge of the sheet. Press Esc.

Sheets of large sizes usually have their title blocks on a vertical strip on the right side. We will draw a guideline to indicate the title block.

12. Offset the border rectangle 4" to the inside. Then explode the new rectangle. Erase the top, bottom, and left lines of this new rectangle. Then use the Extend command to extend the remaining line up and down to the rectangle that will serve as the border (see Figure 13.19b).

T I P   Don't worry about the left side of the title block almost coinciding with the right edge of the viewport. This is a coincidence. It makes it a little more difficult to pick the lines, but you now know techniques that can help you with this problem.

13. Start the Pedit command (type pe↵) and select the rectangle that is the new border. Use the Width option to change the width of the borderline to ¹⁄₁₆". Type ↵↵ to stop and restart the Pedit command. Then pick the new line that represents the left side of the title block. When asked if you want to make this line into a polyline, press ↵ to accept the default of Yes.

Use the Width option again and set this line to the same width as you used for the border. You now have a border and title block area set up in Layout1 and are ready to work with the viewports (see Figure 13.19c).

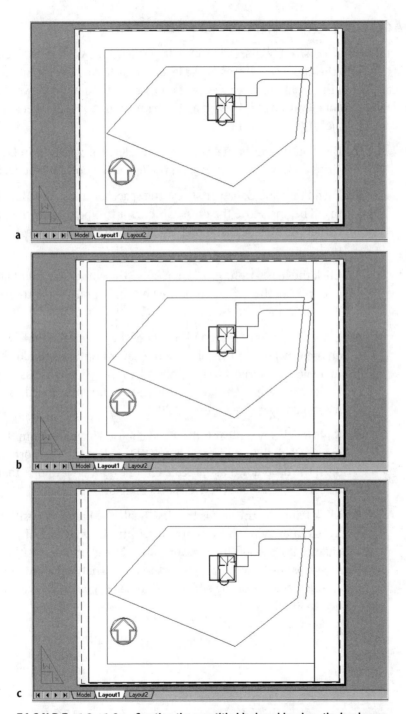

FIGURE 13.19: Creating the new title block and border: the border rectangle (a), the strip for the title block (b), and the finished title block and border (c)

Adjusting a Viewport for the Site Plan

On the 30" × 42" sheet, we already have a large viewport. We'll move it and resize it to fit into the upper two-thirds of the layout in order to view the site plan at ⅛" scale. You'll then make smaller viewports across the bottom for views of the floor plan and front elevation at ¼" scale and the bathroom at 1" scale. Let's resize and reposition the larger viewport first.

1. Click on the viewport's boundary to select the viewport in Layout1. Grips appear. Click the grip on the upper-left corner to activate it.

2. Turn Polar and Osnap off. Press the spacebar once. The Move command begins. Move the crosshair cursor to a point near the upper-left corner, just inside the border, and then click. The viewport is moved to the upper left.

3. Click the lower-right grip. Then move the cursor to a point about one-third of the way up from the bottom boundary line to the top boundary line, next to the title block (see Figure 13.20a).

4. Click to position the second corner of the viewport. Then, with grips on the viewport still visible, use the Layer Control drop-down menu to move the viewport to the Vports-L1 layer. Finally, press Esc to remove the grips. The viewport is resized, is repositioned, and is on its proper layer (see Figure 13.20b).

5. Right-click any toolbar button and choose Viewports from the toolbar menu. Click the viewport's boundary to select the viewport, and then open the drop-down list of scale options on the Viewports toolbar. Select ⅛" = 1'. Close the Viewports toolbar.

6. Click Paper on the status bar. Use Realtime Pan to reposition the Site12a drawing more centrally within the viewport. If you need to enlarge the size of the viewport, click Model on the status bar, and use grips to stretch the viewport to a size that will allow you to fit all the elements of the site plan in the viewport at ⅛" scale (see Figure 13.20c).

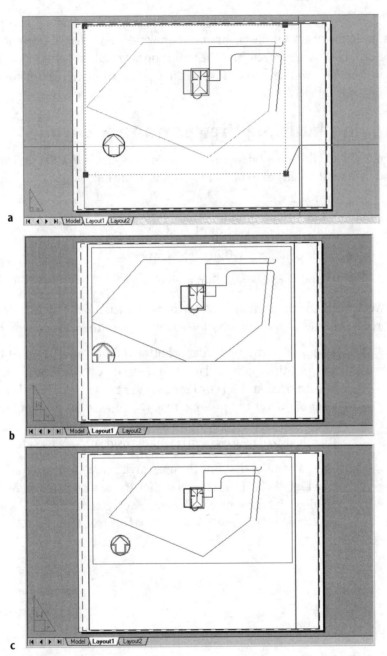

FIGURE 13.20: Adjusting a viewport with grips on (a), after the adjustment (b), and after the zoom (c)

The view of the site plan is just like the drawing before Paper Space was activated. Remember that the cabin in this drawing is an external reference. Many of the cabin layers are frozen, and the visible ones are all the same color, except the new deck. This will have to change when we set up other viewports for the floor plan and front elevation.

Adding Multiple Viewports to a Layout

Now we'll add three new viewports to the empty space below the first viewport, and then we'll modify each of them in terms of the following:

▶ Viewport size

▶ Content of each viewport

▶ Scale of objects within each viewport

▶ Visibility of layers within each viewport

We'll create the three viewports together and then modify them individually, starting with the leftmost viewport where we'll place the floor plan of the cabin.

1. Be sure that the Model/Paper button on the status bar is set to Paper. Then set the Vports-L1 layer to be current. Choose View ➤ Viewports ➤ 3 Viewports. At the [Horizontal/Vertical/Above/Below/Left/Right] <Right>: prompt, type v↵. You see the prompt Specify first corner or [Fit]:. This means you need to make a window that the three new viewports will fit inside of, side by side.

2. Make a window that fills the open area below the existing viewport (see Figure 13.21a). When you click the second point to define the window, the three new viewports are created, and each has a view of the Site12a drawing zoomed to Extents (see Figure 13.21b).

All my logical sense tells me that the Horizontal/Vertical/etc. option that you select here should be horizontal, but AutoCAD requires you to select the Vertical option to get a horizontal row of viewports.

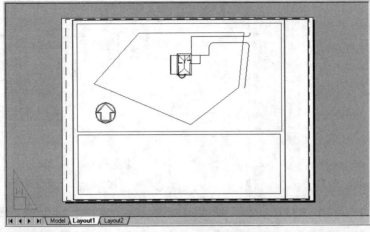

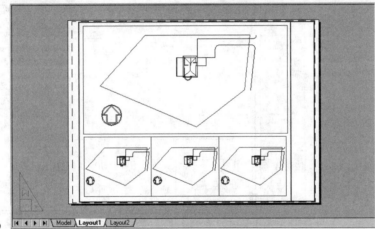

FIGURE 13.21: Windowing the area in which to insert the viewports (a) and the inserted viewports (b)

3. Click the Model/Paper button on the status bar to move to Model Space and click in the leftmost viewport to make it active. Type ucs↵ z↵ -90↵. Then type plan↵↵. The site plan is rotated 90° counterclockwise. The cabin is now oriented the way it was before being inserted as an external reference into the site plan (see Figure 13.22a).

4. Pan the cabin to the middle of the viewport, and then move back to Paper Space. Open the Viewports toolbar as you did in step 5 of the previous section. Click the lower-left viewport boundary to select the viewport; then, in the Viewports toolbar, set the scale to ¼" = 1'. The floor plan fills the viewport (see Figure 13.22b). Close the Viewports toolbar, remove the grips, switch back to Model Space, and pan again if necessary.

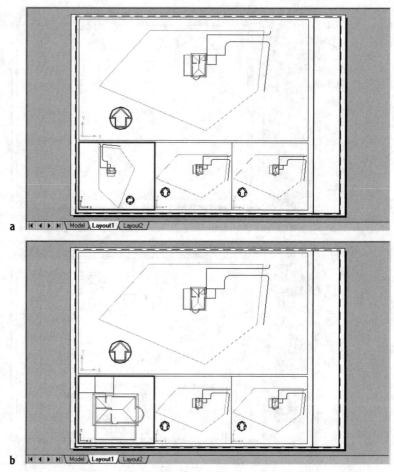

FIGURE 13.22: The left viewport with a rotated site plan (a), and the floor plan zoomed to ¼" scale in the viewport (b)

N O T E   You can control the visibility of the UCS icon in each viewport and in Paper Space by choosing View ➢ Display ➢ UCS Icon and then clicking On. When the check mark next to On is visible, the UCS icon is displayed. When the layout is active, the icon is a triangle and sits outside the layout.

To complete this view, you'll need to do a few things. You need to resize the viewport and pan the view so everything that you want to see is visible. You also need to determine which layers you want visible in this viewport and freeze the ones whose objects you don't want to see. We'll work with the layers first because we need to make all the objects to be displayed visible in order to tell how big the viewport needs to be.

Controlling Layers in Viewports

You can control which layers are visible in each viewport, so two viewports can have a different combination of layers visible. To do so, first thaw all frozen layers and make sure all layers are turned on. Then, with Model Space current, make a viewport active and freeze the layers you don't want visible in that viewport. When finished, move to the next viewport and freeze layers you don't want visible in that viewport. In this situation, you'll eventually have to reset the visibility of the layers in all viewports.

1. On the Layout1 tab, be sure that Model Space is active and the lower-left viewport is current. Then click the Layer Properties Manager button on the Layers toolbar. When the Layer Properties Manager dialog box opens, click and drag the right edge of the dialog box to the right to widen it enough to see the Current VP Freeze column. Use the horizontal slider if necessary.

TIP   The Current VP Freeze column might be compressed in such a way that the entire column title is not displayed. It may say "Curr…" or something like that. You can widen the column by clicking and dragging the divider at the right of the title farther to the right.

2. Thaw all currently frozen layers and turn on all layers. (Right-click any layer, and then choose Select All from the menu that appears in the drawing area. All layers are highlighted. Then click a snowflake in the Freeze column and a turned-off light bulb in the On column. All layers are thawed and turned on. Scroll back to the top and click the Cabin layer. The rest of the layers are deselected.)

    Now that all layers are visible, you need to go down the list of layers. When you see a layer that needs to be frozen in the current viewport, click the sun in the Current VP Freeze column for that layer. The lower-left viewport is current, so let's start with the layers for that one.

3. Move down the list and click the sun in the Current VP Freeze column for these layers:

    ▶ Cabin12a| layers: Dim1, F-elev, Roof, Tblk1, Text1, and all the hatch layers *except* Hatch-plan-walls

    ▶ Prop-line and Road layers

    Click OK when finished. You are returned to your drawing (see Figure 13.23a). The smaller viewport looks OK, but it needs resizing. All the layers are visible in the other two small viewports and in the larger one. Let's set the layers for the larger viewport now.

4. Click the larger viewport to make it active. Then click the Layers button again. In the Layer Properties Manager dialog box, go down the list again, clicking the suns in the Current VP Freeze column, as you did before, to make the following layers invisible in this viewport: all Cabin12al layers except Balcony, Deck, Roof, Steps, and Walls. Click OK when finished. The drawing in this viewport is what we want (see Figure 13.23b).

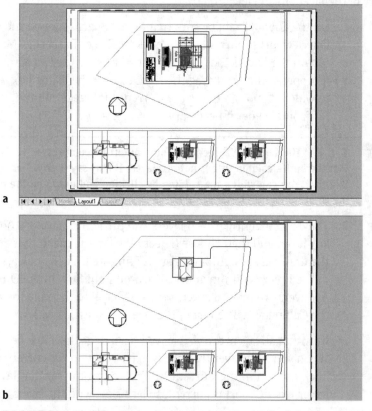

FIGURE 13.23: Layer changes made in the smaller left viewport (a), and in the larger viewport (b)

Now you need to adjust the size and view of the smaller left viewport so the structural grid will be fully displayed. You're going to stretch the viewport up to a point where it will overlap the larger viewport. While the larger viewport is active, move the north arrow to the other side of the site plan to get it out of the way.

1. Start the Move command and select the north arrow. Press ↵. Click the middle of the arrow, and click again to place it in a clear space in the lower-right corner of the larger viewport.

2. Switch to Paper Space. Click the small viewport on the left to make grips appear.

3. Click the upper-right grip. With Polar and Ortho off, move the cursor up and a little to the right, pick a point just below the property line, and click (see Figure 13.24a). Press Esc to remove the grips.

4. Switch to Model Space. Click the lower-left viewport to make it active. Use the Pan command to move the floor plan around in the viewport until the deck and the grid are completely visible. Leave some room below the deck for text. Press Esc to end the Pan command.

5. Switch back to Paper Space and do a final adjustment of the viewport's size with grips, making it as small as possible while still showing everything (see Figure 13.24b). Press Esc to remove the grips.

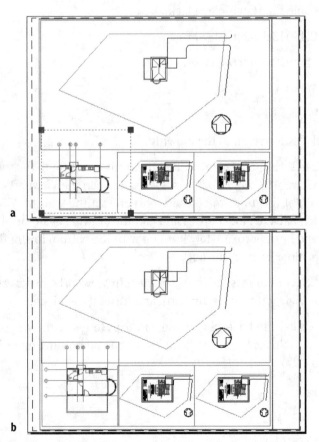

FIGURE 13.24: Stretching the viewport with grips in the layout (a), and panning the view in Model Space (b)

The layers are now set up so they are visible in all viewports (the Freeze In All VP column), except where frozen in particular viewports (the Current VP Freeze column). The other two small viewports have all layers visible, because we have yet to make these viewports current and work on them.

Let's move to those viewports now and set them up using the procedures we've just used for the first two.

1. Switch to Model Space. Click the smaller viewport that's in the middle to make it active. Then click the Layer Properties Manager button. Freeze all layers in the Current VP Freeze column, except the following:

   ▶ Cabin

   ▶ Cabin12a|F-elev

   ▶ Cabin12a|Hatch-elev-black

   ▶ Cabin12a|Hatch-elev-brown

   ▶ Cabin12a|Hatch-elev-gray

   ▶ Tblk-L1

   ▶ Vports-L1

   Click OK to return to the drawing.

2. Type **ucs.⏎ z⏎ -90⏎ plan.⏎⏎**. Pan the front elevation to the middle of the viewport. Switch to Paper Space and open the Viewports toolbar. Highlight the lower-middle viewport and set the scale to ¼" = 1'. Switch back to Model Space and pan the drawing again until the ground line approximately lines up with the bottom line of the deck in the floor plan on the left.

3. If UCS icons are visible in any of the four viewports, make each of those viewports current in turn, and turn off each icon.

4. Switch back to Paper Space and use grips to resize the viewport so that it includes the entire front elevation and nothing more (see Figure 13.25).

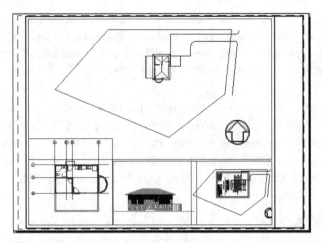

FIGURE 13.25: The front elevation in the middle small viewport

5. Move to the viewport in the lower-right corner, and make adjustments to display the bathroom at a scale of 1" = 1'-0". Follow these steps:

   A. To work on the fourth viewport, switch to Model Space and activate the right small viewport.

   B. Use the UCS and Plan commands to rotate the drawing 90° counterclockwise, as you did for the other two small viewports.

   C. In the Current column of the Layer Properties Manager dialog box, freeze the following layers: all the Cabin12a1 layers, except for Doors; Fixtures; Hatch-plan-floor; Hatch-plan-walls; Headers; Walls; Windows; and all layers not prefaced by Cabin12a except the Cabin and 0 layers.

   D. In Paper Space, use the Viewports toolbar to set the scale to 1" = 1'.

   E. In Model Space, pan the drawing until the bathroom is centered in the viewport. Try to line up the bottom bathroom wall with the ground line in the front elevation.

   F. Switch to Paper Space and adjust the size and position of the viewport. Try to make the right and bottom boundary lines of the viewport coincide with the right and bottom edges of the wall lines. Zoom in close if you need to.

N O T E   Once a scale has been set for a viewport, the final adjustment has two steps: panning the drawing in Model Space, and adjusting the size and location of the viewport with grips in Paper Space.

If you're using LT, you can open Cabin12a, **make the same repair, and then save your work. Back in the site drawing, choose Insert ➤ Xref Manager to reload the Xref.**

G. Repair the bathroom door using the same technique we used in Chapter 12, when we repaired the roof hip lines. Turn off the Hatch-plan-floor layer temporarily, and zoom in to the area around the bathroom door. Switch to Model Space. Choose Modify ➤ Xref And Block Editing ➤ Edit Reference In-Place, and then click an object in the viewport.

In the Reference Edit dialog box, select Prompt To Select Nested Objects, and then click OK. Select the two pieces of the door swing and the left header line, and then press ↵. The Refedit toolbar opens. Erase the small swing line. Use the header line as a boundary line and extend the swing to it. Save changes back to the reference file. Turn the Hatch-plan-floor layer back on.

H. Switch back to Paper Space, and then zoom out to a full view of the layout. Be sure Polar is on. If necessary, move any of the small viewports horizontally to space them evenly on the layout. Then select all viewports and use the Properties palette to lock them.

The results should look something like Figure 13.26.

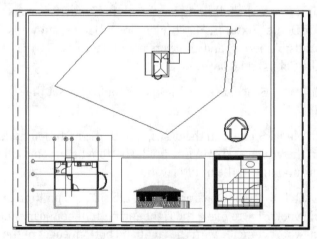

F I G U R E 1 3 . 2 6 :   All viewports completed

T I P   Because viewports are usually made to be invisible, it isn't important to line them up evenly. Viewports can overlap as long as the visible objects in one viewport do not overlap visible objects in another.

Adding Text to Paper Space

Now you'll add titles to the views in a style that matches the style of the front elevation title. Underneath each title, we will put the scale of the view.

1. Switch to Model Space. Make the viewport containing the front elevation active. Then thaw the Cabin12a|Text1 layer in the Current VP Freeze column. The FRONT ELEVATION text appears.

T I P   If the GENERAL NOTES or the FLOOR PLAN text also appears, you can stretch the viewport to hide it the next time you are in Paper Space.

2. Create a new layer called Text-L1. Assign it the same color as the Cabin12a|Text1 layer and make it current.

3. Create a new text style called Title-L1. (Remember, you start the Style command by choosing Format ➤ Text Style on the menu bar.) We want the new style to be identical to the Title text style we used in Model Space, but the height has to be adjusted for use in a layout. It was 1'-6" high in Model Space. The front elevation is now at ¼" scale. If you divide 1'-6" by 48, you have the Paper Space text height: ⅜". Assign this text style the romand.shx font and a ⅜" height. Click Apply, and then click Close.

4. Switch to Paper Space. Then choose Draw ➤ Text ➤ Single Line Text from the menu bar. Type j↵, and then type c↵. To activate point filters, type .y↵.

5. Select the Insert Osnap and click the FRONT ELEVATION text. Select the Midpoint Osnap and click one of the horizontal deck lines in the floor plan.

6. Press ↵ for the Rotation prompt. With Caps Lock on, type **floor plan**↵↵. The floor plan title is placed on the drawing. Zoom in to see it better (see Figure 13.27a).

7. With Polar on, copy this text down ¾". Click the new text, and then open the Properties palette. Change the height of this text to ¼". Highlight the FLOOR PLAN text in the Contents box and type, with Caps Lock on: **scale:** 1/4" = 1'-0" (see Figure 13.27b). Leave a space before and after the = sign. Close the Properties palette and remove the grips.

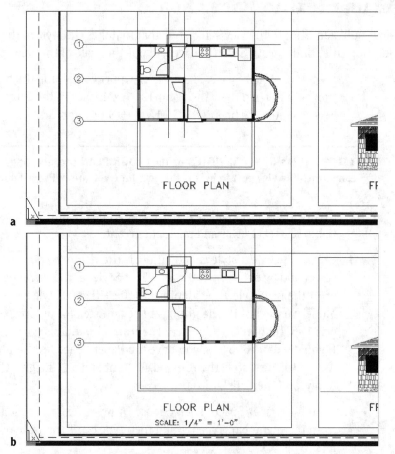

FIGURE 13.27: A title is placed on the floor plan (a), and a scale is added (b).

8. Zoom Previous. Use the Copy command and the Insertion Osnap to copy the scale to the front elevation.

9. With Polar on, use the Copy command with the Multiple option to copy both the view title and the scale from the floor plan to the bathroom viewport. Then turn off Polar and place the second copy of the text under the site plan.

10. Choose Modify ➤ Object ➤ Text ➤ Edit to start the Ddedit command. Use this command to change the titles to BATHROOM and SITE PLAN and to change the scales to 1" = 1'-0" and ⅛" = 1'-0", respectively.

11. Turn off the Vports-L1 layer. The results should look like Figure 13.28a. The drawing looks complete. The only problem is that the roof lines and property line in the site plan look continuous. With Paper Space, you need to set the global linetype scale to 1. AutoCAD will then adjust the linetype scale for each viewport, depending on the scale it's zoomed to.

12. Type ltscale↵ 1↵. The phantom linetype is now visible for the site plan, and the roof lines are dashed (see Figure 13.28b).

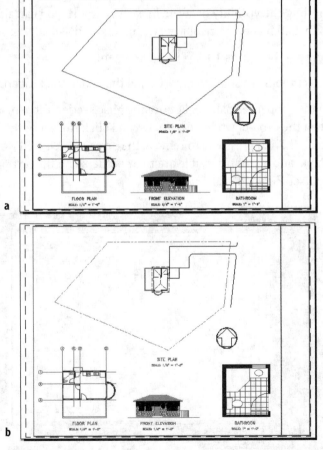

FIGURE 13.28: The 30" × 42" drawing complete with titles and scales of views (a), and with the ltscale setting adjusted for Paper Space (b)

You added one line of text on the layout and then copied and changed it to make six more lines of the text.

If you have been using a black Model Space background, some of your colors may appear faded on the layout. Feel free to assign darker colors to the layers.

As you have just seen, you can place text and lines on a layout on top of viewports. The viewport is like a window through which you can view the Model Space drawing, but the window has a transparent surface, like glass or cellophane, on which you can place text or other AutoCAD objects.

A layer can have some objects on a layout and some in Model Space. But arranging the drawing like this is not a good habit to get into because it can make the drawing harder to manage.

Turning Off Viewports

Beyond controlling the visibility of layers in each viewport, you can also turn off a viewport so that all Model Space objects within it are invisible.

1. Turn on the Vports-L1 layer for a moment.

2. Select the three small viewports, and then click the Properties button.

3. In the Properties palette, be sure the Misc section is open, and then open the drop-down list next to On and click No. Close the Properties palette. Then press Esc to remove the grips. All selected viewports go blank, and all that is visible are their borders and the text on the layout (see Figure 13.29).

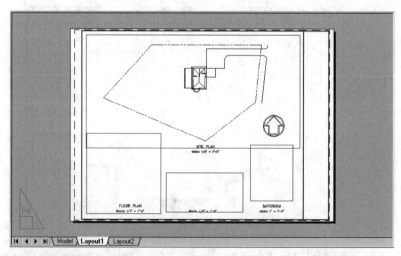

FIGURE 13.29: Layout1 with the smaller viewports turned off

4. Reselect the three small viewports and click Properties to turn them back on. Turn off the Vports layer again. Your drawing should look like Figure 13.28b (shown earlier).

5. Save this drawing as Site13.

Being able to turn off viewports can be an advantage for a complex drawing with many viewports or for one with a lot of information in each viewport. Remember that even though all four views in this drawing are based on one drawing, AutoCAD is drawing at least part of that drawing in each viewport. In a complex drawing, this can slow down the computer, so it's handy to be able to temporarily turn off any viewports you aren't working on. It's also an easy way to check which objects are in Model Space and which are on the layout (or in Paper Space).

We will work with the viewports and layouts again in the next chapter, where you will round out your knowledge of AutoCAD by learning the principles of plotting and printing AutoCAD drawings.

WHAT YOU DO IN MODEL SPACE AND PAPER SPACE (LAYOUTS)

Here's a partial list of some of the things you do in the two environments.

In Model Space

▶ Zoom to a scale in a viewport (1/*scale factor*xp).

▶ Work on the building (or the project you are drawing).

▶ Make a viewport current.

▶ Control layer visibility in the current viewport.

In Paper Space (Layouts)

▶ Create viewports.

▶ Modify the size and location of viewports.

▶ Lock/unlock the scale of the display in a viewport.

▶ Turn viewports on or off.

▶ Add a title block and border.

If You Would Like More Practice...

Create a second layout for Site13 that is similar to Layout2 in Cabin13b (see Figure 13.30). Use the Layout Wizard to create the layout. Then copy the border and title block from Layout2 of Cabin13b and the title and scale of the site plan from Layout1 of Site13. Here's an outline of the procedure.

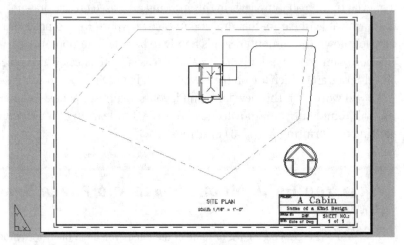

FIGURE 13.30: A second layout for Site13

Create a new layer called Tblk_B-size and make it current. Then, in the Layout Wizard, follow these steps:

1. Delete Layout2, and then choose Insert ➤ Layout ➤ Create Layout Wizard.

2. In the Begin screen, replace Layout2 with B-size.

3. In the Printer screen, select DWF6 ePlot.pc3.

4. In the Paper Size screen, select ANSI B (17.00 × 11.00 inches).

5. In the Orientation screen, select Landscape.

6. In the Title Block screen, select None.

7. In the Viewport Setup area, select Single.

8. In the Viewport Scale drop-down list, select ¹⁄₁₆" = 1'-0".

9. In the Pick Location screen, make a rectangle that covers the printable area except for the bottom 2".

In the B-size layout, follow these steps:

1. Switch to Model Space.

2. Open the Layer Properties Manager, and in the Current VP Freeze column, freeze all Cabin12al layers except Balcony, Deck, Roof, Steps, and Walls.

3. Create two new layers called Text_B-size, and Vports_B-size, and make the last one current.

4. Switch back to Paper Space.

To copy the title block and border from Cabin13b, follow these steps:

1. Open Cabin13b, and then right-click.

2. Choose Copy With Base Point.

3. For base point, type 0,0↵.

4. Select the border and title block, and then press ↵.

5. Use the Window menu to switch to Site13.

6. Right-click, and then choose Paste from the menu.

7. For the insertion point, type 0,0↵.

8. Adjust the viewport to fit neatly inside the border top and sides while still displaying the entire site drawing.

9. Use the Properties palette to lock the scale of the viewport.

10. Switch to Model Space while Layout1 is still visible, and if necessary, pan the site drawing to fit in the viewport.

To copy the site plan view title and scale from Layout1, follow these steps:

1. Switch to Layout1.

2. Right-click and choose Copy With Base Point.

3. Use the Insert Osnap and select the insert point of SITE PLAN.

4. Click SITE PLAN and SCALE: ⅛" = 1'-0" text. Press ↵.

5. Switch to the B-size layout.

6. Right-click, and choose Paste.

7. Click the blank area to the left of the title block to place text. Move this text onto the Text_B-size layer.

8. Use the Scale command to reduce the text by half.

9. Double-click the SCALE text to change it to $\frac{1}{16}$" = 1'-0".

10. Right-click the Layout1 tab and choose Rename.

11. Change Layout1 to 30×42.

12. Save this drawing as Site13-extra.

Are You Experienced?

Now you can...

☑ **create a layout and associate it with a page setup**

☑ **draw a border and title block on a layout**

☑ **set up viewports on layouts**

☑ **cut and paste in AutoCAD**

☑ **zoom to a scale in a viewport**

☑ **lock the display of a viewport**

☑ **align viewports**

☑ **control layer visibility in individual viewports**

☑ **control the visibility of viewport boundaries**

☑ **use the Layout Wizard**

☑ **set up a text style for layouts**

☑ **add text to a layout**

☑ **turn viewports off and on**

CHAPTER 14

Printing an AutoCAD Drawing

▶ Setting up a drawing to be printed

▶ Using the Plot dialog box

▶ Assigning lineweights to layers in your drawing

▶ Selecting the part of your drawing to print

▶ Previewing a print

▶ Printing a layout

▶ Looking at plot styles

irst of all, with today's equipment, there is no difference between printing and plotting. *Printing* used to refer to smaller-format printers, and *plotting* used to refer to pen plotters, most of which were for plotting large sheets. But the terms are now used almost interchangeably. Pen plotters have a few extra settings that other printing devices do not have. Otherwise, as far as AutoCAD is concerned, the differences between plotters and laserjet, inkjet, dot-matrix, and electrostatic printers are minimal. So in this book, printing and plotting mean the same thing.

Getting your drawing onto paper can be very easy or very hard, depending on whether your computer is connected to a printer that has been set up to print AutoCAD drawings and depending on whether AutoCAD has been configured to work with your printer. If these initial conditions are met, you can handily manage printing with the tools you will learn in this chapter. If you do not have the initial setup, you will need to get some help either to set up your system to make AutoCAD work properly with your printer or to find out how your system is already set up to print AutoCAD drawings.

We will be using a couple of standard setup configurations between AutoCAD and printers to move through the exercises. You may or may not be able to follow each step to completion, depending on whether you have access to an 8.5" × 11" laserjet or inkjet printer, a larger-format printer, or both.

We have four drawings to print:

Cabin11a   A drawing with Model Space only, to be printed on an 8½" × 11" sheet at ⅛" scale

Cabin13a   The same drawing as Cabin11a, except with the title block and border on Layout1, to be printed from Layout1 on an 8½" × 11" sheet at a scale of 1:1

Cabin13b   The 11" × 17" drawing, to be printed on an 11" × 17" sheet from a layout

Site13   To be printed on a 30" × 42" sheet from a layout

Even if your printer won't let you print in all these formats, I suggest that you follow along with the text. You'll at least get to preview how your drawing would look if printed in these formats, and you will be taking large strides toward learning how to set up and run a print for your drawing. The purpose of this chapter is to give you the basic principles for printing whether or not you have access to a printer.

The Plot Dialog Box

The job of getting your AutoCAD file onto hard copy can be broken into five tasks. You will need to tell AutoCAD the following:

- ▶ The printing device you will use
- ▶ The lineweight assigned to each object in your drawing
- ▶ The portion of your drawing you are printing
- ▶ The sheet size you are printing
- ▶ The scale, orientation, and placement of the print on the sheet

You handle most of these tasks in the Plot dialog box.

1. Open Cabin11a. Zoom to Extents, and then zoom out a little (see Figure 14.1). This drawing is not quite ready to print.

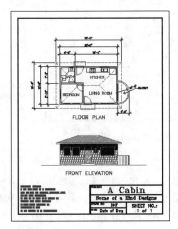

FIGURE 14.1: Cabin11a zoomed to Extents and then zoomed out a little

2. Click the Plot button on the Standard toolbar to open the Plot dialog box. The title bar includes "Model" because, in this case, we are printing a drawing from Model Space. Later, when we print from Layouts, the title bar displays the name of the layout. This dialog box is similar to the Page Setup dialog box that you worked with in Chapter 13 when you were setting up layouts (see Figure 14.2). But there are some differences:

You can also open the Plot dialog box by choosing File ➣ Plot, by pressing Ctrl+P, or by typing plot.↵ or print.↵.

> ► It's smaller, but you can expand it to include four more areas of information and settings on the right side. Yours might come up in expanded form.

> ► It has an additional area called Number of Copies.

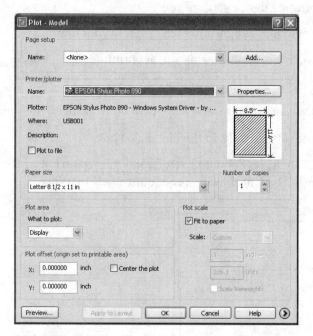

FIGURE 14.2: The Plot dialog box

When we get to the point in this chapter where we are printing layouts, you'll find that much of the setup work has already been done. But before we do, let's take a quick tour of this dialog box. Then we'll start setting up to print.

There are seven areas of settings on this unexpanded version of the dialog box. Some of the buttons and boxes won't be activated. I'll mention others only in passing, because their functions are for more advanced techniques than those covered in this book. I'll save discussion of the Page Setup area at the top of the dialog box until we begin printing drawings with layouts.

Printer/Plotter

In this area, the Name drop-down list contains the various printing devices to which AutoCAD has been configured, with the current one, the EPSON Stylus Photo 890, displayed in Figure 14.2. Yours might say None or display a different printer. Just below the list, the name of the driver and port are displayed for the selected printer. Clicking the Properties button to the right opens the Plotter Configuration Editor dialog box, which has three tabs of data specific for the current printer. Most of these will already be set up by your Windows operating system. Back in the Plot dialog box, the Plot To File check box, when selected, directs AutoCAD to make and save the print as a `.plt` file, rather than sending it to a printer.

Paper Size and Number of Copies

In the Paper Size area, the Paper Size drop-down list contains paper sizes that the current plot device can handle. To the right is the Number Of Copies area, which is self-explanatory.

The Plot Area

In the Plot Area area, a drop-down list contains the options for specifying what to print in your drawing. We have already decided which layers will be visible when the print is made by freezing or turning off the layers whose objects we don't want to print. Now we must decide how to designate the area of the drawing to be printed. As we go through the options, it will be useful to think about the choices with regard to two printing possibilities: printing the whole drawing and printing just the floor plan.

To illustrate how these options work, we will make a couple of assumptions. First, the Fit To Paper check box is selected in the Plot Scale area, so AutoCAD will try to fill the sheet with the drawing. Second, the drawing will be in portrait orientation.

The Display Option

The Display option will print what's currently on the screen, including the blank area around the drawing. With both drawing and sheet in portrait orientation, and with the origin in the lower-left corner of the sheet, the plot would look like Figure 14.3. The dashed lines represent the edge of what was the drawing area on the screen. (You won't see the dashed line in your own drawing; it was put in to illustrate the point.) The drawing doesn't fit well on the sheet with this option. It's oriented correctly, but it's forced to be too small on the sheet. The blank space in the drawing area on the left and right of the print is brought into the print with this option, and that's what creates the misfit. Printing to Display is a good method if the drawing is in landscape orientation, if it is proportional in size to the drawing area, and if the printer is also set to landscape orientation.

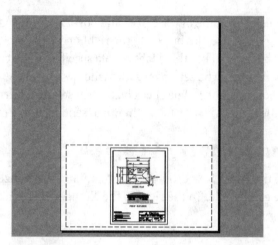

FIGURE 14.3: The Cabin11a drawing printed to Display

The Extents Option

You can use the Preview option to view how the drawing will print for Extents and the three following printing options.

When you select the Extents option, AutoCAD tries to fill the sheet with all visible objects in the drawing. If you print Cabin11a using the Extents method of selecting what to print, the results will look like Figure 14.4. This is a good method to use if the border has been drawn with the same proportions as the printable area of the sheet. It was in this case because you offset a rectangle that represented the sheet to make the border, but the rectangle that represented the sheet was also printed, and we didn't want that. You would have to erase the outer rectangle before printing to Extents.

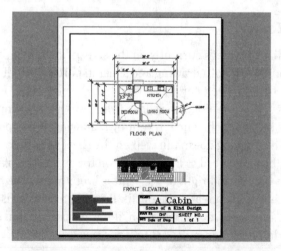

FIGURE 14.4: The Cabin11a drawing printed to Extents

The Limits Option

Do you remember the drawing limits for the cabin drawing that you set in Chapter 3? As a refresher, perform the following steps:

1. Click Cancel to cancel the plot.

2. Click the Grid button on the status bar to make the grid visible. It's still there, around the floor plan, just as you first set it in Chapter 3 (see Figure 14.5a). When you print to Limits, AutoCAD prints only what lies within the limits (or, in another way of saying it, what's on the grid), and it will push what's within the limits to the corner that is the origin of the print.

3. Click the Plot button again, and make the Plot Settings tab active. In the Plot dialog box, click Limits in the Plot Area area, and be sure Portrait is selected in the Drawing Orientation area. Then click the Preview button in the lower-left corner (see Figure 14.5b). This print won't work here because the limits don't cover the entire drawing. Also, the limits are in Landscape orientation, so the portion of the drawing to be printed doesn't fit properly on the paper. Printing to Limits can be a good tool for setting up a print, but you will usually reset the limits from their original defining coordinates to new ones for the actual print.

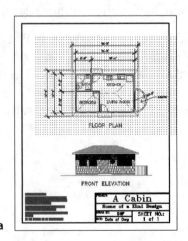
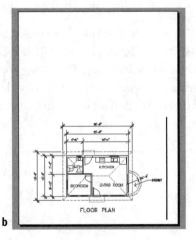

a   b

FIGURE 14.5: The grid showing the limits of Cabin11a (a), and a preview of the drawing printed to Limits (b)

4. Right-click and choose Exit from the shortcut menu to exit the preview. Cancel the plot, and then press F7 to turn off the grid.

If Layouts have been set up for a .dwg file, the Limits option will be replaced by Layout in the What To Print drop-down list in the Plot Area area.

The View Option

When printing to View, you tell AutoCAD to print a previously defined view that was saved with the drawing. Right now, the View option is not displayed in the What To Plot drop-down list because we haven't defined and saved any views yet. We'll save a view, and then we'll see what the print looks like.

1. If the Plot dialog box is still on the screen, cancel it. Choose View ➤ Named Views to open the View dialog box.

2. Click the New button to open the New View dialog box, and type plot1.

3. Click the Define Window radio button.

4. Back in the drawing, make a window around the left half of the floor plan, not including the dimensions, as shown in Figure 14.6a.

5. Click OK to close the New View dialog box. The saved view, called plot1, is listed in the Views list box of the View dialog box.

6. Click OK. Then click the Plot button and continue reading along.

Now, to plot the plot1 view of this drawing, open the What To Plot drop-down list in the Plot Area area of the Plot dialog box and click View. Then move to the right and select plot1 from the drop-down list of saved views. At the settings for scale and orientation that we have been using, the print will look like Figure 14.6b. The View option for What To Plot is a valuable tool for setting up partial prints of a drawing.

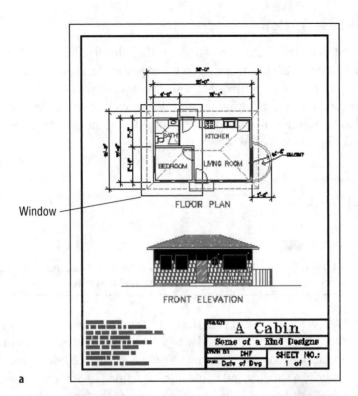

Window

a

b

F I G U R E   1 4 . 8 : Using a window to define a view (a), and the print to this view (b)

The Window Option

Using a window to define the area of a plot is the most flexible of the five methods being described. It's like using a zoom window in the drawing. When you select this option, you are returned to your drawing. In your drawing, make a window around the area you want to print. When you return to the Plot dialog box, a Window button is displayed in the right side of the Plot Area area (see Figure 14.7), in case you need to redo the window.

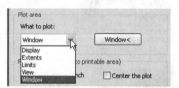

FIGURE 14.7: The Plot Area area in the Plot dialog box with its drop-down list open and the Window button displayed next to it

AutoCAD will print only what is in the window you made, regardless of how it fits on the sheet. This method is similar to the View method just discussed. The difference is that the View method prints a previously defined view (one that was possibly defined by a window, but could also be defined in other ways), and the Window method prints what is included in a window that you define as you are setting up the plot. The window used by the Window method can't be saved and recalled at a later time.

These are the five ways to specify what to print. We'll use the Window option in the first exercise that follows.

Plot Scale

Moving to the right, we come to the Plot Scale area, where you control the scale of the plot. When the Fit To Paper check box is selected, AutoCAD will take whatever area you have chosen to print and automatically scale it so that it will fit on the selected page size. When it is unchecked, the Scale drop-down list becomes available. This list contains 32 preset scales to choose from, plus Custom. Some of the scales in the list are displayed as pure ratios, such as 1:50. Others are shown in their standard format, such as ¼" = 1'-0". Below the drop-down list is a pair of text boxes for setting up a custom scale. When you choose a preset scale, these text boxes display the true ratio of the current scale.

To set up a custom scale, you enter a plotted distance in the Inch = text box. Then, in the Units text box, enter the distance that, in your drawing, will be represented by the distance that you entered in the Inches text box. The inches distance will be an actual distance on the plotted drawing, and the units distance is the distance the plotted units represent. For ¼" scale (¼" = 1'-0"), you could enter several combinations:

Inch =	Units
¼	1'
1	4'
1	48

Layouts are plotted at a scale of 1:1. We'll come back to this and other scale issues as we prepare a drawing for printing.

Plot Offset and Plot Options

Below the Plot Area area is the Plot Offset (Origin Set To Printable Area) area, which contains two text boxes and a check box. Place a check mark in the Center The Plot box to center the plot on the printed sheet. If this check box is not selected, by default, AutoCAD will place the lower-left corner (or the origin) of the area you have specified to plot at the lower-left corner (or origin) of the printable area of the current paper size. By changing the settings in the X and Y text boxes, you can move the drawing horizontally or vertically to fit on the page as you wish. When the Center The Plot check box is selected, the X and Y text boxes display any movement from the lower-left corner of the sheet that was necessary to center the drawing.

Just as each drawing has an origin (0,0 point), each plotter creates an origin for the plot. Usually it's in the lower-left or upper-left corner, but not always. When the plot is being made, the printer first locates the origin and starts the print there, moving outward from the origin. If the origin is in the lower-left corner, the print may come out looking like Figure 14.8a. If the origin is the upper-left corner, the print will look like Figure 14.8b.

By using the X and Y settings in the Plot Offset area, you can make one margin wider for a binding. To center your drawing on the page, place a check mark in the Center The Plot box (see Figure 14.8c). If Layouts are set up and being use for printing, they determine this setting, and the Center The Plot check box is unavailable.

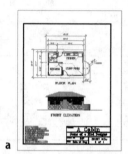 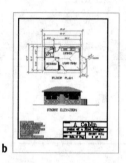 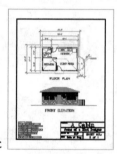

a   b   c

FIGURE 14.8: A print with its origin in the lower-left corner (a), in the upper-left corner (b), and with the drawing centered (c)

  T I P   Usually, 8.5" × 11" format printers are configured to the portrait orientation. If your drawing is also set to that orientation, the origin of the plot will be in the lower-left corner. If your drawing is in the landscape orientation, the plot origin will move to the upper-left corner of the page because the plot has been rotated to fit on the page.

Setting the material to be printed accurately on the page will be a result of trial and error and getting to know your printer. We will return to this topic shortly, when we get ready to print.

The Expanded Plot Dialog Box

If the Plot dialog box hasn't already been expanded, click the right-pointed arrow in the lower-right corner to expand it to include four additional areas. For now, we are concerned only about the one on the bottom.

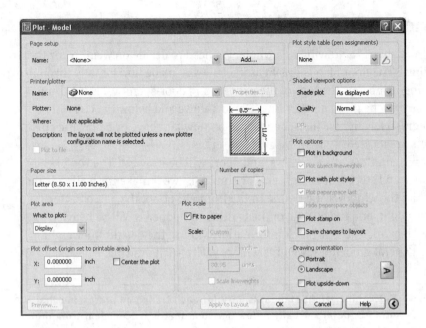

Drawing Orientation   The settings in this area are self-explanatory. The radio buttons serve as a toggle between the portrait and landscape orientation, and the Plot Upside-Down check box serves as an on/off toggle.

Plot Options   This area has six check boxes that don't concern us now.

Shaded Viewport Options   This area has settings to control the plot for renderings and shaded views, which will be covered in the Appendix.

Plot Style Table (Pen Assignments)   Plot styles and pen assignments will be discussed later in this chapter.

We have taken a quick tour of the Plot dialog box, and we still have a drawing, Cabin11a, to print. Let's print it. As we set up the print, refer to this section for explanation of the steps, if necessary.

Printing a Drawing

Our task is to print Cabin11a.dwg at a scale of ⅛" = 1'-0" for an 8.5" × 11"–format inkjet printer. In this exercise, we will use the default system printer, which is set up for an 8.5" × 11"–format laserjet printer. If you have an 8.5" × 11"–format printer, you should be able to follow the steps. If you don't have a printer, you can still get familiar with printing by following along with the steps.

The first step is to assign lineweights to the visible layers.

Determining Lineweights for a Drawing

Look at the Cabin11a drawing as a whole. We need to decide on weights for the various lines. The floor plan is drawn as if a cut were made horizontally through the building just below the tops of the window and door openings. Everything that was cut will be given a heavy line. Objects above and below the cut will be given progressively lighter lines, depending on how far above or below the cut the objects are located.

In this system, the walls, windows, and doors will be heaviest. The roof, headers, fixtures, and steps will be lighter. For emphasis, we'll make the walls a little heavier than the windows and doors. In the front elevation, the hatch pattern will be very light, and the outline of the various components will be heavier, for emphasis. Text and the title block information will use the default lineweight. These are general guidelines; weights will vary with each drawing.

 N O T E Lineweight standards vary for each trade and profession that uses AutoCAD. Details usually follow a system that is independent from the one used by other drawings in the same set. Section lines, hidden lines, center lines, cutting plane lines, break lines, and so on all will be assigned specific lineweights.

We will use four lineweights for this drawing:

Weight	Thickness In Inches
Very light	0.005
Light	0.008
Medium	0.010
Heavy	0.014

In Cabin11a, 15 layers are visible in the drawing as it is currently set up. Their lineweights will be assigned as follows:

Layer	Lineweight
Balcony	Light
Dim1	Very light
Doors	Medium

F-elev	**Medium**
Fixtures	**Light**
Hatch-elev-42	**Very light**
Hatch-elev-black	**Very light**
Hatch-elev-gray	**Very light**
Headers	**Light**
Roof	**Very light**
Steps	**Light**
Tblk1	**Medium**
Text1	**Medium**
Walls	**Heavy**
Windows	**Medium**

When we look at the lineweights currently assigned to these layers, and at the thickness we need these lineweights to be, we can generate a third chart that will show us what lineweight needs to be assigned to each group of layers:

Thickness	Layers
0.005	Dim1, all visible hatch layers, Roof
0.008	Balcony, Fixtures, Headers, Steps
0.010 (default)	Doors, F-elev, Tblk1, Text, Windows
0.014	Walls

Now it's time to assign the lineweights to the layers in the drawings.

1. Click Cancel to close the Plot dialog box. Then click the Layer Properties Manager button on the Object Property toolbar to open the Layer Properties Manager dialog box.

2. Click the Dim1 layer to highlight it. Hold down the Ctrl key and click the three Hatch-elev layers and the Roof layer to select them. Then release the Ctrl key.

3. In the Lineweight column, click one of the highlighted Default words to open the Lineweight dialog box.

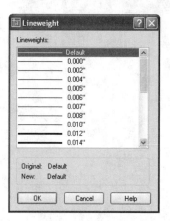

 N O T E   If the lineweights listed in the Lineweight dialog box are in millimeters, cancel to get back to your drawing and type **lw**↵. Then, in the Lineweight Settings dialog box, click the Inches radio button in the Units For Listing area and click OK.

4. Click 0.005". Then click OK. The Lineweight dialog box closes. In the Layer Properties Manager dialog box, the five highlighted layers now have a lineweight of 0.005" assigned to them.

5. Click the Balcony layer near the layer's name.

6. Hold down the Ctrl key and click Fixtures, Headers, and Steps.

7. Click one of the highlighted Default words. The Lineweight dialog box opens.

8. Click 0.008". Then click OK. The newly highlighted layers now have a lineweight of 0.008" assigned to them.

9. You can leave Default as the linetype for the Doors, Windows, and Text1 layers because the thickness they need is the default thickness of 0.010". Click the Walls layer, and use the same procedure to assign it the thickness of 0.014".

10. Click OK to close the Layer Properties Manager dialog box.

11. Type lw↵ to open the Lineweight Settings dialog box.

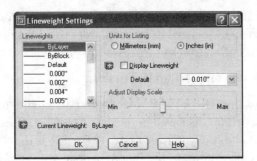

Notice the Default drop-down list on the right, in which 0.010" is displayed. This tells you that the default lineweight thickness is 0.010", which is what we are assuming.

12. Click Cancel to close the dialog box.

The lineweights have been assigned. When the print is complete, you can judge whether these lineweight assignments are acceptable or need to be adjusted. In an office, a lot of time is invested in developing a lineweight standard that can be used in most drawings.

Other Properties of Layers

Two other properties of layers deserve mentioning: Plot and Description. Both are displayed in the Layer List window of the Layer Properties Manager dialog box.

The Plot feature is a two-way toggle that controls whether the objects on a layer are printed. By default, the control is off. When this features is activated for a particular layer, objects on that layer are not printed but remain visible on your screen. You might designate a layer for in-house notes and data that you do not intend to be seen by those who will eventually view your printed drawings, and then set the layer to not be printed.

A column titled Description is at the far right of the Layer List window. Clicking in this column on the blue bar of a highlighted layer opens a text box in which you can enter a description of the layer. Layer names are often in code or use abbreviations that do not fully describe what objects are on that layer. Here's a place to do that.

Setting Up the Other Parameters for the Print

Now that we have set the lineweights, it's time to move to the Plot dialog box and complete the setting changes we need to make in order to print this drawing. We will use the Window option to select what we will print.

1. Click the Plot button on the Standard toolbar.

2. In the Plot dialog box, check the Printer/Plotter area to be sure you have the correct printer displayed in the drop-down list. Check the Paper Size area to be sure you have Letter (8.5 × 11) as the selected paper size. Then move down to the Plot Area area, open the What To Plot drop-down list, and select Window.

3. In the drawing, disable any running Osnaps. To start the window, pick a point outside the border, as close to the lower-left corner of the border as you can without touching it.

4. To complete the window, click a point above and to the right of the border, also as close to the border as you can without touching it. Back in the Plot dialog box, Window will be displayed in the What To Plot drop-down list, and a new Window button is now on the right side of the Plot Area area. Click this button if you need to redo the window after viewing a preview of the plot.

5. If you have not already done so, click the right-pointing arrow in the lower-right corner of the Plot dialog box to display another column of areas. In the Drawing Orientation area in the lower-right corner, be sure Portrait is selected.

6. In the Plot Scale area, uncheck Fit To Paper, open the Scale drop-down list, and select ⅛" = 1'0". Notice that the text boxes below now read 1 and 96, the scale factor for ⅛" scale.

7. In the Plot Offset area, click the Center The Plot check box.

   This completes the setup for the first plot. Before we waste paper, let's preview how it will look as a result of our setup changes.

Previewing a Print

The Preview feature gives you the opportunity to view your drawing exactly as it will print.

1. Click the Preview button. The computer takes a moment to calculate the plot and then displays a full view of your drawing as it will fit on the page (see Figure 14.9).

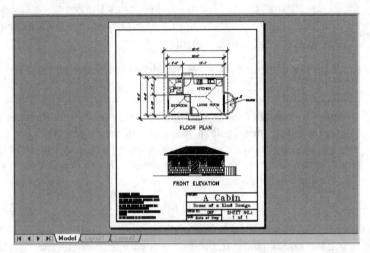

FIGURE 14.9: The preview of Cabin11a, ready to print

2. Right-click and choose Zoom Window from the shortcut menu.

3. Make a window that encloses the bathroom and a couple of the dimensions. You have to left-click and hold down the mouse button, drag open the window, and then release. The new view displays the lineweights you have set up (see Figure 14.10).

FIGURE 14.10: The zoomed-in view of Cabin11a showing the lineweights

4. Right-click and choose Zoom Original from the shortcut menu to return to the first preview view.

5. Right-click again and choose Exit to return to the Plot dialog box. If your print was oriented correctly on the sheet, you are ready to print. If not, recheck the setup steps for errors.

6. At the bottom of the Plot dialog box, click the Apply To Layout button, then click OK. The computer will begin calculating the print and eventually send it to the printer.

7. After the print is done, save this drawing as Cabin14a.

 N O T E   You can change a setting in the Lineweight Settings dialog box to be able to see lineweights in your drawing before you preview a plot, but they are not very accurate unless you are using layouts. When you print from Model Space, you have to preview the drawing in the Plot dialog box to see how the lineweights display.

When your print comes out, it should look like Figure 14.9 (shown earlier). Take a close look at the border. Is the space outside the border equal on the left and right and top and bottom? It should be, if you put a check mark in the Center The Plot box. If not, or if you need to widen one of the margins to make room for a binding, go to the Plot Offset area of the Plot dialog box and uncheck the Center The Plot box. Then change the settings for X and Y.

Just be sure that you don't move the drawing to a point where one of the border lines gets lopped off. It takes a little trial and error. The Preview features will help you. Figure 14.11 illustrates what you will see in the Preview window when you try to print Cabin11a with the landscape orientation.

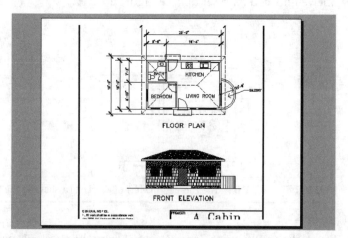

FIGURE 14.11:   Preview of Cabin11a set up to be printed in the wrong orientation

Check the lineweights of the various components on the print. You may have to make adjustments for your particular printer.

Next you'll plot a similar drawing that uses layouts for its border and title block.

Printing a Drawing Using Layouts

As a comparison to the previous exercise, we'll print a drawing that has a layout set up. When a Layout tab has been set up properly and is active, you print at a scale of 1:1. The elements of the drawing on the layout are then printed actual size, and the Model Space portion of the drawing is printed at the scale to which the viewport has been set.

1. Open Cabin13b. Be sure the Layout1 tab is active. Check the status bar to be sure that the Paper/Model button is set to Paper. This drawing is similar to Cabin11a. The only difference in appearance is that this one displays the dashed lines just outside the border, and the sheet is resting on the gray background with a shadowing effect, similar to how a Preview appears (see Figure 14.12). These differences are the result of this drawing having a layout that contains the title block and border, with a viewport through which the model of the cabin is seen. The viewport is on a layer that's been frozen, so you can't see its border. (For a review of layouts and viewports, see Chapter 13.)

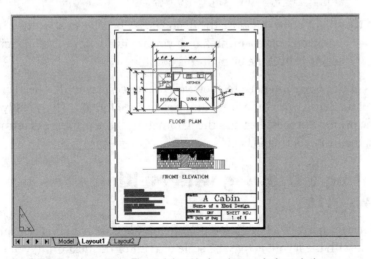

FIGURE 14.12: The Cabin13b drawing ready for printing

The Tblk1 layer in Cabin11a **is replaced in this drawing by the Tblk-L1 layer.**

2. Open the Layer Properties Manager dialog box, and set the lineweights for the layers as you did for Cabin11a. Then click OK.

3. Start the Plot command to open the Plot dialog box. All the parameters you set for the last print will still be in effect (if you actually executed the print), so you have to determine what settings need to be changed to accommodate Paper Space.

4. We are using the same printer, paper size, and orientation as before, so those stay the same.

5. Notice that in the Plot Area area the top radio button is labeled Layout instead of Limits. Layout is also the active button. AutoCAD has sensed that this drawing has layouts set up and made this change automatically.

6. In the Plot Scale area, the scale has been set to 1:1. This is what we want.

7. In the Plot Offset area, the Center The Plot check box is grayed out; it is not needed when using a layout to plot.

8. There are no changes to make. Because Layout1 has been set up for printing when it was created, all the settings in the Plot dialog box are automatically taken care of.

9. In the lower-left corner, select Preview. Your preview should look like Figure 14.9, shown earlier in this chapter.

10. Right-click and close the dialog box. Click OK to start the print. If you don't have a printer, or if you are just following along, click Cancel to cancel the print at this point.

This exercise was intended to show you that once a layout has been created, most of the setup work for printing is already done for you. This greatly simplifies the printing process because the parameters of the print are determined before the Print command begins.

Printing a Drawing with Multiple Viewports

Multiple viewports in a layout don't require any special handling. The print will be made with the layout active at a scale of 1:1. For the next print, you will use a different printer—one that can handle larger sheet sizes. If you don't have access to a large-format printer, you can still configure AutoCAD for one and preview how the print would look. In fact, that's what we did in Chapter 13, in order to set up Layout2, so this task is already completed.

Printing with a Large-Format Printer

The procedure here varies little from the one you just followed to print Layout1.

1. Save the current drawing to your training folder as Cabin14b, but don't close it yet.

2. This drawing has two Layout tabs. We just printed Layout1. Layout2 consists of an 11" × 17" drawing in landscape orientation. You'll print this one, so be sure Layout2 is active (see Figure 14.13).

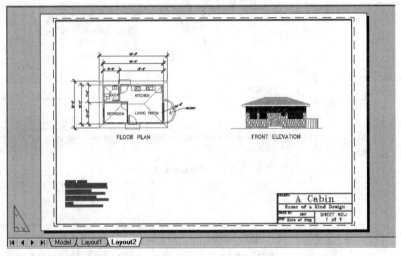

FIGURE 14.13: Cabin13b with the Layout2 tab active

3. Check the Layer Properties Manager dialog box to see that the lineweight assignments you made for Layout1 are still there.

4. Click the Plot button on the Standard toolbar to start the Plot command.

5. In the Plot dialog box, look in the Printer/Plotter and Paper Size areas. The plot device is now listed as DWF6 ePlot.pc3 or that of your own large-format plotter. Also, the paper size has been set for 11 × 17. This was all done when you set up Layout2 in the previous chapter.

6. Note the orientation of the drawing. It's now landscape.

7. In the rest of the dialog box, the settings are the same as they were for Layout1. There are no changes to be made. Again, by setting up a layout, all parameters for printing are done in advance.

8. Click the Preview button. The preview looks fine (see Figure 14.14).

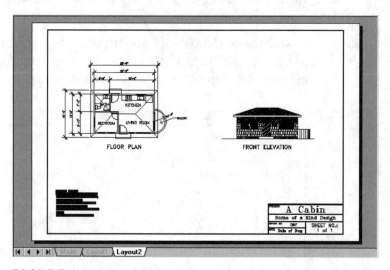

FIGURE 14.14: Preview of the Layout2 tab

N O T E   The DWF6 ePlot.pc3 printer that we have been using for a large-format plotter is set up to plot to a file that can later be posted on a website. If you tell AutoCAD to plot when this is the selected printer, AutoCAD displays a Select File Type dialog box called Browse For Plot File to specify the location and name of the new web plot file (.dwf extension).

9. Right-click and choose Exit from the shortcut menu to cancel the preview. If you have a large-format printer configured and can plot this drawing on an 11" × 17" sheet, click OK to start the print. Otherwise, click Cancel.

10. Resave this drawing as Cabin14b.

For the last exercise in this chapter, you will set up a print for Site13, using the large-format printer.

Printing the Site Plan

The site plan was also set up with a layout and based on a 30" × 42" sheet in landscape orientation. As in the last two prints, we shouldn't have to do much to print this drawing. Follow along even if you can't make the print.

1. Open Site13. The Layout1 tab should be active. If it's not, click it to activate it.

2. Type lw↵. In the Lineweight Settings dialog box, put a check mark in the Display Lineweight box and click OK.

3. Open the Layer Properties Manager dialog box and assign to the Prop_line layer a lineweight of 0.055. Click OK to close the dialog box. Click OK again.

4. While in Paper Space, zoom in to a view of the place where the driveway meets the property line. Include the top borderline in the view to see the contrast in lineweights (see Figure 14.15). The borderline has a thickness because it is a polyline assigned a width of ⅟₁₆", or 0.0625.

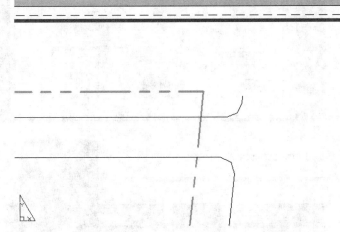

FIGURE 14.15: Zooming in to check the lineweights

5. Zoom Previous, and then start the Plot command to open the Plot dialog box. There are no changes that need to be made.

6. Click Preview. You see how the print sits on the sheet. We want the margins to be the same on the top and bottom, and we want the right

margin to be as small as possible so that there is extra room on the left side for the binding strip.

7. Right-click and choose Exit from the shortcut menu to return to the Plot dialog box. In the Plot Offset area, change the X setting from 0.00 to 0.15.

8. Click Preview again. The drawing is positioned fairly well, but the right margin may be partially lopped off (see Figure 14.16a).

9. Right-click, choose Zoom Window, and then click and drag a Zoom window around the lower-right corner of the border (see Figure 14.16b). The right border has been partially cut off. We'll have to readjust the X value in the Plot Offset area.

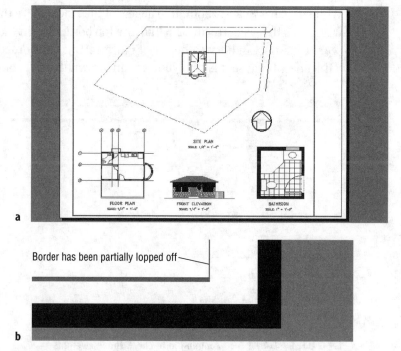

FIGURE 14.16: The plot preview after adjusting the X value in the Plot Offset area (a) and zooming in to check the border (b)

10. Right-click again and choose Exit. Change the X setting to 0.09. Click Preview again. Right-click and choose Zoom Window again. Zoom in to the corner and confirm that the border is now OK. Right-click and choose Zoom Original to return to the preview (see Figure 14.17).

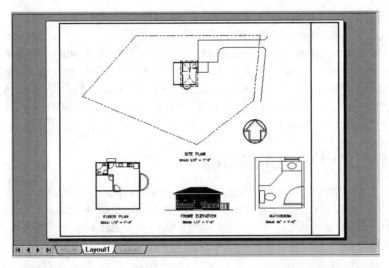

FIGURE 14.17: Preview of the site plot after readjusting the X value to 0.09

11. Feel free to make minor adjustments to the Origin settings. You could also use the Stretch command to move the left side of the border to the right in order to gain a little more space for the binding. Because the border so closely fits the printable area, we could move the drawing on the sheet only a little more than ⅛" without lopping off the right side, so the results are barely noticeable. Normally you make these adjustments when you set up the layout.

12. When you are finished making adjustments, return to the Plot dialog box. Click OK to start the print, or click Cancel to cancel it.

13. Save this drawing as Site14a.

The last section in this chapter will consist of a discussion on a more advanced feature of plotting—plot styles.

A Few Words About Plot Styles

So far in this chapter, we have assigned lineweights to layers. We have assumed that any printer was monochromatic and was converting all colors in the Auto-CAD drawing to black. Laserjet printers usually are monochromatic, but they may print the lighter colors in your drawing as screened. If you have access to a large-format inkjet plotter, you may have the option to print in monochrome or color. And you may have objects in your drawing that are one color, but you want them printed in another color. Plot styles offer a means to handle these kinds of situations. You don't have to use plot styles in AutoCAD, but you may need to work on a drawing that uses them. We'll finish this chapter with a tour of the various dialog boxes and procedures for setting up and assigning plot styles.

Plot Style Table Files

A *plot style* is a group of settings that is assigned to a layer, a color, or an object. It determines how that layer, color, or object is printed. Plot styles are grouped into plot style tables that are saved as files on your hard drive. There are two kinds of plot styles:

- ▶ Color-dependent, which are assigned to colors in your drawing
- ▶ Named, which are assigned to layers or objects

Leave AutoCAD for a moment, and use Windows Explorer to navigate to the following folder: `C:\Documents and Settings\`*your name*`\Application Data\Autodesk\AutoCAD 2005\R16.0\enu\Plot Styles`. Open the subfolder called `Plot Styles`. Figure 14.18 shows the contents of the `Plot Styles` folder. Thirteen plot style table files are already set up. Nine of them are color-dependent Plot Style Table files, with the extension `.ctb`, and four are named Plot Style Table files, with the extension `.stb` and called AutoCAD Plot Style Table File. (You may not be able to see the `.ctb` and `.stb` extensions.) Finally, there is the shortcut to the Add-A-Plot Style Table Wizard, which you use to set up custom plot style tables. Close Windows Explorer and return to AutoCAD.

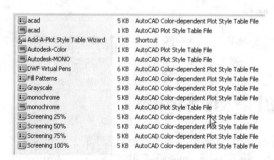

FIGURE 14.18: The contents of the `Plot Styles` folder

How Plot Style Table Files Are Organized

Plot style table files are assigned to a drawing and contain all the plot styles needed to control how that drawing is printed. Color-dependent plot styles control printing parameters through color, so there are 255 of them in each color-dependent plot style table, one for each color. Named plot style tables, on the other hand, have only as many plot styles as are necessary, possibly only two or three. Let's look at a plot style table and see how it's organized.

1. In AutoCAD, choose File ➤ Plot Style Manager to open the Plot Styles dialog box. It is much like the Windows Explorer view of AutoCAD's Plot Styles subfolder. In fact, it is another view of the same folder. Your view may have large icons and may not display all the details.

2. Double-click the first acad file in the list. It's the one that says Auto-CAD Color-dependent Plot Style Table File in the right column of Figure 14.18. This opens the Plot Style Table Editor dialog box with acad.ctb in its title bar (see Figure 14.19). This dialog box has three tabs. The General tab displays information and a Description text box for input.

FIGURE 14.19: The General tab of the Plot Style Table Editor dialog box for the acad.ctb file

3. Click the Table View tab (see Figure 14.20). Now you see the actual plot styles across the top and the plot style properties listed down the left side. This tab organizes the information like a spreadsheet. Use the scroll bar to assure yourself that there are 255 plot styles here. Notice that there are 12 properties for each plot style. This tab displays the plot style information in a way that gives you an overview of the table as a whole.

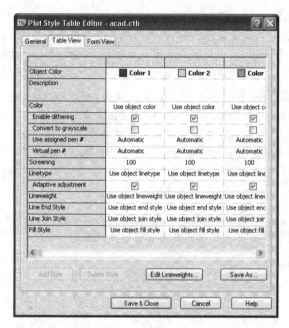

FIGURE 14.20: The Table View tab of the Plot Style Table Editor dialog box for the acad.ctb file

4. Click the Form View tab (see Figure 14.21). The same information is organized in a slightly different way. Here the plot styles are listed in the box on the left. You can highlight one or more plot styles at a time. The properties of the highlighted styles are shown on the right. This view is set up to modify the properties of chosen plot styles. Notice that the first property, Color, has Use Object Color assigned for all plot styles.

5. Close this plot style table and open the color-dependent monochrome file. Click the Table View tab. Now look at the Color property. All plot styles have the color Black assigned (see Figure 14.22).

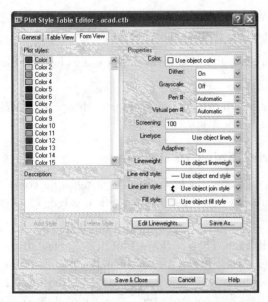

FIGURE 14.21: The Form View tab of the Plot Style Table Editor dialog box for the acad.ctb file

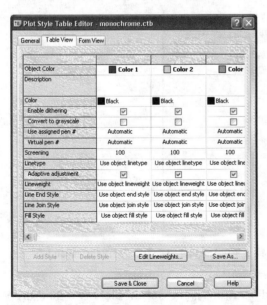

FIGURE 14.22: The Table View tab of the Plot Style Table Editor dialog box for the monochrome.ctb file

6. Close that plot style table file and open acad.stb and monochrome.stb to see how few plot styles they contain. (If you don't see the .stb extension

on the filenames, these files have a listing of AutoCAD Plot Style Table File in the column on the right in Figure 14.18, shown earlier.)

7. Close the Plot Style Table Editor dialog box and close the Plot Styles dialog box.

The monochrome.ctb file will print all colors in your drawing as black, but won't change them in the AutoCAD file.

Assigning Plot Style Tables to Drawings

Each drawing can be assigned only one kind of plot style table file: color-dependent or named. This is determined when the drawing is first created.

1. Choose Tools ➤ Options to open the Options dialog box and click the Plot And Publish tab. Then click the Plot Style Table Settings button that's near the lower-right corner of the dialog box. This opens the Plot Style Table Settings dialog box. In the uppermost area are the two radio buttons that control which type of plot style a drawing will accept, color-dependent or named (see Figure 14.23). New drawings will accept only the type of plot style that is selected here.

FIGURE 14.23: The Plot Style Table Settings dialog box

2. Below the radio buttons is the Default Plot Style Table drop-down list. Here you can select a plot style table file (of the type that is selected by the radio buttons) to be automatically assigned to new drawings. One of the options is None.

3. Close the Plot Style Table Settings dialog box.

N O T E Even though the type of plot style for a new drawing is fixed in the Plot Style Table Settings dialog box, two utility commands let you switch the type of plot style that a drawing can have and assign a different one. They are the Convertpstyles and the Convertctb commands.

Throughout this book, all the drawings that you created (or downloaded) were set up to use color-dependent plot styles, so we can assign this type of plot style to the drawing. Usually this is done by assigning a particular plot style to a layout or to Model Space. To finish our tour, and this chapter, we'll assign one of the available plot style table files to the Cabin14b drawing and use the Preview option to see the results.

1. Make Cabin14b the current drawing, if it isn't already.

2. Click Layout1 to make it current, if it isn't already.

3. Start the Plot command, and make sure that the extension of the dialog box at the right is open. If it's not, click the right-pointing arrow in the lower-right corner to open it. In the upper-right corner, make sure None is displayed in the Plot Style Table drop-down list, and then click the Preview button. AutoCAD displays the preview in the same colors used in the drawing (see Figure 14.24).

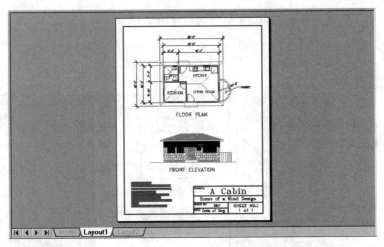

FIGURE 14.24: Preview of Layout1 without a plot style table assigned to it

4. Exit the Preview display, and then click the Cancel button to cancel the plot.

5. Right-click the Layout1 tab, and choose Page Setup Manager. In the Page Setup Manager dialog box, highlight Cabin11a-L1 in the Page Setups list and click Modify. This opens the Page Setup dialog box.

6. Notice that in the Plot Style Table (Pen Assignments) area, None is selected. No plot style table file has been assigned to this layout.

7. Open the drop-down list.

All the available .ctb (color-dependent plot style table) files are listed. You can choose one or click New at the bottom of the list and create your own. Once one is chosen, you can click the Edit button to modify it and make a new plot style out of it.

8. Select monochrome.ctb, and then click OK.

9. Click Preview in the lower-left corner. All lines and filled areas in the drawing are solid black (see Figure 14.25).

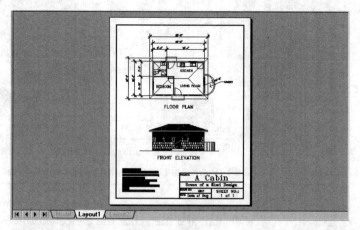

FIGURE 14.25: Preview with the monochrome.ctb plot style table assigned to Layout1

10. Exit Preview.

11. Repeat steps 5 through 10 and select a different .ctb file from the Plot Style Table drop-down list. (I recommend trying Screening 50%.ctb.) When you get back to the preview, you will see the difference.

12. Exit the Plot dialog box and close the drawing without saving any changes.

This has been a quick tour of and introduction to the Plot Style feature that helps control how your drawing will plot. Getting consistently good output from your AutoCAD drawings involves an investment of time by you or the office CAD Manager/IT (Information Technologist) to set up the best configuration of your printers and AutoCAD. As you have seen, layouts provide a good tool for setting up plots, once the configuration is right.

The Appendix that follows contains tutorials and discussion about drawing in 3D (for AutoCAD users only). You will also find a glossary of terms related to AutoCAD, AutoCAD LT, building construction, and design that have been mentioned in the book. The Sybex website (www.sybex.com) offers the following downloads related to this book:

▶ A collection of all AutoCAD drawing files and adjunct files that are used or generated by the reader through the course of this book. Advanced readers can download these files and begin reading anywhere in the book.

▶ A bonus chapter that presents a survey of the various features of AutoCAD that will facilitate your use of the Internet with AutoCAD.

▶ A bonus Appendix that serves as an introduction to the AutoCAD attribute feature. This includes instructions on extracting attribute data from an AutoCAD drawing, calculating areas of rooms or closed spaces in your drawing, and an exercise in setting up a title block using attributes.

I hope that you have found the book useful in learning AutoCAD 2005 and AutoCAD LT 2005. Good luck in your future with AutoCAD. Please contact Sybex with any questions that arise while you work your way through the book (www.sybex.com).

Are You Experienced?

Now you can...

☑ **set up a drawing to be printed**

☑ **assign lineweights to layers in your drawing**

☑ **select the area of your drawing to print**

☑ **choose a sheet size to print your drawing on**

☑ **control the orientation and origin of the print**

☑ **set the scale of the print**

☑ **preview a print**

☑ **print a layout**

☑ **navigate through the Plot Style features**

A Look at Drawing in 3D

Because AutoCAD LT does not have any capacity to draw in three dimensions, this entire appendix does not apply to users of that program.

ACAD ONLY

Nothing in CAD is quite so fascinating as drawing in 3D. Compared with a traditional 3D rendering of a building on a drafting board that uses vanishing points and projection planes, a true 3D computerized model of a building that can be rotated and viewed from any angle, as well as from the inside, is a world of difference. Many architectural firms still use the drafting board to create 3D presentation drawings, even though they use AutoCAD for their construction drawings. But more and more of them are using AutoCAD's 3D features to create either perspective drawings or simple 3D models that are then traced over by hand in the process of creating the final presentation drawing. So it's useful to acquire some skills in working in 3D. It's also a lot of fun.

Constructing a 3D model of a building requires many of the tools that you have been using throughout this book and some new ones that you will be introduced to in this appendix. Your competence in using the basic drawing, editing, and display commands is critical to your successful study of 3D for two reasons. First, drawing in 3D is more complex and difficult than drawing in 2D, and it can be frustrating. If you aren't familiar with the basic commands, you will become that much more frustrated. Second, accuracy is critical in 3D drawing. The effect of errors is compounded, so you must be in the habit of using tools, such as the Osnap modes, to maximize your precision.

Don't be discouraged; just be warned. Drawing in 3D is a fascinating and enjoyable process, and the results you get can be astounding. I sincerely encourage you to make the effort to learn some of the basic 3D skills presented here.

Many 3D software packages are on the market today, and some are better for drawing buildings than others. Many times, because of the precision that AutoCAD provides, a 3D .dwg file will be exported to one of these specialized 3D packages for further work, after being laid out in AutoCAD. Other drawings will be created in 2D, converted to 3D, and then refined into a shaded, colored, and textured rendering with specific lights and shadows. In this appendix, we will look at the basic techniques of *solid modeling* and touch on a couple of tools used in *surface modeling*. In the process, you will learn some techniques for viewing a 3D model. At the end of the appendix, we will introduce the processes of setting up and rendering a 3D model.

3D Modeling

We will begin by building a 3D model of the cabin, using several techniques for creating 3D *solids* and *surfaces*. When using solid modeling tools, the objects you create are solid, like lumps of clay. They can be added together or subtracted from one another to form more complex shapes. By contrast, 3D surfaces are a composite of two-dimensional planes that stretch over a frame of lines the way a tent surface stretches over the frame inside.

As you construct these 3D objects, you will get more familiar with the User Coordinate System, learn how it is used with 3D, and begin using the basic methods of viewing a 3D model.

Viewing a Drawing in 3D

Let's start with Cabin07b. This version of the cabin has all the basic components of the floor plan on their respective layers, with no hatch patterns and no front elevation or title block. If you haven't been following through the whole book and saving your work progressively, you can download this file from Sybex's website, www.sybex.com. You can still follow along if you have another floor plan to use for the exercise that isn't too much more complex than that of the cabin.

1. Open Cabin07b. When the floor plan displays, make the Walls layer current and turn off all other layers. Your drawing will look like Figure A.1. Try to start thinking of it in three dimensions. The entire drawing is on a flat plane parallel to the monitor screen. When you add elements in the third dimension, they will project straight out of the screen toward you if they have a positive dimension, and straight through the screen if they have a negative dimension. The line of direction is perpendicular to the plane of the screen and is called the z-axis. You are familiar with the x- and y-axes, which run left and right and up and down, respectively. Think of the z-axis for a moment as running in and out of the screen.

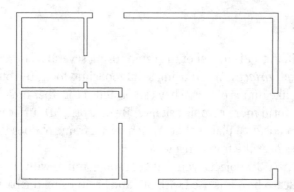

FIGURE A.1: Cabin07b with all layers turned off except Walls

2. If the User Coordinate System icon is not visible on your screen, choose View ➤ Display ➤ UCS Icon ➤ On to place a check mark next to On. The UCS icon appears again. We turned it off in Chapter 5 and then used it in Chapter 8, to help construct some of the elevations, and we'll be using it again in a moment. For now, just keep an eye on it as the drawing changes. Remember that the icon's arrows indicate the positive direction for the x-, y-, and—in 3D—z-axes.

3. Now you'll change the view from a plan view of the drawing—looking straight down at it—to one in which you are looking down at it from an angle. Choose View ➤ 3D Views ➤ SW Isometric. (SW means from the southwest.) The view changes to look like Figure A.2. Notice how the UCS icon has changed with the change of view. The X and Y arrows still run parallel to the left side and bottom of the cabin, but the icon and the floor plan are now at an angle to the screen. And the z-axis is visible.

4. Zoom out and pan down to give yourself some room to put the walls in 3D.

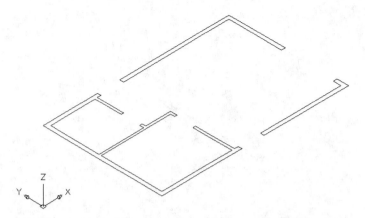

FIGURE A.2: The walls as seen from the SW Isometric view

Making the Walls

The main task ahead is to create what is called a *3D model* of the cabin. We will be using solid elements for the cabin's walls, doors, windows, floor, and steps. You will learn several ways of viewing your work as you progress. To make the walls, we'll start with a solid box and then, like a sculptor, remove from the box everything that is not an interior or exterior wall. The elements to be removed will be the spaces of the rooms and the openings for the doors and windows.

1. Set the Endpoint Osnap to be running, and be sure Polar and Ortho are turned off. Create a new layer called 3D-Walls, assign it color 22, and make it current.

2. Choose Draw ➢ Solids ➢ Box. Click the lowest corner of the walls, and then click the uppermost corner. At the `Specify height:` prompt, type 9'↵. A box is drawn over the entire floor plan, and Auto-CAD displays it as a *wireframe* (see Figure A.3a). Wireframes are 3D drawings in which the lines represent the intersection of walls or other planes. What you are viewing is actually a solid block, a fact that will become apparent as we move along.

   > ◀
   >
   > For the various heights of the windows, doors, roof, and so on, see Figure 8.1 in Chapter 8.

3. Restart the Box command and repeat step 2 to make another 9'-high box in the living room. Pick the inside corner to the left of the front door and the inside corner where the refrigerator stands (see Figure A.3b).

4. Repeat step 2 again and create a third box in the remaining part of the living room that wasn't included in the second box (see Figure A.3c).

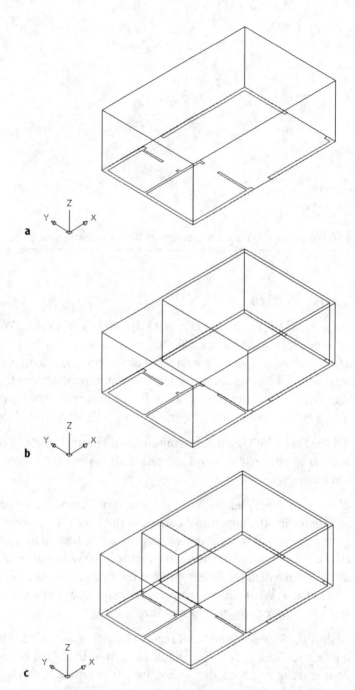

F I G U R E   A . 3 : The first box covers the floor plan (a), a box fills most of the living room (b), and a third box fills the rest of the living room (c).

5. Repeat step 2 twice more to create 9' boxes at the interior corners of the bedroom and bathroom (see Figure A.4).

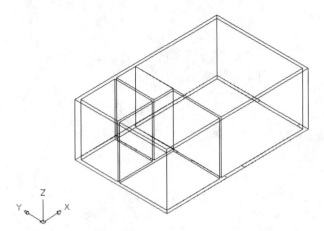

FIGURE A.4: The interior spaces of the cabin are filled with boxes.

Notice that the empty spaces between the boxes' vertical faces are the exterior and interior walls. Because all five boxes are solid, we can subtract the four inside boxes from the larger outside box and be left with the walls.

6. Choose Modify ➤ Solids Editing ➤ Subtract. Pick the large outside box, and then press ↵. Pick the four smaller inside boxes and press ↵. The smaller volumes are subtracted from the larger volume, creating your walls (see Figure A.5a).

7. You need a better view to really see what has happened. Choose View ➤ Hide. Hidden lines are removed, and you can see solid walls (see Figure A.5b). The walls are one object, consisting of the large box after the smaller boxes were subtracted from it.

> When I instruct you to "pick" an object when working in 3D, you need to click on an edge of the object, or on a line that helps define the object.

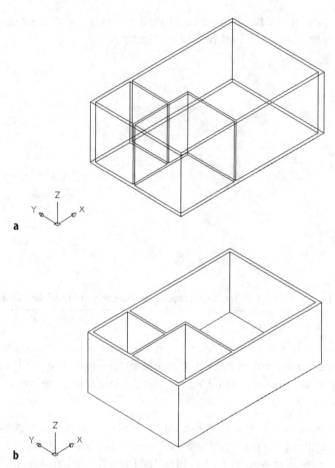

a

b

FIGURE A.5: The solid after subtracting the interior boxes (a) and the view after using the Hide command (b)

8. Choose View ➢ Regen to restore the hidden lines. We'll use a similar procedure to put in the doorway openings.

When you choose View ➢ Regen, AutoCAD recalculates all the geometry of the drawing as if you were just opening it. This process is called a *regeneration*. Choosing View ➢ Redraw merely refreshes the screen.

Cutting Doorway Openings

The five doorway openings vary in width but have the same height. We can make boxes where the openings should be and then subtract them from the wall solid object.

1. Create a new layer called 3D-Doors and make it current. Assign White as this layer's color.

2. Freeze the 3D-Walls layer. Make a zoom window that includes just the five openings in the floor plan of the walls. Be sure Endpoint Osnap is running.

3. Display the Solids toolbar and dock it on the right side of the drawing area, next to the Object Snap toolbar. Click the Box icon to start the Box command.

4. Make a box for the front, bedroom, and balcony door openings. Click opposite corners of each opening, and then enter 7'6⏎ at the Specify height: prompt. Copy the front door box to the back door opening, and copy the bedroom box to the bath opening.

5. Zoom Previous (see Figure A.6a).

6. Thaw the 3D-Walls layer.

7. Choose Modify ➢ Solids Editing ➢ Subtract. Click the wall solid, and then press ⏎.

8. Click the five boxes that are serving as openings, and press ⏎ (see Figure A.6b).

9. Choose View ➢ Hide (see Figure A.6c). The doorway openings have been cut.

10. Choose View ➢ Regen. The window openings can be made in the same way, after a modification to the floor plan.

> ◄
>
> **You can also start the Box command by choosing Draw ➢ Solids ➢ Box or by typing box⏎.**

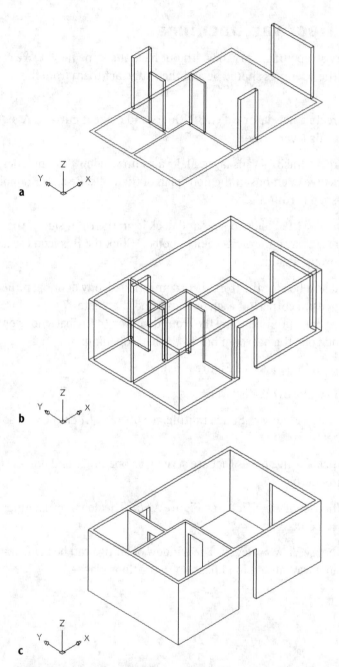

FIGURE A.6: The boxes in all five openings (a), the wall solid after subtracting the boxes (b), and the view after a Hide

Subtracting Window Openings

As you might expect, the window openings will be cut out of the walls just as the doorway openings were. The only difference is that the bottoms of the window openings sit above the 2D floor plan.

1. Create a new layer called 3D-Windows and make it current. Let it take on the default color. Before you leave the Layer Properties Manager dialog box, turn off the Walls layer, turn on the Windows layer, and freeze the 3D-Walls layer. Only window blocks should be visible (see Figure A.7). If the screen doesn't display what is illustrated in the book or what you expect, choose View ➢ Regen.

> When you want to make 2D layers invisible, it doesn't matter whether you freeze them or turn them off. But when working with 3D layers, it is best to freeze them. When they are frozen, they won't interfere with the appearance of a 3D model during a Hide.

F I G U R E A . 7 : The cabin drawing in 3D with only the Windows layer visible

2. Zoom in to a closer view as you did for the doorway openings.

3. Use the Box command to create six box solids that are 3'-6" high at each of the windows except the 2'-wide window in the front wall of the living room, then Zoom Previous (see Figure A.8a). The 2' window in the living room is round and will be dealt with separately.

4. Start the Move command. Select the six boxes, and then press ↵. Click any point on the screen, and then type @0,0,4'↵. The window boxes are moved up 4'.

5. Thaw the 3D-Walls layer and zoom out if necessary. The drawing should look like Figure A.8b.

6. Choose Modify ➢ Solids Editing ➢ Subtract. Click the wall solid, and then press ↵.

7. Pick the six window boxes, and then press ↵. The window openings are cut out of the walls. After hiding, the drawing looks like Figure A.8c.

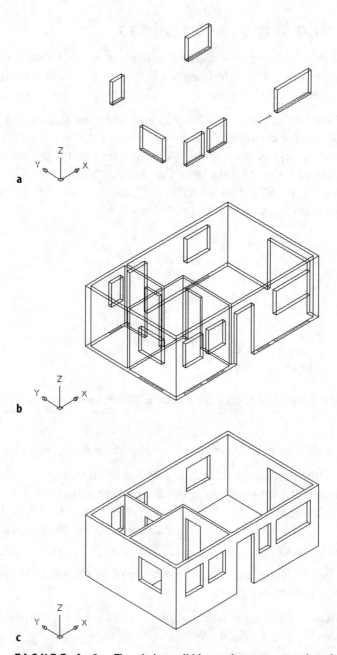

FIGURE A.8: The window solid boxes that were created on the floor plan (a), the wall solid and the window boxes after being raised (b), and the view after a Hide (c)

Now we need to create a circular window opening for the front wall. We'll use a second basic solid shape, or *primitive*, to cut this circular hole. AutoCAD has six primitive shapes that are solids. When you choose Draw ➤ Solids, the top of the cascading menu displays them.

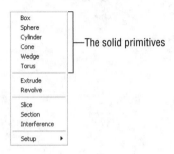

On the Solids toolbar, the primitives have icons that illustrate their basic shapes.

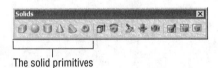

The solid primitives

So far, we've used only the box. For the circular window, we'll use the cylinder.

1. Zoom in close to a view of the front wall, as shown in Figure A.9a. We will need to change the UCS icon to make the cylinder.

2. Type ucs↵ x↵ –90. The UCS icon rotates such that the plane defined by the x- and y-axes is parallel to the front wall and the z-axis points away from you (and is therefore dashed) (see Figure A9.b).

3. Click the Cylinder icon on the Solids toolbar. Then follow the prompts in the Command window.

4. Use Insertion Osnap to locate the center point for the base of the cylinder at the insertion point of the 2' window.

5. Specify the radius for the base of the cylinder by using Endpoint Osnap and clicking the point where one of the window jamb lines meets the front wall.

6. Specify the height of the cylinder by typing 6↵. The cylinder is placed (see Figure A.9c). It has an abbreviated, almost abstract form.

After a hide, zooming or panning automatically changes the view back to the wireframe.

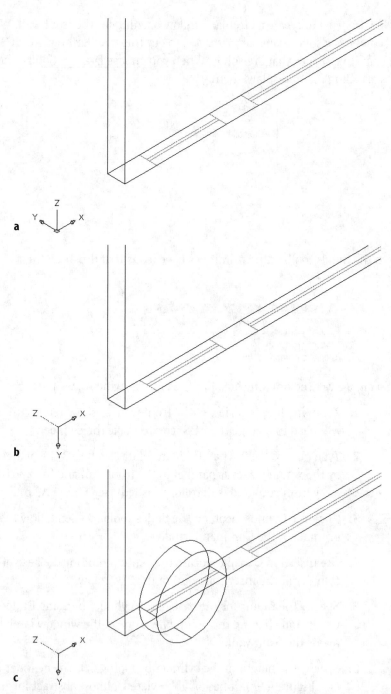

FIGURE A.9: A close view of the 2' window (a), the UCS after reorientation (b), and the cylinder placed in the wall (c)

7. Zoom Previous. Use the Move command, Polar Tracking, and Direct Distance entry to move the cylinder up 6'.

8. Type ucs↵↵ to return the UCS icon to the World Coordinate System orientation.

9. Choose Modify ➤ Solids Editing ➤ Subtract. Click the walls solid, press ↵, click the round window, and press ↵ again.

10. Choose View ➤ Hide. The shell of the cabin walls is complete (see Figure A.10).

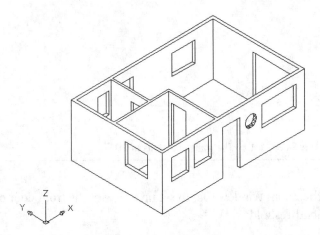

FIGURE A.10: The finished cabin walls solid, after a Hide

You are still looking at one object, the walls solid. Solids that represented doorway and window openings and spaces in rooms have been subtracted from it.

Creating a Floor for the Cabin

In designing our cabin, we didn't draw a floor, but one was implied. The three exterior doorway openings have thresholds that indicate a change in level from the cabin floor down to the steps and the balcony. We'll now use those thresholds to make a 3D solid for the floor.

1. Continuing from the previous set of steps, click the Layer Properties Manager icon on the Object Properties toolbar and do the following:

   ▶ Create a new layer called 3D-Floor, assign it a brownish color, and make it current.

▶ Freeze the 3D-Walls and 3D-Windows layers, and turn off the Windows layers.

▶ Turn on the Walls and Steps layers.

The drawing will look like Figure A.11. If lines are missing, choose View ➢ Regen to regenerate all the lines. We're going to create a series of solid primitives with the Box command that will represent parts of the floor. Then we'll combine them.

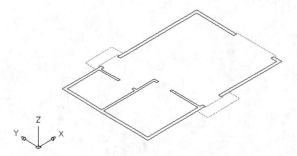

FIGURE A.11: The walls and steps in 2D

2. Use the Zoom Window tool to set up a view of the front door opening and its threshold.

3. Start the Box command and create a box that sits in the opening, between the jamb lines. Give it a height of 2". Then make a second box, also 2" high, that sits on the threshold overhang (see Figure A.12).

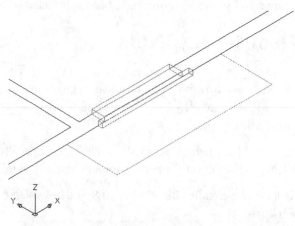

FIGURE A.12: The front door opening with two solid boxes

4. Repeat step 3 for the back door and the sliding glass door openings. Then make similar boxes that fit in the bedroom and bathroom door openings.

5. Finally, make 2"-high boxes for the three rooms, using the inside corners and Endpoint Osnap. There will be two boxes for the living room. You will end up with 12 boxes (see Figure A.13).

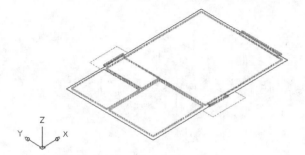

FIGURE A.13: The full floor with 12 solid boxes

6. Turn off the Walls and Steps layers. Choose Modify ➢ Solids Editing ➢ Union, and then use a selection window to select all the boxes. Press ↵. The 12 boxes unite to form a 2"-thick floor solid (see Figure A.14).

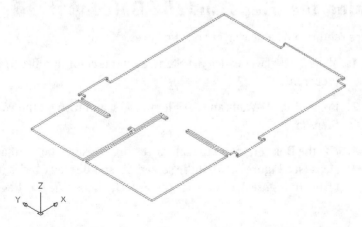

FIGURE A.14: The 12 boxes unite to form a new floor solid object.

7. Start the Move command, select the floor, and press ↵.

8. Click any blank location on the drawing area, and then type @0,0,10↵. The floor will be moved up 10".

9. Thaw the 3D-Walls layer. Choose View ➢ 3D Views ➢ SE Isometric.

10. Choose View ➢ Hide. The drawing should look like Figure A.15.

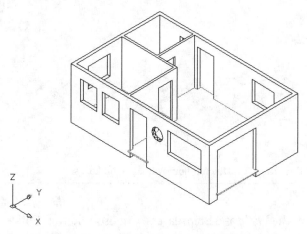

FIGURE A.15: The 3D walls and floor after a Hide

Forming the Steps and the Balcony in 3D

The steps require only a new layer and two boxes.

1. Make a new layer called 3D-Steps, assign it color number 8, and make it current.

2. Freeze the 3D-Walls and 3D-Floor layers, and turn on the Walls and Steps layers.

3. Use the Box command to make a 10"-high box for the front and back steps (see Figure A.16). If the screen doesn't display what is illustrated in Figure A.16 or what you expect, choose View ➢ Regen.

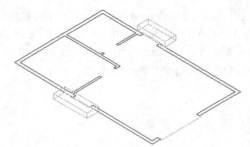

FIGURE A.16: The front and back steps as 3D solids

For the balcony, we'll use the cylinder primitive and the Subtract Solids editing command.

1. Make another new layer called 3D-Balcony, assign it color number 24, and make it current. Zoom in to the area around the balcony, leaving a little extra room for the 3D view. Turn on the Balcony layer.

2. Choose the Cylinder tool to create a cylinder solid to represent the space enclosed by the balcony wall. Use Center Osnap to locate the center at the center point of the arcs that represent the balcony wall. Select a radius of 4'-6" and a height of 3'-2".

3. Move this cylinder up 10" (see Figure A.17a).

4. Draw a second cylinder using the same center point, with a radius of 5' and a height of 4'.

5. Choose Modify ➤ Solids Editing ➤ Subtract. Select the larger cylinder, press ↵, select the smaller cylinder, and press ↵. A shape that looks like a bowl or a hot tub is created (see Figure A.17b).

6. Click the Slice button on the Solids toolbar, select the balcony, and press ↵.

7. At the first prompt, type yz↵. This defines the plane that we'll use to slice the balcony.

8. At the second prompt, pick the bottom corner of the cabin wall, where the bottom of the balcony meets the corner. This positions the yz cutting plane in line with the exterior wall surface that the balcony wall butts against.

9. At the third prompt, click a blank spot below and to the right of the balcony. This tells AutoCAD the side of the cutting plane where the desired objects are. The shape is cut in half, the inside half is deleted, and the balcony is complete (see Figure A.17c).

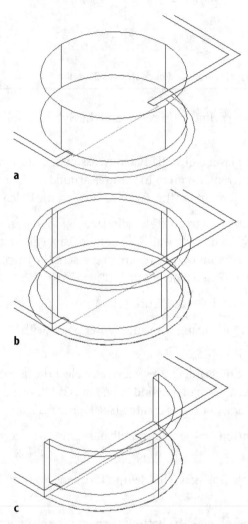

a

b

c

FIGURE A.17: The first cylinder of the balcony (a), the balcony solid after subtraction (b), and the finished balcony after using the Slice tool (c)

10. Zoom Previous, turn off the Balcony, Walls, and Steps layers, and thaw the 3D-Walls and 3D-Floor layers. Then choose View ➢ Hide (see Figure A.18a). Note the series of flat, triangular surfaces that compose the curved surface of the balcony.

11. Choose View ➢ Shade ➢ Gourard Shaded, Edges On. This type of shading blends the shades of two adjacent surfaces that define a curve at their adjoining edges and creates a realistic appearance (see Figure A.18b).

12. Choose View ➢ 3D Orbit. A green circle called an *arcball* is superimposed over your 3D model. There are smaller circles at the quadrant points of the larger circle. This is a viewing tool in which the view of the 3D model is controlled by the movement of the cursor. How the cabin moves in 3D space depends on whether you click and drag inside or outside the big circle or within one of the small circles.

13. Place the cursor inside the circle, and then click and hold down the left mouse button. As you move the cursor, the model turns in space. Release the mouse button to fix a view (see Figure A.18c). Play around with this feature for a bit.

14. When finished, right-click and choose Reset View from the shortcut menu. Choose View ➢ Shade ➢ 2D Wireframe to restore the view to that of the wireframe.

The 3D model is taking shape. To finish it, we will add doors, windows, and the roof.

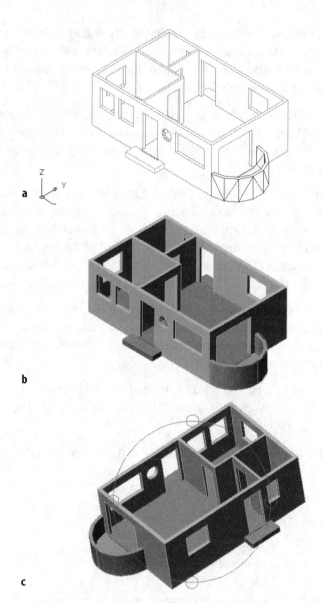

FIGURE A.18: The balcony, walls, and floor after a Hide (a), after using the Shade command (b), and while using 3D Orbit (c)

Finishing the 3D Model

The 3D solids of the swinging doors are constructed with the box primitive that we have been using. There is no need for any step-by-step instructions here. Just follow the same procedure that you did for creating the floor, steps, and balcony. You can use the 3D-Doors layer that you created earlier for the openings, but change its color to No. 34. Construct the swinging doors over the 2D doors on the Door layer, with a height of 6'-5½". Then move them up 12½". Use the Shade command and the 3D Orbit tool to check your work.

The sliding glass door and the windows are similar in construction. They both have a frame and a piece of glass held in the frame. Once we do the sliding glass door, you can apply the same method to the windows. Our strategy will be to create a frame by subtracting a smaller box from a larger one. Refer to Chapter 4 for the dimensions of the opening. The frames are 2" wide and 1½" thick.

1. Set the view to SE Isometric (choose View ➤ 3D Views).

2. Turn on the Doors layer and freeze all 3D layers except 3D-Walls and the current layer, 3D-Doors.

3. Zoom in to the sliding glass door panel that is closest to the corner (see Figure A.19a).

4. Use the Box tool to make a solid box that sits on the outside corners of the door panel frame, with a height of 6'-6".

5. Make a second box that sits inside the frame. To do this, snap to the opposite inside corners of the little rectangles that represent the frame. Give this box a height of 6'-2" (see Figure A.19b).

6. Move the smaller box up 2" (in the positive Z direction).

7. Subtract the smaller box from the larger one.

8. Create a new layer called 3D-Glass, assign it color 151, and make it current.

9. Choose Draw ➤ Surfaces ➤ 3D Face.

Remember: to make 3D layers invisible, freeze them. This ensures that Hides will display properly.

A *3D Face* is a three- or four-sided two-dimensional surface object that turns opaque in a Hide.

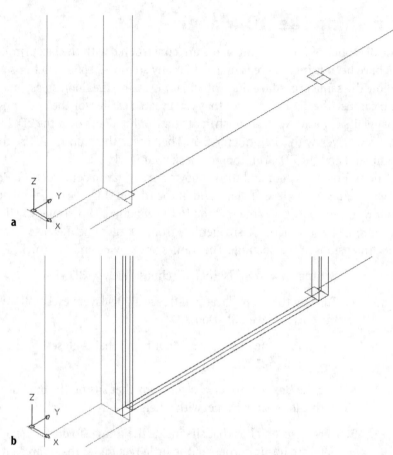

FIGURE A.19: A close view of one sliding glass door panel (a) and two new box solids on the 2D view of the panel (b)

10. Set Midpoint to be the only running Osnap, and then click the midpoints of the lines representing the lower inside corners of the frame (see Figure A.20a).

11. Pan up and pick the midpoints of the upper inside corners of the frame in a circular fashion to complete the 3D face (see Figure A.20b). Press ↵ to end the 3D Face command.

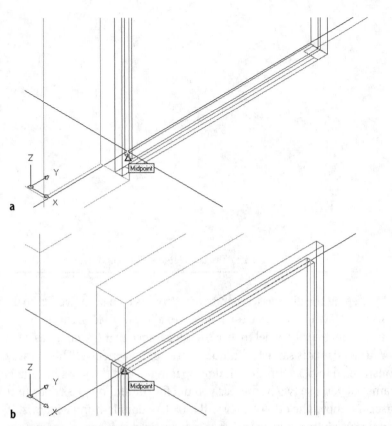

FIGURE A.20: Beginning the 3D face at the bottom of the frame (a) and finishing it at the top of the frame (b)

12. Zoom Previous until you are back at the view of the bottom of the frame. Make Endpoint the only running Osnap, and copy the frame and glass to the other sliding glass door panel.

13. Zoom out to a view of the whole opening, and then move the two doors with their glass up 12".

14. Turn off the Doors layer, and thaw all 3D layers except 3D-Balcony. Use Hide to get a view of the completed sliding glass door in 3D (see Figure A.21).

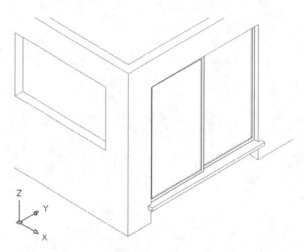

FIGURE A.21: The completed sliding glass door

By keeping the glass as a separate object on its own layer, we can make it invisible while leaving the frame unchanged, to allow us to look through the window. You can move either panel to give the appearance that the door has been slid open.

You can use this same technique to create the windows. The frames can be constructed in place (in the window openings), and the glass installed in the frames. If you use two frames, as you did for the sliding glass door (but in this case, one above the other), they will look like double-hung windows. If only one panel is used, the window will appear to be fixed in place.

Figure A.22 shows a partial view of the cabin. The front living room window is fixed in place, and the bathroom window is double hung. The bathroom window has the addition of a sill at the bottom of the opening.

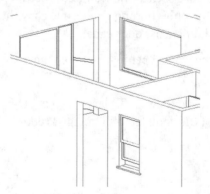

FIGURE A.22: A partial view that shows two windows and the sliding glass door

Putting a Roof on the Cabin

We'll finish the 3D model of the cabin by constructing a roof. The edge of the roof will be a different color than the roof surface, so we'll make them as two separate objects, each on its own layer. The edge will be a solid, and the sloping part will be a set of surfaces.

1. Create two new layers: 3D-Roof_Edge with color 32, and 3D-Roof with color 114. Make 3D-Roof_Edge current.

2. Freeze all 3D layers except the two new ones, and turn off all other layers except Roof. Choose View ➢ 3D Views ➢ SE Isometric. Just the roof will be visible. (If it's not, the Roof layer may be frozen, so thaw it.)

3. Use the Box icon on the Solids toolbar to make a box that is 6" high and sits on the four corners of the roof (see Figure A.23a).

4. Move the box up 9'. Then copy the ridge line and hip lines of the roof up to the top edge of the box.

5. Use Properties to change these copied lines to the 3D-Roof_Edge layer. Then turn off the Roof layer (see Figure A.23b).

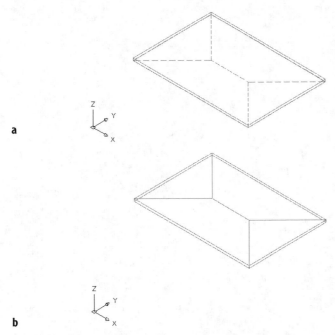

a

b

FIGURE A.23: The solid box is made (a) and the copied roof lines are moved to the 3D-Roof_Edge layer (b).

6. Start the Stretch command (on the Modify toolbar), and use a crossing window to select just the ridge line and the ends of the four hip lines that touch the ridge line.

7. Press ↵. Click a blank part of the drawing area for the base point, and then type @0,0,3'↵. The roof is stretched up 3' (see Figure A.24a).

8. Make the 3D-Roof layer current, and then choose Draw ➤ Surfaces ➤ 3D Face.

9. With Endpoint Osnap, start at the leftmost corner of the sloping planes and pick the four corners of the front plane of the roof. Then, at the `Specify third point or [Invisible] <exit>:` prompt, move to the rightmost corner and click this point twice. Follow the diagram in Figure A.24b. Press ↵ to end the 3D Face command.

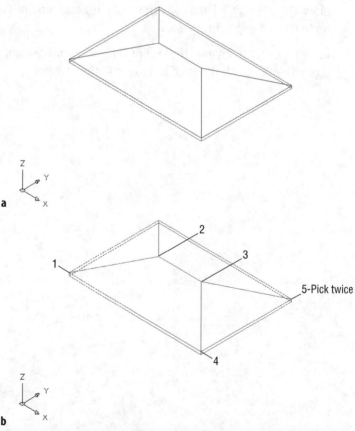

FIGURE A.24: The ridge and hip lines are stretched up (a) and the sequence of picks for the first two 3D Faces (b)

10. Repeat steps 8 and 9 for the back and left surfaces of the roof.

11. Momentarily turn off the 3D-Roof layer, erase the ridge and hip lines, turn the 3D-Roof layer back on again, and thaw all 3D layers except the 3D-Glass layer.

12. Zoom to Extents, and then choose View ➢ Hide to view the cabin (see Figure A.25).

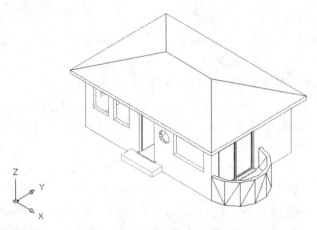

FIGURE A.25: The completed cabin after a Hide

13. Use the Shade options and 3D Orbit to view the model in color and at different angles.

14. Save this file as CabinA1.

Further Directions in 3D

Covering 3D in real depth is beyond the scope of this book, but I can mention a few other tools and features that you might enjoy investigating. First, I'll summarize a few of the solids and surface modeling tools that I didn't cover in the tutorial on the cabin. Then we will take a quick look at the rendering process as it is approached in AutoCAD.

Other Solids Modeling Tools

We used the Box and Cylinder primitive solid tools to build up the model of the cabin. There are four other primitive shapes, all found on the Solids toolbar:

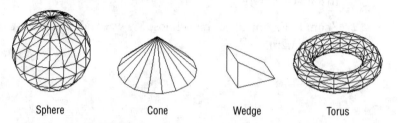

Sphere   Cone   Wedge   Torus

Sphere   You specify the center point and radius or diameter.

Cone   You specify the center point of the base, the radius of the base, and the height of the pointed tip. The base is parallel to the XY plane, and the height is perpendicular to it.

Wedge   It has a rectangular base and a lid that slopes up from one edge of the base. You specify the base as you do in the Box tool and then enter the height.

Torus   This is a donut. You specify a center point for the hole, the radius of the circular path that the donut makes, and the radius of the tube that follows the circular path around the center point.

   Two other tools exist for creating solids by moving 2D shapes in the third dimension:

Extrude   Select a closed 2D shape such as a rectangle or a circle. Then specify a height of the extrusion or a path to extrude along. If the extrusion is straight up, you enter an angle to taper the edges away from the vertical.

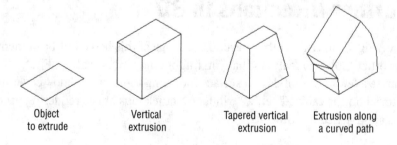

Object
to extrude

Vertical
extrusion

Tapered vertical
extrusion

Extrusion along
a curved path

Revolve   Select a closed 2D shape, and then define the axis and the angle of rotation.

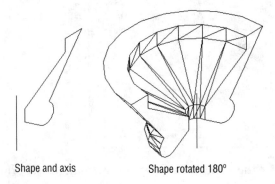

Shape and axis   Shape rotated 180°

There are many tools for modifying solids. When we formed the cabin walls, floor, and balcony, we used Union and Subtract, as well as Slice. Another solids editing tool, Intersect, finds the volume that two solids have in common when they partially occupy the same space. It's at the top of the Modify ➢ Solids Editing menu, with Union and Subtract. Click the solids that are "colliding," and AutoCAD creates a solid from their intersection.

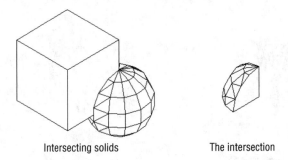

Intersecting solids   The intersection

These are only a few of the many tools for creating and modifying solids, but should be enough to get you started.

Surface Modeling Tools

Surface modeling has its own set of tools, some of which are similar to those for solid modeling. Choose Draw ➢ Surfaces ➢ 3D Surfaces to open the 3D Objects dialog box.

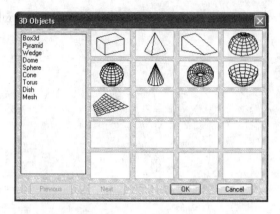

Most of these shapes are the same as, or vary slightly from, the six primitive solid shapes. But 3D Surface objects can't be joined using the Union, Subtract, and Intersection tools. Here is a brief description of a few of the other tools on the Surfaces menu.

In the 3D Objects dialog box, selecting Mesh creates a rectangular three-dimensional surface mesh when you pick four points in 3D space and specify the number of divisions of faces.

When you choose Draw ➤ Surfaces, you have the following choices at the bottom of the submenu:

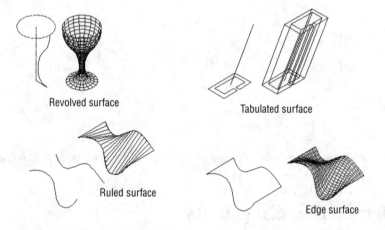

Revolved surface

Tabulated surface

Ruled surface

Edge surface

Revolved Surface   Creates a 3D surface mesh by rotating a 2D curved line around an axis of revolution.

Tabulated Surface Creates a 3D surface mesh by extruding a 2D object in a direction determined by the endpoints of a line, an arc, or a polyline.

Ruled Surface Creates a 3D surface mesh between two selected shapes.

Edge Surface Creates a 3D surface mesh among four lines that are connected at their endpoints. Each line can be in 2D or 3D, and the original shape must be a boundary of a shape that does not cross or conflict with itself.

Most 3D models today use the solid modeling tools for their basic shapes because the tools for adding, subtracting, slicing, and so forth are easy to use and allow complex shapes to be fabricated quickly. Still, surface modeling has its uses, and sometimes a shape will lend itself to surface over solid modeling. Any serious 3D modeler will be familiar with both sets of tools.

Rendering with AutoCAD

The next step after developing a 3D model is to render it. This process has several parts:

- ▶ Setting up a 3D view of the scene to be rendered
- ▶ Creating a lighting scheme
- ▶ Enabling and controlling shadow effects
- ▶ Assigning material textures to surfaces
- ▶ Possibly choosing a background view
- ▶ Putting in auxiliary objects such as people and trees
- ▶ Saving setup views and lights as restorable scenes
- ▶ Outputting a rendering to a file

In this appendix, I'll just give you a quick tour of some of these rendering steps, as we set up a view of the cabin and render it. Developing a full rendering takes time and patience, but touching on a few of the many steps involved will give you a feel for the process. You have put in a lot of time working your way through this book, and you deserve to have a rendered 3D view of your cabin, however simple, to complete the process.

Setting Up a 3D View to Render

We'll create a rectangle to serve as the land the cabin sits on, and then we'll adjust our view.

1. With CabinA1 as the current drawing, type ucs, and then press ↵ twice to return to the World Coordinate System, if you weren't already there.

2. Choose View ➤ 3D Views ➤ Plan View ➤ World UCS to return to a plan view of your drawing. Turn off the UCS icon.

3. Create a new layer called 3D-Land, assign it color 74, and make it current.

4. Zoom out and create a rectangle around the cabin that is 160' wide and 140' high. To be sure the rectangle is created at "ground level," don't snap to any parts of the cabin.

5. Move that rectangle to a position relative to the cabin approximately as shown in Figure A.26. Again, don't snap to any parts of the cabin yet.

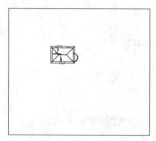

FIGURE A.26: A plan view with the rectangle around the cabin

6. Choose Draw ➤ Region, select the rectangle, and then press ↵. This creates a 2D object called a *region* that behaves like a 3D object. It turns opaque in a Hide, Shade, or Render, and holes can be cut out of it.

7. Choose View ➤ 3D Views ➤ SE Isometric. This is one of the standard 3D views we used to construct the 3D model of the cabin. Now we'll modify it slightly.

8. Choose View ➤ 3D Views ➤ Viewpoint Presets to open the Viewpoint Presets dialog box. Here you can fine-tune the rotation of the view in

the XY plane and the angle of the view relative to the XY plane. The rotation is all right, but we will make the angle flatter.

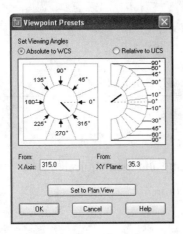

9. On the right, in the XY Plane text box, change 35.3 to 5, and then click OK.

10. Use a Zoom Window to bring the cabin in closer, as shown in Figure A.27.

FIGURE A.27: A close view of the cabin after zooming in

A standard isometric view uses an angle relative to the XY plane of 35.3°.

11. Pan the view down so only the back lines of the rectangular region are visible.

12. Be sure all 3D layers are thawed and turned on.

13. Select View ➢ 3D Orbit. Right-click in the drawing area, and choose Projection ➢ Perspective. Exit 3D Orbit. This completes the view setup for the render (see Figure A.28).

FIGURE A.28: The view ready to be rendered

Creating a Light Source

Here are AutoCAD's three kinds of lighting and their equivalents:

► Point Light, a hanging light bulb

► Distant Light, the sun

► Spotlight, a floodlight

Each has unique setup parameters. We'll set up a Distant light, which will light the cabin as the sun would. To do this, we have to march through a series of dialog boxes.

 1. Display the Render toolbar and let it float in the drawing area. On this new toolbar, click the Lights button to open the Lights dialog box (see Figure A.29).

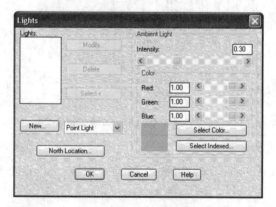

FIGURE A.29: The Lights dialog box

2. On the left side, next to the New button, open the drop-down list and select Distant Light. Then click the New button to open the New Distant Light dialog box (see Figure A.30).

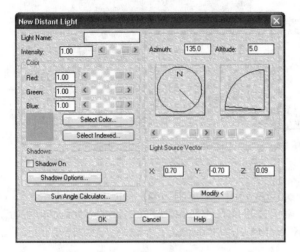

FIGURE A.30: The New Distant Light dialog box

3. Enter Sunlight for the Light Name, and then click the Sun Angle Calculator button to open the Sun Angle Calculator dialog box (see Figure A.31).

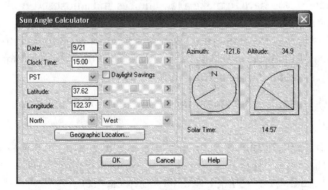

FIGURE A.31: The Sun Angle Calculator dialog box

4. Change the date to 9/8 and the time to 11:00, and then click the Geographic Location button to open the Geographic Location dialog box (see Figure A.32).

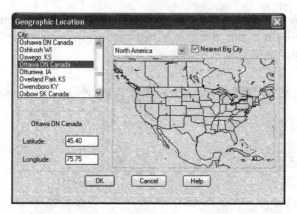

FIGURE A.32: The Geographic Location dialog box

5. In the drop-down list above the map, select North America. Then scroll down the list of cities on the left, and select San Francisco, CA. Click OK to close this dialog box.

6. Click OK twice more to get back to the Lights dialog box (see Figure A.29, shown earlier). In the Ambient Light area, change the intensity from .30 to .50. You can change the Intensity setting by using the scroll bar or by typing it. Then click OK to return to your drawing.

Enabling Shadows

To control shadows, you have to make a few choices and adjust several settings. Shadows can be soft- or hard-edged, and you can calculate them using a couple of methods. This part of the rendering process is too technical to go into in this book, but you can follow along and end up with at least one setup for shadows that will enhance the rendering of the cabin.

1. Click the Lights button on the Rendering toolbar to bring back the Lights dialog box.

2. With Sunlight highlighted, click the Modify button to open the Modify Distant Light dialog box. It's almost identical to the New Distant Light dialog box in Figure A.30 (shown earlier).

3. In the Shadows area, put a check mark in the Shadow On box. Then click the Shadow Options button to open the Shadow Options dialog box (see Figure A.33).

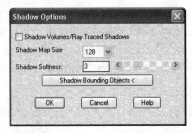

FIGURE A.33: The Shadow Options dialog box

4. Put a check mark in the Shadow Volumes/Ray Traced Shadows box, and then click OK. This will give the shadows harder edges.

5. Click OK to return to the Lights dialog box. Then click OK again to return to the drawing. When we start to render, we will have a few more changes to make for the shadows.

The First Render

Let's make the adjustments for shadows and then make a preliminary render. We'll then add a background and try again. First, we need to check our layers to be sure they are colors that render well. The following is a list of the 3D layers and the colors that I have found work well with a white background in the drawing area for the rendering that we are setting up here.

Layer	Color
3D-Balcony	24
3D-Doors	34
3D-Floor	42
3D-Glass	132
3D-Land	76
3D-Roof	250
3D-Roof-Edge	32
3D-Steps	8
3D-Walls	40
3D-Windows	22

These colors don't all match the colors that I instructed you to assign to these layers as we were building the 3D model earlier in this appendix. You can save the current assignments by using the Save Layer States Manager button in the Layer Properties Manager dialog box. Then, for the rendering, change the colors to match the table.

 1. Click the Render button on the Render toolbar to open the Render dialog box (see Figure A.34).

FIGURE A.34: The Render dialog box

2. At the top, be sure the Rendering Type drop-down list displays Photo Raytrace.

3. In the Rendering Options area, put a check mark in the Shadows box.

4. Click the Render button. After a few moments, the rendering appears (see Figure A.35).

The building looks fine, but it would be nice to have something in the background other than the blank screen.

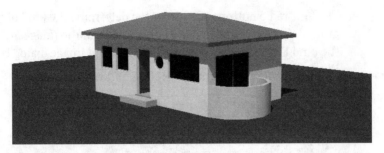

FIGURE A.35: The preliminary render

Controlling the Background of the Rendering

The following are some of the options in choosing a background for the rendering:

The AutoCAD Background   This is what we used for the preliminary rendering.

Another Solid Color   You use slide bars to choose it.

A Gradient   You can use varying colors (usually light to dark) blended together.

An Image   You can supply or choose a bitmap image.

We'll choose the last option and use a file that is supplied with AutoCAD.

1. Click the Background button on the Render toolbar to open the Background dialog box (see Figure A.36).

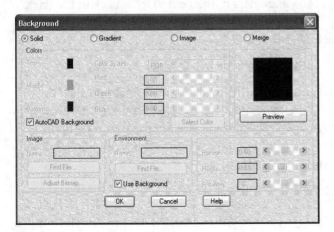

FIGURE A.36: The Background dialog box

2. The four radio buttons across the top determine the kind of background. Click the Image radio button; then in the Image area, click the Find File button to open the Background Image dialog box (see Figure A.37). It's a Select File type of dialog box.

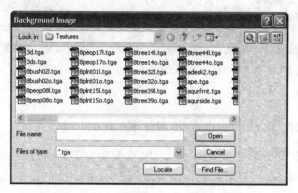

FIGURE A.37:   The Background Image dialog box

3. Navigate to the Textures subfolder. Here is the path if you need it: C:\Documents and Settings*your name*\Local Settings\Application Data\Autodesk\AutoCAD 2005\R 16.0\enu\Textures. Open the Files Of Type drop-down list and select the *.tga type. Quite a few .tga files are listed.

4. Find valley_1.tga and select it, then click Open. Back in the Background dialog box, the file and its path will be displayed in the Name text box in the Image area.

5. Click OK to close the Background dialog box.

6. Click the Render button on the Render toolbar, and then click the Render button in the Render dialog box. Your rendering now has a photographic scene as a background (see Figure A.38). The lighting on the cabin is slightly different from that in the photograph, but the overall effect works well enough.

Now you need to save this view and this rendering.

FIGURE A.38: The complete rendered scene

Saving a Rendering Setup

You need to save two things in order to re-create this rendering at a later time: the view that was set, and the light or lights that were used for the rendering. First, we'll save the view, and then we'll save the view and distant light as a *scene*.

1. Choose View ➢ Named Views to open the Views dialog box.

2. Click the New button. In the New View dialog box, enter **Render1** for the view name. Click the Current Display radio button, and then click OK. The view is saved and now displayed in the list of views. Click OK again to close the Views dialog box.

 3. Click the Scenes button on the Render toolbar to open the Scenes dialog box. Click the New button to open the New Scene dialog box. In the left box, views are listed; in the right, the one light we have set up is listed (see Figure A.39).

FIGURE A.39: The New Scene dialog box

4. Enter Scene_A in the Scene Name box. Select Render1 under Views, select Sunlight under Lights, and then click OK. You are returned to the Scenes dialog box. Scene_A is now on the list (see Figure A.40). Click OK.

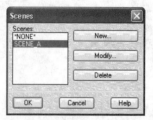

FIGURE A.40: The Scenes dialog box with Scene_A listed

Now you can change the view and add new lights to create a second scene.

Rendering to a File

The Render feature creates a rendering on the drawing area. The picture itself can't be saved (except by a screen grab), but we can re-render the scene to a file. Then it is saved and can be viewed by various applications.

1. Click the Render button on the Render toolbar. In the Render dialog box, go to the Destination area, open the drop-down list, and select File. Then click the More Options button that is in the same area to open the File Output Configuration dialog box (see Figure A.41).

FIGURE A.41: The File Output Configuration dialog box

2. Set your preference for the file type, pixel size, color, and so on, and then click OK.

3. Back in the Render dialog box, click the Render button to open the Rendering File dialog box.

4. Designate a folder and a name, and then click Save. The scene is rendered and saved to the chosen folder.

Trying Another View

Let's finish by changing our view and turning off a layer to see a slightly different result.

1. Freeze the 3D-Glass layer.

2. Choose View ➤ 3D Orbit.

3. Change the view of the cabin so that it's a little flatter and you can see through windows and doors into the cabin and out to the background scene.

4. Right-click and choose Projection ➤ Perspective. (Perspective may already be selected.)

5. Right-click again and choose Exit.

6. Click the Render button on the Render toolbar.

7. In the Scene To Render area, select Current View.

8. In the Destination area of the Render dialog box, open the drop-down list and select Viewport. Then click the Render button in the dialog box. AutoCAD renders this scene (see Figure A.42).

FIGURE A.42: The second rendered scene

9. If the view or lighting needs modification, make the change and try another render. If you like the results, re-render the scene to a file. Save the view as a named view, and then save the view and lights as a scene.

This has been a brief introduction into the world of 3D and rendering in Auto-CAD, but you should now be oriented to the general way of doing things and have enough tools to experiment further. For a more in-depth discussion of the entire process, including rendering, see *Mastering AutoCAD 2005 and AutoCAD LT 2005* (Sybex, 2004) by George Omura.

3D face

A triangular or four-sided flat surface that is the basic unit of a 3D surface.

3D mesh

A set of adjacent flat surfaces that together form a geometrical depiction of a three-dimensional curved surface.

3D model

An AutoCAD drawing file containing Auto-CAD objects that occupy 3D space and represent building components or geometrical objects in the real world. See also *object*.

A

absolute coordinates

Values for locating a point in space that describe its displacement from the *origin* (0,0,0) point of the drawing.

alias

A shortcut for starting commands. It is a set of one or two letters that you can enter at the *command line* instead of the full command.

aligned dimension

A linear dimension measuring the distance between two points. The dimension line for an aligned dimension is parallel to a line between the two points.

angular dimension

A dimension that measures the angle between two lines or the angle inscribed by an arc segment.

Angular unit

The unit in which angle values are displayed. The choices are Decimal Degrees, Degrees-Minutes-Seconds, Grads, Radians, and Surveyor units.

associative dimension

A dimension that updates automatically when the object being dimensioned changes size.

associative hatch pattern

A hatch pattern that updates automatically when the shape of the hatched area is modified. See also *hatch patterns*.

attribute

An *object* inside a block that contains text data. You specify the value of an attribute (*attribute value*) when you insert the block. See also *block reference*.

attribute definition

A special AutoCAD *object* that is included in a *block definition* so that varying text information can be included in the *block reference* when a block is inserted in a drawing.

attribute extraction file

A text file in which extracted attribute data is stored.

attribute extraction template file

A text file (.txt) that is used to organize the data in an *attribute extraction file*.

attribute prompt

The part of the *attribute definition* that instructs the user what to enter at the *command line* or in a dialog box when they are entering attribute values. See also *attribute value*.

attribute tag

A part of the *attribute definition* that represents the field of the table into which attribute data is extracted.

attribute value

The data that is the content of an attribute. It is always text and appears in the Auto-CAD drawing or in the record or rows of the table into which attribute data is extracted.

AutoCAD object

See *object*.

AutoSnap

A feature of AutoCAD that works with the Object Snap tools by displaying a symbol on the places in the drawing that can be snapped to. Each of these Object Snap modes has a different AutoSnap symbol. The symbol appears when the cursor is near a location where the active Object Snap can be used. See also *Object Snap mode*.

B

baseline dimension

A dimensioning option that allows you to do multiple measurements from a designated baseline.

base point

1. The initial point of reference for a number of modify commands, including Copy, Move, Rotate, Stretch, and Scale. 2. The insertion point for a drawing, as designated by the Base command.

bearings

See *Surveyor units*.

block

See *block reference*.

bind

To transform an external reference file into a permanent part of the host file as a block. See *external reference*.

block definition

The description of a grouping of AutoCAD objects that is stored with the drawing file and includes a name, an *insertion point*, and a listing of objects in the grouping.

block reference

An instance of a grouping of objects that is inserted into a drawing and is based on the block definition for that grouping. Casually called a block.

ByLayer

A value that can be assigned to colors and linetypes so that objects will receive their color and linetype properties according to the layer they are on.

C

Cartesian coordinate system

A 2D system of locating points on a plane. It uses a horizontal (x) and a vertical (y) component to locate a point relative to the 0,0 point, or origin.

command line

A text window at the bottom of the screen that displays command prompts. This is where you see what you are entering through the keyboard. Also called the *Command window*.

Command: prompt

The prompt at the *command line*, when no commands are currently running.

Command window

See *command line*.

continued dimension

A dimensioning option that allows you to place sequential dimensions that are adjacent to each other so that the dimension lines are aligned.

crosshair cursor

A form of the *cursor* that consists of a horizontal line and a vertical line intersecting at their midpoints, resembling the crosshair in a sighting device.

crossing window

A selection tool that selects an area defined by two points acting as opposite corners of a rectangle. All objects within or crossing the rectangle are selected.

current UCS

The *User Coordinate System* that is active in a drawing. It determines the positive x, y, and z directions.

cursor

The pointing symbol on the computer monitor that is moved by moving the mouse. It can appear as, among other things, an arrow, a *pickbox*, and a crosshair. See also *crosshair cursor*.

cutting edge

The role certain objects can be temporarily assigned to play in a trimming operation. If an object is designated as a cutting edge, lines or other objects being trimmed will be trimmed back to the point where they intersect the cutting edge.

cycling

A procedure for selecting a particular line when it coincides with one or more lines. To cycle, hold down the Ctrl key, make the first selection, release the Ctrl key, continue to select in the same place until the object you want is selected, and then press ↵.

D

default

A value or option in a command that will be used unless you designate otherwise. In AutoCAD, default values and options are enclosed in angle brackets (< >).

dimension style

A collection of settings for *dimension variables* that is saved in a drawing under a specified name. Dimensions placed in the drawing follow the settings of the current dimension style.

dimension text

The text in a dimension. It expresses the measurement that the dimension is displaying.

dimension variables

A group of settings and values that control the appearance of dimensions in AutoCAD.

direct entry

An option for specifying the next point in a series of points, by using the cursor to indicate direction and the keyboard to enter the distance from the last point.

docking

Relocating a toolbar or a palette to a place outside the *drawing area* so it won't interfere with the AutoCAD drawing or other items on the screen.

donut

A command on the Draw menu that draws filled rings, like the donut pastry. If you specify an inside diameter of 0, it draws a filled circle.

drawing area

The portion of the monitor screen where you draw objects and view your drawing.

drawing extents

The minimum rectangular area with the same proportions as your *drawing area* that will enclose nonfrozen objects in your drawing. When you *Zoom* to Extents, the rectangular area fills the drawing area.

drawing limits

The area in a drawing that is covered by the *grid*. It can be defined by the user. It is stored as the coordinates of the lower-left and upper-right corners of the rectangular area covered by the grid.

drawing units

The intervals of linear and angular measurements chosen for use in a drawing.

.dwg

The file extension and format for the standard AutoCAD drawing.

E

Edge

1. The side of a 3D face or a *3D mesh*. 2. A command for controlling the visibility of the edges of 3D faces.

Elevation view

A view of a building that viewers get when they look at it horizontally, perpendicular to an interior or exterior wall.

entity

See *object*.

Explode

A command to undo a grouping of objects. It can be used on blocks, *multiline text*, *polylines*, and dimensions. Exploded multiline text becomes single-line text. Exploded polylines become lines. Exploded blocks become the individual objects that make up the block. See also *polyline* and *multiline text*.

external reference

A drawing file that has been temporarily attached to another drawing for read-only purposes. Also called an Xref.

external reference host file

The drawing file to which external references have been attached.

extrusion

1. A 2D object that has been given *thickness*. 2. A 3D solid object created with the Extrude command, by sliding a closed 2D shape along a path that is usually perpendicular to the 2D shape. If you use the Path option of the Extrude command, the extrusion need not be perpendicular to the 2D shape.

F

fill

A display mode that can be set to on or off. When it is set to on, it displays a solid color for shapes made with wide polylines, 2D solids, *donut*, and *hatch patterns* using the Solid pattern. When it is set to off, the solid color area is invisible, and only the boundary of the fill is displayed. See also *donut* and *polyline*.

floating toolbar

A toolbar that is located in the drawing area. You can move it around by dragging its title bar.

floating viewports

Openings created in the *Paper Space* of a drawing that allow you to view a drawing in *Model Space*.

font

A group of letters, numbers, and other symbols all sharing common features of design and appearance.

freeze

The Off portion of a setting called Freeze/Thaw that controls the visibility of objects on layers and determines whether AutoCAD calculates the geometry of these objects during a *regeneration*. See also *layer*.

G

ghosting

The fuzzy or hazy appearance that a line or another object takes on when it's selected.

graphical user interface

See *graphics window*.

graphics window

The appearance of your screen when AutoCAD is running. It consists of the *drawing area* and surrounding toolbars, menu bars, the *Command window*, and the status bar. Also called the graphical user interface. See also *menu bar*.

grid

1. A drawing aid that consists of a regularly spaced set of dots in the *drawing area*.
2. A series of horizontal and vertical lines in a floor plan or section that locate the main structural elements of a building, such as columns and walls. Also called a column grid or a structural grid.

grips

An editing tool that allows you to perform five Modify commands on selected objects without having to start the commands themselves. When grips are enabled, small squares appear on selected objects. By clicking a square, you activate the first of the available commands. To access the five commands, press the spacebar to cycle through the commands or right-click and choose from the shortcut menu.

H

hatch patterns

Patterns of lines, dots, and other shapes that fill in a closed area.

host file

See *external reference host file*.

hyperlink

An electronic connection between an Auto-CAD object and any of several places, including another drawing, a Word document, a website, and so on.

I

icon

One of a set of small pictures on a toolbar. When the cursor rolls across an icon, it takes on the appearance of being a picture on a button.

insertion point

A reference point that is part of a block and is used to locate the block when it is inserted into a drawing. It is attached to the cursor while a block is being inserted. Once a block has been inserted, use the Insertion *Osnap* to snap to the insertion point of the block.

Isometric view

A pictorial view of a 3D object in which all lines that are parallel on the object appear parallel in the view. See also *Perspective view*.

J

jamb

A surface that forms the side or top of an opening for a door or window in a wall.

justification point

A reference point on a line of single-line text or a body of multiline text that acts like the *insertion point* for blocks.

L

layer

An organizing tool that operates like an electronic version of transparent overlays on a drawing board. Layers can be assigned color and *linetype*, and their visibility can be controlled.

layout

An optional interface that serves as an aid to the user in setting up a drawing for printing. It rests "on top of" the *Model Space* in which the drawing of the building resides. It contains the title block, notes, scale, and other information. Users view a drawing through openings in the layout called *viewports*. A single drawing file may have multiple layouts, one for each print to be made from the file. The layout interface is sometimes referred to as *Paper Space*. See also *viewport*.

Layout tab

A tab at the lower-left corner of the drawing area that you use to switch from a *Model Space* view of the drawing to a Layout view.

limits

See *drawing limits*.

linetype

The style of appearance of a line. AutoCAD styles include continuous, dashed, dash-dot, and so on.

linetype scale

A numeric value for noncontinuous line-types that controls the size of dashes and spaces between dashes and dots. In an AutoCAD drawing, a global linetype scale controls all noncontinuous linetypes in the drawing, and an individual linetype scale can be applied to one or more selected lines.

lineweight

The value of a line's width. AutoCAD offers 24 lineweights in a range from 0.00" to 0.083".

M

menu bar

The set of drop-down menus at the top of the AutoCAD graphics window.

Mirror

This command makes a copy of selected objects and flips it around a specified line to produce a mirror image of those objects.

mirror line

An imaginary line about which an object is flipped by the Mirror command.

Model Space

The portion of an AutoCAD drawing that contains the lines representing the building or object being designed, as opposed to the notes and title block information, which are kept on a *layout*.

Mtext

See *multiline text*.

multiline text

A type of text in which an entire body of text is grouped together as one object. Casually called Mtext, it can be edited with word-processing techniques. Individual characters or words in the Mtext can have different heights, fonts, and colors from the main body of Mtext. *Dimension text* is Mtext. When exploded, Mtext becomes *single-line text*.

N

Named view

A view of your drawing that is saved and given a name so that it can be restored later.

O

object

A basic AutoCAD graphical element that is created and manipulated as part of the drawing, such as a line, an arc, a dimension, a block, or text. Also called an entity.

Object Snap mode

Any of a set of tools for precisely picking strategic points on an *object*, including Endpoint, Midpoint, Center, and so on. It is casually called *Osnap*.

Object Snap Tracking

See *tracking*.

origin

The point with the coordinates 0,0,0, where the x-, y-, and z-axes all meet.

orthogonal drawing

A system of creating views in which each view shows a different side of a building or an object, such as top, front, left side, right side, and so on.

Ortho mode

An on/off setting that, when on, forces lines to be drawn and objects to be moved in a horizontal or vertical direction only.

Osnap

See *Object Snap mode*.

Otrack

See *tracking*.

P

Pan

A command that slides the current drawing around on the drawing area without changing the magnification of the view.

Paper Space

A term sometimes used to refer to the interface for a drawing that contains layouts. See also *layout*.

path

The hierarchy of drive, folder, and subfolders where a file is stored, along with the file's name, such as C:\Program Files\AutoCAD2005\Training Data\ Cabin8a.dwg.

Perspective view

A pictorial view of a 3D object in which parallel lines that are not parallel to the plane of the screen appear to converge as they move farther from the viewer, similar to the way objects appear in the real world, such as railroad tracks in the distance. See also *Isometric view*.

pickbox

A form of the cursor as a small square that occurs when AutoCAD is in *selection mode*.

pick button

The button on the mouse (usually the left one) that is used to pick points, buttons, or menu items, as well as select objects in the drawing area.

Plan view

A view of a drawing in which the viewer is looking straight at the *XY plane* in a direction parallel to the z-axis.

plot style

A group of settings that are assigned to a layer, a color, or an object. The settings determine how that layer, color, or object is printed.

plot style table

A set of plot styles that control the way in which a layout or drawing is printed.

point filters

A set of tools that allow you to specify a point in the drawing by using some of the X, Y, and Z coordinates from another point or points to generate the coordinates for the point you are specifying.

Polar Tracking

A tool for temporarily aligning the cursor movement to preset angles while drawing. See also *tracking*.

polyline

A special type of line that (a) treats multiple segments as one object, (b) can include arcs, (c) can be smoothed into a curved line, and (d) can have width in 2D applications.

precision of units

The decree of accuracy in which linear and angular units are displayed in dialog boxes, at the command line, or in dimensions.

prompt

The text at the command line that asks questions or tells you what action is necessary to continue the execution of a command. The Command: prompt tells you that no command is currently running.

R

Redraw

A command to refresh the *drawing area* or a particular *viewport*, thereby ridding it of any blip marks or graphic distortions that show up on the monitor while you're drawing.

regeneration

A process in which the geometry for the objects in the current drawing file is recalculated.

regular window

A selection tool that selects an area defined by two points acting as opposite corners of a rectangle. All objects completely within the rectangle are selected. See also *crossing window*.

relative coordinates

Values for locating a point in space that describe its displacement from the last point picked in the drawing rather than from the *origin*.

rubberbanding

The effect of a line extending between the last point picked and the crosshair cursor, stretching like a rubber band as the cursor is moved.

Running Object Snap

An *Object Snap mode* that has been set to be continually activated until turned off.

S

scale factor

The number that expresses the *true ratio* of a scale. For example, 48 is the scale factor for quarter-inch scale (¼" = 1'-0").

selection mode

The phase of a command that requires the user to select objects, and thereby build up a *selection set* of objects, to be modified by or otherwise used in the function of the command.

selection set

Any object or group of objects that have been selected for modification or have been selected to be used in a modification process.

selection window

A tool for selecting objects whereby the user creates a rectangular window in the *drawing area* and objects are selected in two ways, depending on whether the selection window is a *crossing window* or a *regular window*.

shortcut menu

A menu that appears on the drawing area—usually as the result of a right-click—and contains options relevant to what the user is doing at that moment.

single-line text

A type of text *object* in AutoCAD in which each line of text is treated as a single object, with its own *justification point*, whether it be a sentence, word, or letter.

Snapbase

A command (and setting) used to reset the origin of a hatch pattern. By default, Snapbase is set to 0,0,0.

Snap mode

An on/off setting that locks the cursor onto a spatial grid, which is usually aligned with the *grid*, allowing you to draw to distances that are multiples of the grid spacing. When the grid spacing is set to 0, the grid aligns with the snap spacing.

soffit

The underside of the roof overhang that extends from the outside edge of the roof, back to the wall.

Solid

1. The name of a hatch pattern that fills a defined boundary with a solid color. 2. A three-dimensional object in AutoCAD that has properties similar to those of a solid block of material, such as mass, centroid, volume, and so on.

stud

A vertical piece of lumber or metal used in framing walls. It is usually 2" × 4" or 2" × 6" in cross dimension and extends the height of the wall.

Surveyor units

An angular unit of direction in which the value is the angle that the direction deviates away—or "bears"—from true north or south, toward the east or west.

T

template drawing

A drawing that has been set up to serve as a format for a new drawing. This allows the user to begin a new drawing with certain parameters already set up, because various settings have been predetermined.

text style

A collection of settings that controls the appearance of text and is saved in a drawing under a specified name. Text placed in the drawing will follow the settings of the current text style.

thaw

The On portion of a setting called Freeze/Thaw that controls the visibility of objects on layers and determines whether AutoCAD calculates the geometry of these objects during a *regeneration*. See also *layer*.

thickness

The distance that a 2D object is extruded in a direction perpendicular to the plane in which it was originally drawn, resulting in a 3D object. For a floor plan of a building, wall lines can be extruded to a thickness that is the wall's actual height. See also *extrusion*.

tracking

The process by which the user sets up temporary points or angles as guides for the cursor, used to locate desired points in the process of drawing. Object Snap Tracking (or Otrack) creates the temporary points, and *Polar Tracking* sets the angles. See also *Object Snap mode*.

tracking points

The temporary points that are set up for use in Object Snap Tracking. See also *tracking*.

transparent command

A command that can be executed while another command is running, without interfering with the running command. Display commands, such as *Zoom* and *Pan*, are transparent.

true ratio

An expression of two numbers that defines the actual size differentiation in a scale, that is, the number of units represented by a single unit. See also *scale factor*.

U

UCS

See *User Coordinate System*.

UCS icon

The double-arrow icon in the lower-left corner of the *drawing area* that indicates the positive directions of the x- and y-axes for the current *User Coordinate System*. In 3D views, the z-axis is also represented in the icon.

User Coordinate System (UCS)

A definition for the orientation of the x-, y-, and z-axes in space relative to 3D objects in the drawing or to the *World Coordinate System*. UCSs can be named, saved, and restored.

V

view

A picture of the current drawing from a particular user-defined perspective that is displayed on the screen or in a *viewport*. Views can be named, saved, and restored.

viewport

An opening—usually rectangular, but not always—through which the user can view their drawing or a portion of it. There are two kinds of viewports: tiled viewports (used in *Model Space*) and *floating viewports* (used in layouts). See also *layout*.

W

wireframe

A view of a 3D object that uses lines to represent the intersections of planes. The planes defined by these lines represent surfaces of building components, machine parts, and so on.

World Coordinate System

The default *User Coordinate System* for all new drawing files, in which the positive directions for the x- and y-axes are to the right and upward, respectively, and in which the positive direction for the z-axis is toward the user and perpendicular to the plane of the screen.

WYSIWYG

An acronym for "what you see is what you get." It's a description applied to preview features that show you exactly what a screen will look like when printed.

X

XY plane

The 2D flat surface, defined by the x- and y-axes, that is parallel to the monitor screen in a new AutoCAD drawing file.

Z

Zoom

The name of a command with several options, all of which allow the user to increase or decrease the magnification of the *view* of the current drawing in the *drawing area* or in a *viewport*.

INDEX

Note to the Reader: Throughout this index **boldfaced** page numbers indicate primary discussions of a topic. *Italicized* page numbers indicate illustrations.

D

G

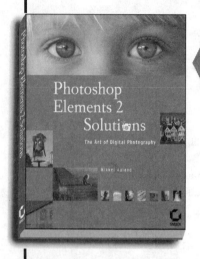
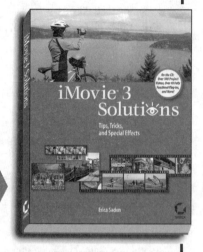

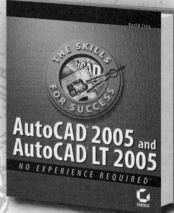

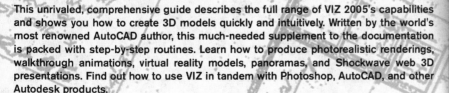

Shooting Digital: Pro Tips for Taking Great Pictures with Your Digital Camera

By Mikkel Aaland
ISBN: 0-7821-4104-8
US $35.00

Noted photographer and best-selling author Mikkel Aaland has drawn on his 28 years of experience in the field to bring you *Shooting Digital: Pro Tips for Taking Great Pictures with Your Digital Camera*. Containing wisdom and images from more than 30 contributors, this tutorial covers all the bases to help you get consistently great results. Through simple instruction and illustrative examples you'll learn how to:

- Use digital-specific techniques to take great pictures of virtually everything

- Fully exploit the minimovie capabilities of your digital camera

- Recognize and compensate for the dreaded shutter release lag

- Use the LCD preview to turn portrait subjects into collaborators

- Create stunning panoramas and object movies

- Work with RAW data, the holy grail of digital photography

- Extend the tonal range of digital cameras

- Archive your digital images while on the road. And much more...

"You can't go wrong with Mikkel when it comes to working with digital imagery."

— Russ Walkowich, MyMac.com

Mikkel Aaland is an award-winning photographer and author of eight books, including *Digital Photography, Photoshop for the Web,* and *Photoshop Elements 2 Solutions*. His photography has been published in *Wired, Newsweek,* and has also been exhibited in major institutions around the world, including the Bibliothèque Nationale in Paris and the former Lenin Museum in Prague.

SYBEX®
www.sybex.com